MW01225831

Visual Basic 5

OBJECT-ORIENTED
PROGRAMMING

Visual Basic 5

OBJECT-ORIENTED PROGRAMMING

Gene Swartzfager

THE CORIOLIS GROUP

Publisher	Keith Weiskamp
Project Editor	Scott Palmer
Cover Artist	Gary Smith/Performance Design
Cover Design	Anthony Stock
Layout Design	Nicole Birney
Layout Production	April Nielsen
Copyeditor	Jenni Aloi
Proofreader	Gary Finkel
Indexer	Caroline Parks

Trademarks: Trademarked names appear throughout this book and on the accompannying compact disk. Rather than list the names and entities that own the trademarks or insert a trademark symbol with each mention of the trademarked name, the publisher states that it is using the names only for editorial purposes and to the benefit of the trademark owner with no intention of infriging upon that trademark.

Copyright © 1997 by The Coriolis Group, Inc. All rights reserved.

No part of this book may be reproduced, stored, or transmitted by any means, mechanical, electronic, or otherwise, without the express written consent of the publisher. Reproduction or translation of any part of this work beyond that permitted by section 107 or 108 of the 1976 United States Copyright Act without the written permission of the copyright owner is unlawful.

Requests for permission or further information should be addressed to:

The Coriolis Group, Inc.
14455 N. Hayden Road, Suite 220
Scottsdale, AZ 85260
Phone: (602) 483-0192
Fax: (602) 483-0193

Web address: http://www.coriolis.com

Printed in the United States of America

ISBN 1-57610-106-1 $49.99

10 9 8 7 6 5 4 3 2

Dedicated to my partner and wife, Judy Ford. When you listen to me talk about my work in computer programming, you make me believe I can do anything. You are the best listener I have ever known.

Acknowledgments

This book is the result of a lot of effort and enthusiasm, a couple of fortunate job assignments, and the encouragement of my wife and partner, Judy Ford.

In January of 1994, I started teaching Visual Basic for the University of Washington in Seattle. I thank Judith Frye of the U Of W for hiring me as an instructor and for her support when I approached her with an idea for an advanced VB course, with the title *Object-Oriented Programming With Visual Basic*. I have used earlier drafts of this book for that course throughout 1996; the book has improved every quarter, as I have incorporated into it the suggestions of over 100 students who have taken the course.

In the summer of 1994, Randy Holbrook of Microsoft hired me to help write the VB4 Help file. Thanks, Randy, for giving me an early look at VB4; from the start, I was just blown away by the language's object-oriented programming features, flexibility and ease of use.

Many thanks are due to Scott Palmer and the other members of the Coriolis Group's editing and publishing team. This is my first published book and, at the start of the process, I didn't really appreciate how many different individuals are involved in such an effort. It was a pleasure working with all of them and I hope we can do another book together.

I want to thank my wife Judy most of all. When I first said to her, in the fall of 1995, that I was going to write a VB book, she encouraged me. Ever since, her support has been unflagging. I would not have finished the book without her.

The last persons to acknowledge are Julia Heiman and Stuart Wachter, both good people who care passionately about their professions. For the past nine years, off and on, they have been my role models and mentors. I believe that I am like them now, with this book being the profession of that belief.

CONTENTS

INTRODUCTION

This book was written for the Visual Basic developer who wants to become a better, more productive programmer. Whether you are a corporate developer in the Fortune 500 or just an entrepreneur with a dream of writing a cool new ActiveX control, you and your clients or customers will benefit if you can become a more productive programmer.

The easiest way to become a more productive Windows programmer is to learn the new object-oriented development methodology (or object-based methodology, if you are a purist) that VB5 supports. This book, *Object-Oriented Programming With Visual Basic 5*, was specifically written to help developers master VB5's object-oriented syntax as quickly as possible. The material in the book has been field-tested by over 100 VB programmers who in 1996 used this book as part of a University of Washington course on VB object-oriented programming.

Prerequisites For Using The Book

To use this book successfully, it really helps to be an experienced Visual Basic programmer. You also need to have access to a computer with the Professional Edition of VB5 installed on it and to be willing to work through the sample code that comes with the book in a methodical and detailed manner. If you are an experienced Windows programmer but have never used Visual Basic, it's also possible to work your way through the book, but you would probably benefit by augmenting this text with a general reference book on VB such as *The Visual Basic 5 Programming EXplorer* (The Coriolis Group, 1997).

What The Book Covers

This book covers all the major capabilities and features that VB5 supports for object-oriented programming. More specifically, the book explains how to:

- Grasp the fundamental concepts of object-oriented programming (class, instance, object, encapsulation, polymorphism, inheritance).

- Use VB5 to write class libraries of reusable code; that is, create ActiveX components (known as OLE Automation servers under VB4) which can expose their objects for reuse by other ActiveX programming languages. These objects are of two general types: those whose members (that is, methods and properties) are VB-specific and can be reused only by other VB applications and those whose members are generic and can be reused by any ActiveX-compliant language (for example, Excel VBA, Delphi 2, or PowerBuilder 5).

- Test and reuse the members of a **ClassModule** object, both internally and externally.

- Use the new VB5 syntax that enables the creation of ActiveX components.

- Use the new VB5 syntax that enables the creation of ActiveX controls.

Note: For a complete list of all VB5 and VB4 syntactical elements that are either entirely new or have new characteristics, see the New Syntax In VB 4.0/5.0 jump on the Contents topic of EFS.HLP, the Help file that comes with the book's class library. It includes all the new syntax related to VBA and to VB's intrinsic controls.

- Implement commercial-quality, industrial-strength error-handling and syntax-checking code in the procedures of a class.
- Use Windows API functions to optimize the speed of the members exposed by ActiveX components.
- Create a commercial-quality Windows Help file for an ActiveX component's class library and link individual Help topics to an object or an object's members.

Registering The ActiveX Components

Before you proceed with these steps under VB5, you should know that once you have saved a project's files with VB5, you will no longer be able to open that project with VB4. To register the two major versions of the ActiveX component that come on the book's CD-ROM in the Windows 95 or Windows NT registry, follow these steps:

1. Assuming that you have installed the files from the book's CD-ROM, start VB5.

2. Select File|Open Project, point-and-click to the file EFSD.VBP on the path C:\VBOOPEFS\VBCLSLIB, and choose Open.

3. Select File|Make EFSD.DLL (under VB4, it was File|Make OLE DLL File) and choose OK to make and register the in-process version of the book's ActiveX component.

4. Select File|Save Project to save the changes to EFSD.VBP.

5. Select File|Open Project, point-and-click to the file EFSE.VBP on the path C:\VBOOPEFS\VBCLSLIB, and choose Open.

6. Select File|Make EFSE.EXE (under VB4, it was File|Make EXE File) and choose OK to make and register the out-of-process version of the book's ActiveX component.

7. Select File|Save Project to save the changes to EFSE.VBP.

That's how easy it is to make and register an ActiveX component with VB5. You're now ready to reuse any of the objects in the book's class library.

In the retail release of VB5, Microsoft changed the Language Reference Help file's name from VEENLR3.HLP (its name in the Beta 2 release) to VBENLR3.HLP. Consequently, some of the book's demonstration code in EFS.HLP no longer runs correctly. Before you run any of the book's demonstration code, do a project-wide, search-and-replace operation on the code, substituting VBENLR3.HLP for VEENLR3.HLP. Also, about three of the demo code routines use BIBLIO.MDB as a data file. Microsoft changed the version of BIBLIO.MDB in the retail release of VB5. If it doesn't work with the demo code, use the VB4 or VB3 version of BIBLIO.MDB.

Conventions Used

The following lists information on various conventions mentioned in this book.

Typographic Conventions

The typographic conventions used in this book are listed in Table I.1.

Programming Conventions

The programming conventions used in the sample code listings in this book are:

- An apostrophe (') followed by a space introduces a code *comment*:

```
' Create instance of class.
```

Table I.1 Typographic conventions.

Example	Description
Err.Raise 3	This font is used for code samples.
. . .	This font and three dots separated by spaces indicates code that exists in a procedure in the book's class library but is not listed in the book.
"MYCLSLIB"	Non-code words appearing in quotation marks are to be typed or indicate a quotation (in code, quotation marks indicate a string).
TypeName, VarType	Words in bold with the initial letter capitalized indicate VB language-specific or class-library specific identifiers or keywords.
method	A word in italics indicates a word or words being used as a term, a technical term, or a reference to a section or chapter of this book. If it indicates a technical term, it is italicized the first time it is used in the book and its formal definition appears in the Glossary topic of EFS.HLP, the Help file that comes with the book's class library.
Prompt	In syntax, a word in italics indicates the name of an argument in a procedure.
[*HelpFile*]	In syntax, an argument inside square brackets is optional.
[Public I Private]	In syntax, a straight slash or pipe symbol (I) indicates that the parts on either side of the slash are mutually exclusive.
EFSD.DLL	Words in all capital letters indicate directory and/or file names.

- All comments are set off by one blank line before the comment and appear above the lines of code to which they are related. No endline comments are used.

- Control-flow code blocks are indented three spaces from the enclosing code and are preceded by a blank line:

```
Private Sub Command1_Click()

   ' Variables.
   Dim Results As Variant

   Results = ClientApp.CheckSecurity

   If Results(1) = "Cancel" Then
      MsgBox "You chose Cancel to close Security dialog box."
   Else
      Msg = "Login ID and password you input were:" & vbCr & vbCr
      Msg = Msg & Results(1)
      MsgBox Msg, vbInformation
   End If

End Sub
```

- VB4 and VB5 support the use of a *line-continuation character*, a space followed by an underscore (_). Code statements too long for one line are continued on the next line using the line-continuation character. Each continuation line is indented to line up logically with the code in the line above it. An example is:

```
' Center form:
Me.Move (Screen.Width - Me.Width) * .5, _
        (Screen.Height - Me.Height) * .5
```

- When a call is made to a procedure using *named arguments*, the line-continuation character is often used to set off each named argument. Each continuation line contains another named argument and is indented in line with the position of the previous named argument. An example is:

```
List.FillWithDAO(CboOrLst:=List1, _
                 Dbs:=Dbs, _
                 Rst:=Rst, _
                 Field:="Title", _
                 Sort:=SORT_ASC)
```

- Each *variable* is explicitly declared. The assumption is that Require Variable Declaration is checked on the Editor tab of VB's Options dialog box (Tools|Options).

- All variable declarations follow the format

```
Dim Results As Variant
```

where the data type is explicitly stated using the **As** keyword. The only exception to this rule is the declaration of a *Windows API* function. In this case, the suffix approach is used to conserve space and so, as much as possible, to minimize the use of the line-continuation character. For example:

```
Declare Function LockWindowUpdate& Lib "USER32" (ByVal hWndLock&)
```

- If a VB *intrinsic constant* exists, it is used. Examples:

```
' Warn user there will be a delay.
Screen.MousePointer = vbHourglass

' Reset default cursor.
Screen.MousePointer = vbDefault
```

- If a *constant* or constants exist for a Windows API function's arguments or return values, this book uses them. Examples:

```
' Constants for SetWindowPos Windows API function:
Const HWND_TOPMOST = -1
Const HWND_NOTOPMOST = -2
Const SWP_NOSIZE = &H1
Const SWP_NOMOVE = &H2
```

- If no VB intrinsic or Windows API function constants exist, this book's code declares its own constants and assigns most numeric or string literals and control array index values to these constants.
- Whenever coding steps are listed in this book, the assumption is that VB5 is being used. However, all of the source code that comes on this book's CD-ROM will run unchanged under the 32-bit or 16-bit versions of VB4. The only exceptions are the source code for the two ActiveX controls (TBARICON.VBP and LSTBOXSC.VBP), which cannot be read by VB4.

Naming Conventions For Code

Naming conventions are akin to religious beliefs. Every VB programmer can give you several good reasons why his or her naming conventions are better than all the rest. Most programmers do not waste time preaching to the unconverted. Still, you cannot help but feel when you read books on VB or Microsoft Access programming that, if you do not adhere to the prescribed naming conventions, you will be excommunicated from the VB flock.

Some of the most widespread and commonly-used naming conventions are:

- The Hungarian convention is named after the legendary Microsoft C developer, Michael Simonyi, who happens to be of Hungarian descent. It is used by many C and C++ programmers.

- Microsoft's suggested conventions for VB and Visual Basic For Application (VBA) are explained briefly in the *Visual Basic Programmer's Guide* and are used in the book *Microsoft Office 95 Data Access Reference*, published by Microsoft Press.

- The Leszynski conventions are used by many Microsoft Access programmers and are based on and expand upon Microsoft's suggested conventions.

The naming conventions in this book for VB's built-in objects are based on Microsoft's suggested conventions for VB and VBA and the fundamental Leszynski naming conventions when Microsoft does not have a suggestion.

However, the rest of the book's naming conventions are based on the assumption that you are going to use VB5 to write encapsulated, object-oriented code that will be compiled into an *ActiveX component.* When you do this, you want to write members which, when viewed from VB's Object Browser dialog box (F2), appear the same with regard to names/syntax as VB's and VBA's members appear. To achieve this, this book names:

- A *member* that is a *method* with a verb. If necessary, the verb is followed by a noun that specifies a related *object.*

- A member that is a *property* with a noun.

- An *argument* with a noun or, occasionally, a verb. The name of the argument is not preceded by a three-letter prefix indicating the data type of the variable because the arguments for VB's and VBA's members do not use three-letter prefixes.

NAMES FOR VARIABLES

Variables are given descriptive names when they are explicitly declared and are not given any prefix to indicate their data type. This sounds like heresy of the worst sort compared to the commonly-used VB naming conventions, which all use prefixes of some kind. The rationale for not using prefixes in the book's class library is threefold: first, all the procedures are part of an object-oriented design; second, 99 percent of all the class library's variables are declared with procedure-level scope; third, the code is meant, as much as is possible, to be readable like a natural language.

Today's generation of Windows programming languages and the ActiveX component software protocol Microsoft is promoting make it easy to write highly cohesive, encapsulated procedures/modules/classes. If you adhere to the object-oriented programming paradigm, the procedures composing the members of a class library should be relatively short and should not be coupled with the code of other procedures except through message passing. No public/global variables should be used and module-level variables, except for those required in conjunction with VB's **Property Get**, **Let** and **Set** procedures, should only be rarely declared (and then closely commented to document their use).

For those VB developers who commit themselves to the OOP paradigm, programmers who continue to clutter their procedures with elaborate and esoteric variable naming conventions and broadly-scoped variables seem very much like those who continue to observe an antiquated religious dogma.

The *scope* of variables is specified in this way:

- Any variable declared to have **ClassModule** object-level scope has the prefix *c*. The only exception to this is an object variable that is assigned a reference to one of the **ClassModule** objects in the book's class library.

- Any variable declared to have form-level scope has the prefix *f*.

- All variables of form-level or **ClassModule** object-level scope are declared with the **Private** statement. Procedure-level variables, declared with the **Dim** statement, are private by definition. This practice conforms with the encapsulation characteristic of object-oriented programming, which forbids the use of any variables declared with the **Public** statement (in VB3, the **Global** statement).

NAMES FOR FORM AND CONTROL OBJECTS

All *form* and *control* objects intrinsic to VB are identified by a generic, lowercase, three-letter prefix specifying the class of the object. These prefixes are listed in Table I.2.

Controls that are part of a *control array* simply use the control's three-letter prefix as their **Name** property. Their **Index** property value is then identified by a constant. For example, two **CommandButton** objects for OK and

Table I.2 Prefixes for VB's Form and intrinsic control objects.

Class/Object Name	Prefix	Example
Form	frm	frmBrowse
MDIForm	mdi	mdiEditor
CheckBox	chk	chkWholeWord
ComboBox	cbo	cboBrowse
CommandButton	cmd	cmdReplace
Data	dat	datBiblio
DirListBox	dir	dirBrowse
DriveListBox	drv	drvBrowse
FileListBox	fil	filBrowse
Frame	fra	fraOptions
HScrollBar	hsb	hsbRate
Image	img	imgLogo
Label	lbl	lblEmpName
Line	lin	linVertical
ListBox	lst	lstFiles
Menu	mnu	mnuEdit
OptionButton	opt	optEnglish
PictureBox	pic	picLogo
Shape	shp	shpCircle
TextBox	txt	txtEmpName
Timer	tmr	tmrGetWindowInfo
VScrollBar	vsb	vsbRate

Close which are part of a control array would be identified in code by Cmd(OK) and Cmd(CLOSE), with OK and CLOSE being the constants.

How This Book Is Organized

This book consists of an Introduction, 21 chapters, and a CD-ROM that contains sample code and a Help file.

The Introduction and Chapter 1 give a general overview of the theory and practice of object-oriented programming. They lay out the assumptions and conventions used in writing this book, the class library that comes with it, and the Windows Help file that documents the class library (EFS.HLP). They also introduce and explain, in general terms, the essential concepts that govern object-oriented programming and the creation of ActiveX components with VB5.

Chapters 2 through 4 explain the fundamentals of how to create classes, write members, and make a VB project containing public classes into two kinds of ActiveX components, the in-process DLL version and the out-of-process EXE version. This section demonstrates how to instantiate a public class and call/reuse public members contained in that class. It also shows how to encapsulate a **Form** object in an ActiveX component, how to display a form with code in a public member, and how to return information from a form to a client application.

Chapters 5 through 9 introduce the concept of the public interface of an ActiveX component; that is, the information that the class library itself makes available about how to reuse its members. The design principles that should govern the creation of classes, members, and arguments (required and optional) are discussed in detail; returned values; an exception-handling scheme (syntax and run-time errors); and Help topics that document the functional specifications of public members.

Chapters 10 through 13 discuss how to write members that subclass VB's **Form** and control objects and enhance their functionality. The concepts and techniques involved in subclassing with members from the **Dialog**, **Graphic**, and **List** classes (included in the book's class library) are demonstrated in these chapters. It explains how to write polymorphic methods, which present a single, consistent public interface to the client application programmer, but which implement different kinds of functionality.

Chapters 14 through 17 explain and illustrates a variety of advanced techniques that you can use when writing members in an ActiveX component. Some of these advanced techniques are:

- Displaying modeless **Form** objects from an out-of-process ActiveX component and the various purposes this technique can serve.
- Displaying hidden **Form** objects from an ActiveX component so that only a control object on the form is visible.
- Running other applications and calling functions contained in third-party DLLs, from an ActiveX component.

- Using polling and callback techniques when an ActiveX component is performing batch (that is, asynchronous) processing.

- Returning object references from a member of an ActiveX component to the client application and using them, in the client, to manipulate control objects.

The final portion of this book, Chapters 18 through 21, introduce the concept of the reusable application framework in object-oriented Programming development, and offers Windows-based examples in the form of the **File** and **Text** classes of the book's class library. It also demonstrates how to use the new IDE extensibility features of VB5, including the creation of ActiveX controls and Add-Ins.

The book's CD-ROM includes a commercial-quality ActiveX component. This ActiveX component is designed as a class library of methods that enhances VB's own programming language, and the component includes a Windows Help file to assist you in reusing its members. The CD-ROM also includes a separate **Error** class that you can reuse from any application to handle VB errors, and it has examples of ActiveX controls and Add-Ins created with VB5. Finally, the CD-ROM contains a free demo version of my Windows API Browser utility. You can purchase the full-featured, 32-bit version of this utility for only $9.99 plus $5.00 shipping and handling by writing to me at 75521.3130@compuserve.com.

Object-Oriented Programming Concepts

C hapter 1 introduces you to the fundamental concepts and terminology of object-oriented programming (OOP) and development. The computer software industry is notorious for its tendency to hype new programming techniques, approaches, and languages as they come along. However, in the case of object-oriented programming, there is real substance behind the hype.

Object-oriented programming, as Microsoft has implemented it with Visual Basic and ActiveX components, is a methodology and framework for developing programs that:

- Are composed of a greater number of reusable modules or objects.
- Have fewer bugs.
- Are easier to maintain, enhance, and scale up.

For the corporate programmer and IS (Information Systems) department, adopting the object-oriented programming paradigm can, over the long term, improve programmer productivity by 50 to 100 percent. Because much of the code written the object-oriented way is reusable and more easily maintained, corporate programmers enjoy their work more and get to write new code a greater percentage of the time. For the individual programmer or utility developer, the object-oriented approach (in conjunction with ActiveX components and Add-Ins) makes it easier to write that one "hot" utility. Your utility is so easy to reuse by other programmers that, in your dreams, you sell 500,000 copies of it at $10 per copy and then retire to a life of leisure and game playing.

The rest of Chapter 1 familiarizes you with the basics that you need to know to understand the rest of the material in this book. After a brief look at the history of object-oriented programming, I discuss the terminology of OOP, both as generally used by the software industry and as used by Microsoft. The key OOP attributes of encapsulation, polymorphism, and inheritance are introduced, along with the larger OOP-related issues of COM, OLE and ActiveX. Finally, because Windows API functions are an important part of writing OOP code with Visual Basic, I discuss the essential concepts you need to know to use Windows API functions in your VB code.

History Of Object-Oriented Programming

Although object-oriented programming has assumed a very high profile among developers in the last few years, it is actually more than 25 years old. All the essential concepts of the object-oriented approach to programming were introduced in the Simula language, developed in Norway during the late 1960s. Simula, an acronym for *simulation language*, was created to support simulations of real-world processes. Modularization in Simula was based on the physical objects being modeled in the simulation, not on procedures, as in conventional programming languages. The concept of software objects arose from the requirement to model or abstract real-world objects and their relationships.

A Look At The Basics

An object is a software package that contains a collection of related procedures and data. In object-oriented programming, procedures are termed *methods* and the data elements are termed *properties*. The concept of an object is simple, yet powerful and flexible. Objects make ideal software modules because they can be defined and maintained independently of one another, with each object forming a self-contained, independent unit.

Everything a software object knows is expressed in its properties and everything it can do is expressed in its methods.

Software objects interact with each other by sending messages requesting that methods be carried out, or that properties be set or returned. A *message* is simply the name of an object followed by the name of one of its members. A message can have three parts:

- The name of the receiving object.
- The name of the object's member (method or property).
- The values specified by the arguments of the member.

In Visual Basic syntax, an example of a message is

```
List.FillWithDAO CboOrLst:=List1, _
                 Dbs:=Dbs, _
                 Rst:=Rst, _
                 Field:="Title", _
                 Sort:=SORT_ASC
```

where **List** is the receiving object, **FillWithDAO** is the name of the member, and the remainder of the code specifies the named arguments of the **FillWithDAO** member and the values passed to them. An object-oriented program consists of some number of objects interacting with each other by passing messages back and forth. Because everything an object can do or know is expressed by its members (that is, methods and properties), this programming model supports all possible interactions between objects.

An extremely simple simulation might require only a single example of a particular kind of object, but most real-world simulations require several instances of each kind of object. It would be extremely inefficient to have to redefine and recode the same members for every occurrence of a kind of object. An efficient solution to this problem is the concept of a class. A class specifies, once and for all, the members to be included in a particular kind of object. Thereafter, each instance of a class need contain only the particular values or settings that differentiate it from its sibling object instances.

As OOP evolved and different object-oriented languages like Smalltalk and C++ were written, the classes these languages created came to exhibit three key attributes that define the purest form of OOP: *encapsulation, polymorphism,* and *inheritance.* We'll cover these attributes in detail later in the chapter, but for now, let's stick with the basics.

The Microsoft Connection

Microsoft has recently added a new twist to OOP—an attempt to structure all object-oriented programming around the low-level abstraction of an *ActiveX component* (formerly known as an OLE Automation server). An ActiveX component, which we'll discuss in more detail later on, is an application that exposes programmable objects and their members for reuse by any application containing an OLE Automation-compliant programming language. Microsoft has designed Visual Basic 5.0 (VB5) to easily create class libraries that, at a lower level of abstraction, are ActiveX components.

The history of software development seems to go through cycles of evolution, with each cycle characterized by a greater degree of abstraction. Some of the major steps in this evolutionary process include:

- Machine language programming.
- Assembly programming.
- Higher-level language programming (Cobol, Fortran, Basic, C, and so on).
- Procedural language programming (Focus, dBASE, VB3, and so on).
- Structured programming techniques (capable of being adhered to in almost any language).
- Pure OOP languages (Simula, Smalltalk, C++, and so on).
- OOP techniques (capable of being added on to almost any higher-level or procedural language; for example, object-oriented versions of Ada, Cobol, Visual FoxPro, VB5, and so on).
- ActiveX components.

Microsoft is staking its future and the future of the various versions of its Windows operating systems on the ActiveX component implementation of OOP. Given Microsoft's dominance and influence in the software industry, I am certain that OOP as embodied in ActiveX components is more than just a passing fancy—it is here to stay.

Understanding Classes

As I briefly discussed earlier, a class is a template or formal definition that defines the properties of an object and the methods used to control that object's behavior. The description of these members is done only once, in the definition of the class. The objects that belong to a class, called *instances* of the class, share the code of the class to which they belong, but contain only their particular settings for the properties of the class. You create, or *instantiate*, an instance as an object at runtime with the same inherent methods and default property settings with which the class was designed. You then can change the settings of the properties of the class as necessary.

Visual Basic Class Specifics

Visual Basic has three generic kinds of classes:

- **Control**. When instantiated, this is an object that you draw on a **Form** object to enable or enhance user interaction with an application. Control objects appear in the toolbox and are placed on a **Form** object by double clicking them or by clicking and then dragging them onto a Form object. To place a Menu control object on a **Form** object, you use the Menu Editor (found in the Tools menu). Control objects have three general attributes. First, they accept user input, respond to *events* initiated by the user or triggered by the system, or display output. Second, they have properties that define aspects of their appearance, such as position, size, and color, and aspects of their behavior, such as how they respond to user input. Third, they can be made to perform certain actions by applying methods to them in code.

- **Object**. When instantiated, this is an object that supports members, but that does not have its own recognized set of events.

- **Collection**. When instantiated, this is an object that contains a set of related objects. An object's position in the Collection object can change whenever a change in the Collection object occurs; therefore, the position of any specific item in the Collection object may vary.

Now that you understand the types of classes available, let's look at some VB-specific points regarding the concept of classes:

- The terms *class* and *type* are synonymous. All the tools on the toolbox represent control classes.

- After a control class is instantiated on a **Form** object, the class name of the control object appears in the drop-down list at the top of the Properties window, to the right of the **Name** property of the control object. **TextBox**, **CommandButton**, and **Label** are examples of class names for commonly used control objects.

- VB5 contains over 100 different classes, including the built-in ActiveX controls **CommonDialog**, **DBCombo**, **DBGrid**, **DBList**, **Grid**, and **OLE** container. You can add other ActiveX controls/classes to VB. To see an alphabetic list of all classes contained in VB5, start Visual Basic and select Help|Microsoft Visual Basic Help Topics to display the Help Topics dialog box. Select the Contents tab and then select Language Reference/Objects.

Understanding Objects

An object is a unit of code and data that can be accessed, manipulated, and reused. An object is composed of two types of entities. First, it has procedures or members, called methods, that define the tasks that the object can perform. Second, it has variables, called properties, that are used to return or set attributes of the object.

As you learned in the previous section, an object is an instance of a class. Multiple instances of a class are created or instantiated at runtime with the same inherent methods and default property settings with which the class was designed.

Visual Basic Object Specifics

Now that you understand objects a little bit better, I'd like to point out some VB-specific points regarding the concept of instantiating a class:

- When you take a control or class from the toolbox and add it to a **Form** object, an object (an instance of that class) is created.
- You can create an object instance of some classes with the **As New** syntax. The following statement creates a new object instance of the **Form** class:

```
Dim Form2 As New Form1
```

- You can create an object instance of public classes in ActiveX components by using VB's **CreateObject** function. First you declare an object variable, then you use **CreateObject** to assign an object instance to the variable, as shown here:

```
Dim Dialog As Object
Set Dialog = CreateObject("EFSD.Dialog")
```

- Once an object instance of a class exists, you can modify the default settings of the properties of the class.
- All controls can be instantiated as objects, but not all object instances of classes are controls. For example, the DAO syntax of VB's Jet database

engine is composed of many classes, but the great majority of these DAO classes are not controls.

Collection Objects

A Collection is an object that contains a related set of objects. An object's position in the Collection can change whenever a change occurs in the Collection object. Therefore, the position of any specific object in the Collection may vary. All Collection objects have a single property **Count** that specifies the number of items in the Collection. Collection objects that you instantiate have three methods: **Add**, **Item**, and **Remove**.

VISUAL BASIC'S BUILT-IN COLLECTION OBJECTS

VB's three built-in Collection objects—Controls, Forms, and Printers—support the **Count** property, as well, but they don't have the methods associated with Collection objects you create. Let's briefly discuss the Collection objects built into VB:

- **The Controls Collection Object**. The items within this Collection object represent each control object on a **Form** object, including elements of control arrays. You can use the Controls collection object to iterate through all loaded control objects on a **Form** object.
- **The Forms Collection Object**. The items within this Collection object represent each loaded **Form** object in an application. You can use the Forms collection object to iterate through all loaded **Form** objects.
- **The Printers Collection Object**. The items within this Collection object represent all the available printers on the system. The Printers collection object enables you to query the available printers to specify a default printer for your application.

CREATING AND USING COLLECTION OBJECTS

You can instantiate your own Collection objects from VB's **Collection** class using the **As New** syntax:

```
Dim Ctls As New Collection
```

Once you've created the object, the **Count** property returns the number of items in a Collection object:

```
Print Ctls.Count
```

You work with a Collection object by using its methods: You add items to the Collection object with the **Add** method and delete items from the object

with the **Remove** method. For example, you could clone Visual Basic's built-in Controls collection object with the following snippet:

```
' Variables:
Dim Ctl    As Variant
Dim Ctls   As New Collection

For Each Ctl In Form1.Controls
    Ctls.Add Ctl
Next Ctl

Print Ctls.Count
```

Although a Collection object doesn't have a **Clear** method, you can clear the contents of the object by setting the object variable containing the Collection object to **Nothing**. In addition, you can return specific items from the Collection object, either by key or by position, using the **Item** method.

OTHER FEATURES OF COLLECTION OBJECTS

A Collection object has features of both an array—because it contains a set of items—and a **ListBox** object—because it provides a predefined set of methods (**Add**, **Item**, and **Remove**) to process its items. However, a Collection object is more useful and flexible than an array in cases where items must be added and removed.

Because a Collection object stores its items as **Variant** data types, it can store data of almost any type, including the **Object** data type. You can even store other Collection objects within a Collection object, allowing you to create very complex data structures. You can also use a Collection object to simulate a control array, which allows you to mix various kinds of controls into the Collection object.

The ClassModule Object

The **ClassModule** (*filename*.CLS) object is Visual Basic's way of allowing you to create your own classes and reusable objects. You use a **ClassModule** object to define a class that can contain members, which you code using **Event**, **Function**, **Sub**, and **Property** procedures. You can have many different **ClassModule** objects in a single Visual Basic project.

A **ClassModule** object is similar to a standard (.BAS) module. However, the members in a **ClassModule** object can be called and returned or set from any other Visual Basic project without physically loading them into the project. Depending on the types of arguments a specific method or property in a **ClassModule** object takes, you can also call some of them from other applications or languages that are OLE Automation client-enabled. When Visual Basic compiles a project containing a **ClassModule** object, it can automatically create an ActiveX component and register it in the Windows registration database.

Examining The Attributes Of Object-Oriented Programming

As I mentioned earlier, software objects exhibit three characteristics: polymorphism, inheritance, and encapsulation. I guess you could say these attributes are as easy as "pie" to remember (programming is not only useful, it's entertaining, too!). At a very high level of abstraction, we can define these three attributes as follows:

- *Encapsulation* is the process of combining logically related procedures and data in one class/object. In this way, each object is insulated from the rest of the program. Because the object is only using data contained within it or passed to it, and it executes only internal procedures, an encapsulated object is said to implement *data hiding* or *information hiding*.

- *Polymorphism* is a characteristic of an object's method that allows a programmer to call a single method (for example, **Center**) and apply it to many different classes/objects. It is not necessary for you to understand the details of how this is implemented in the object's method in order to call and use the polymorphic method.

- *Inheritance* is the process by which all *subclasses* of a given *superclass* can make use of the members of that superclass/object. Inheritance results in common code being written in a super, base, or parent class, and specialized code being written in sub, derived, or child classes. The final result of creating an object-oriented application while adhering to inheritance is a hierarchy of classes.

Encapsulation

Now that you have a clear idea of encapsulation from our previous description, let's examine this attribute in more detail. Encapsulation means that an object is not coupled to or dependent upon any other object or procedure; instead, it is independent and internally cohesive. It does not contain any global or public variables, and does not require any external procedures to execute its members. The data and behaviors of an encapsulated object can only be accessed and manipulated through its public interface.

In VB, for example, the public interface of a class library composed of **ClassModule** objects includes:

- The hierarchy of classes (**ClassModule** objects) that comprise the class library; these classes are able to expose their public members for reuse.
- The arguments of a **ClassModule** object's public **Event**, **Function**, and **Sub** members.
- The arguments of a **ClassModule** object's public **Property Get**, **Property Let**, and **Property Set** members.
- The values returned, upon success or failure, by a member. These possible values include the error codes returned to describe a syntax or runtime error.

As I pointed out in the previous section, objects are said to exhibit data or information hiding. No one except the programmer who created the object knows the details about what is hidden inside the object. An encapsulated object communicates with another object or part of the program only by receiving and sending messages. In VB, this messaging activity is a two-way street: The object accepts values from calling procedures as arguments for the object's members and returns value(s) to the calling procedure as the result of a **Function** procedure or **Property Get** procedure.

Encapsulation provides several advantages to object-oriented programmers. Specifically, programmers can:

- Protect data from corruption by other objects or parts of the program.
- Hide low-level, complex implementation details from the rest of the program and encourage data abstraction, which results in the ability to implement a simple public interface to a more complex set of private members. It is also easier to maintain legacy code or add new members to the object without affecting any procedures that currently call the object.
- Make it easier to debug individual objects and ensure that a bug in one object will not affect some other part of the system in an apparently unconnected way.
- Promote reuse of the object by other programmers, improving their productivity.

Polymorphism

Moving right along, we're ready to see a more detailed view of polymorphism. If two or more classes have behaviors that share the same name and have the same basic purpose, but are implemented differently, the method/code used to implement the behaviors is said to be polymorphic. The ability to hide the implementation details of an object's method behind a common public interface is known as polymorphism. If an object's method has the characteristic of polymorphism, then a programmer can call or invoke that method for any other object that the method supports, without knowing or caring about the type of object to which the method is applied.

In VB, the **Move** method is polymorphic because it can be applied to over 20 different classes. When you apply the **Move** method to a **Form** object, you pass it the same number of arguments and the same data types as when you apply it to a **PictureBox** object. As a programmer, you don't need to worry about any of the low-level implementation details of a polymorphic method; instead, all you do is apply it to a supported object and pass it the correct values as arguments.

As with encapsulation, polymorphism provides several advantages for object-oriented programmers. Specifically, programmers can:

- Simplify the public interface to an object by minimizing the number of its members and hiding low-level, complex implementation details from the client application programmer.
- Reduce the size and optimize the speed of the EXE or DLL file containing the object.
- Maintain legacy code more easily.
- Promote reuse of the object by other programmers, improving their productivity.

Inheritance

You've conquered the first two attributes without any major blood loss. This third attribute, inheritance, is a piece of cake (or is that "pie"), as well. Although it is possible to define classes independently of each other, inheritance in an OOP language allows you to base, or define, one or more classes as special cases of a more general class. These special cases are known as subclasses, derived classes, or children of that class. The more general class, in turn, is known as the superclass, base class, or parent class of its special cases.

Through inheritance, a subclass can use all the members of its superclass, override any of the inherited members, and define its own new members. Inheritance increases efficiency because behavior or methods that are characteristic of larger groups of objects are programmed only once, in the superclass. Subclasses add to or modify the behavior of a superclass only as required for their special cases.

Of course, inheritance provides its own set of advantages to object-oriented programmers. Specifically, programmers can:

- Minimize redundant programming. Behavior that is characteristic of larger groups of objects is coded only once—in the definition of the higher-level class. Such legacy code is maintained more easily.
- Reduce the size and optimize the speed of the EXE or DLL file containing the objects.
- Increase programming flexibility. Subclasses that exhibit specialized behaviors or that may exhibit new behaviors in the future can merely add to or modify the behavior of their superclass as required.
- VB5 still doesn't support inheritance in the classic sense of the term, but you can subclass existing objects with it. Also, Sheridan Software Systems, Inc., one of the pre-eminent ActiveX control software manufacturers, sells a product for Visual Basic, called ClassAssist, that implements inheritance and subclassing to a useful degree.

An Introduction To COM, OLE, And ActiveX

Before we move on, I'd like to explain several concepts that you, the object-oriented programmer, need to understand: COM, OLE, and ActiveX.

The Component Object Model (COM) is Microsoft's low-level software protocol for code modules/objects that are cross-platform and cross-language capable. Until recently, most COM development has been done with C++ on Intel-based PCs, but now, Windows NT also supports COM on MIPS, DEC Alpha, and PowerPC RISC systems.

OLE (Object Linking and Embedding) is Microsoft's high-level implementation of COM. In the most general sense, OLE defines and implements a set of software technologies that allows applications to connect to or communicate with each other. This process of communication is accomplished via messaging from various kinds of objects. The many manifestations of OLE (linking, embedding, ActiveX components, ActiveX controls, and so on), taken as a whole, comprise COM.

ActiveX is Microsoft's name for a group of software technologies built on top of OLE. Microsoft touts ActiveX as the best way to add powerful Internet connectivity capabilities to traditional business applications, and to endow traditional Internet communications programs with true computational power. ActiveX essentially takes the diverse capabilities of OLE's object sharing-and-messaging model and expands them to function in the environment of the Internet.

One of the major objectives of the COM/OLE/ActiveX model is to facilitate and encourage the development of future component applications. The huge applications that currently make up the Microsoft Office suite are obvious candidates to be deconstructed into components because they require a long time to load and consume a large amount of Windows resources.

The only significant alternative to the COM/OLE/ActiveX model is OpenDoc, a cross-platform object protocol that is being funded and developed by a consortium of Microsoft's major competitors, including IBM, Apple, Novell, Lotus, and several other notable software manufacturers. Unfortunately for the OpenDoc adherents, COM/OLE has been evolving for almost three years and has gained a significant market share; OpenDoc is just emerging from beta testing and is still not available in any applications.

OLE/ActiveX Terminology

To fully understand OLE/ActiveX, you need to get a few definitions under your belt. The following items represent some important terms related to the OLE/ActiveX software technologies:

- An *ActiveX document* is a file containing an OLE link(s). This link enables the automatic launching of a program, which can then interact with the file's contents. An ActiveX document permits an application to share data created by another ActiveX-enabled application. A document containing data created by another application is called a *compound document*. Data can be embedded in an ActiveX document and contained entirely within it or created by a link to a file containing the data.

- An *ActiveX document container* application (called an OLE client application in the past) is one that can display and manipulate ActiveX document files. All of Microsoft's major 32-bit and 16-bit applications and programming languages, including Visual Basic, are ActiveX document container applications. Most of the other major software manufacturers' applications are also ActiveX document container-enabled.

- An *ActiveX component* (for example, an EXE or DLL file created with Visual Basic that contains a **ClassModule** object) exposes programmable objects for reuse by a client application containing an ActiveX component-compliant programming language. There are two types of ActiveX components: *in-process components*, which share the same address or memory space as the client application, and *out-of-process components*, which run in a memory space separate from the client. ActiveX components were formerly known as OLE Automation servers.

- A *remote ActiveX component*, also called a Remote Automation Object (RAO), is an out-of-process component that communicates with networked client applications via Remote Procedure Calls (RPCs). RAO ActiveX component technology can be used to develop three-tier, client/server database applications, where an RAO is used in the middle tier to implement business rules. It is also the forerunner of Network OLE, which will appear in a more fully realized implementation in the version of Windows NT that is code-named Cairo.

- An *ActiveX control* (formerly known as a custom control) is a special kind of in-process ActiveX component that also exposes events. Members (events, methods, and properties) exposed by an ActiveX control are accessible only to applications like Visual Basic, Delphi 2.0, and PowerBuilder 5.0, which are ActiveX control container-enabled. In its most recent implementation in VB5, an ActiveX control can also easily be embedded within a Web page on the Internet.

Using Windows API Functions

When a Visual Basic programmer writes object-oriented code, the performance of that code must be a high priority. The speed at which the members of an ActiveX component's object run is never as fast as the same code included within the application's own executable (EXE) file. Some constraints on an object's performance include the programming overhead associated with the abstraction layer of the ActiveX component, the time required to create an object instance of the class to be used, and the time required to do the extra syntax checking necessary to resolve late-binding, data type mismatch problems.

As a result of these and other constraints on performance, you need to use every trick in the Visual Basic programmer's toolkit to optimize the code composing an object's members. One of the best sources of optimization comes from the Windows API functions. For example, a simple Windows API function like **SendMessage** can speed up some of the common algorithms related to **ListBox** objects by 200 to 400 percent. And, as with Visual Basic programming in general, sometimes the only way to accomplish certain tasks is to use one or more Windows API functions.

Windows API functions are used throughout the code that comprises this book's class library/ActiveX component. It is not necessary that you learn as much about Windows programming as a C or C++ developer in order to use Windows API functions effectively. However, if you have not dealt with Windows API functions much in the past, then some background information about the concepts underlying them will help you to better understand how they are used in the book's class library. The following sections will arm you with all the information you'll need.

The Windows API

We'll begin with the basics: *API* is an acronym for Application Programming Interface. An API is a set of procedures, both functions and subs, that are part of one application or operating system, but that can be called by another application.

Many software products have their own APIs, through which third-party programmers can access specific functionality. For example, the server database program Microsoft SQL Server has its own API. As a VB programmer, if you purchase a copy of the *SDK* (system development kit) for Microsoft SQL Server (and a couple books that explain how to use it), you can write VB code that will directly access and manipulate the functionality of SQL Server. This code would, generally speaking, run faster than any other kind of VB code that you could write to use SQL Server (for example, ODBC code) because it directly accesses the core procedures of the product and does not get slowed down by any layers of code abstraction.

The Windows operating system has its own API, whose procedures can be called by any Windows programming language. A Windows programming language like Visual Basic (or, for that matter, PowerBuilder or Delphi) is, in reality, a huge layer of code abstraction that implements the most commonly used Windows API functions. The gory details of all the calls that VB is incessantly making to hundreds of Windows API functions are hidden from you.

Of course, you pay for this easy-to-use, intuitive layer of abstraction—and the price is slower performance overall. In certain situations, however, you can fruitfully bypass Visual Basic itself (and its layer of code abstraction) and directly access the Windows API by calling one or more of its hundreds of procedures.

The current sets of Windows APIs are:

- **Win16**. The 16-bit API for Windows 3.x. This API also runs under Windows 95 and Windows NT in 16-bit mode. The 16-bit versions of VB and VBA (Visual Basic for Applications) can access this API.

- **Win32**. The 32-bit API for Windows NT. The 32-bit versions of VB and VBA can access this API.

- **Win32c**. A subset of the Win32 API that runs under Windows 95. You can call any Win32 procedure under Win32c, but some of them are not implemented and will not do anything. Some Windows 95-specific procedures that are included in Win32c are not part of Win32 on Windows NT. The 32-bit versions of VB and VBA can access this API.

- **Win32s**. A subset of Win32 that is supported under Windows 3.x. No version of VB or VBA can access the Win32s API.

Dynamic Link Libraries (DLLs)

A *dynamic link library* (DLL) file is one containing a library of procedures that are specifically designed and written to be called under the Windows operating system. Windows DLL files, when they are compiled, use a process called *dynamic linking*. Dynamic linking allows the programmer to specify which of the many procedures included in the file are to be accessible from other applications. This technique is termed *exporting* the procedure.

When VB creates a Windows executable file from a project's source code, it uses a technique termed *importing* the function. It scans the source code, lists all the references to procedures that are not part of its own library of procedures, and notes the DLL files in which these procedures can be found.

If the path of code execution in a VB executable file requires a call to a procedure that is not in the executable, Windows loads the dynamic link library (.DLL) file that contains that procedure. At that point, all the public procedures in the DLL file become accessible, and memory addresses are specified and dynamically linked into the executable file.

This technique of dynamic linking contrasts with the more traditional approach called *static linking*. Statically linking a library of procedures to an executable file created with Fortran for Unix, for example, means that all the information needed by the executable to access the library procedures is fixed at compile time. This information then remains unchanged (that is, *static*) while the executable is running. Dynamic linking provides several advantages over static linking:

- Changes or enhancements to libraries of procedures are easier to make. If you don't disturb the existing public interface to the procedures in the DLL library file, all you have to do is replace the older version with the new one. You do not have to go back and recompile all the executables that use it (as would be necessary with statically linked libraries).

- DLL files are efficient in their use of RAM because they are active in memory only when they are being called or dynamically linked to.

- DLL files are efficient in their use of hard disk space because the same DLL library file can be used by the software products of many different manufacturers.

Dynamic link library files typically have the extension DLL, but this is not necessary. ActiveX controls (which use the extension .OCX) are also DLL files, although they have some special features of their own. Windows device drivers are contained in DLL files but typically have the extension .DRV. Some Windows operating system DLL files, especially the 16-bit versions, use the standard executable file extension .EXE.

Table 1.1 lists the most common 32-bit Windows DLL files. Table 1.2 lists the most common 16-bit Windows DLL files.

The Declare Statement

To call a Windows API function from Visual Basic, you must first declare the name of the procedure you want to use in the General Declarations section of a code module. You do this by declaring a reference to an external procedure in a DLL file with VB's **Declare** statement. For example, **GetVersionEx** is a 32-bit Windows API function that obtains information

Table 1.1　32-bit Windows DLL files.

File Name	Description
GDI32.DLL	Graphics procedures
KERNEL32.DLL	System procedures
USER32.DLL	User-interface management procedures
COMDLG32.DLL	Common dialog box procedures
WINMM.DLL	Multimedia procedures
MAPI32.DLL	Mail and messaging procedures
TAPI32.DLL	Telephony and communications procedures
WING32.DLL	3D games procedures
COMCTL32.DLL	Windows 95 and Windows NT control procedures
NETAPI32.DLL	Network procedures
ODBC32.DLL	ODBC (Open Database Connectivity) procedures

Table 1.2　16-bit Windows DLL files.

File Name	Description
GDI.EXE	Graphics procedures
KRNL386.EXE	System procedures
USER.EXE	User-interface management procedures
SHELL.DLL	Windows shell procedures
TOOLHELP.DLL	Task and other low-level procedures
COMMDLG.DLL	Common dialog box procedures
MMSYSTEM.DLL	Multimedia procedures
MAPI.DLL	Mail and messaging procedures
TAPI.DLL	Telephony and communications procedures

about the version of the operating system that is running. Its declaration is:

```
Private Declare Function GetVersionEx& Lib "KERNEL32" _
                    Alias "GetVersionExA" _
                    (VerInfo As OSVERSIONINFO)
```

VB's **Declare** statement can have these major syntactical parts (brackets denote optional items and the pipe symbol denotes an either | or choice):

- [**Public** | **Private**]. **Public** (the default) indicates that the procedure is accessible to all other procedures in all modules. **Private** indicates it is accessible only to other procedures in the module where it is declared.

- **Sub** | **Function**. **Sub** indicates that the procedure does not return a value. **Function** indicates that the procedure returns a value that can be used in an expression.

- *name*. Indicates the name of any valid procedure in the DLL file.

- **Lib**. Indicates that a DLL file contains the procedure being declared.

- *"libname"*. Indicates the name of the DLL file containing the declared procedure. This name must be enclosed within quotation marks.

- [**Alias**]. Indicates that the procedure being called has another name in the DLL file. This is useful when the external procedure name is the same as a Visual Basic keyword or the name of a constant or variable.

- [*"aliasname"*]. Indicates the name of any valid procedure in the DLL file. This name must be enclosed within quotation marks.

- [([*arglist*])]: Indicates a list of variables representing arguments that are passed to the procedure when it is called.

- [**As** type]. Indicates the data type of a value returned by a function procedure.

For a more detailed explanation of the **Declare** statement, see VB's Help file for the help topic titled *Declare Statement*.

User-Defined Data Types And Constants

Some Windows API functions require predefined user-defined data types and many of them use predefined constants. For example, the 32-bit Windows API function **GetVersionEx**'s declaration requires that the user-defined data type OSVERSIONINFO be declared above it in the General Declarations section of a module. The declaration would look like this:

```
Private Type OSVERSIONINFO

    TypeSize As Long
    MajorVer As Long
    MinorVer As Long
    BuildNbr As Long
    ID As Long
    CSDVer As String * 128

End Type
```

GetVersionEx also uses predefined constants to specify the values that some of the elements of its user-defined data type can assume. For example:

```
' Constants for Windows API functions:
Const WF_WINNT = &H4000&
Const VER_PLATFORM_WIN32_WINDOWS = 1
Const VER_PLATFORM_WIN32_NT = 2
```

Windows API function constants have been defined by Microsoft. It is conventional Windows programming practice to use them to enhance the readability of your code. These constants are contained in the files WIN31API.TXT, WIN32API.TXT, and WINMMSYS.TXT that come with Visual Basic. Next time you have a few minutes to spare, I suggest you take the time to read these files to familiarize yourself with the constants.

Windows Objects, Handles, And Device Contexts

Once you have declared a Windows API function and any user-defined data types and constants that it requires, you are able to call it from any Visual Basic procedure. Any Visual Basic programmer who has worked with Windows API functions knows that you have to learn to call them the old-fashioned way: one-at-a-time, by working through examples. Because there are so many of them (almost 2,000 of the 32-bit variety), and almost all of them are codependent on others when being used, it takes a long time and a lot of hard work to conceptually and intuitively grasp how they work together.

There are three high-level concepts that you as a Visual Basic programmer must understand about the Windows operating system in order to use Windows API functions. These three concepts are Windows objects, Windows handles, and Windows device contexts. Let's take a look at these concepts in more detail.

WINDOWS OBJECTS

Windows itself is object-oriented. When a Visual Basic programmer calls Windows API functions, some abstract object(s) is being manipulated. For example, a pen is a graphical object that Windows uses to encapsulate the style, width, color, and other properties of lines that are drawn on a **Screen** or **Form** object.

Windows works with many abstract objects. Each object has a different use and behaves in differently than the others. Some objects are exclusive to an application, while others can be shared among several applications. After being used, some objects are automatically removed from memory by Windows; other objects, however, must be explicitly destroyed and removed from memory by the programmer.

Table 1.3 lists some of the most common objects used by Windows.

WINDOWS HANDLES

Windows identifies and keeps track of all objects with *handles*. In 16-bit Windows, a handle is a 16-bit **Integer**. In 32-bit Windows, a handle is a 32-bit **Long**. When Windows itself is started, it assigns unique handles to its startup objects. Then, when a Windows application is run, Windows assigns unique handles to all the objects that application uses. If a user terminates an application and later restarts it, Windows assigns different handles to the application's objects the second time it is run. According to VB's Help file, in the help topic titled *hWnd Property*, you should never store a handle in a variable because its value can change even while a program is running.

In VB itself, the **hWnd** property of the **Form**, **MDIForm**, and certain control objects returns the handle that Windows has assigned to that object. The **hWnd** property is used when calling many Windows API functions because it is how Windows knows which VB object to apply the function to. In addition, most non-VB objects (that is, Windows objects) have handles. In order to manipulate these objects with Windows API functions, you must identify them by their handles.

Table 1.3 Common Windows objects.

Object	Description
Bitmap	Area in memory that specifies the attributes of a bitmap
Brush	Used to fill areas while drawing other objects
Cursor	The mouse pointer's image
Device context	Describes attributes of current drawing environment
Memory	Specifies a block of memory
Menu	A menu bar or item
Pen	Specifies attributes of a line while drawing an object
Window	Represents a window displayed on the screen

Windows Device Contexts

A *device context* object in Windows specifies the attributes of the area in which Windows is currently drawing text or graphics. Some of the attributes of a device context are its size, the foreground and background colors, and the type of device (screen display or printer), and so on.

Visual Basic itself automatically provides access to three kinds of device context objects and their properties. These three Visual Basic objects—**Form**, **PictureBox**, and **Printer**—each have an **hDC** property, which returns a handle provided by Windows to the device context of an object.

Some of the properties and methods of these three Visual Basic objects allow you to easily draw on them. However, there is also a large set of Windows API functions that get and set device context object attributes. These functions can, given certain situations and requirements, provide a greater degree of control over device context objects, and, of course, they can perform some tasks significantly faster than native Visual Basic code.

Conditional Compilation

Both VB4 and VB5 support conditional compilation; that is, the ability to compile the same source code to run on different Windows platforms. The **#If**, **#ElseIf**, **#Else**, and **#End If** directives and the **Win16** and **Win32** intrinsic compiler constants enable conditional compilation. As of its Beta 2 release, VB5 seems to no longer support conditional compilation for 16-bit Windows. However, it still supports conditional compilation for possible future versions of Windows.

Conditional compilation is necessary in three situations:

- If your Visual Basic source code uses Windows API functions, you need to use conditional compilation. The DLL file names and data types (**Longs** vs. **Integers**) are different for 32-bit and 16-bit Windows API functions.

- If your project uses any ActiveX controls, then you would need to use the 16-bit version of the ActiveX control when compiling under 16-bit Visual Basic and the 32-bit version of the ActiveX control when compiling under 32-bit Visual Basic.

- If you want to code a feature that Windows 3.x supports but Windows 95 does not (for example, a system modal message box), you will have to conditionally compile that code.

In the sample code of the book's CD-ROM, I have kept the conditionally-compiled 16-bit code. I have done this for two reasons. First, all the book's code also runs under VB4, which continues to support 16-bit compilation. Second, there is a possibility that the final version of VB5 will include 16-bit Window support.

You can't do conditional compilation with VBXs

Because the old VBX custom controls can only be 16-bit, they cannot support conditional compilation.

Information About The Windows API

This section lists places where you can seek more information on the WAindows API.

VISUAL BASIC FILES

The Professional Edition of VB5 provides information on the Microsoft Windows API in several files located in the \WINAPI subdirectory of your Visual Basic directory. Be sure to check out the following files:

- **WIN31API.TXT**. This file contains function declarations, user-defined data type declarations, and the values for constants used in the functions for the 16-bit Windows API.

- **WIN31WH.HLP**. This file documents each 16-bit function in terms of the C programming language. This file is found only in 16-bit versions of VB and is the same file that came with the Professional Edition of VB3.

- **WIN32API.TXT**. This file contains function declarations, user-defined data type declarations, and the values for constants used in the functions for the 32-bit Windows API.

- **WINMMSYS.TXT**. This file contains declarations, user-defined data type declarations, and constants for Windows 3.1 multimedia API functions.

Unfortunately, Microsoft did not distribute the API32.HLP file with any edition of VB5—and it is the *only* Help file in existence that documents the 32-bit functions of the Windows API. If you want a copy of this file, you must buy the Microsoft Visual C++ programming language. Even then, API32.HLP is written for C and C++ programmers.

VISUAL BASIC'S TEXT API VIEWER

The Professional Edition of VB5 also comes with 32-bit and 16-bit versions of a utility called the Text API Viewer. This utility provides access to the WIN31API.TXT, WIN32API.TXT, and WINMMSYS.TXT files. You use the utility to copy and paste API functions, user-defined data types, and the values for constants into your Visual Basic code. Figure 1.1 shows the Text API Viewer.

Unfortunately, the Text API Viewer is not a commercial-quality utility. I've found several deficiencies, which are shown here:

- The Available Items list is single-select enabled, which means that you can only pick the functions you need one at a time.

- The Copy button only copies the selected functions from the Selected Items list to the clipboard. You must then manually paste the items into the General Declarations section of a Visual Basic code module.

- The API Type drop-down list has selections for Constants and Types, but selecting one of these items only fills in the Available Items list with all the possible constants or user-defined data types associated with a given Windows API set; the utility doesn't seem to know which constants or which user-defined data types go with which Declarations.

- The utility does not include a Help file, sample code, or any examples of how to use any of the API functions.

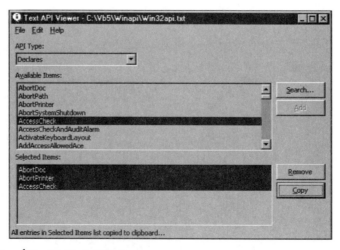

Figure 1.1   Visual Basic's Text API Viewer.

THE WINDOWS API BROWSER UTILITY

The best Windows API utility on the market for Visual Basic and VBA programmers is the Windows API Browser. I know it's a great utility because I developed it myself (a little self-promotion is good for the soul). The Windows API Browser is meant for the professional Visual Basic or VBA developer who uses Windows API functions when programming. It is modeled on Microsoft's Object Browser in VB4, Excel 5 and 7, and so on. Figure 1.2 shows the browser in action. The Windows API Browser includes many helpful features. The browser:

- Runs under Windows 3.1, Windows For Workgroups 3.11, Windows 95, and NT Workstation/Server (3.5 and higher).

- Automatically pastes Windows API information into a Visual Basic or VBA code module. With one click of a command button, the browser pastes the declaration and any associated user-defined data types, constants and call arguments for the selected Windows API function(s) directly into the current code module.

- Supports multifunction copy-and-paste capability. You can paste a maximum of 20 API functions and associated data.

- Contains a Help file that includes sample code for more than 350 of the 32-bit API functions and 320 of the 16-bit API functions most commonly used by Visual Basic programmers. Running these sample code demonstrations is an excellent way to learn how to call the Windows API from within Visual Basic or VBA. The Help file also contains a comprehensive, cross-referenced index to Windows API tips, tricks, and information.

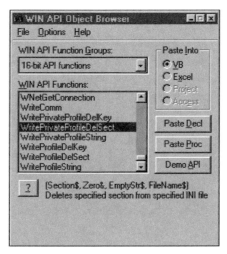

Figure 1.2 The Windows API Browser utility.

- Allows you to select or deselect options for pasting user-defined data types, constants, and call arguments.

- Senses whenever any of the four supported programming environments is opened or closed and enables or disables pasting to it accordingly.

- Displays, for each API function, the sequence and data types of its arguments and its purpose.

- Displays a context-sensitive help topic for each API function if you have Microsoft's WIN31WH.HLP file (16-bit functions) or API32.HLP file (32-bit functions) on your system.

- Allows you to search for and paste any Windows API constants listed in Microsoft's WIN31API.TXT, WIN32API.TXT, and WINMMSYS.TXT files.

- Can be placed on top of other windows.

If you like the Help file and example code that comes with this book's class library, you will love the Windows API Browser and its Help file, which is available for $9.99 + $5.00 (S/H).

You can get information about how to purchase the Windows API Browser from these sources:

- The advertising blurb at the back of this book.

- The demonstration copy of the Windows API Browser included with this book.

- Via email. For CompuServe users, send email to 75521,3130. For all others, use the address INTERNET:75521.3130@compuserve.com. Enter *Want To Buy* as the subject of the message.

BOOKS

Next time you're browsing in a bookstore, I recommend that you pick up one of the following books to learn more about calling and using Windows API functions from within Visual Basic. Both books are some of the finest resources around.

- *Visual Basic 4 API How-To*, Jerky & Brierley, ISBN 1-57169-072-7, CD-ROM

- *Visual Basic Programmer's Guide To The Win32 API*, Daniel Appleman, ISBN 1-56276-287-7, CD-ROM

Appleman's book is the standard reference work for using the Windows API from within Visual Basic; no Visual Basic programmer should be without it.

CREATING A PROCEDURE 2

An important point to understand about object-oriented programming is that it evolved from, and is founded upon, the concepts of *structured programming.* Two decades ago, structured programming was being touted as the best way to write and develop complex software applications. In the most general sense, the term refers to an approach to programming that produces software with clean flow, clear design, and a high degree of modularity and hierarchical structure.

Structured programming was a reaction to the prevalence at that time of what was termed *spaghetti code.* Spaghetti code is code that is characterized by convoluted program flow, usually resulting from excessive or inappropriate use of **goto** or **jump** statements, or some other similar language construct. To address the problems inherent in the spaghetti-code approach to writing code, the adherents of structured programming emphasized the importance of using a *procedural language* and writing procedural code.

A procedural language is one in which the basic programming construct is the procedure. The most widely used high-level languages, such as C, Pascal, Basic, FORTRAN, COBOL, and Ada, are all (in their present incarnations) procedural languages. All object-oriented programming languages, such as C++, Smalltalk, VB5, PowerBuilder 5, and Delphi 2, are also, first and foremost, procedural languages. So, we will start our discussion of object-oriented programming with VB5 by reviewing the concept of the procedure and how it is used in Visual Basic.

Characteristics Of A Good Procedure

The term "good" in the heading for this section is by no means subjective. A good procedure has certain elements. In this section, we'll discuss exactly what elements make up a "good" procedure. However, before we tackle what makes up a procedure, we must first examine what a procedure actually is.

A *procedure* (or routine) is a sequence of code statements executed as a unit. All code written in a Visual Basic form (FRM), standard (BAS), or class (CLS) *module* should be in the form of procedures (or functions, a variation on the idea of procedures). A procedure performs a specific, precisely defined task. Well-designed procedures divide complex code tasks into more manageable units.

There are two general kinds of procedures used in VB and Windows programming:

- An *event procedure* is code that remains idle until called upon to respond to events caused by the user, triggered by the operating system, or raised by code. In VB4 and earlier versions, you could only write an event procedure in a form module; the events themselves were predefined by the programming language. With VB5, however, you can declare user-defined events in a form, class, or user-document (DOB) module. You use the new **Event** statement to declare the user-defined event and the **RaiseEvent** statement to fire it and execute the event procedure it contains. Each **Form** object and control object still has the set of predefined events that it can recognize (for example, the **Load** and **Unload** events of a **Form** object).

- A *general procedure* tells an application how to perform a specific task. Once a general procedure is declared, it must be explicitly called or invoked by a statement in an event procedure or another general procedure. It can be placed in any Visual Basic code module. There are two kinds of general procedures: public and private. Public general procedures can be called from any module in your application, providing you qualify the name of the procedure with the name of the module that contains the procedure. Private general procedures can only be called from within the module that contains the private general procedure.

Attributes Of A Procedure

A well-designed and well-written event or general procedure, by common consensus, has certain attributes. It should:

- Implement a formal specification. The specification of a procedure should precisely define what the procedure is to do. It should not define with what algorithms or syntax the programmer is to implement the specification.
- Do one thing and do it well; that is, the procedure should meet its specifications and run sufficiently fast on the specified hardware platform.
- Have an appropriate name. If the procedure is a **Function** procedure, the name should be a clear, verb-plus-object name. If the procedure is a **Property** procedure, the name should include the name of the property that is set or returned. A good procedure returns some value under all circumstances.
- Have a reasonable number of arguments. The maximum number of arguments is debatable, but a good rule-of-thumb is that it should not exceed seven. These arguments should be an optimal combination of required and optional arguments.
- Protect itself from bad input values passed as its arguments, handle exceptions gracefully, and trap all runtime errors. If a runtime or syntax error does occur, it should return an error code which the calling statement can read and react to.
- Exhibit abstraction; that is, all parts of the procedure that can be used by more than one procedure should be put into procedures of their own.

- Exhibit encapsulation; that is, any variables or other procedures that it depends on should be contained in the same code module or ActiveX component.
- Allow for quick-and-easy code changes and maintenance.
- Document its interface assumptions and the logic of its algorithm with comments in the procedure itself and with a Help file topic that can be accessed online.

Optimal Placement Of A Procedure

As a Visual Basic programmer, you should strive to write every procedure's code so that it can be declared and placed in a standard or class module. When you write a procedure this way, you ensure that it is not dependent on or coupled with any form module and that it can be called from any other procedure (if it is declared as **Public**). Also, a form module loads and displays itself most quickly when it contains as little code as possible.

Placing a procedure in a standard or class module conforms to the object-oriented programming paradigm. Communication with the procedure is accomplished via message-passing—by passing values from the calling statement to the procedure's arguments and, for the **Function** and **Property Get** procedures, by returning some value(s) from the procedure to the calling statement. A procedure written in a class module, which is part of an ActiveX component becomes a method of a reusable object. Such a method can be encapsulated to any degree desired, and can be designed and written to exhibit polymorphism.

Creating A Sample Procedure

Now that you are fully versed on the elements of a procedure, let's try our hand at creating one. First, we'll cover the syntax used for declaring a procedure, then we'll actually get our feet wet and write some simple code.

Syntax For Declaring A Procedure

The **Function**, **Property**, and **Sub** statements that declare a procedure, and their identifiers and keywords, are Visual Basic's most versatile and powerful syntactical elements. These identifiers and keywords are described in the following list (brackets denote optional items and the pipe symbol denotes an either | or choice):

- [**Public** | **Private**]. As I mentioned earlier, **Public** (the default) indicates that the procedure is accessible to all other procedures in all modules; **Private** indicates it is accessible only to other procedures in the module where it is declared.

- [**Static**]. Indicates that the method's local variables are preserved between calls. The **Static** attribute does not affect variables that are declared outside the procedure, even if they are used in its procedure.

- [**Optional**]. Indicates that an argument is not required. If used, all subsequent arguments must also be optional and declared using the **Optional** keyword. All **Optional** arguments must be of the **Variant** data type. **Optional** cannot be used for any argument if the **ParamArray** keyword is used.

- [**ByVal** | **ByRef**]. **ByVal** indicates that an argument is passed by value, allowing a method to access a copy of the variable. This technique ensures that the variable's actual value (if it is not an object variable) cannot be changed by the method. **ByRef** (the default) indicates that an argument is passed by reference or memory address, allowing a method to access and change the actual variable that is passed.

- [**ParamArray**]. Is allowed only as the last argument. This keyword indicates that the final argument is an **Optional** array of **Variant** elements. **ParamArray** allows you to provide an arbitrary number of arguments. It may not be used with **ByVal**, **ByRef**, or **Optional**.

- [**Exit Function** | **Exit Property** | **Exit Sub**]. These keywords cause an immediate exit from the respective type of procedure. Program execution continues with the statement following the statement that called the **Function**, **Property**, or **Sub** procedure. Any number of **Exit** statements can appear anywhere in a procedure.

The CenterForm Procedure

Whenever a dialog box or a form other than a multiple-document interface form is displayed, Windows programming convention dictates that it should initially appear in the center of the screen. The single statement required to perform this task is usually written in the **Form_Load** event procedure and is shown in Listing 2.1.

Listing 2.1   Simple procedure to center form.

```
Private Sub Form_Load()

   Move (Screen.Width - Width) * .5, (Screen.Height - Height) * .5

End Sub
```

No name required

*Any statement that applies a method or property to the **Form** object whose code is currently executing need not explicitly specify the **Name** property of that **Form** object. In the code in Listing 2.1, the references to the **Move** method and **Width** and **Height** properties utilize this technique, which improves performance by one to two percent.*

Although the code in Listing 2.1 does center a **Form** object, it has some limitations:

- It will only center a **Form** or **MDIForm** object. It will not center a MDI child form within a **MDIForm** object.
- It cannot be called from any other event procedure in the **Form** object. If a user has temporarily dragged the form off to the side of the screen and now wants to recenter it, this statement cannot be re-executed without reloading the **Form** object.
- It does not trap for any possible runtime errors.
- It is not encapsulated in its own procedure, so it cannot be reused. Many VB programmers have written this same line of code, or some variation on it, hundreds of times.

The objective of this chapter is to create a reusable procedure named **CenterForm** that exemplifies the attributes of a good procedure and overcomes the limitations of the code in Listing 2.1. To do this, however, you need to write more code and place it in a standard module. You also need to understand Visual Basic's object hierarchy as it pertains to the **Form** and **MDIForm** objects. Of the two types of forms, the **Form** object is the more generic object data type. Although the Visual Basic documentation does not explicitly say so, you can assume from their behavior that the **Form** object and **MDIForm** object are an example of a superclass and subclass relationship.

To begin, start VB5. If this is the first time you are running the application, the dialog box in Figure 2.1 appears. For our **CenterForm** procedure example, double click on the Standard EXE icon.

Because you can use VB5 to create many different kinds of applications (each of which requires a different configuration of modules), Microsoft has provided the New Project dialog box to facilitate the selection of the module configuration required by each kind of application. If you select the

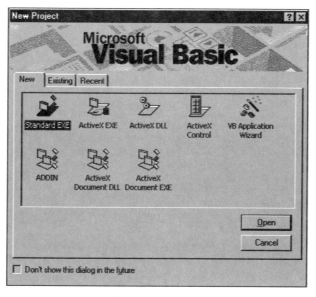

Figure 2.1 The VB5 New Project dialog box.

"Don't show this dialog in the future" checkbox, the New Project dialog box will not display when you first start VB. If you select this option and then change your mind, simply select Tools|Options to display the Options dialog box, shown in Figure 2.2. Select the Environment tab and then select the "Prompt for project" checkbox.

Now that you have a Standard EXE project opened, select Project|Add Module. Again, if this is your first time running VB5, the Add Module dialog box displays. This dialog box lists the two types of modules available (Module and ADDIN). For this example, double click the Module icon to add a standard module to the project. As with the New Project dialog box, if you select the "Don't show this dialog in the future" checkbox, the Add Module dialog box will not display again. If you want this dialog box to display when you select Project|Add Module, select Tools|Options to display the Options dialog box. Select the Environment tab and then select the Show Templates For Modules checkbox.

Declare a **Function** procedure in Module1 by typing "Function CenterForm (Frm As Form) As Boolean" at the bottom of the code window and pressing Enter. Visual Basic then creates the beginning and ending statements of the procedure. The code that makes up the **CenterForm** procedure is in Listing 2.2.

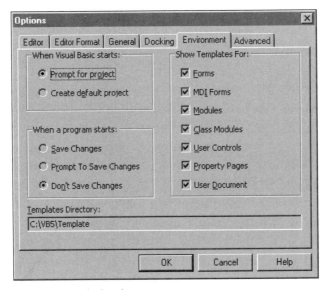

Figure 2.2 The VB5 Options dialog box.

Why Frm is a Form

*The **Frm** argument is declared as the **Object** data type **Form** so that you can pass it a reference to either the **Name** property of a **Form** or **MDIForm** object. This works because, in VB, the **MDIForm** class is actually a subclass of the **Form** superclass.*

Listing 2.2   Code for CenterForm procedure.

```
Function CenterForm (Frm As Form) As Boolean

    ' Constants for literals:
    Const MB_ICONEXCLAMATION = 48
    Const FIFTEEN = 15
    Const ONE_HALF = 0.5

    ' Variables:
    Dim X          As Integer
    Dim Y          As Integer
    Dim ParWid     As Integer
    Dim ParHgt     As Integer
    Dim ChildFrm   As Boolean
    Dim Msg        As String
    Dim Rct        As RECT

    ' Enable in-line error-handling.
    On Error Resume Next
```

```
' * If Frm argument is MDI child:
'    a) Get handle of MDIForm object and its client coordinates.
'    b) Compute height and width of client portion of MDIForm
'       and convert pixels to twips (15 twips per pixel).
'    c) Compute X and Y coordinates of MDI child to center.
' * If Frm argument is not MDI child, compute coordinates normally.

If Frm.MDIChild Then

    If Err = False Then
        On Error GoTo ET
        ChildFrm = True
        GetClientRect GetParent(Frm.hWnd), Rct
        ParWid = (Rct.Rgt - Rct.Lft) * Screen.TwipsPerPixelY
        ParHgt = (Rct.Bot - Rct.Top) * Screen.TwipsPerPixelX
        X = (ParWid - Frm.Width) * ONE_HALF
        Y = (ParHgt - Frm.Height) * ONE_HALF
    End If

End If

If Not ChildFrm Then
    On Error GoTo ET
    X = (Screen.Width - Frm.Width) * ONE_HALF
    Y = (Screen.Height - Frm.Height) * ONE_HALF
End If

' Center form and return True to indicate success:
Frm.Move X, Y
Err = False
CenterForm = True
Exit Function

ET:

' If run-time error occurs, trap and return False:
Msg = "Run-time error " & Err & " occurred."
MsgBox Msg, MB_ICONEXCLAMATION, "CenterForm"
Err = False

End Function
```

Besides the execution of the algorithm itself (which is straightforward), there are three points to note about the code in Listing 2.2:

- The **On Error** statement's **GoTo** line variation no longer requires that the line label be unique within a code module. Every error handler that is enabled with the **On Error GoTo** line syntax in this book's class library is named *ET* (for Error Trap).

- In any procedure where a runtime error can occur and that has an error handler, always reset the value of **Err** to **False** (zero) before exiting the procedure. Exiting the procedure automatically disables the procedure's error handler, but it does not reinitialize the properties of the **Err** object.

- Because you want this procedure to be as flexible as possible and, so, be able to center MDI child forms on a **MDIForm** object, the code uses the **GetParent** and **GetClientRect** Windows API functions, which need to be declared in the General Declarations section of the standard module. **GetParent** returns the handle of the parent/container object (a **MDIForm** object) of the MDI child form to be centered. The handle that **GetParent** returns is then used by **GetClientRect** to fill the user-defined data type RECT, represented by the variable **Rct**, with the coordinates of the upper-left and lower-right corners of the client portion of the parent/container object. The declarations for the two Windows API functions are shown in Listing 2.3. Note that they are conditionally declared so that the **CenterForm** procedure will run under both 32-bit and 16-bit Visual Basic.

Listing 2.3 Declarations of Windows API functions.

```
' User-defined data types:
#If Win32 Then

    Private Type RECT
        Lft As Long
        Top As Long
        Rgt As Long
        Bot As Long
    End Type

#Else

    Private Type RECT
        Lft As Integer
        Top As Integer
        Rgt As Integer
        Bot As Integer
    End Type

#End If

' DLL functions:
#If Win32 Then

    Private Declare Function GetClientRect& Lib "USER32" _
                            (ByVal hWnd&, Rct As RECT)
    Private Declare Function GetParent& Lib "USER32" _
                            (ByVal hWnd&)
#Else

    Private Declare Function GetClientRect% Lib "USER" _
```

```
                                (ByVal hWnd%, Rct As RECT)
    Private Declare Function GetParent% Lib "USER" _
                                (ByVal hWnd%)
```

```
#End If
```

Applying A Procedure To Different Objects

We've learned a lot about procedures in a very short time. Now that we have a working procedure, let's practice applying it to some objects to see what it is we've done.

Applying CenterForm To A Form

To call the **CenterForm** procedure and apply it to a **Form** object, select Form1 and write the code shown in Listing 2.4 in its **Form_Load** event procedure.

Listing 2.4   Applying CenterForm procedure to Form.

```
Private Sub Form_Load()

    ' Variable.
    Dim Result As Boolean
    Result = CenterForm(Me)

End Sub
```

Select Run | Start to execute the procedure (you can also press F5 or click on the toolbar's shortcut button). The procedure centers the normal **Form** object. Notice that in the calling statement, you can pass either the **Name** property setting of the **Form** object or the keyword **Me** to the **CenterForm** procedure.

Applying CenterForm To A MDIForm And Child

To call the **CenterForm** procedure and apply it to a **MDIForm** object, select Project | Add MDI Form. VB displays the Add MDI Form dialog box. Double click on the MDI Form icon, select MDIForm1, and write the code shown in Listing 2.5 in its **MDIForm_Load** event procedure.

Listing 2.5   Applying CenterForm procedure to MDIForm.

```
Private Sub MDIForm_Load()

    ' Variable.
    Dim Result As Boolean
    Result = CenterForm(Me)
    Load Form1

End Sub
```

To run the project and call the procedure, follow these steps:

1. Select Form1 and set its **MDIChild** property to **True** in the Properties window.

2. Select Project|Project1 Properties to display the Project Properties dialog box, which lists the current property settings of the project. Figure 2.3 shows VB5's new Project Properties dialog box.

3. From the Startup Object list, select MDIForm1.

4. Select Run|Start.

The **CenterForm** procedure first centers the **MDIForm** object on the **Screen** object and, when it's called the second time, centers the MDI child on the **MDIForm** object.

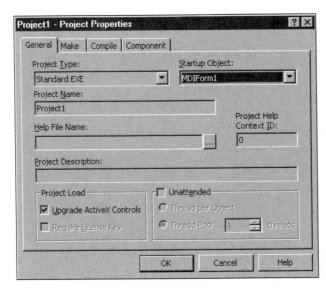

Figure 2.3   The VB5 Project Properties dialog box.

Handling Errors When Calling A Procedure

The code in any **Function** or **Sub** procedure in VB can, depending on the circumstances, cause two general types of errors: syntax errors and runtime errors. VB defines a syntax error as an error that occurs when you enter a line of code that Visual Basic doesn't recognize. It normally occurs either when you move the insertion point off of the offending line of code or when you try to execute the code in run mode.

VB defines a runtime error as an error that occurs when code is running. It normally occurs when a code statement attempts an invalid operation. The invalid operation is usually related to some characteristic of the hardware or software that is subject to change and over which the code statement has no control.

Microsoft recommends that you set two switches for Visual Basic's IDE (*integrated development environment*) to facilitate the detection of syntax errors and enhance development efficiency. To set these switches, select Tools | Options to display the Options dialog box. Select the Editor tab and select the Auto Syntax Check and Require Variable Declaration checkboxes if they are not already selected. Click on OK to save your selections and exit the dialog box. All of the examples and sample code in this book assume that both of these switches are turned on. Until you become very familiar with VB5's new IDE, use the settings on the Editor tab shown in Figure 2.4.

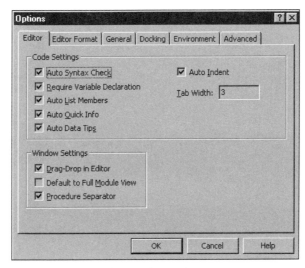

Figure 2.4 The VB5 Options dialog box (Editor tab).

Runtime Errors

Runtime errors are illegal operations that occur after the application starts to execute. Every VB runtime error is identified by an error number and is listed in the help topic in Visual Basic's Help file titled *Trappable Errors*. Some examples of common runtime errors include:

- Dividing a number by a variable that is currently assigned the value of zero (error 11).
- Writing to a file that may once have existed on a hard disk but no longer does (error 53).
- Trying to move a form that is currently maximized or minimized (error 384).

There are almost 1,000 possible runtime errors in VB. Any untrapped runtime error that occurs is fatal; that is, an error message is displayed and program execution stops. To avoid crashing your application, you should trap for runtime errors by following these general steps:

1. Enable an error-handling routine in any procedure where an error could possibly occur, by using either the **On Error GoTo** or the **On Error Resume Next** statements. This prevents the program from crashing.
2. In the error-handling routine, read the value of **Err**. If **Err** does not equal **False**, then a runtime error has occurred.
3. Based on the numeric value of **Err**, react to the error and alert the user by displaying a message box.
4. After the user closes the message box, reinitialize the value of **Err** to zero.

Syntax Errors

A syntax error is one that occurs when you enter a line of code that VB doesn't recognize. It normally is triggered either when you move the insertion point off of the offending line of code, or when you try to execute the code in run mode. If you plan on doing object-oriented development with VB, it is important that you be familiar with the different ways that its IDE reacts to kinds of syntax errors.

IMMEDIATE RECOGNITION OF SPECIFIC SYNTAX ERRORS

If you type an incorrect statement and move the insertion point off of the line, Visual Basic normally detects the syntax error immediately. To see an example, modify the statement in the **MDIForm_Load** event procedure you wrote in the preceding section by removing the closing parenthesis, as shown here:

```
Result = CenterForm(Me
```

Then, move the insertion point off the line of code and VB displays the syntax error message box shown in Figure 2.5.

Because Visual Basic 5 now supports compilation, most of its syntax error messages and many other features of its IDE have been affected. Each time we initially encounter one of these changes or differences in the course of this book, I will note it.

DELAYED RECOGNITION OF SYNTAX ERRORS

If you type an incorrect statement, but don't move the insertion point off of the line, you are able to run the procedure. In this case, VB detects the syntax error in a more general way. To see an example, in the **MDIForm_Load** event procedure, change the statement as you did in the previous section, but *do not move the insertion point off of the line.* Select Run|Start. VB displays the syntax error message *Compile error: Syntax error.*

Data Type Mismatch Errors: The Differences Between VB3 And VB5

When programmers upgrade from VB3 to VB5, they are often surprised to find that there are important differences between the ways VB3 and VB5 handle errors when a statement makes a call to a procedure. The great

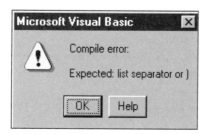

Figure 2.5 VB5's new kind of syntax error message.

majority of errors that can occur when calling a procedure fall into the category of data type mismatch errors; that is, there is a conflict between the data type of the value being passed to a procedure and the data type that an argument in the procedure requires.

VB3 is precise and consistent in the way it handles data type mismatch errors. VB5 is less stringent in its handling of such errors, and it will actually compile a project's code that includes such a data type mismatch. The reasons why VB5 differs from VB3 in its treatment of data type mismatch errors are noted here:

- In VB3, each project is self-contained. Therefore, prior to runtime or to making an EXE file, VB3 can syntax check for all possible mismatches between the data types of values being passed and the data types of arguments in procedures.

- In VB5, calls can be made to external public members in a DLL or EXE ActiveX component. If a reference to the ActiveX component has not been set (Project References command), VB5 cannot syntax check for data type mismatches. Instead, it uses an OLE technique called *late binding* and only becomes aware of any mismatches at runtime.

- Although VB5 must use late binding to resolve data type mismatches when calls to unreferenced ActiveX components are made, it seemingly could syntax check for all data type mismatches within the project itself. However, Microsoft's Visual Basic development team chose not to do this.

Because of the less stringent data type mismatch checking that Visual Basic 5 does, application programmers who make calls to a procedure in an ActiveX component must take extra measures when testing and debugging the code to defend against data type mismatch errors:

- Run and test every possible code execution path where a call to a procedure is made. Because VB5's syntax checking routine no longer catches many data type mismatches, you must catch them manually.

- Enable an error-handling routine at the beginning of any procedure that makes a call to an ActiveX component. You can no longer assume that you know whether such a procedure's execution can result in a runtime error or what kind of runtime errors can occur.

If you are writing procedures in a **ClassModule** object that are going to be members in an ActiveX component, you must write your own syntax-checking code to protect against late-bound, data type mismatches. Debugging and writing error-handling code have always been important, if tedious, parts of the programmer's job, but in VB5, they have assumed an even greater importance. In the next chapter, we'll rewrite the **CenterForm** procedure as a method in a **ClassModule** object. We'll be making changes to implement more stringent, crash-proof error handling.

CREATING CLASSES AND METHODS

3

This chapter first introduces you to the new Object Browser included with VB5, which is a major improvement over VB4's Object Browser. The Object Browser is Microsoft's preferred utility for viewing the type or class libraries encapsulated in an ActiveX component. You learn how easy it is to view the reusable members of a class library and to determine how to call them by looking at two different type libraries: the one that is VB5 itself and the one that is the class library found on the CD-ROM included with this book.

You then walk through the steps of how to create classes, methods and ActiveX components with VB5 and how to register ActiveX components in the Windows registration database. There are two types of ActiveX components that VB can create: an in-process, ActiveX DLL project and an out-of-process, ActiveX EXE project. When you open a new project, you must first decide which of these two kinds of ActiveX components you want to make (of course, you can also still make the standard, standalone EXE file). Each kind of ActiveX component serves different purposes, and you will learn the differences between them.

After you decide which kind of ActiveX component you want to make, you will use VB's **ClassModule** object to create a class. After making a few property settings to the **ClassModule** object, you can write a procedure in it that becomes one of its methods. Then, after you make a few entries to the General and Make tabs of the Project Properties dialog box, VB automatically handles all the gory details of creating an ActiveX component and registering it. All you have to do is select File | Make DLL (for an in-process component) or File | Make EXE (for an out-of-process component) and VB does the rest.

The last thing you look at in in this chapter is how to call and reuse a method in an ActiveX component from another VB project. We demonstrate how to reuse the public members of two objects included in the book's class library. One is the **Browse** method of the **File** object, which displays a customizable common dialog box and returns the string specifying the path and file name you select. The second is the **ShowSplash** method of the **ClientApp** object, which displays a customizable splash screen. When you have finished this chapter, you will have mastered the mechanics of creating and registering ActiveX components, and reusing their objects.

Creating A ClassModule Object

At the beginning of a journey to a foreign country, many people like to try and get a feel for what the country is like by looking at photographs of the indigenous peoples who live there and the cultural artifacts that they share. Before you start to learn how to create classes with Visual Basic and instantiate and use them as objects in your code, it is a good idea to take a look at that foreign country.

The best way to see snapshots of what Microsoft's Visual Basic OOP paradigm can accomplish is to view existing ActiveX components and the classes they contain. You can do this from Visual Basic by opening the Object Browser dialog box. We will view two groups of libraries/classes/members from the Object Browser: those constituting VB5 itself and those contained in this book's class library.

Visual Basic 5's Class Library Hierarchy

Start a new project in Visual Basic and select View | Object Browser (or press F2) to display the Object Browser dialog box. Then follow these steps to view the VB5 ActiveX component and the classes and members it contains:

1. From the All Libraries list, select VB. The Object Browser fills the other lists with information about the VB ActiveX component.

2. From the Classes list, select CheckBox. The Object Browser fills the Members list with the members of Visual Basic's **CheckBox** class/object.

3. From the Members list, select Drag (toward the bottom of the list). The Object Browser should appear as shown in Figure 3.1.

At this point, you have drilled down through the hierarchy of the Object Browser to its lowest level, which is comprised of the members of the class. There are three kinds of members listed in the Members list: properties, methods, and events. You can view these members either grouped by the three categories (the default view) or sorted by alpha. To change the order in which the members are listed, right click on the Members list and select or deselect the Group Members item on the pop-up menu. If the members are listed by group, the order they appear in is properties/methods/events. Each group has its own icon. Select the **Drag** method from the methods group and click on the yellow ? button on the Object Browser's toolbar to see its associated help topic, which is shown in Figure 3.2.

To see which objects (that is, instantiated classes) this method can be applied to, click on the Applies To hotspot on the help topic. Because of polymorphism, a member can apply to more than one object. The **Drag** method, for example, applies to more than 25 different objects. To see sample code that demonstrates how to use the method, click on the Example hotspot.

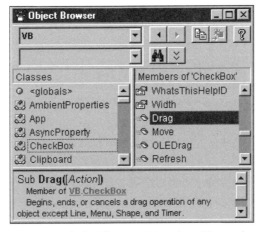

Figure 3.1 VB's Object Browser dialog box—VB5's class library hierarchy.

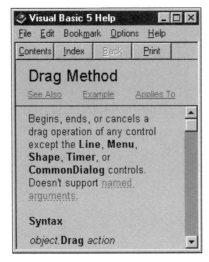

Figure 3.2 VB's help topic for the **Drag** method.

The Book's Class Library Hierarchy

To see the book's class library hierarchy in the Object Browser dialog box, you must first set a reference to its ActiveX component. Begin this process by selecting Project|References. Find the book's class library items (toward the bottom of the Available References list) and select one. The book's *Visual Basic 5.0 Class Library* reference can have four possible listings (DLL, EXE, RAO, or 16), depending on which versions of the class library you registered when you installed the files from the book's CD-ROM. After you have selected a reference to the book's ActiveX DLL component, the References dialog box should appear as shown in Figure 3.3.

Click on OK to close the References dialog box and save the reference to the book's ActiveX component. Select View|Object Browser and follow these steps:

1. From the All Libraries list, select EFSD (the DLL version of the book's ActiveX component). The Object Browser fills the other lists with information.

2. From the Classes list, select File. The Object Browser fills the Members list with the members of EFSD's **File** class/object.

3. From the Members list, select Move. The Object Browser should now appear as shown in Figure 3.4.

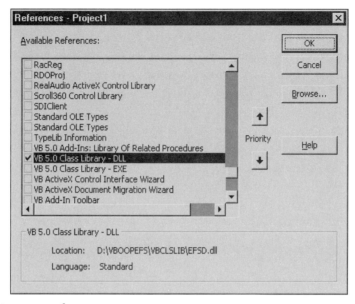

Figure 3.3 Setting a reference to an ActiveX component.

Click on the yellow ? button on the Object Browser's toolbar to see the help topic for the **Move** member, as shown in Figure 3.5.

As you can see, the way the book's class library hierarchy is structured and the way the elements of the hierarchy appear in the Object Browser is exactly the same as VB5 itself. Microsoft has designed Visual Basic to create object-oriented class libraries (that is, ActiveX components) that function

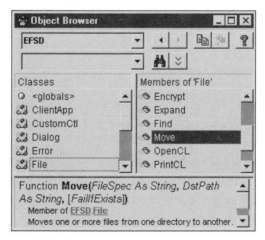

Figure 3.4 VB's Object Browser dialog box—The book's class library hierarchy.

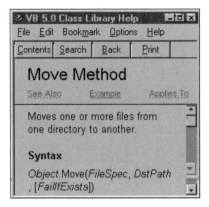

Figure 3.5 The class library's help topic for the **Move** method.

and appear exactly like Visual Basic itself. What this book is meant to do and what we begin to discover in this chapter is:

- How to use VB5 to write class libraries of reusable code; that is, how to create ActiveX components that can, just like VB5, expose their objects for reuse by OLE Automation-compliant programming languages.

- How to use the VB5 syntax that enables the creation of class libraries.

- How to create a commercial-quality Windows Help file for an ActiveX component's class library and link individual help topics to objects or objects' members to be viewed from the Object Browser dialog box.

Overview Of A ClassModule Object

A **ClassModule** object is a unique kind of object in the Visual Basic object hierarchy. You add one to a Visual Basic project by selecting Project | Add Class Module. In many respects, a **ClassModule** object behaves much like a standard module. You write procedures in it, which are considered its members. These members can be either methods (procedures created with the **Function** or **Sub** statements), properties (procedures created with the **Property Let**, **Property Get**, or **Property Set** statements), or events (procedures created with VB5's new **Event** statement).

A **ClassModule** object defines only one class; however, you can have more than one of them in a project, so you can create as many classes as your design requires. Using **ClassModule** objects, you can assemble classes, with their members, into a hierarchical class model. This class model can include custom collections, built using Visual Basic's **Collection** object.

You can use a **ClassModule** object in many ways in a Visual Basic project. However, there are three general kinds of applications that you will most commonly use them in. First, you can use one in a normal project that runs as an executable file. Second, you can make the project that contains one into a special kind of EXE or DLL file called an ActiveX component. Third, you can use one as part of a Visual Basic Add-In application. In this book, we use **ClassModule** objects primarily in the second way, as part of the class library's ActiveX component, but we will also examine how to use them as part of a normal EXE file or an Add-In.

ActiveX components expose the public members of their **ClassModule** objects to development tools, macro languages, and other applications that can function as OLE Automation clients. Visual Basic, Visual C++, Excel, Project, and Access are all examples of OLE Automation client-enabled applications that can reuse members of a **ClassModule** object.

Making A New ClassModule Object

Now, we're going to make a new **ClassModule** object. Start Visual Basic, select File|New Project and double click on the ActiveX DLL icon. Then select the **ClassModule** object named Class1. Go to the Properties window, which should appear as in Figure 3.6.

A **ClassModule** object has two properties that need to be set (in VB4, there were three properties). Double click on the **Name** property, type *MiscExs*, and press Enter. The **Name** property of the **ClassModule** object becomes the second half of the programmatic ID string that Visual Basic writes to the registration database when it makes an ActiveX component. Next, select the **Instancing** property, click on its drop-down arrow, and select 5 - MultiUse.

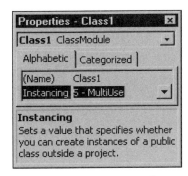

Figure 3.6 The initial Properties window for the new **ClassModule** object.

Note that the possible settings of the **Instancing** property have changed from three in VB4 to six in VB5, and that the **ClassModule** object no longer has a **Public** property.

The **Instancing** property of the **ClassModule** object is only available at design time and has these six possible settings:

- *Private.* The default setting. Other applications aren't allowed access to type library information about the class, and cannot create instances of it. Private objects are only for internal use within your application or component.

- *PublicNotCreatable.* Other applications can use objects of this class only if your component creates the objects first. Other applications cannot use the **CreateObject** function or the **New** operator to create objects from the class.

- *SingleUse.* For EXE ActiveX components only. Allows other applications to create objects from the class, but every object of this class that a client application creates starts a new instance of your component.

- *GlobalSingleUse.* For EXE ActiveX components only. Similar to SingleUse, except that properties and methods of the class can be invoked as if they were simply global functions.

- *MultiUse.* Allows other applications to create objects from the class. One instance of your component can provide any number of objects created in this fashion, regardless of how many applications request them.

- *GlobalMultiUse.* Similar to MultiUse, with one addition: Properties and methods of the class can be invoked as if they were simply global functions. It's not necessary to explicitly create an instance of the class first because one will automatically be created.

Making an ActiveX DLL

*In order to make a Visual Basic project into an ActiveX DLL component, the **Instancing** property must be set to 5 - MultiUse or 6 - GlobalMultiUse.*

Once you have set the two properties (**Name** and **Instancing**) of a **ClassModule** object, you can write procedures in it that become its members (its methods, properties, or events). Before you do that, however, you should save your new project and **ClassModule** object. Save the project under the name MYCLSLIB.VBP and the CLS module under the name MISCEXS.CLS. Ensure that you save both files (and all new files that you add to this project during the course of this book) to the same subdirectory.

Adding A Method To A ClassModule

In Visual Basic's OOP terminology, a method is a **Function** or **Sub** procedure in a **ClassModule** object. A method does something and its name usually is a verb or begins with a verb. One **ClassModule** object can contain many methods. You can create different kinds of methods to do different things. For example, methods can:

- Execute traditional kinds of algorithms for sorting, string manipulation, calculations, file I/O, and so on. The books *Visual Basic Algorithms: A Developer's Sourcebook Of Ready-To-Run Code* (ISBN 0-471-13418-X) and *Mathematical Algorithms In Visual Basic For Scientists And Engineers* (ISBN 0-07-912003-2) are excellent sources of Visual Basic implementations of traditional algorithms for inclusion in a class library.

- Perform data processing operations on databases.

- Act upon one or more objects. You do this by passing a reference to the **Name** property of the object as one of the method's arguments. For example, passing the **Name** property of a **Form** object to a **CenterForm** method causes the method to center the **Form** object on the screen.

- Display a **Form** object that has been encapsulated inside the **ClassModule** object project's ActiveX component. For example, you can create a **ShowAbout** method which, when called, displays the conventional Windows About dialog box (customized for the specific client application, based on the values passed to the method's arguments).

- Use a custom control object that has been encapsulated inside the **ClassModule** object project's ActiveX component. For example, you can display any of the six dialog boxes of the **CommonDialog** custom control object. Once such a method exists in a **ClassModule** object, you will never have to add a **CommonDialog** custom control to a Visual Basic project again.

The procedure that constitutes a method can be declared with either the **Function** statement or the **Sub** statement. It is conventional practice in OOP to declare all public methods with the **Function** statement. Whether declared with a **Function** statement or a **Sub** statement, most methods take one or more arguments (that is, support message passing). These arguments specify what the method is to do and to which object or objects, if any, it applies.

When you declare a method as a **Function**, you design it to be very flexible in the way it reacts to the call from the client application. Upon success, it can return a value that represents the result of the execution of the method. For example, a method that displays a Windows file browser dialog box would need to return a string specifying the path and file name(s) the user chose. Upon failure, it might return a value or error code that the calling statement can read to determine what occurred. All the methods in this book's class library are designed to return a **Variant**, which can contain an array with several elements of information; in this way, a very sophisticated set of error codes can be returned upon failure, or different kinds of information or data types can be returned upon success.

Adding A Copy Method To A ClassModule

The first method we'll create is called **Copy**. This method will copy a file from one directory to another. To create the **Copy** method, select MISCEXS.CLS and declare a **Function** procedure at the bottom of the General Declarations Section, by typing

```
Function Copy (FileSrc As String, FileDst As String) As Boolean
```

and pressing Enter. Visual Basic then creates the beginning and ending statements of the procedure. The code that comprises the **Copy** function is shown in Listing 3.1.

Listing 3.1   Code for Copy method.

```
Function Copy (FileSrc As String, FileDst As String) As Boolean

  ' Enable error handler.
  On Error GoTo ET

  ' Depending on whether 32-bit or 16-bit Visual Basic is running,
  ' use two different approaches to copy file:
  ' * If 32-bit, use new 32-bit Windows API function.
  ' * If 16-bit, use Visual Basic's FileCopy statement.

  #If Win32 Then

     If CopyFile(FileSrc, FileDst, False) Then Copy = True

  #ElseIf Win16 Then
```

```
    FileCopy FileSrc, FileDst

      If Err = False Then Copy = True

  #End If

  Exit Function

ET:

  Err = False

End Function
```

Because a Windows API function is used in the **Copy** method, you need to declare it, as well. To preserve the OOP attribute of encapsulation, you should declare all Windows API functions in the General Declarations section of the module from which they are called. Select the General Declarations section of MISCEXS.CLS and enter the declaration shown in Listing 3.2.

Listing 3.2   Declaration of Copy API function.

```
' DLL functions:

#If Win32 Then

    Private Declare Function CopyFile& Lib "KERNEL32" _
                            Alias "CopyFileA" _
                            (ByVal ExistingFileName$, _
                            ByVal NewFileName$, _
                            ByVal FailIfExists&)

#End If
```

The Windows API function **CopyFile** can only be called from 32-bit Windows (a similar function does not exist in the 16-bit Windows API). Its first argument specifies the path and name of an existing file. Its second argument specifies the path and name of the new file. Its third argument specifies how this operation is to proceed if a file of the same name as that specified by the second argument already exists: If the third argument is **True** and the new file already exists, the function fails; if it is **False** and the new file already exists, the function overwrites the existing file and succeeds.

There are three advantages to using the 32-bit Windows API function **CopyFile** in the code in Listing 3.1. First, it runs slightly faster than the Visual Basic **FileCopy** statement. Second, it has an argument that enables you to turn on a flag that causes the copy operation to fail if the specified destination path/file already exists. Third, its execution cannot cause a runtime error. If the **CopyFile** API function fails, it simply does not copy the file. When you use Visual Basic's **FileCopy** statement, however, you must enable an error handler to deal with any runtime error.

Don't forget the Private keyword

*When you declare a Windows API function or a user-defined data type in a **ClassModule** or **Form** object, the **Private** keyword must precede the **Declare** statement or **Type** statement. If you do not use **Private**, Visual Basic displays an incredibly long syntax error message that is not particularly helpful; the bottom line, however, is that you will not be allowed to do it.*

Making An ActiveX DLL File

Before we get into making an ActiveX DLL file, we need to understand what an ActiveX DLL *component* is. An ActiveX DLL component exposes OLE Automation objects and their members to OLE Automation clients for their use. Like all DLL files, it is loaded in and uses its OLE client application's stack and process space. When a client application uses one of a **ClassModule** object's members, the operation remains in the client's process or memory space, hence the name *in-process component*. The terms in-process component and ActiveX DLL component are synonymous as far as VB5 is concerned. A project containing a **ClassModule** object that Visual Basic makes into an ActiveX DLL is, at a lower level of abstraction, really an in-process OLE Automation server.

Because an ActiveX DLL component runs as a DLL file, no new process needs to be created and none of the runtime DLL files need to be loaded. This allows an in-process component to load considerably faster than an equivalent out-of-process, ActiveX EXE component. Also, no out-of-process call overhead is incurred by in-process components when referring to the **ClassModule** object's members because the message-sending is not occurring between processes. This allows an ActiveX DLL component's method to run 3 to 10 times faster than the same method would run in an ActiveX EXE component.

An ActiveX DLL component must meet several requirements:

- It can only be developed and run on 32-bit Windows operating systems.
- It must run on the same machine as the client application that calls it.
- It must contain one or more **ClassModule** objects.
- At least one **ClassModule** object's **Instancing** property must be set to either 5 - MultiUse or 6 - GlobalMultiUse.
- The **End** statement may not be used in an ActiveX DLL component and will cause a compile-time error.

Steps To Make An ActiveX DLL

The making of an ActiveX DLL file involves several tasks. To help you follow along, I've split these tasks into several separate topics.

SETTING THE PROJECT'S PROPERTIES

Before you set the project properties, you need to add a standard module to the project. Select Project | Add Module and add a **Sub Main** procedure to it. You don't have to add any code to this procedure, but you should have it in the project because it is a conventional ActiveX component programming practice to use **Sub Main** as the component's startup object. Name this BAS module MiscExs and save it under the file name MISCEXS.BAS.

> *Note: VB4 required that an ActiveX DLL's startup object be **Sub Main**. VB5 no longer requires this and will allow you to set the startup object to (None), but this is not conventional practice and is not advisable.*

To specify certain settings for the properties of the **ClassModule** object's project, select Project | Project1 Properties and then select the General tab from the Project Properties dialog box. You must set the following properties before making the project into an ActiveX DLL component:

- **Project Type**. Ensure that the ActiveX DLL item is selected.
- **Startup Object**. Ensure that **Sub Main** is selected.
- **Project Name**. This entry serves two purposes. First, it is the initial part of the programmatic ID string, which identifies the component and class, that Visual Basic writes to the Windows registration database when it creates an ActiveX DLL component. Second, it is part of the

name displayed in the Object Browser dialog box when a reference is set to a Visual Basic ActiveX DLL component. Set the Project Name entry to MYLIBDLL.

- **Help File Name**. The name of the Help file associated with the ActiveX component's project. It does not need to be preceded by a fully qualified path. Because you do not have a Help file of your own, set this entry to EFS.HLP (the book's class library Help file).

- **Project Help Context ID**. The context ID for the specific help topic to be called when the user clicks on the ? button while the ActiveX component is selected in the Object Browser dialog box. This is normally the context ID associated with the Contents topic. Set the context ID entry to zero (the number of the Contents topic of EFS.HLP).

- **Project Description**. A brief description of the ActiveX component that appears when it is displayed in the References dialog box (Project|References). Set the Project Description entry to My First Class Library - DLL.

- **Upgrade ActiveX Controls**. Enables upgrading of the ActiveX controls. Ensure that this checkbox is selected.

- **Require License Key**. Enables licensing for a project that produces ActiveX components (automation servers, user controls, or ActiveX controls). A Visual Basic license file (*.VBL) will be created when you build the file. The VBL file must be registered on the user's machine for the components to be used. The SetUp Wizard registers the VBL file. Leave this entry unchecked.

- **Thread per Object**. For a component with no interface elements, indicates that each instance of a class marked as MultiUse in the **Instancing** property will be created on a new and distinct thread. Each thread has a unique copy of all global variables and objects, and will not interfere with any other thread. Leave this entry unchecked.

- **Thread Pool**. For a component with no interface elements, indicates that each instance of a class marked as MultiUse in the **Instancing** property will be created on a thread from the thread pool. The choice of thread is determined in a round-robin fashion. Each thread has a unique copy of all global variables, but multiple instances reside on a given thread and can potentially interfere with each other. Leave this entry unchecked.

- **Number of Threads**. For a component with no interface elements, determines the maximum number of threads created for the thread pool. When a MultiUse class is instantiated, threads are created as needed up to the number set here. After the maximum number is reached, Visual Basic begins assigning new instances to existing threads. Leave this entry unchecked.

> *Note:* Any ActiveX component that contains a **Form** object or displays a message box has an interface element. For such ActiveX components, the Unattended Execution items on the General tab of the Project Properties dialog box (that is, Thread per Object, Thread Pool and Number of Threads) are disabled. The book's ActiveX components all contain interface elements.

Figure 3.7 shows a typical profile of settings for the General tab of the Project Properties dialog box for an ActiveX DLL component.

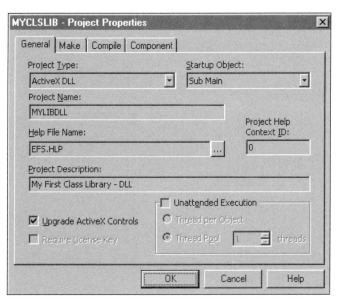

Figure 3.7   General tab settings for the Project Properties dialog box (DLL).

MAKING THE ACTIVEX DLL

After you have set the project's properties, you can follow these steps to
make the ActiveX DLL file:

1. Select File | Make MYLIBDLL.DLL to display the Make Project dialog
    box.

2. In the Make Project dialog box, click on the Options button to display
    the Make tab of the Project Properties dialog box.

3. Under Version Number, ensure that Auto Increment is checked.

4. For the Application Title, ensure that the entry is the same as the entry
    you made for the Project Name on the General tab (that is, MYLIBDLL).
    They do not have to be the same, but it is easier and makes more
    sense to use the same names.

5. Click on OK to store the entries you made and close the dialog box.
    Figure 3.8 shows a typical profile of settings for the Make tab of the
    Project Properties dialog box.

6. In the Make Project dialog box, ensure that MYLIBDLL.DLL is the
    file name.

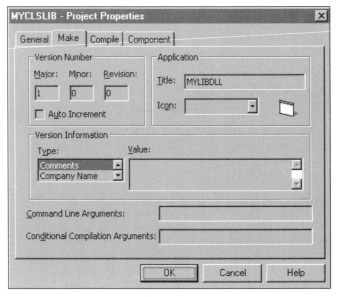

Figure 3.8   Make settings for the Project Properties dialog box.

7. Click on OK to make the ActiveX DLL file and then register the ActiveX DLL component in the Windows registration database.

8. Select File|Save Project to save the project's files.

EXAMINING THE POSSIBLE ERRORS ENCOUNTERED WHEN MAKING AN ACTIVEX DLL COMPONENT

Visual Basic can display the following error messages when you try to make an ActiveX DLL component:

- If you try to make an ActiveX DLL component that does not have a **ClassModule** object in the project, or if there is a **ClassModule** object but its **Instancing** property is not set to 5 - MultiUse or 6 - GlobalMultiUse, Visual Basic displays the syntax error *No creatable public class module detected. Press F1 for more information.*

- If there is an **End** statement or some other statement not supported by an ActiveX DLL component anywhere in the project's files, Visual Basic displays the syntax error message *Functionality not supported in DLL.*

> **Note:** *In VB4, if you instantiated a class in an ActiveX DLL component, called/reused one of its public members from another project, -and then opened that ActiveX component's project and tried to remake it, VB4 would display the syntax error message Permission denied 'file name'. Microsoft has fixed this bug in VB5.*

Making An ActiveX EXE File

Before we get into making an ActiveX EXE file, we need to understand what an ActiveX EXE *component* is. An ActiveX EXE component is one whose operation does not remain in the client application's process or memory space. Out-of-process ActiveX EXE components have performance problems compared to in-process ActiveX DLL components. These performance problems manifest themselves as slow startup speed and out-of-process call overhead. The terms out-of-process component and ActiveX EXE component are synonymous as far as VB5 is concerned. A project containing a **ClassModule** object that Visual Basic makes into an ActiveX EXE is, at a lower level of abstraction, really an out-of-process OLE Automation server.

An ActiveX EXE component will always be slower to start than an ActiveX DLL component, and every reference to a **ClassModule** object's method or property in an out-of-process, ActiveX component is slower than an equivalent reference to an object or procedure in the calling application itself or in an in-process ActiveX component. Because of the performance penalty associated with an ActiveX EXE component, the only practical reasons why you would want to use one are to:

- Create a class library and ActiveX component with 16-bit VB4 that will run under Windows 3.x. The 16-bit version of VB4 cannot create, and Windows 3.x cannot run, an in-process ActiveX DLL component.

- Create a Remote Automation Object (RAO) with Visual Basic's Enterprise Edition. An RAO must be an out-of-process component because, as the term *Remote* implies, it runs on a different machine than the client does.

- Enable asynchronous code execution (a form of multitasking or threading).

Steps To Make An ActiveX EXE

The making of an ActiveX EXE file involves several tasks. To help you follow along, I've split these tasks into several separate topics.

Configuring An ActiveX EXE Project

First, open a new ActiveX EXE project with VB5. Then, before you set the project's properties, add a standard module to the project by selecting Project | Add Module. Add a **Sub Main** procedure to the module. You don't have to add any code to this procedure, but you should have it in the project simply because it is a conventional ActiveX component programming practice to use **Sub Main** as the component's startup object. Name this BAS module MiscExs and save it under the file name MISCEXS.BAS.

If, as described previously in this chapter, you made the ActiveX DLL component, select Project | Add File and add the MISCEXS.CLS file from the MYLIBDLL.VBP project to this project. Otherwise, follow the instructions listed previously in this chapter under the sections titled *Making A New ClassModule Object* and *Adding A Copy Method To A ClassModule*.

Setting The Project's Properties

To specify certain settings for the properties of the **ClassModule** object's project, select Project | Project1 Properties and then select the General tab of the Project Properties dialog box. You must set these properties before making the project into an ActiveX EXE component. The settings are:

- **Project Type**. Ensure that the ActiveX EXE item is selected.

- **Startup Object**. Ensure that **Sub Main** is selected. It is possible for an out-of-process ActiveX component to have a modeless form as the startup object; but, for the time being, it will help keep things simple to select **Sub Main**.

- **Project Name**. This entry serves two purposes. First, it is the initial part of the programmatic ID string, which identifies the component and class, that Visual Basic writes to the Windows registration database when it creates an ActiveX EXE component. Second, it is part of the name displayed in the Object Browser dialog box when a reference is set to a Visual Basic ActiveX EXE component. Set the Project Name entry to MYLIBEXE.

- **Help File Name**. The name of the Help file associated with the ActiveX component's project. It does not need to be preceded by a fully qualified path. Because you do not have a Help file of your own, set this entry to EFS.HLP (the book's class library Help file).

- **Project Help Context ID**. The context ID for the specific help topic to be called when the user clicks on the ? button while the ActiveX component is selected in the Object Browser dialog box. This is normally the context ID associated with the Contents topic. Set the Context ID entry to zero (the number of the Contents topic of EFS.HLP).

- **Project Description**. A brief description of the ActiveX component that appears when it is displayed in the References dialog box (Project|References). Set the Project Description entry to My First Class Library - EXE.

The functionality of the remaining items on the General tab (Upgrade ActiveX Controls, Require License Key, Thread per Object, Thread Pool, and Number of Threads) is the same as described in the previous section in this chapter titled *Steps To Make An ActiveX DLL*. You should leave these five entries unchecked/unset.

Figure 3.9 shows a typical profile of settings for the General tab of the Project Properties dialog box for an ActiveX EXE component.

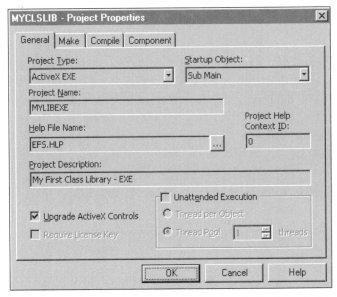

Figure 3.9 General tab settings for the Project Properties dialog box (EXE).

MAKING THE ACTIVEX EXE

After you set the project's properties, you can follow these steps to make the ActiveX EXE file:

1. Select File|Make MYLIBEXE.EXE to display the Make Project dialog box.

2. In the Make Project dialog box, click on the Options button to display the Make tab of the Project Properties dialog box.

3. Under Version Number, ensure that Auto Increment is checked.

4. For the Application Title, ensure that the entry is the same as the entry you made for the Project Name on the General tab (that is, MYLIBEXE). They do not have to be the same, but it is easier and makes more sense to use the same names.

5. Click on OK to store the entries you made and close the dialog box.

6. In the Make Project dialog box, ensure that MYLIBEXE.EXE is the file name.

7. Click on OK to make the ActiveX EXE file and register the ActiveX EXE component in the Windows registration database.

8. Select File|Save Project to save the project's files.

Calling An Object's Method

There are two general ways to call a **ClassModule** object's method: internally, from within the **ClassModule** object's project, or externally, from another Visual Basic project. Both ways are equally important, but they serve different purposes. As you develop a new method's code, for the sake of convenience, you want to be able to run it on the fly from within its own project. You need to set breakpoints and single-step through the code's execution path in debug mode. Until you have the code screwed down tight, you will call and test it internally.

Later, when you have the method's code completely debugged, you (or someone else) will call and test it externally from another Visual Basic project. This, of course, is the way the object and its method will be used by other Visual Basic programmers. Complex ActiveX component class libraries should always be subjected to a formal, structured testing methodology. This means that its methods should be tested by a person or persons who didn't develop the code.

Calling A Method Externally

Because you are just starting your Visual Basic OOP journey, we will focus on how to call a method externally. Later in the book, you will learn how to call and debug a method internally. The usual way to externally call and test a method from a **ClassModule** object is to call it from an ActiveX DLL component. The advantages of using an in-process component whenever possible are twofold. First, methods execute faster in an ActiveX DLL component than in an ActiveX EXE. Depending on the method, the rate of increase in speed can be from 300 to 1000 percent. If you are calling/testing a lot of methods, you want to do it as quickly as possible. Second, a **Form** object that is displayed modally normally appears having the focus, on top of the **Form** object from whose procedure it was called. With ActiveX EXE components, however, a **Form** object that is displayed modally will not have the focus and may be hidden behind another **Form** object. This is an unnecessary nuisance that will also slow you down.

At this point in the book, we will examine how to call both kinds of ActiveX components. To ensure that the demonstrations run correctly, we'll call two different methods in the book's class library:

- For the ActiveX DLL component, we'll call the **Browse** method of the **File** class.

- For the ActiveX EXE component, we'll call the **ShowSplash** method of the **ClientApp** class. Note that the **ShowSplash** method displays a modeless **Form** object from the ActiveX component and, so, can only be called and run from an out-of-process ActiveX component.

Instead of writing the code yourself, for these first demonstrations we'll use the example code contained in the book's class library Help file (EFS.HLP). This approach serves two purposes at this point on your learning curve. First, it demonstrates how easy it is to write sample code and encapsulate it inside a Help file. As the Windows programming community inexorably devotes more and more resources to the development of ActiveX components, it is imperative that these components be documented well and consistently. There is no more effective tool for doing this than a Windows Help file like the one that accompanies this book's class library. Second, it allows you to concentrate on understanding the calling code and to follow its execution in single-step mode, rather than worrying about getting the calling syntax correct the first time you write it.

CALLING A METHOD FROM AN ACTIVEX DLL

Follow these steps to call the **Browse** method of the **File** class:

1. Open a new project in Visual Basic and select the Standard EXE project template.
2. Select Project | References.
3. Toward the bottom of the Available References list, select the item VB5.0 Class Library - DLL and click on OK.
4. Select View | Object Browser.
5. From the All Libraries list, select EFSD.
6. Select the **File** class and the **Browse** member, and then click on the yellow ? button to display the help topic for **Browse**.
7. Click on the Example hotspot to display the **Browse** method's example code in a secondary Help window.
8. Follow the instructions in the Help window and copy and paste the code into the General Declarations section of Form1.
9. Select Run | Start. When Form1 is displayed, double click on it. The code in the **Form_DblClick** event procedure calls the **Browse** method and the method displays the common dialog box shown in Figure 3.10.

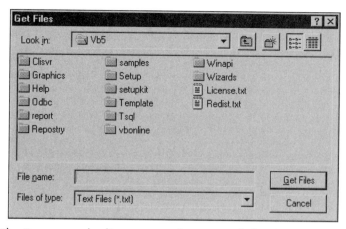

Figure 3.10 The **Browse** method's customized common dialog box.

10. Select a file(s) and click on Browse. The code in the **Form_DblClick** event procedure reads the file names returned by the **Browse** method and displays them in a message box.

To call the **Browse** method, you must first declare an object variable to which you will assign an instance of the **File** class. It is best to do this in the General Declarations section of the form module, so that the object instance remains in scope until the form is unloaded. You declare the object variable with the statement

```
Dim File As Object
```

where **File** is the name of the object variable. It also happens to be the name of the class in the ActiveX DLL component, but Visual Basic is able to distinguish between the two similar names (and this naming convention makes the calling code more readable).

After you have declared an object variable, you use the **CreateObject** function and **Set** statement to instantiate the class and assign the object instance to the object variable. The best place to do this is in the **Form_Load** event procedure, with the statement

```
Set File = CreateObject("EFSD.File")
```

where **File** is the object variable and the string **EFSD.File** is the programmatic ID of the class in the Windows registration database. EFSD is the name of the ActiveX component's project and File is the setting of the **Name** property of the **ClassModule** object.

The last major step is to call the method, done here from the **Form_DblClick** event procedure. The **Browse** method takes the optional arguments **Filter** and **Caption**, which in this example are the strings "Text Files (*.txt)|*.txt" and "Get Files", respectively. The actual call is made with the statement

```
Results = File.Browse(Filter:=FileType, Title:="Get Files")
```

where **Results** is a **Variant** variable that catches the returned values, **File** is the object variable, and **Browse** is the method being called with named arguments. The remainder of the code in the **Form_DblClick** event procedure reads the returned file names and displays them in a message box. The entire **Form_DblClick** procedure appears in Listing 3.3.

Listing 3.3 Procedure to call Browse method.

```
Private Sub Form_DblClick()

    ' Constants for values returned from members:
    Const MBR_SUCCESS = 0
    Const MBR_FILES = 1

    ' Variables:
    Dim Msg        As String
    Dim TmpStr     As String
    Dim Results    As Variant
    Dim FileType   As String

    ' Assign values to variables:
    FileType = "Text Files (*.txt)|*.txt"
    Hide

    ' Call object's member using named arguments:
    Results = File.Browse(Filter:=FileType, Title:="Get Files")

    ' If method executes successfully, read whether user chose
    ' Cancel or some file name(s) and display appropriate message:
    If Results(MBR_SUCCESS) Then
        If Results(MBR_FILES) = vbNullString Then
            Msg = "User chose Cancel."
        Else

            #If Win32 Then
                Results = Text.Replace(Results(MBR_FILES), vbNullChar, vbCr)
            #Else
                Results = Text.Replace(Results(MBR_FILES), Chr$(vbKeySpace), vbCr)
            #End If

            Msg = "Path/file(s) user chose are: " & vbCr
            Msg = Msg & Results(MBR_FILES)

        End If
```

```
Else
   Msg = "Member failed."
End If

MsgBox Prompt:=Msg, Buttons:=vbInformation, Title:="Class Library Demo"
Show
```

```
End Sub
```

We will study the **Browse** method and related members of the **File** class in more detail later on in the book. The last important thing to note is the code in the **Form_Unload** event procedure. When you instantiate a class from an ActiveX component and assign it to an object variable in a client application, you must remember to deinstantiate it and free any system resources used by it. This is normally done in the **Form_Unload** event procedure by using the **Set** statement to assign **Nothing** to the object variables:

```
Private Sub Form_Unload(Cancel As Integer)

   ' Free system resources associated with objects:
   Set File = Nothing
   Set Text = Nothing
   Set Form1 = Nothing

End Sub
```

CALLING A METHOD FROM AN ACTIVEX EXE

Follow these steps to call the **ShowSplash** method of the **ClientApp** class:

1. Open a new project in Visual Basic and select the Standard EXE project template.

2. Select Project | References.

3. Toward the bottom of the Available References list, select the item VB5.0 Class Library - EXE and click on OK.

4. Select View | Object Browser.

5. From the All Libraries list, select EFSE.

6. Select the **ClientApp** class and the **ShowSplash** member, and then click on the yellow ? button to display the help topic for **ShowSplash**.

7. Click on the Example hotspot to display the **ShowSplash** method's example code in a secondary Help window.

8. Follow the instructions in the Help window and copy and paste the code into the General Declarations section of Form1.

9. Select Run|Start and watch as the **ShowSplash** method displays a splash screen for a specified amount of time. The **CancelSplash** method is then called to unload the splash screen and the client application's startup form is displayed. The splash screen that the **ShowSplash** method displays is shown in Figure 3.11.

You follow the same basic steps to call the **ShowSplash** method as you used to call the **Browse** method. First, you declare, in the General Declarations section, an object variable to which you will assign an instance of the **ClientApp** class. Second, in the **Form_Load** event procedure, you use the **CreateObject** function and **Set** statement to instantiate the class and assign the object instance to the object variable. Third, you call the method, passing it the appropriate arguments. In this case, because of the nature of the method, the call is also made from the **Form_Load** event procedure. The entire **Form_Load** procedure appears in Listing 3.4. Note that the code in the top half of the procedure is fail-safe code that you would not write in a normal client application. It is included in every code example in the class library's Help file to provide feedback to you if something is wrong with the entries in the Windows registration database.

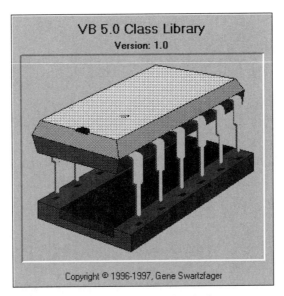

Figure 3.11 The **ShowSplash** method's customized splash screen.

Listing 3.4   Procedure to call ShowSplash method.

```vb
Private Sub Form_Load()

    ' Constants for elements in Captions() argument:
    Const SS_APP_NAME = 1
    Const SS_VER_NBR = 2
    Const SS_COPYRIGHT = 3

    ' Variables:
    Dim Msg              As String
    Dim Graphic          As String
    Dim Duration         As Integer
    Dim Start            As Long
    Dim Captions(1 To 3) As String

    ' Enable in-line error handler.
    On Error Resume Next

    ' Instantiate class. Programmatic ID has two parts delimited by dot:
    ' * Project Name on General tab of Project Properties dialog box.
    ' * Name property of ClassModule object.
    #If Win32 Then
        Set ClientApp = CreateObject("EFSE.ClientApp")
    #ElseIf Win16 Then
        Set ClientApp = CreateObject("EFS16.ClientApp")
    #End If

    If Err <> False Then
        Msg = "The ActiveX component cannot create object." & vbCr & vbCr
        Msg = Msg & "The programmatic ID "

        #If Win32 Then
            Msg = Msg & "'EFSE.ClientApp'"
        #ElseIf Win16 Then
            Msg = Msg & "'EFS16.ClientApp'"
        #End If

        Msg = Msg & " does not" & vbCr & "exist and "
        Msg = Msg & "its associated class is not registered" & vbCr
        Msg = Msg & "correctly in the Windows database." & vbCr & vbCr
        Msg = Msg & "Open the file "

        #If Win32 Then
            Msg = Msg & "'EFSE.VBP' with 32-bit VB and" & vbCr
        #ElseIf Win16 Then
            Msg = Msg & "'EFS16.VBP' with 16-bit VB and" & vbCr
        #End If

        Msg = Msg & "reregister the ActiveX component."
        MsgBox Prompt:=Msg, Buttons:=vbExclamation, Title:="Class Library Demo"
        End
    End If
```

```
' Generate error to find VB's path (this finds
' it without using Windows API functions):
Err.Raise Number:=3
Graphic = Err.HelpFile

If Right$(Graphic, 6) = "VB.HLP" Then
    Graphic = Mid$(Err.HelpFile, 1, Len(Err.HelpFile) - 6)
ElseIf Right$(Graphic, 11) = "VEENLR3.HLP" Then
    Graphic = Mid$(Err.HelpFile, 1, Len(Err.HelpFile) - 16) & "GRAPHICS\"
End If

Graphic = Graphic & "METAFILE\BUSINESS\MICRCHIP.WMF"

' Assign other variables:
Duration = 3
Captions(SS_APP_NAME) = "VB5.0 Class Library"
Captions(SS_VER_NBR) = "1.0"
Captions(SS_COPYRIGHT) = "1995-1997, Gene Swartzfager"

' Call object's member using named arguments:
ClientApp.ShowSplash Graphic:=Graphic, Captions:=Captions()

' Get current time.
Start = Timer

' Simulate startup processing for three seconds and
' then call object's member to unload splash screen:
Do Until Timer > (Start + Duration)
    DoEvents
Loop

ClientApp.CancelSplash

Msg = "Now that startup processing is complete," & vbCr
Msg = Msg & "client app's Form object will be displayed."
MsgBox Prompt:=Msg, Buttons:=vbInformation, Title:="Class Library Demo"

' Center Form object.
Move (Screen.Width - Width) \ 2, (Screen.Height - Height) \ 2
Err.Clear

End Sub
```

Try the Copy method

*Here's a challenge: Having practiced calling members of the book's class library, you might be ready to try and call the **Copy** method that you wrote earlier in this chapter. Assuming that you were able to get the ActiveX component MYLIBDLL registered, the syntax to call it is exactly like the two preceding examples. It takes just three lines of code to do* *these three things: the declaration of the object variable, the assignment of the instantiated class to the object variable, and the call to the* **Copy** *method (passing it two arguments: path/name of a source file and of a destination file). Give it a try!*

DISADVANTAGES OF USING THE ACTIVEX EXE COMPONENT

Unless you need to use an out-of-process ActiveX EXE component to meet a special requirement that an in-process ActiveX DLL component cannot fulfill, you should not use an ActiveX EXE component. To reiterate, the major disadvantages of using out-of-process OLE components are twofold. First, their methods run significantly slower than those in an in-process component. Second, if a member of an ActiveX EXE component modally displays a **Form** object or a message box, it will not have the focus when it appears. As a result, the **Form** object or message box may be hidden behind another window. This can confuse the user/tester.

Follow these steps to demonstrate for yourself the out-of-focus problem associated with an ActiveX EXE component:

1. Open a new project in Visual Basic and select the Standard EXE project template.
2. In the General Declarations section of Form1, type the statement:

    ```
    Dim MiscExs As Object
    ```

3. In the **Form_Load** event procedure, type the statement:

    ```
    Set MiscExs = CreateObject("EFSE.MiscExs")
    ```

4. In the **Form_DblClick** event procedure, type the statement:

    ```
    MiscExs.CenterForm Me
    ```

5. Select Run | Start.
6. Maximize the **Form** object.
7. Double click on the **Form** object. The **Form_DblClick** event occurs but, after a few seconds, nothing seems to happen.
8. Try to minimize the **Form** object. Windows displays the Component Request Pending dialog box, as shown in Figure 3.12.

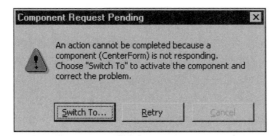

Figure 3.12   Component Request Pending dialog box.

9.   Select Switch To. The **CenterForm** method displays runtime error message 384, which it trapped. However, because of the out-of-focus problem associated with an ActiveX EXE component, the error message box was hidden behind the maximized **Form** object.

As you can see, this out-of-focus problem can cause quite a bit of confusion the first time you encounter it; and, even after you know what is going on, it is quite irritating. Because externally calling and testing members of an ActiveX component is so important and time-consuming, it only makes sense not to waste any unnecessary time or energy. So, do not test members from an ActiveX EXE component until they have been thoroughly tested and debugged first from an ActiveX DLL component. The only exception to this general rule would be in the case of a member like **ShowSplash**, which can only be run from an ActiveX EXE component.

Also, I cannot overemphasize the importance of rigorously and systematically testing all members externally. Although it is true that calling and testing a member in a **ClassModule** object internally normally results in the same behavior and error messages that occur when you test it externally, you cannot always count on this being the case. In addition, the major difference between calling and testing a member externally vs. internally is that often the person testing it externally will not be the programmer who wrote the member. To this programmer, an object and its members is like a black box; all that is known is what goes into the box and what comes out of it. This part of the black box is referred to as the member's public interface. It is comprised of:

- The arguments that the member requires when it is called and the value(s) that it returns.
- Any information about the member that is available in a Windows Help file created by the programmer who wrote the member.

- Any feedback that the member's code provides in the form of syntax or runtime error messages.
- Any printed documentation that might exist.

One of the major benefits of object-oriented programming is its potential for improving the frequency of code reuse. However, the degree to which your objects and methods will be reused depends a lot on how easy the public interface is for another programmer/tester to use and call externally. Testing and debugging members internally is like a practice for an athletic team. Every coach knows that the rubber doesn't hit the road until game time. Likewise, you cannot put a class library and its members to the acid test unless you test them externally.

USING A FORM IN AN ACTIVEX COMPONENT

4

Chapter 4 introduces you to the fundamental techniques for using visual GUI objects in ActiveX components. You will learn how to encapsulate a **Form** object in an ActiveX class library and how to display that form from an associated method. This is done by applying VB's **Show** method modally to the **Form** object from code within the method and, after the user is done with the form, applying VB's **Hide** method to return code execution back to the calling method. To master these techniques, you will create a **Delete** method and a Delete Files **Form** object and add them to the book's class library.

Chapter 4 also shows you how to internally test and debug a method in an ActiveX component. In Chapter 3, we stressed the importance of having someone other than the ActiveX component's developer externally test its public members. However, at design time, the developer also needs an easy way to debug and test a member's code. VB5 supports two different techniques for doing this and we examine both in depth.

We also discuss the pros and cons of the two different ways (the **CreateObject** function and **As New** statement) of instantiating a class in an ActiveX component. Finally, Chapter 4 takes a closer look at the private **CL** class of the book's class library and some of the **Form** object-related methods that it contains. The **CL** class contains many different general-purpose methods that you will find useful when you develop your own ActiveX components.

Encapsulating A Form Object

In Chapter 3, you learned how to write methods in a **ClassModule** object and call them externally by passing the required arguments. Many of the methods that you will write work in that way; that is, they take the arguments passed in to them, execute their algorithms, and return some value signifying success or failure. However, because Windows is a GUI operating system, there will be situations where you will want to write a method that displays some kind of **Form** object while the method is executing in order to accept input from the user.

Also, if you are a typical Visual Basic programmer, you have spent a lot of time creating and coding the same types of **Form** objects over and over again. Most of us have repeatedly designed and written code for such generic **Form** objects as:

- Splash screen
- File browser dialog box
- About dialog box
- Text editor
- Security password dialog box
- Search-and-select dialog box

Depending on the type of application programming you do, you can probably add several more types of **Form** objects to the preceding list. In the past, using VB3, you could create one of these **Form** objects in a generic fashion, but it was not easy to do or to maintain.

The obstacles to creating and using reusable **Form** objects with VB3 were many. The **Form** object's module had to be physically added to each new project to be able to be reused. And, if the code in the **Form** object's module was not completely encapsulated, a related standard module might have to be added to the project. Because most Visual Basic programmers like to keep all the files related to a project in the same directory, copies of the generic **Form** object and any related files proliferated. Because of the proliferation of copies, maintaining and enhancing the code was difficult to do on a systematic basis.

In a large-scale VB3 project, the logistics of trying to create and control the reuse of generic **Form** objects were a nightmare for any project manager. But that was then, and this is now. Project managers and Visual Basic programmers will be glad to know that VB5 makes it quite easy to encapsulate a reusable **Form** object inside a class library.

To show you how easy encapsulating a **Form** object is, I've provided the general steps to encapsulate a **Form** object in a class library and to enable it to be displayed from a client application:

1. Add a new **Form** object to the ActiveX component's project.

2. Add the control objects required by the **Form** object to perform its functionality.

3. Set the design-time properties of the **Form** object and its control objects.

4. Write the code for the **Form** object's and control objects' event procedures.

5. Write the required **Property Get**, **Property Let**, or **Property Set** procedures and general procedures.

6. Create and write a method that displays the encapsulated **Form** object using Visual Basic's **Show** method (*style* argument set to **vbModal**). It is at this point that code execution branches to the **Load** event procedure of the encapsulated **Form** object and temporarily pauses in the calling method.

7. When the user finishes with the **Form** object, an event is triggered (usually the **Click** event for a **CommandButton** object) and the **Hide** method is applied to the **Form** object. At this point, code execution reverts back to the calling method.

8. The calling method reads the **Tag** property or a custom property of the **Form** object, where any value(s) to be returned to the client application was stored, and then unloads the encapsulated **Form** object.

9. The calling method returns the value(s) to the client application that called it.

Encapsulating A Delete Files Form

Our first example of encapsulating a **Form** object in an ActiveX component will be to create a simple dialog box that enables a client application to select files located on a hard or floppy disk and delete them. Figure 4.1 shows how the **Form** object will look when it is displayed.

The **FileListBox** object will have its **MultiSelect** property set to 2 - Extended at design time. After the user selects some files to delete, the **Form** object will look like the one shown in Figure 4.2.

When the user clicks on Delete, the code in the **Click** event procedure of the **CommandButton** object deletes the selected files. Once this process takes place, the **Form** object will appear as shown in Figure 4.3.

When the user is done deleting files, clicking on OK or Close causes the **Hide** method to be applied to the encapsulated **Form** object. Then execution reverts back to the calling method, which will return **True** to the client application.

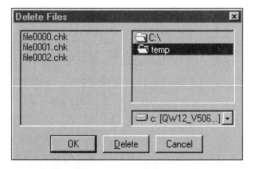

Figure 4.1 The Delete Files dialog box.

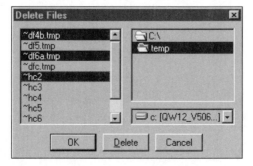

Figure 4.2 The Delete Files dialog box after the user selects files to delete.

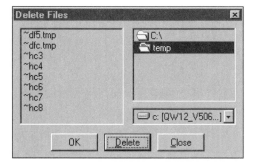

Figure 4.3   The Delete Files dialog box after files have been deleted.

ADDING THE FORM AND ITS CONTROLS TO AN ACTIVEX COMPONENT

Start VB5 and open the book's ActiveX EXE component project EFSE.VBP.

Select Project | Add Form and, from the Add Form dialog box, double click on the Form icon. Next add the following control objects from VB's toolbox to the form:

- **DriveListBox**, **DirListBox**, and **FileListBox**. Set their **Name** properties to drvDelete, dirDelete, and filDelete, respectively.

- Three **CommandButton** objects. Set their **Name** properties to cmdOK, cmdDelete, and cmdCancel, respectively.

You can set the various properties of the **Form** object and its control objects to mimic the size and organization of the dialog box pictured in Figure 4.1. A few properties, however, must be set to specific values in order to support the functionality of the dialog box as implemented by the code in the next section of this chapter. The properties and their settings are listed in Tables 4.1 and 4.2.

Only set the **Icon** property to (None) if you are running 32-bit Visual Basic. You can do this by selecting the (Icon) setting in the Properties window and pressing Delete.

WRITING THE CODE FOR THE FORM AND ITS CONTROLS

The code needed to enable a **Form** object and its controls to display and delete files is not extensive. In the process of writing it, you will learn some generic concepts about code for a class library that you will use repeatedly in this book. The first step is to make two declarations that enable the encapsulated **Form** object to call and use the services of members in **ClassModule** objects in the class library. When you instantiate an internal

Table 4.1   Settings for the **Form** object's properties.

Property	Setting
BorderStyle	3 - Fixed Dialog
Caption	Delete Files
Icon	(None)
Name	frmDelete

Table 4.2   Setting for the **FileListBox** object's properties.

Property	Setting
MultiSelect	2 - Extended

class that is part of your current Visual Basic project, you use a different syntax than when you are instantiating a class in a separate ActiveX component.

Write the code shown in Listing 4.1 in the General Declarations section of frmDelete.

Listing 4.1   Instantiating internal classes.

```
' Instantiate internal classes to reuse their members:
Private CL       As New CL
Private Dialog   As New Dialog
```

You should note these points about the code in Listing 4.1. First, the **Private** keyword is used to make the declarations. This ensures that encapsulation is not violated for these form-level object variables. Second, the **As New** statement is used to declare the object variable and to instantiate the class at the same time. Third, the type of object variable declared is the specific **ClassModule** object types **CL** and **Dialog** (that is, the **Name** properties of these two classes in the book's ActiveX component).

Using As New instead of CreateObject

*You can only use the **As New** statement, instead of the more commonly used **CreateObject** function, when you are instantiating an internal class or if you have previously set a reference in your Visual Basic project to the class library (Project | References). In ActiveX component terminology, this technique is called* early binding. *See* The As New Statement *section later in this chapter for more details.*

In the interest of writing readable, English-like Visual Basic code, the object variables in Listing 4.1 are given the same names (that is, **CL** and **Dialog**) as the names of the classes that will be instantiated and assigned to them. This is the only type of module-level declaration in the book's class library whose variable name is not preceded by a prefix indicating scope. Visual Basic has no problem keeping the same names straight when it executes calls to members of the classes.

Now we will continue with the rest of the code required for **frmDelete** and its controls. The code for the **CommandButton** objects is pretty straightforward. The **cmdOK** and **cmdCancel** Click event procedures are shown in Listing 4.2.

Listing 4.2   Code for the Click event of the command buttons.

```
Private Sub cmdCancel_Click()

    ' Reroute code execution back to calling method.
    Hide

End Sub

Private Sub cmdOK_Click()

    ' Reroute code execution back to calling method.
    Hide

End Sub

Private Sub cmdDelete_Click()

    ' Constants for literals:
    Const FIRST_FILE = 0

    ' Variables:
    Dim File        As Integer
    Dim LastFile    As Integer
    Dim Path        As String

    ' Enable error handler.
    On Error GoTo ET

    ' Delete selected files, repaint FileListBox
    ' object and change caption of Cancel button:
    Path = dirDelete & "\"

    If Right$(Path, 2) = "\\" Then Path = Left$(Path, Len(Path) - 1)

    LastFile = filDelete.ListCount - 1
```

```
      For File = LastFile To FIRST_FILE Step -1

         If filDelete.Selected(File) Then
            Kill Path & filDelete.List(File)
         End If

      Next File

      filDelete.Refresh
      cmdCancel.Caption = "&Close"
      Exit Sub

ET:

   Err = False

End Sub
```

You should note in Listing 4.2 that the **cmdDelete_Click** event procedure actually deletes files with Visual Basic's **Kill** statement. There are two points to note here. First, when you test this code, be careful to delete only files that you have made copies of or do not need (like those on the Windows temporary path). Second, this kind of code needs to be error trapped, and it is, but all the error handler does is set the **Number** property of the **Err** object to zero (**False**). We won't be dealing with implementing commercial-quality, error-handling routines in this chapter; that sort of code will come later in the book.

The code for the **DirListBox** and **DriveListBox** objects, in Listing 4.3, is minimal and goes in their **Change** event procedures.

Listing 4.3 Code for DirListBox and DriveListBox.

```
Private Sub drvDelete_Change()

   ' Update list of directories when drive changes.
   On Error GoTo ET
   dirDelete = drvDelete
   Exit Sub

ET:

   Err = False

End Sub

Private Sub dirDelete_Change()

   ' Update list of files when directory changes.
   filDelete = dirDelete

End Sub
```

Finally, there is the code for the **Form** object's event procedures. You need to write code for the **Form_Load**, **Form_QueryUnload**, and **Form_Unload** event procedures. Each one of these code blocks illustrates some generic techniques in coding class libraries.

The **Form_Load** event procedure has code that calls a method in the **Dialog** class called **ShowCL**. This method sets attributes of a **Form** object and its control objects to mimic the functionality of the dialog boxes in Microsoft's Office applications. The **ShowCL** method takes two required arguments: **Frm**, which is the **Name** property of the **Form** object to apply the method to, and **Properties()**, which is a boolean array. This boolean array may have from one to three elements, each of which is set to either **True** or **False**. The code for the **Form_Load** event procedure is in Listing 4.4.

Listing 4.4   Code for Form_Load procedure.

```
Private Sub Form_Load()

    ' Constants for literals:
    Const MS_BOLD = 0
    Const MS_DLG = 1
    Const MS_ONTOP = 2

    ' Variables:
    Dim Properties(2) As Boolean

    ' Subclass appearance/behavior of Form object:
    Properties(MS_BOLD) = True
    Properties(MS_DLG) = True
    Properties(MS_ONTOP) = True
    Dialog.ShowCL Me, Properties
    Dialog.Center Me

End Sub
```

You will learn more about the **ShowCL** method later in this book. Remember, however, that you can access the Help file topic for any member of the book's class library by viewing it from Visual Basic's Object Browser or by starting the class library's Help file EFS.HLP from the Explorer or File Manager.

The **Form_QueryUnload** event procedure has code that calls a method in the private, internal **CL** class. The **CL** class, which we'll cover in more detail later in the chapter, contains all of the methods that are called by more than one member of the public classes or their encapsulated **Form** objects. The **IsUnloadFromApp** method checks to see how the client application's user is trying to close and unload the **Form** object, and only proceeds to unload it if the user selected a **CommandButton** object or Control|Close. Finally, the code for the **Form_Unload** event procedure demonstrates how you should always explicitly free the system resources associated with any objects before unloading the **Form** object. The code for the **Form_QueryUnload** and **Form_Unload** event procedures is in Listing 4.5.

Listing 4.5 Code for procedures unloading form.

```
Private Sub Form_QueryUnload(Cancel As Integer, UnloadMode As Integer)

    ' Call object's member:
    If Not CL.IsUnloadFromApp(UnloadMode) Then
        Cancel = True
    Else

        If UnloadMode = vbFormControlMenu Then
            Cancel = True
            cmdCancel_Click
        End If

    End If

End Sub

Private Sub Form_Unload(Cancel As Integer)

    ' Free system resources associated with objects:
    Set CL = Nothing
    Set Dialog = Nothing
    Set frmDelete = Nothing

End Sub
```

The one tricky bit of code in Listing 4.5 is in the **Form_QueryUnload** event procedure. If the user tries to unload the form from the Control menu, the code cancels the request to unload and reroutes execution to the **cmdCancel_Click** event procedure. This must be done so that the **Hide** statement there can execute and reroute execution back to the calling method.

When you unload a Form object ...

*Visual Basic's Knowledge Base Help file recommends that when you unload a **Form** object, you set all its object references to **Nothing** (including itself) to avoid memory leaks and reinitialize any form-level variables.*

Writing Code For The Delete Method

Now that you have created the encapsulated **Form** object and written its code, you must declare and write a method that the client application can call and that displays the **Form** object modally. To begin this process, select the MISCEXS.CLS and, at the bottom of the General Declarations section, type

```
Function Delete() As Boolean
```

and press Enter. Visual Basic creates the opening and closing statements for the method. Write the code shown in Listing 4.6 for the **Delete** method.

Listing 4.6   Code for Delete method.

```
Function Delete() As Boolean

    ' Enable error handler.
    On Error GoTo ET

    ' Display frmDelete Form object modally so code execution pauses
    ' on this line until Hide method is applied to Form object.
    frmDelete.Show vbModal

    ' When Hide method is executed in delete files Form object—
    ' * Unload Form object.
    ' * Return True to indicate success.
    Unload frmDelete
    Delete = True
    Exit Function

ET:

    Err = False

End Function
```

Testing A Method Internally

In Chapter 3, we learned how to test a method externally by calling it from another Visual Basic project. It is now time to learn how to test and debug a method internally, from within the ActiveX component project that contains the method. There are two techniques that you can use to test an ActiveX component internally. The first technique works with both EXE and DLL ActiveX components under VB4, but it only works with an EXE component under VB5. The second technique works with both EXE and DLL components under either VB4 or VB5.

Technique #1—One VB Instance

With the first technique, you can test an ActiveX component internally without being required to start another instance of Visual Basic. To test the **Delete** method and its associated **Form** object with technique #1 internally, follow these steps:

1. Select Form1 and then select Project | Remove Form1.
2. Select Project | Add Form and, from the Add Form dialog box, double click on the Form icon.

Steps 1 and 2 are a quick way of cleaning out any previous test code and ensuring that you have a blank test form, which will simulate a client application's **Form** object.

3. Write the code in Listing 4.7 in the various event procedures of Form1.
4. Ensure that the **Form1.Show** statement in the **Sub Main** procedure in STARTUP.BAS is uncommented.
5. Select Project | EFSE Properties and, on the Component tab, ensure that Start Mode is set to Standalone.
6. Select Run | Start to display the simulated client application's **Form** object.

From here on, the process of testing a method internally is the same, whether you are using technique #1 or technique #2.

> **Note:** *When you save, make and register an ActiveX EXE component's project, you can leave Start Mode on the Component tab of the Project Properties dialog box set to Standalone to facilitate internal testing. This is because an ActiveX EXE component's actual Start Mode setting is determined by how it is started at runtime, not by its nominal setting on the Component tab. For an ActiveX DLL component in VB5, however, the Start Mode setting is always disabled (a change from VB4).*

Technique #2—Two VB Instances

With the second technique, you must start another instance of Visual Basic to test an ActiveX component internally. To test the **Delete** method and its associated **Form** object with technique #2, follow these steps:

1. Select Run | Start to run the ActiveX component's project.

2. Start a second instance of Visual Basic and open a standard EXE project that will function as a simulated client application.

3. Write the code in Listing 4.7 in the various event procedures of Form1 of the client application.

4. Select Run|Start to display the simulated client application's **Form** object.

From here on, the process of testing a method internally is the same, whether you are using technique #1 or technique #2.

Listing 4.7   Code for test form.
Code in General Declarations section:

```
' Form-level variable.
Dim MiscExs As Object

Private Sub Form_Load()

    ' Instantiate class. Programmatic ID has two parts delimited by dot:
    ' * Project name's entry on Options tab of Project dialog box.
    ' * Name property of ClassModule object.
    #If Win32 Then
       Set MiscExs = CreateObject("EFSE.MiscExs")
    #ElseIf Win16 Then
       Set MiscExs = CreateObject("EFS16.MiscExs")
    #End If

End Sub

Private Sub Form_DblClick()

    ' Call object's member.
    MiscExs.Delete

End Sub

Private Sub Form_Unload(Cancel As Integer)

    ' Free system resources associated with object variable.
    Set MiscExs  = Nothing

    ' Force ClassModule object's project to unload completely.
    ' This is only done when testing a method internally.
    End

End Sub
```

At this point in the book, the code in Listing 4.7 should be clear. You are following the usual three steps: the declaration of the object variable in the General Declarations section, the assignment of the instantiated class to the object variable in the **Form_Load** event procedure, and the call to the object's method in the **Form_DblClick** event procedure.

After you select Run|Start to display the client application's **Form** object, double click it, and watch as the **Delete** method displays the Delete Files dialog box. Use the **DirListBox** object to find the Windows temporary directory (or some other directory) and select some files that you can safely delete. Once you have selected a file or files, click on the Delete button. The code in the **cmdDelete_Click** event procedure deletes the files and repaints the **FileListBox** object to confirm that they have been deleted.

When you test an ActiveX component internally, you can set a breakpoint on the calling statement by selecting Debug|Toggle Breakpoint, pressing F9 or clicking the toolbar button. You may then single-step through the method's code by pressing F8 or clicking the toolbar button. You can also set breakpoints in the method's code or do any other kind of debugging that you would do in a standard EXE project.

You can use the same code in Listing 4.7 to externally call and test the **Delete** method and its associated **Form** object, but you cannot debug the method's code when testing externally. For a review of external testing of procedures, see the section *Calling A Method Externally* in Chapter 3.

Now that you have internally tested the new **Delete** method and its associated **Form** object, you need to save the changes to the book's ActiveX component project. Be sure that the new form is saved to the same directory that contains the other project files (that is, C:\VBOOPEFS\VBCLSLIB).

Different Ways To Instantiate A Class

Our next step is to examine the ways to instantiate a class. In this section, we will discuss the **CreateObject** function and the **As New** statement.

The CreateObject Function

The **CreateObject** function is used to create a new instance of an externally creatable ActiveX component. **CreateObject** only creates a new instance of the object. You must first declare an object variable to which you then assign the instance of the object returned by **CreateObject**. In OLE Automation terminology, this way of creating an instance of an object is referred to as *late binding*. Using the **CreateObject** function to instantiate a class has several advantages:

- You do not need to set a reference to the ActiveX component in the References dialog box (Project | References).

- Version incompatibilities are not an issue.

- If you are instantiating an in-process, ActiveX DLL component, perceived performance is basically the same using the **CreateObject** function as when you use the **As New** statement.

Of course, we must also consider the other side of the coin—the disadvantages:

- Visual Basic does not provide syntax checking if a client application calls an invalid member or passes an invalid data type to an argument of a member. Instead, the ActiveX component must provide the exception-handling capabilities.

- The **CreateObject** function is slightly slower than when you use early binding and the **As New** statement on an out-of-process ActiveX EXE component.

Optimizing object performance

You can optimize perceived performance by declaring the object variable with form-level scope and instantiating the class with **CreateObject** *in the* **Form_Load** *event of the* **Form** *object that uses a member of the class. In this way, the instantiation (and the time required to do it) occurs only once.*

The As New Statement

The **As New** statement is used to indicate that a declared object variable is a new instance of an externally creatable object (for example, an ActiveX component). This statement can be used with these types of variable declarations:

- **Dim As New**. This declaration defaults to a public variable if declared in a standard module.

- **Private As New**. This declaration limits the scope to the module in which it is declared.

Used with a **ClassModule** object, **Dim As New** and **Private As New** both declare the **Object** variable and create a new instance of the object at the same time. In OLE Automation terminology, this way of instantiating a class is referred to as *early binding*. The early binding approach and the **As New** syntax are always faster than using the **CreateObject** function.

You can only use the **As New** syntax to instantiate a class externally if you first set a reference to the ActiveX component containing the class in the References dialog box (Project|References). If you do not set the reference first, Visual Basic displays the syntax error message *User-defined type not defined* when you try to run your project. When you instantiate a class internally, inside the class library itself, it is not necessary to set a reference because Visual Basic automatically sets a reference to the current project.

Regardless of whether you prefer to use early binding or late binding to instantiate an ActiveX component's class and reuse its members, the members should still provide their own syntax checking. There are two reasons for this approach. First, you cannot assume that everyone who uses the ActiveX component you write will use the early binding technique. If they use late binding, then Visual Basic cannot perform syntax checking. Second, some OLE Automation-compliant languages do not support the early binding technique (for example, Excel VBA).

Understanding The Private CL Class

Because you used the **IsUnloadFromApp** method of the **CL** class in the previous code related to the **Delete** method, I think this is a good time to discuss the difference between private and public **ClassModule** objects. The private **CL ClassModule** object can only be instantiated and used from inside the book's class library. A public **ClassModule** object can be instantiated externally and its public methods can be called from another Visual Basic project. If you select CL.CLS in the class library's project, you see that it is the only **ClassModule** object whose **Instancing** property is set to 1 - Private. All the other classes in the book's class library have their **Instancing** property set to 5 - MultiUse.

The private **CL** class (the *CL* stands for Class Library) contains all procedures that are called more than once by members of the public classes. Strictly speaking, this approach violates the OOP attribute of encapsulation, but in practice, most developers code this way in order to minimize the size of the ActiveX component. As long as all unencapsulated procedures are located in one private class, it is not difficult to understand what is happening or to re-encapsulate the common procedures within each individual class (if you so desire). You need to understand how some of the more broadly applicable methods of the **CL** class work because they use techniques that are essential to Visual Basic class library development. Some of these techniques are really workarounds that compensate for limitations in VB5.

Table 4.3 lists some of the most commonly used methods of the **CL** class.

HasHandle Method

The **HasHandle** method checks if an object reference has a handle. Three possible generic cases are dealt with. First, if the object reference does have a handle, the method returns a string set to "True". Second, if the object reference does not have a handle and it is one of the built-in Visual Basic objects, the method returns a string corresponding to the class or type name of the object (for example, "ListBox"). Third, if the object reference does have a handle and the handle evaluates to zero, then it must be Visual Basic's **OLE** container control object. In this case, the method returns the string "OLE". The code for the **HasHandle** method is in Listing 4.8.

Table 4.3 **CL** class methods.

Method	Description
HasHandle	Determines if an object reference passed as an argument to a member of a public class has an hWnd property (handle) and, therefore, whether certain Windows API functions can be applied to it.
IsForm	Determines if an object reference passed as an argument to a member of a public class is a Visual Basic Form object.
IsMDIForm	Determines if an object reference passed as an argument to a member of a public class is a Visual Basic MDIForm object.
IsDrv	Determines if a path-and-file specification passed as an argument to a member of a public class contains a valid drive.
IsDir	Determines if a path-and-file specification passed as an argument to a member of a public class contains a valid path.
IsUnloadFromApp	Determines how a client application is trying to unload a Form object from the class library.
IsWinNT	Determines if the client application is running under Windows NT.
IsWin95Shell	Determines if the client application is running under the new shell used by Windows 95 and Windows NT 4.

Listing 4.8   HasHandle method of CL class.

```
Function HasHandle(Obj) As String
' ─────────────────────────────
' Purpose: Determines if an object/control has an hWnd
'          property (handle) and, so, whether certain Windows
'          API functions can be applied to it. Also serves as
'          indirect way to determine if object reference is to
'          ClassModule object.

' Called:  Internally from members of class library.

' Accepts: Obj: Variant that evaluates to VB object.

' Returns: String: "True" if object has hWnd property or else
'                  class name of Obj argument.
' ─────────────────────────────


' Enable in-line error handling.
On Error Resume Next

' Try to get handle of object passed to Obj argument (causes
' error 438 if object does not have hWnd property):
If Obj.hWnd <> False Then

    ' If no error, then object has handle; so
    ' set function's return value to "True":
    If Err = False Then
       HasHandle = "True"

    ' Else if object does not have handle:
    Else

       ' Clear property settings of Err Object.
       Err = False

       ' Find its type name from groups below and
       ' set function's return value to that name:
       Select Case TypeName(Obj)

          ' Add-in objects:
          Case "Application", "Component", "Components", _
               "ControlTemplate", "ControlTemplates", _
               "FileControl", "FormTemplate", "MenuItems", _
               "MenuLine", "ProjectTemplate", "Properties", _
               "Property", "SelectedComponents", _
               "SelectedControlTemplates", "SubMenu"
                  HasHandle = TypeName(Obj)

          ' Custom control object:
          Case "CommonDialog"
                  HasHandle = TypeName(Obj)

          ' Data Access objects:
          Case "Column", "Columns", "Container", _
               "Containers", "Database", "Databases", _
```

```
                    "DBCombo", "DBEngine", "DBGrid", "DBList", _
                    "Document", "Documents", "Dynaset", "Error", _
                    "Errors", "Field", "Fields", "Group", _
                    "Groups", "Index", "Indexes", "Parameter", _
                    "Parameters", "Properties", "Property", _
                    "QueryDef", "QueryDefs", "Recordset", _
                    "Recordsets", "Relation", "Relations"
                        HasHandle = TypeName(Obj)
                Case "RowBuffer", "SelBookmarks", "Snapshot", _
                    "Table", "TableDef", "TableDefs", "User", _
                    "Users", "Workspace", "Workspaces"
                        HasHandle = TypeName(Obj)

                ' OLE Automation objects (Controls, Forms, Printers):
                Case "Object"
                        HasHandle = "Object"

                ' OLE Automation objects whose types are unknown:
                Case "Unknown"
                        HasHandle = "Unknown"

                ' Other objects:
                Case "App", "Clipboard", "Collection", "Data", _
                    "ErrObject", "Font", "Image", "Label", "Line", _
                    "Picture", "Printer", "Screen", "Shape", "Timer"
                        HasHandle = TypeName(Obj)

                ' Some other object (Form, MDIForm or ClassModule
                ' object), in which case VB's TypeName function
                ' either returns Name property of object (for Form
                ' or MDIForm) or results in run-time error (for
                ' ClassModule). Instead, HasHandle returns class
                ' name of object.
                Case Else
                    If IsForm(Obj) Then
                        HasHandle = "Form"
                    ElseIf IsMDIForm(Obj) Then
                        HasHandle = "MDIForm"
                    Else
                        HasHandle = "ClassModule"
                    End If
            End Select
        End If

    ' The OLE Container Control Properties topic in VB.HLP says
    ' the OLE Container object has an hWnd property; but, VB.HLP's
    ' hWnd Property topic says the hWnd property is no longer
    ' supported for the OLE container control. When you read it,
    ' it always returns zero and you cannot find its parent. This
    ' code returns its class name:
    ElseIf Obj.hWnd = False Then
        HasHandle = TypeName(Obj)
    End If

End Function
```

There are several things to note about how the **HasHandle** method is written. First, because it is a member of a private class and is not documented in the class library's Help file, a brief template at the top of the procedure documents the purpose of the member and its interface (that is, arguments accepted and values returned). Second, the three built-in Visual Basic collection objects (**Controls**, **Forms**, and **Printers**) are actually, at a lower lever of abstraction, OLE Automation objects. This type of object has the class name **Object**, which is how you must declare any argument in a member of an ActiveX component that accepts an object reference. Third, to determine if an object reference is to a **Form** or **MDIForm** object, **HasHandle** calls two other methods in the **CL** class: **IsForm** and **IsMDIForm**. We will discuss those methods in the next section. Fourth, there is no easy way to determine if an object reference is to a **ClassModule** object. The **HasHandle** method does it by brute force, so to speak, because it assumes that if an object reference is not to any of the other possible Visual Basic objects, then it must be to a **ClassModule** object.

Passing an object to OLE

*If you pass an object reference to Visual Basic's **OLE** container control object to **HasHandle**, it determines that the **OLE** container has an **hWnd** property, but that the handle is zero. This is a contradiction in terms because any handle Windows assigns must be a positive **Integer** or **Long**. In one topic, the Visual Basic Help file says the **hWnd** property applies to this object; in another topic, it says that it no longer applies. When you read the **OLE** container control with Visual Basic code, the control does have an **hWnd** property; however, it always returns zero and you cannot find its parent. This confusing situation probably reflects a bug in Visual Basic.*

IsForm And IsMDIForm Methods

The **IsForm** and **IsMDIForm** methods compensate for the fact that Visual Basic itself has no certain way of determining if an object reference passed as an argument to a member of an ActiveX component is a **Form** or **MDIForm** object. If you use Visual Basic's **TypeName** function on a reference to a **Form** or **MDIForm** object, it returns its **Name** property (for example, frmDelete) but not its generic class or type name. Visual Basic's **TypeOf** keyword will return the generic class name, but only if an in-process ActiveX DLL component is running. For some reason, **TypeOf** does not work correctly on a **Form** or **MDIForm** object in an out-of-process ActiveX EXE component.

Both the **IsForm** and **IsMDIForm** methods use the same technique. The code tries to read a property of the object reference (**KeyPreview** for the **Form** object and **AutoShowChildren** for the **MDIForm** object). This property is unique to the object that is being checked. If the object reference has the property, no runtime error occurs and **IsForm** or **IsMDIForm** returns **True**. If the object reference does not have the property, runtime error 438 (Object doesn't support this property or method) occurs and **IsForm** or **IsMDIForm** returns the default value of **False**. The code for the two methods is shown in Listing 4.9.

Listing 4.9   IsForm and IsMDIForm methods of CL class.

```
Function IsForm(Frm) As Boolean
    ' _____

    ' Purpose: Checks whether or not object is Form object.
    '
    ' Called:  Internally from members of class library.
    '
    ' Accepts: Frm: Variant that must evaluate to VB's
    '               Form object.
    '
    ' Returns: If it is Form object, True. If not, False
    '          (uninitialized/default value of function).
    '
    ' Notes:   a) VB's TypeName function returns Name property of
    '             Form object, not generic class name.
    '          b) VB's TypeOf function returns generic class name,
    '             but it fails when used in out-of-process,
    '             ActiveX component.
    ' _____


    ' IsForm method follows these steps—
    ' * Tries to return value of property of Frm argument that is
    '   unique to its VB class (that is, KeyPreview).
    ' * If property applies to Frm argument, no error occurs and
    '   method returns True.
    ' * If property does not apply, error 438 occurs and method
    '   returns False.
On Error Resume Next

If Frm.KeyPreview = True Or Frm.KeyPreview = False Then
    If Err = False Then IsForm = True
End If

Err = False
```

```
End Function

Function IsMDIForm(MDIFrm) As Boolean
    ' ─────────────────────────────
    ' Purpose: Checks whether or not object is MDIForm object.
    '
    ' Called:  Internally from members of class library.
    '
    ' Accepts: MDIFrm: Variant that must evaluate to VB's
    '                  MDIForm object.
    '
    ' Returns: If it is Form object, True. If not, False
    '          (uninitialized/default value of function).
    '
    ' Notes:   a) VB's TypeName function returns Name property of
    '             MDIForm object, not generic class name.
    '          b) VB's TypeOf function returns generic class name, but
    '             but it fails when used in out-of-process,
    '             ActiveX component.
    ' ─────────────────────────────

    ' IsMDIForm method follows these steps—
    ' * Tries to return value of property of MDIFrm argument that
    '   is unique to its VB class (that is, AutoShowChildren).
    ' * If property applies to MDIFrm argument, no error occurs
    '   and method returns True.
    ' * If property does not apply, error 438 occurs and method
    '   returns False.
    On Error Resume Next

    If MDIFrm.AutoShowChildren = True Or MDIFrm.AutoShowChildren = False Then
        If Err = False Then IsMDIForm = True
    End If

    Err = False

End Function
```

A trick with IsForm and IsMDIForm

*Both **IsForm** and **IsMDIForm** use a generic coding trick that every Visual Basic programmer should know. Sometimes the easiest way to determine if an argument is passed a valid value or if an object has a certain member is to enable an inline error handler and then force a runtime error to occur if the argument's value or the member being tested is invalid.*

IsDrv And IsDir Methods

The **IsDrv** and **IsDir** methods validate whether a string passed to an argument contains a valid drive or a valid path. The code for the two methods is shown in Listing 4.10.

Listing 4.10   IsDrv and IsDir methods of CL class.

```
Sub IsDrv(PathFiles As String, _
          Member As String, _
          Arg As String)
'  _____
'
' Purpose: Validates existence of drive.
'
' Called:  Internally from members of class library.
'
' Accepts: PathFiles: String expression specifying path or
'                     path and file name(s) to check for
'                     valid drive.
'          Member:    String expression specifying name of
'                     member from which this method is called.
'          Arg:       String expression specifying name of
'                     argument being checked.
'  _____

' Constants for literals:
Const NO_DRIVE = 1

' Variables:
Dim Drive As String
Drive = Left$(PathFiles, 1)

#If Win32 Then

    If Drive = "A" Or Drive = "B" Then
       Drive = Drive & ":"
    Else
       Drive = Drive & ":\"
    End If

    If GetDriveType(Drive) = NO_DRIVE Then
       E.TrapSyntax 44, Member, Left$(PathFiles, 1), Arg
    End If

#Else

    If GetDriveType(Asc(PathFiles) - vbKeyA) = False Then
       E.TrapSyntax 44, Member, Left$(PathFiles, 1), Arg
    End If

#End If
End Sub
```

```
Sub IsDir(Path As String, _
          Member As String, _
          Arg As String)
    ' _____
    '
    ' Purpose: Validates existence of directory.
    '
    ' Called:  Internally from members of class library.
    '
    ' Accepts: Path:    String expression specifying directory
    '                   to validate.
    '          Member:  String expression specifying name of
    '                   member from which this method is called.
    '          Arg:     String expression specifying name of
    '                   argument being checked.
    ' _____

    ' Constants for literals:
    Const WILDCARD1 = "*.*"
    Const ATTRIBS = vbHidden + vbSystem + vbDirectory
    Const NO_DIR = vbNullString

    ' Variables:
    Dim DirName As String
    DirName = Path
    DirName = DirName & WILDCARD1

    If Dir$(DirName, ATTRIBS) = NO_DIR Then
        E.TrapSyntax 43, Member, "Path", Arg
    End If

End Sub
```

There are several things to note about how the **IsDrv** and **IsDir** methods are written. First, **IsDrv** uses the Windows API function **GetDriveType** to validate the existence of the drive. Unfortunately, like many Windows API functions, **GetDriveType** behaves differently under the 32-bit API than under the 16-bit API. The 32-bit version takes a **String** data type as its argument (for example, "G:\") and returns 1 if the drive does not exist. The 16-bit version takes an **Integer** data type as its argument (for example, 2 signifies drive C) and returns zero if the drive does not exist. Second, each of the methods is declared as a **Sub** procedure (unlike all the members of the public classes and the majority of the members of the **CL** class, which are declared as **Function** procedures). Three, no error handler is enabled in either of these procedures (or, for that matter, in any of the other procedures in the private **CL** class). The reasons behind the second and third points have to do with the error-handling scheme that the book's class library uses; you will learn more about that topic in Chapters 5 and 8.

Constants in the IsDir method

*Note the use of the Visual Basic intrinsic constants **vbNullString**, **vbHidden**, **vbSystem**, and **vbDirectory** in the **IsDir** method. Using these and other Visual Basic intrinsic constants makes your code more readable and reduces the amount of system resources used by an application or class library.*

IsUnloadFromApp Method

The **IsUnloadFromApp** method determines how a client application/user is trying to unload a **Form** object in the class library. Unless the **QueryUnload** event is triggered from the Control menu or from code in the **Form** object, the **Unload** event is canceled. There are five actions that can cause the **QueryUnload** event of a **Form** object to occur. These actions and their intrinsic constants are:

- **vbFormControlMenu** (0). The user selects Control | Close on the **Form** object.

- **vbFormCode** (1). The **Unload** statement is invoked from code.

- **vbAppWindows** (2). The current Windows operating environment session is ending.

- **vbAppTaskManager** (3). The Windows Task Manager is closing the application.

- **vbFormMDIForm** (4). A MDI child form is closing because its MDI parent form is closing.

The code for the method is shown in Listing 4.11.

Listing 4.11   IsUnloadFromApp method of CL class.

```
Function IsUnloadFromApp(UnloadMode As Integer) As Boolean
    ' ─────────────────────────────────────────────
    ' Purpose: Checks how client application is trying to unload
    '          Form object in class library.
    '
    ' Called:  From Form_QueryUnload event of all Form objects
    '          encapsulated in class library.
    '
    ' Accepts: UnloadMode: Integer expression that is argument in
    '                      Form_QueryUnload event procedure.
    '
    ' Returns: If unloading form from Control menu or by code,
    '          True. If not, False (uninitialized/default value
    '          of function).
```

```
'  _____

If UnloadMode = vbFormControlMenu Or _
    UnloadMode = vbFormCode Then
        IsUnloadFromApp = True
End If

End Function
```

Call this kind of code from Query_Unload

You should call this kind of code from the **Query_Unload** *event proce-dure of every* **Form** *object. The best habit to get into is to not let a user close Windows itself without first being warned to close any Visual Basic application that is running.*

IsWinNT And IsWin95Shell Methods

The **IsWinNT** method checks if the client application is running under Windows NT. The **IsWin95Shell** method checks whether the client appli-cation is running under the new shell used by Windows 95 and Windows NT 4. The code for the two methods is shown in Listing 4.12.

Listing 4.12   IsWin95Shell method of CL class.

```
Function IsWinNT() As Boolean
    '  _____

    ' Purpose: Checks whether or not Windows NT is running.
    '
    ' Called:  Internally from members of class library.
    '
    ' Returns: If Windows NT is running, True. If not, False
    '          (uninitialized/default value of function)
    '  _____

    ' If 32-bit VB is running:
    ' * Size user-defined data type and fill it with data.
    ' * Get version and, if it is Windows NT, return True.
#If Win32 Then

        ' Constants for Windows API functions:
        Const VER_PLATFORM_WIN32_NT = 2

        ' Variables:
        Dim Win As OSVERSIONINFO
        Win.TypeSize = Len(Win)
```

```
       If GetVersionEx(Win) Then
           If Win.ID = VER_PLATFORM_WIN32_NT Then IsWinNT = True
       End If

   #End If

End Function

Function IsWin95Shell() As Boolean
   '  ─────────────────────────────
   '
   ' Purpose: Checks whether or not new shell in Windows 95 or
   '          NT 4.0 is running.
   '
   ' Called:  From Form_Load event of all Form objects
   '          encapsulated in class library.
   '
   ' Returns: If Windows 95 or NT 4.0 is running, True. If not,
   '          False (uninitialized/default value of function)
   '  ─────────────────────────────


   If FindWindow("Shell_TrayWnd", vbEmpty) <> False Then
       IsWin95Shell = True
   End If

End Function
```

The **IsWinNT** method uses the **GetVersionEx** Windows API function to determine if the client application is running under Windows NT. Because the Windows API function **GetVersionEx** only exists in the 32-bit API set, the code in the method must be conditionally compiled. **GetVersionEx** loads information about the version of the operating system that is currently running into the OSVERSIONINFO user-defined data type (represented by the variable **Win**). The **TypeSize** element must first be explicitly sized. You can then read the various elements of OSVERSIONINFO. In this method, the element being read is **ID**.

There are several reasons why the members of the class library that display a **Form** object need to know whether the client application is running under the old Windows 3.x shell or the new Windows 95 shell:

- The Control menu of the dialog boxes is slightly different in Visual Basic, depending on whether the new Windows 95 shell is being run or not.

- Certain features of the Windows operating system are only available when running under the Windows 95 shell.

- The dialog boxes in Windows and in the Microsoft Office 95 applications use a bold font for all controls when displayed under Windows 3.x or Windows NT 3.51. The same dialog box uses a normal font when it is

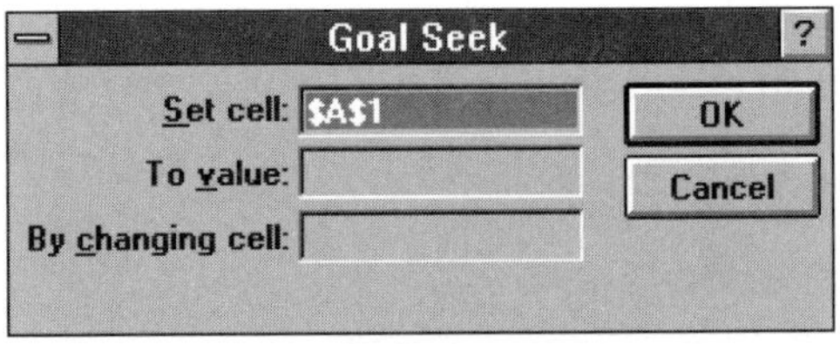

Figure 4.4 Goal Seek dialog box—Windows 3.x shell.

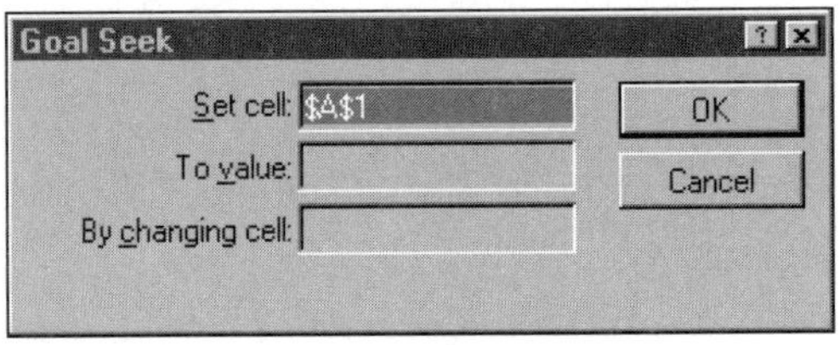

Figure 4.5 Goal Seek dialog box—Windows 95 shell.

displayed under Windows 95 or Windows NT 4. Figures 4.4 and 4.5 show the two different types of font displays (for the Excel 7.0 Goal Seek dialog box). To mimic this behavior, the **Form** objects in the class library call the **IsWin95Shell** method from their **Form_Load** event procedures to determine the version of Windows that is running. They then call the **MimicMS** method of the **Dialog** class to set the font to bold or normal.

The **IsWin95Shell** method uses the Windows API function **FindWindow** to determine under which shell the client application is running. In this usage, **FindWindow**'s first argument is a **String** specifying the class name (**Shell_TrayWnd**) of the taskbar window, which is unique to the new Windows 95-type shell. The second argument, if it is set to Null or the VB intrinsic constant **vbEmpty**, tells **FindWindow** to ignore the argument in its search. In another kind of usage, **FindWindow**'s second argument can be a **String** that specifies the window's title.

That's it for Chapter 4. By this point in the book, you should have a good grasp of the basic techniques of OOP development with Visual Basic and be able to try out some ideas of your own. In the next chapter, we are going to pull back a little from the level of detail in Chapters 2 through 4. Chapter 5 discusses the concept of the public interface of an ActiveX component and the principles that should govern the design of that public interface.

CREATING THE PUBLIC INTERFACE OF AN ACTIVEX COMPONENT

B ased on material in the preceding chapters, I'm sure it's quite clear to you that writing Visual Basic code in the form of reusable objects in an ActiveX component is a more complex task than simply writing **Sub** and **Function** procedures that are contained and called from a single Visual Basic project. Writing object-oriented code with Visual Basic is more challenging and demanding for these reasons:

- VB5 no longer handles many of the syntax and data type mismatch errors that VB3 caught, so we must now assume the responsibility for writing commercial-quality, bullet-proof error-handling routines.

- The code that makes up a method or property of an object is hidden from everyone except the person who wrote it (that is, the code is encapsulated in a black box), so the public interface of the method or property's arguments must be as simple and easy to use as possible. Designing and writing code that is simple and easy to use by anyone, yet sophisticated enough to perform a complex set of tasks on a consistent basis and under all possible conditions, is the ultimate software engineering challenge.

- The objects in a Visual Basic class library, in the form of an ActiveX component, can potentially be reused on a wide variety of hardware and software platforms and by many different programming languages, so general principles of software architectural analysis and design are more important than if you were writing normal Visual Basic code. The ideal is to write a class library that is based on a single set of Visual Basic source code, but that is flexible enough in design and implementation to be used on as many different platforms and by as many programming languages as possible.

- Members exposed by ActiveX components can be run both locally and remotely, so it is important to design and write class libraries that can run gracefully under the restrictions imposed by either of these two different types of platforms.

- A member is part of a black-box object that can communicate with its user only by means of its public interface, so the general principles that govern the architecture of that public interface must also be easy to understand and use. In this regard, Microsoft has helped the Visual Basic object programmer by creating, as part of the ActiveX component protocol, the metaphor of the Object Browser.

Before you make any serious attempt to write object-oriented code with Visual Basic, it is essential that you first consider the options available for meeting these requirements. Once you have found your solutions, choose a set of design features that will both satisfy the requirements and be feasible to implement and maintain on an ongoing basis. The general term that is used to describe such a set of design features is the *public interface*, and that's what we're going to discuss in this chapter.

Designing The Public Interface

In object-oriented programming under Visual Basic and the ActiveX component paradigm, the public interface of a class library composed of **ClassModule** objects includes:

- The hierarchy of classes (**ClassModule** objects) that comprise the class library and that are able to expose their public members for reuse.

- The arguments of a **ClassModule** object's public **Function**, **Sub**, **Property Get**, **Property Let**, **Property Set**, and **Event** procedures.

- The values returned, upon success or failure, by a member. These possible values include the error codes returned to describe a syntax or runtime error, where and when the error occurred, and so on.
- Microsoft's Object Browser, which enables us to display a member's syntax and arguments, a brief description of its purpose, a help topic with a detailed explanation of its specifications, and example code that demonstrates how to call and use it.

Microsoft's Object Browser is becoming a standard design feature associated with all OLE Automation-compliant programming languages.

Understanding The Principles Of Good Class Design

This book is not intended to address the topics of object-oriented analysis and design. Many books have been written on these subjects, and most universities and training centers offer courses on them. However, it is appropriate at this point in our discussion to outline the design and naming scheme used for this book's class library. The choice of classes and their members for the class library was driven by two general objectives. First, I wanted to demonstrate all the essential Visual Basic 5.0 object-oriented syntax. Second, I wanted to provide a class library whose objects would be reusable by as large a number of Visual Basic programmers as possible. This second objective dictated that the class library be designed to function essentially as an application framework; that is, the classes and their members provide most of the functionality that the conventional Windows GUI and menu structure (the application framework) requires.

In meeting these two objectives, I was able to design the 10 public classes of the book's class library. The name of each public class and a description of its purpose are shown in Table 5.1

There is an eleventh public class, the **Thread** class, that is not part of the class library's application framework. Rather, it demonstrates callback and polling techniques used when running an asynchronous or batch processing-type member in an out-of-process ActiveX component. A twelfth public class, the **MiscExs** class, is included only to demonstrate a few code snippets in this book and it is not documented in the class library's Help file (EFS.HLP).

Table 5.1 The public classes of the class library framework.

Class	Description
ActiveXCtl	Embeds certain ActiveX custom controls (status bar, toolbar) on a Form object in a client application.
ClientApp	Performs tasks related to a client application as a whole (displaying a splash screen, message box, or security password dialog box; choosing a color; showing tooltips; and so on).
Dialog	Subclasses the properties and appearance of dialog boxes in both client applications and the class library.
Error	Handles Visual Basic runtime errors and class library syntax errors in both a client application and the class library, and displays their associated help topics.
File	Performs tasks related to files for a client application (compressing, copying, deleting, encrypting, expanding, opening and saving them, and so on).
Graphic	Subclasses and manipulates Visual Basic objects that contain graphics in a client application.
Help	Provides the various kinds of Windows Help for a client application.
List	Subclasses and manipulates Visual Basic objects that contain lists in a client application.
Text	Subclasses and manipulates Visual Basic objects that contain text, and performs the tasks related to the conventional Windows Edit and Format menus for a client application.
Utility	Performs miscellaneous tasks (formatting a floppy disk, displaying a RAM monitor, getting information about windows, and so on) for a client application.

Each of the classes in the book's class library exhibits these general design principles. First, it is self-contained and is not part of a hierarchy. Second, it uses no **Public** or **Global** variables. In fact, no **Public** variables are used anywhere in the ActiveX components EFSD.DLL, EFSE.EXE, EFSR.EXE, and EFS16.EXE. Third (and this follows from the second principle), internal message passing among the classes is done only through instantiation. With regard to naming conventions, although some books (such as Deborah Kurata's *Doing Objects In Microsoft Visual Basic 4.0*) suggest that the names of classes should follow a scheme that includes the prefix *c*, the classes in the book's sample code follow Microsoft's naming scheme—they use simple, descriptive names that reflect the functionality they encapsulate.

Understanding The Principles Of Good Member/Argument Design

The following general principles related to the design of the argument structure of an object's members are both consistent with Microsoft's own programming practices and generally accepted among Windows object-oriented, ActiveX component programmers. Whenever possible, a member of Visual Basic itself is cited as an example:

- Arguments may be either required or optional.

- Required arguments for any specific member are kept to the minimum number needed to implement the portion of the functional specifications that is most fundamental and most commonly used. For example, Visual Basic's **MsgBox** function takes five arguments, but only the first one (the text of the message) is required.

- Optional arguments, when used, are provided in the order of their importance or frequency of potential use. For example, Visual Basic's **Move** method provides three optional arguments (*top*, *width*, and *height*). The *top* argument comes first in the sequence because the assumption is that it will be used more often than *width* or *height*.

- Some optional arguments are designed to be dependent on one another; that is, if a certain optional argument is provided, then another, dependent optional argument must also be provided. If dependent optional arguments are provided, they should normally be at the end of the sequence of arguments. For example, Visual Basic's **MsgBox** function has four optional arguments, the last two of which (*helpfile* and *context*) are dependent on each other.

- An argument should be able to accommodate an array of elements, but this feature should only be used when appropriate because it is potentially more confusing and difficult to document. For example, the data structure that underlies the **List** property of Visual Basic's **ComboBox** and **ListBox** objects is a **String** array. But, when you look at the help topic titled *List Property* in the Visual Basic Help file, it is a little confusing. It is not readily apparent how you can use the **List** property to set an element in the array. In addition, the help topic says to use the **AddItem** method to set an element in the underlying array, even though you can just as easily do it with the **List** property.

- The decision as to the data type of an argument should be governed not by memory-usage considerations, but by the need to validate or syntax-check the value passed in to the argument. Such validation is necessary because of the late binding problem and the potential data type mismatches associated with calling procedures in ActiveX components. Microsoft's solution to the late binding/data type mismatch problem is to use the **Variant** data type. For example, all optional arguments must be of the **Variant** data type. One of the underlying reasons for this is so that syntax checking of the data type passed to the optional **Variant** argument can be done with the **VarType** function. Many of the members of the DAO Jet engine classes in Visual Basic use the **Variant** data type almost exclusively for their arguments.

- Under certain circumstances, functional specifications for a method may be most easily implemented or may only be able to be implemented by using an argument that meets these three requirements. First, the argument must be optional. Second, the argument must be able to accept either an array of elements or individual, discrete expressions. Third, if the argument is passed an array, each of the elements in the optional array must be capable of accepting any data type. Visual Basic provides the **ParamArray** type of argument to address these requirements. Visual Basic and VBA were the first Microsoft programming languages to implement this **ParamArray** type of argument.

Understanding The Principles Of Good Returned-Values Design

The following general principles related to the types of values that an object's member returns are consistent with Microsoft's own programming practices, as implemented in their Windows API functions:

- All methods should be implemented as **Function**s rather than **Sub**s, so that a value returned from the method can be read by the client application (if it chooses to do so).

- A method that is implemented as a **Function** should be able to be called in either of two ways. First, it could be called the usual way—a variable is declared and the returned value from the **Function** method is assigned to the variable and can be read from it. For complex methods or those that can result in runtime errors, this capability is essential in order to correctly route code execution based on whether the method was successful or not. Second, it could be called directly—with no variable in place to store a returned value. This approach allows us to call a simple method without being forced to also declare and read a variable to determine if the method succeeded or failed. The design of Windows API functions has always permitted VB programmers to call them in both ways, but VB3's own **Function** procedure did not permit this. VB5 has corrected this deficiency.

- A method (or VB's **Property Get** procedure, which also can return a value) should be able to return an array of values or elements, and each of these elements should be able to be a different data type, if necessary. VB3 did not support this capability, but VB5 uses the **Variant** data type to do so. This enhancement maximizes your ability to design extremely flexible and powerful members that can return large and diverse data structures, in one transaction, from methods that are run on remote components over distributed networks.

Whatever approach you adopt in regard to returning values from members, it should be consistent across the entire class library, handle any syntax and runtime errors that occur, and be designed to work well with both local and remote implementations of ActiveX components.

Understanding The Principles Of Good Error-Handling Design

The following general principles related to handling syntax and runtime errors in an object's member are consistent with Microsoft's own programming practices, as implemented in their Windows API functions:

- Each member should contain an error handler to trap runtime errors. In the case of an in-process, ActiveX DLL component, an untrapped error would not only crash the component, but also the client application.

- Each member should implement data type mismatch and other syntax checking to provide adequate feedback to the client application programmer who is trying to call a member but is passing it incorrect arguments. The member should also safeguard the client application from unanticipated behavior caused by a member's execution. The golden rule should be this: If there is any chance that a member could do the wrong thing (that is, something not dictated by its functional specifications), then it should do nothing. Ideally, the member should also alert the calling application about its failure by displaying a syntax error message or returning some error code.

- Sufficient information should be returned or made available to the client application when an error occurs in a member's procedure. You can use a combination of the following techniques to accomplish this. You could use VB's **Err** object and its **Raise** method to generate an error in the member's procedure. This, in turn, propagates the error back to the calling procedure where an enabled error handler deals with it and reads the information stored in the properties of the **Err** object. Second, you could write information about the error that occurred to an error log file. Third, you could return an array of error codes that, in addition to the information stored by VB's **Err** object, would contain other types of information (for example, when the error occurred or whether an entry regarding the error was written to an error log file).

Whatever approach you adopt in regard to handling syntax and runtime errors, it should be consistent across the entire class library and be designed to meet the needs/constraints of both local and remote implementations of ActiveX components.

Understanding The Principles Of Good Help-Topic Design

The following general principles related to writing a help topic for an object's member are consistent with the approach that Microsoft uses in Visual Basic's Help file for the topics that document Visual Basic's members:

- Each member should have its own help topic.
- The help topic should contain information about the member's purpose, the syntax of its argument structure (including detailed descriptions of their data types, subtypes, and valid values), the possible values it can return, limitations on where it can be called from, and miscellaneous remarks about the member.
- The help topic should have hotspots or pop-ups, which display other related help topics or the object or objects to which the member applies.
- The help topic should have an Example hotspot which displays a secondary window that contains example code demonstrating how to call and use the member.

In a nutshell, the help topic should document the functional specifications of the member. The days of documenting systems in hard-copy format are rapidly disappearing. Printed documentation is too hard to maintain on a timely basis and not easy enough to use. A well-written Help file is the best way to document the members of any object-oriented development project.

Syntax For An Error-Handling Scheme

Of all the elements of a good public interface for an ActiveX component, the way it handles errors and returns error information to the client application programmer may be the most important. As every programmer is keenly aware, when things are going right with software, people (including other programmers) pretty much take the situation for granted. However, let something go wrong and, psychologically, a completely different reaction occurs (something along the lines of "Who wrote this piece of junk?").

Because Murphy's law tells us that things are always going to go wrong, we know that we can't write error-free software. Rather, it is how an ActiveX component handles an error and provides information about it that dictates how the client application programmer will react. The rest of this chapter consists of a detailed discussion of all the factors you should consider when designing a good error-handling scheme for an ActiveX component. Hopefully, with such a scheme in place, the programmer's reaction to an error when using an ActiveX component will be more like "Cool! Even when something goes wrong, this thing is pretty easy to reuse."

Visual Basic's Err Object Scheme

When Microsoft's development team set out to add object-oriented programming features to the VB language, two of the requirements were to increase the amount of information stored when an error occurred and to make that information available in a way that was consistent with the OLE Automation and ActiveX component protocols.

To achieve these two objectives, the development team created the global, or *system-level*, **Err** object. Similar in scope to other existing VB3 global objects, like **Screen**, **Printer**, and **Debug**, the **Err** object was designed to be upwardly compatible with Visual Basic's existing error-handling syntax.

PROPERTIES AND METHODS OF ERR OBJECT

The **Err** object includes six properties and two methods. To make this section easier for you to reference, I've broken the information down into tables. Table 5.2 describes the properties, Table 5.3 provides details about the methods, and Table 5.4 covers the arguments of the **Raise** method.

Table 5.2 The **Err** object's properties.

Property	Description
Description	Returns or sets a descriptive string associated with a runtime error.
HelpContext	Returns or sets a context ID for a topic in a Microsoft Windows Help file.
HelpFile	Returns or sets a fully qualified path to a Microsoft Windows Help file.
LastDLLError	Returns a system error code produced by a call into a DLL. This property applies only to DLL calls that require a Declare statement within the Visual Basic code. When such a call is made, the called function usually returns a code indicating success or failure, and the LastDLLError property is filled. This property is set only on 32-bit Microsoft Windows operating systems.
Number	Returns or sets a numeric value specifying a runtime error. Number is the Err object's default property.
Source	Returns or sets the name of the object, application, or procedure that originally generated the runtime error.

Table 5.3 The **Err** object's methods.

Method	Description
Clear	Clears all property settings of the Err object. Use Clear to explicitly clear the Err object after an error has been handled. This may be necessary, for example, when you use deferred or inline error handling with On Error Resume Next. Visual Basic calls the Clear method automatically whenever any type of Resume or On Error statement executes. Visual Basic's Help file is incorrect when its Clear Method help topic states that Visual Basic automatically calls the Clear method when an Exit Sub, Exit Function, or Exit Property statement executes.
Raise	Generates a runtime error. Raise takes five arguments: Number, Source, Description, HelpFile, and HelpContext.

Table 5.4 The **Raise** method arguments.

Method	Required/Optional	Description
Number	Required	A Long integer that identifies the nature of the error. Visual Basic errors (both Visual Basic-defined and user-defined errors) are in the range 0 through 65535. When setting the Number property to your own error code in an ActiveX component, you add your error code number to the intrinsic constant vbObjectError. For example, to generate the error number 1050, assign vbObjectError + 1050 to the Number property. The value of the constant vbObjectError is -2,147,221,504.
Source	Optional	A String expression naming the object, application, or procedure that originally generated the error. If nothing is specified, the programmatic ID of the current Visual Basic project is used.
Description	Optional	A String expression describing the error. If unspecified, the value in the Number argument is examined. If it can be mapped to a Visual Basic runtime error code, the string that would be returned by the Error function is used as Description. If there is no Visual Basic error corresponding to Number, runtime error 95 (Application-defined or object-defined error) is used. Although Visual Basic runtime error 95 does exist, it is difficult to find any reference to it in Visual Basic's Help file. To find out more information about this error, use the statement Err.Raise 95 to generate it and then choose Help to display the corresponding help topic.
HelpFile	Optional	The fully qualified path to the Microsoft Windows Help file in which help about this error can be found. If unspecified, Visual Basic uses the fully qualified drive, path, and file name of the Visual Basic Help file.
HelpContext	Optional	The context ID identifying a topic within HelpFile that provides help for the error. If omitted, the Visual Basic Help file context ID for the error corresponding to the Number property is used, if it exists.

DEMONSTRATING THE RAISE METHOD

You can use the **Raise** method of the **Err** object to generate either a Visual Basic runtime error or to fill the properties of the **Err** object with information that defines a syntax error that has occurred in a member of an ActiveX component. When you use the **Raise** method to generate a Visual Basic runtime error in a client application's procedure (normally used this way just for testing purposes), you need to have previously enabled an error handler, or the application will crash and the **Err** object's properties will not be set.

When you use the **Raise** method to generate a syntax error in an ActiveX component, you do not need an enabled error handler in the component. You do, however, need to have an error handler in the procedure in the client application that called the public member in the component. When an error is generated with the **Raise** method in an ActiveX component, this sequence of events occurs:

1. The **Raise** method fills the **Err** object's properties with the information that you specify.

2. The error information is propagated or sent back to the client application from the ActiveX component.

3. Code execution in the procedure that called the ActiveX component is rerouted to the procedure's previously enabled error handler.

4. Code in the error-handling routine reads the properties of the **Err** object and reacts appropriately.

It is easy enough to demonstrate how the **Raise** method works in a normal VB project. Start VB and open a new Standard EXE project. Then select the Form1 module and enter the code shown in Listing 5.1 into the **Form_DblClick** event procedure.

Listing 5.1   Demo of Raise method in client.

```
Private Sub Form_DblClick()

    ' Variable.
    Dim Msg As String

    ' Enable an error handler.
    On Error Resume Next

    ' Generate Visual Basic run-time error 3.
    Err.Raise 3
```

```
' Read settings of properties of Err object:
Msg = "Number: " & Err.Number & vbCr
Msg = Msg & "Description: " & Err.Description & vbCr
Msg = Msg & "Source: " & Err.Source & vbCr
Msg = Msg & "Help File: " & Err.HelpFile & vbCr
Msg = Msg & "HelpContext: " & Err.HelpContext & vbCr
Msg = Msg & "LastDLLError: " & Err.LastDllError

' Display property settings.
MsgBox Msg, vbInformation

End Sub
```

After entering the code, select Run|Start, then double click on the **Form** object. Visual Basic displays the message box shown in Figure 5.1.

To demonstrate how the **Raise** method works in an ActiveX component is a little tedious but, nonetheless, easy enough to do. Start VB5 and open the book's class library ActiveX component EFSE.VBP. Select the MISLEXS.CLS and, at the bottom of the General Declarations section, type

```
Sub DemoRaise
```

and press Enter. Visual Basic creates the opening and closing statements for the procedure. Write the code shown in Listing 5.2 for the **DemoRaise** procedure (the code is patterned after the example code for the help topic in Visual Basic's Help file titled *Raise Method*).

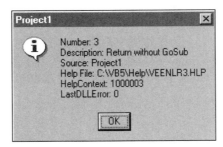

Figure 5.1 Settings of **Err** object from client.

Listing 5.2   Demo of Raise method in component (1).

```
Sub DemoRaise()

    ' Define a constant for context ID and raise
    ' the exception using named arguments:
    Const MyContextID = 1010407

    Err.Raise Number:=vbObjectError + 27, _
            Source:="MyProj.MyObject", _
            Description:="No ""bob"" allowed in your name", _
            HelpFile:="c:\MyProj\MyHelp.Hlp", _
            HelpContext:=MyContextID

End Sub
```

Now, to finish up the demonstration, follow these steps:

1. Ensure that the statement **Form1.Show** in **Sub Main** in STARTUP.BAS is commented out.

2. Remake the ActiveX component, and save all changes when prompted.

3. Open a new Standard EXE project and, in the **Form_Load** event procedure of Form1, enter the code shown in Listing 5.3.

Listing 5.3   Demo of Raise method in component (2).

```
Private Sub Form_Load()

    ' Variables:
    Dim MiscExs   As Object
    Dim Msg     As String

    ' Instantiate class. Programmatic ID has two parts delimited by dot:
    ' * Project name's entry on Options tab of Project dialog box.
    ' * Name property of ClassModule object.
#If Win32 Then
    Set MiscExs = CreateObject("EFSE.MiscExs")
#ElseIf Win16 Then
    Set MiscExs = CreateObject("EFS16.MiscExs")
#End If

    ' Enable an error handler.
    On Error Resume Next

    ' Call object's member to demo Raise syntax in ActiveX server.
    MiscExs.DemoRaise

    ' Read settings of properties of Err object that were
    ' propagated in and sent back from ActiveX server:
    Msg = "Number: " & Err.Number - vbObjectError & vbCr
    Msg = Msg & "Description: " & Err.Description & vbCr
    Msg = Msg & "Source: " & Err.Source & vbCr
```

```
Msg = Msg & "Help File: " & Err.HelpFile & vbCr
Msg = Msg & "HelpContext: " & Err.HelpContext & vbCr
Msg = Msg & "LastDLLError: " & Err.LastDllError

' Display property settings.
MsgBox Msg, vbInformation
```

End Sub

After entering the code, select Run | Start. Visual Basic displays the message box shown in Figure 5.2.

Using the vbObjectError constant

*In order to read the actual syntax error number assigned to the **Err** object by the **Raise** method in the ActiveX component, the intrinsic Visual Basic constant **vbObjectError** must be subtracted from the value of the **Number** property back in the client application. As I mentioned earlier, the value of the constant **vbObjectError** is a negative 2,147,221,504. The reason why the constant **vbObjectError** is added to a syntax error number in the first place is explained in somewhat confusing detail in VB4's Help file in the topic titled **Number Property** (it is not explained at all in VB5's Help file). The simple explanation of why this is done is so that you can consistently parse out or subtract the constant **vbObjectError** back in the client application and then, if the value of the **Number** property is still greater than 0, be sure that it was a syntax error that occurred in the ActiveX component and not a Visual Basic runtime error.*

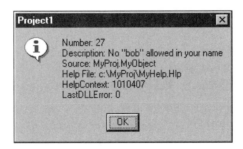

Figure 5.2 Settings of **Err** object from server.

120 VB   Chapter 5

Pros And Cons Of The Err Object Scheme

The advantages of the **Err** object scheme are that the **Err** object and its associated syntax are built into Visual Basic and should be familiar to all Visual Basic programmers. Because the error information contained in the properties of the **Err** object is part of the standard OLE Automation protocol, some form of the **Err** object and its related syntax should be supported by all OLE Automation-compliant programming languages. Also, using the **Err** object scheme to pass error information from an ActiveX component back to the client application eliminates the need to build that type of transmission capability into the returned value from the method itself; that is, the value(s) returned by the **Function** procedure.

The disadvantages of the **Err** object scheme are several. To begin with, this approach limits the amount of error information that can be returned from an ActiveX component to the predefined six properties of the **Err** object. Next, the scheme requires that, even when you are making a call from a client application to the simplest member in an ActiveX component, you go to the trouble of enabling an error handler and writing code to respond to various possible scenarios for syntax and runtime errors. In addition, for syntax errors, the **Err** object scheme is too inflexible and cumbersome. No Visual Basic programmer writing a client application will want to reuse objects from a class library if, even in the earliest prototyping and debugging phase of development, elaborate error-handling code must be written to find out precisely what has gone wrong with a call to a member of an ActiveX component. Finally, this scheme puts too much of the responsibility for syntax and runtime error-handling on the Visual Basic client application programmer. If you write an ActiveX component with Visual Basic, the best way to ensure that other programmers will want to reuse the objects in your class library is to make the public interface (including error-handling) as easy to use as possible.

Class Library's Error-Handling Scheme

The syntax and runtime error-handling scheme used by the class library for this book implements the guidelines outlined in the *Understanding The Principles Of Good Error-Handling Design* section covered earlier in this chapter. Because of the limitations associated with Visual Basic's **Err** object scheme, it plays only a minor role in the class library's proprietary scheme; however, the class library's scheme provides the same information as do the properties of the **Err** object, and it also passes back other useful information about the error that occurred.

The details of the error-handling scheme are discussed and demonstrated in Chapters 8 and 9. In order to appreciate how the scheme works, you must first clearly understand these key issues as they relate to error-handling:

- The different ways you can call a **Function** procedure in VB5.

- How to return an array from a **Function** procedure or **Property Get** procedure in VB5.

Two Ways To Call A Function

In the Help file for VB3, the help topic titled *Call Statement* begins with this description of its purpose: "Transfers program control to a Visual Basic **Sub** procedure or a dynamic-link library (DLL) procedure." In the Help file for VB5, the help topic titled *Call Statement* describes its purpose this way: "Transfers control to a **Sub** procedure, **Function** procedure, or dynamic-link library (DLL) procedure." The ability of VB5 to now invoke a **Function** procedure with the **Call** statement signals a major change in Visual Basic's low-level architecture.

In this regard, Visual Basic now works the same way as the Windows API functions have always worked. All Windows API procedures are written as functions, which means that they do return some value under all circumstances. Normally, a Windows API function is constructed so that it returns two general types of values. If it succeeds, it returns its specified value (or values contained in a user-defined data type). For example, many Windows API functions return the handle of a Windows object. If the function fails, it returns an error code to be read by the client application and handles the error so the client application does not crash.

The key point here is that the Windows API function does not require the client application to read the returned value. Many such function calls are simple enough that the programmer can safely ignore the returned value. It is easy to demonstrate the two different ways to call a Windows API function. Start Visual Basic and open a new Standard EXE project. Place two **CommandButton** objects on Form1, then select the Form1 module and enter the code shown in Listing 5.4 into the various procedures.

Listing 5.4   Calling a Windows API function.

```
' General Declarations section:
#If Win32 Then
    Private Declare Function SetFocusAPI& Lib "USER32" _
                            Alias "SetFocus" _
                            (ByVal hWnd&)
```

```
#Else
    Private Declare Function SetFocusAPI& Lib "USER" _
                            Alias "SetFocus" _
                            (ByVal hWnd%)
#End If

Private Sub Command1_Click()

    ' Call API function, move focus to second
    ' button, and ignore returned value.
    SetFocusAPI Command2.hWnd

End Sub

Private Sub Command2_Click()

    ' Variables:
    Dim Result   As Variant
    Dim Msg      As String

    ' Call API function (passing it nonexistent handle)
    ' and read returned value for error code:
    Result = SetFocusAPI(-1000)

    If Result = False Then
       Msg = "API function failed and returned Null/False (0)."
       MsgBox Msg, vbInformation
       Result = SetFocusAPI(Command1.hWnd)

       If Result <> False Then
          Msg = "API function returned handle "
          Msg = Msg & Result & " for Command2."
          MsgBox Msg, vbInformation
       End If

    End If

End Sub

Private Sub Form_Paint()

    ' Display handles of objects:
    Cls
    Print "Form1 handle: " & Form1.hWnd
    Print "Command1 handle: " & Command1.hWnd
    Print "Command2 handle: " & Command2.hWnd

End Sub
```

After entering the code, select Run|Start. Click on the Command1 button
and the Windows API function succeeds and moves the focus to the second
button. No return value is read by the call. Click on the Command2 button
and the Windows API function fails (a handle cannot be a negative number)

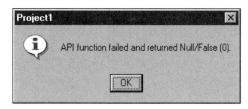

Figure 5.3 Result of reading the API function's returned value.

and returns an error code. The demo code reads the returned value and displays the message box shown in Figure 5.3.

If the erroneous call to the Windows API function in the **Command2_Click** event procedure fails and the programmer does not bother to read the returned value, nothing bad happens. The API function handles the error, ignores the call, and leaves the focus on the object that previously had it.

To demonstrate the same type of syntax for calling a function in VB5, open a new Standard EXE project. Place two **CommandButton** objects and an **Image** object on Form1. Set the **BorderStyle** property of Image1 to 1 - Fixed Single, then select the Form1 module and enter the code shown in Listing 5.5 into the various procedures.

Listing 5.5   Calling A VB function.

```
Function MoveFocus(Ctl As Control) As Boolean

    ' Initialize return value to be True.
    MoveFocus = True

    ' Enable error handler.
    On Error Resume Next
    Ctl.SetFocus

    ' If SetFocus method resulted in run-time error,
    ' return False as value of MoveFocus function:
    If Err <> False Then
       MoveFocus = False
    End If

End Function

Private Sub Command1_Click()

    ' Move focus to second button.
    MoveFocus Command2

End Sub

Private Sub Command2_Click()
```

```
' Variables:
Dim Msg As String

' Try to move focus to Image object (which
' does not support Visual Basic's SetFocus method).
If Not MoveFocus(Image1) Then
    Msg = "MoveFocus failed. Image object cannot have focus."
    MsgBox Msg, vbInformation
End If

End Sub
```

After entering the code, select Run | Start. Click on the Command1 button and the **MoveFocus** function succeeds and moves the focus to the second button. No return value is read by the call. Click on the Command2 button and the **MoveFocus** function fails and returns an error code. The call reads the returned value and displays the message box shown in Figure 5.4.

The differences between the two ways of invoking a **Function** procedure in VB5 are obvious. It should also be clear why this dual syntax related to the **Function** procedure will enable a more flexible and powerful implementation of an error-handling scheme for a class library in an ActiveX component.

RETURNING AN ARRAY FROM A FUNCTION

Returning an array from a **Function** procedure is the key technique that the class library's error-handling scheme uses to pass back error information from an ActiveX component to the client application. VB3 did not permit you to return an array from a **Function** procedure, but new syntax in VB4 and VB5 allows you to assign different data types to different elements in an array, return the array from a **Function** in a **Variant** variable, and read the contents of the returned **Variant** back in the calling procedure.

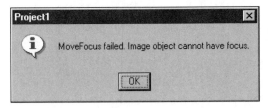

Figure 5.4 Result of reading the Visual Basic function's returned value.

The following steps illustrate the general procedure for returning a **Variant** containing an array from a **Function** procedure and reading the results:

1. Declare the **Function** procedure as a **Variant**.

2. Declare a **Variant** variable as an array in the **Function** procedure and assign each of the values that you want to return from the **Function** to an element in the **Variant** array (or use VB's **Array** function to create a **Variant** containing an array).

3. Set the name of the **Function** equal to the name of the **Variant**, thus returning it as the result of the **Function**.

4. Have a **Variant** variable (but not an array) declared back in the calling procedure to receive the returned **Variant**.

5. Cycle through the elements in the returned array, reading and reacting to them as is appropriate.

I think it would be helpful to demonstrate the two different ways to return an array from a Visual Basic **Function** procedure. Open a new Standard EXE project, put two **CommandButton** objects on the **Form** object, select the Form1 module, and enter the code shown in Listing 5.6 into the various procedures.

Listing 5.6 Returning an array from a function.

```
Function ReturnArray1(ErrNbr As Integer) As Variant

    ' Variables:
    Dim RetVals(4) As Variant

    ' Enable error handler and generate error:
    On Error Resume Next
    Err.Raise ErrNbr

    ' Read properties of Err object, assign them to
    ' elements in Variant array, and return Variant:
    RetVals(0) = Err.Number
    RetVals(1) = Err.Description
    RetVals(2) = Err.Source
    RetVals(3) = Err.HelpFile
    RetVals(4) = Err.HelpContext
    ReturnArray1 = RetVals

End Function

Function ReturnArray2(ErrNbr As Integer) As Variant

    ' Enable error handler and generate error:
    On Error Resume Next
    Err.Raise ErrNbr
```

```
    ' Use VB's Array function to create Variant array,
    ' read properties of Err object, assign them to
    ' elements in Variant array, and return Variant:
    ReturnArray2 = Array(Err.Number, _
                         Err.Description, _
                         Err.Source, _
                         Err.HelpFile, _
                         Err.HelpContext)

End Function

Private Sub Command1_Click()

    ' Variables:
    Dim Msg        As String
    Dim Results    As Variant

    ' Pass Visual Basic run-time error number to function
    ' which will read Err object's properties
    ' and return their settings in an array.
    Results = ReturnArray1(53)

    ' Read elements in returned array and display them:
    Msg = "Number: " & Results(0) & vbCr
    Msg = Msg & "Description: " & Results(1) & vbCr
    Msg = Msg & "Source: " & Results(2) & vbCr
    Msg = Msg & "Help File: " & Results(3) & vbCr
    Msg = Msg & "HelpContext: " & Results(4)
    MsgBox Msg, vbInformation

End Sub

Private Sub Command2_Click()

    ' Variables:
    Dim Msg        As String
    Dim Results    As Variant

    ' Pass Visual Basic run-time error number to function
    ' which will read Err object's properties
    ' and return their settings in an array.
    Results = ReturnArray2(53)

    ' Read elements in returned array and display them:
    Msg = "Number: " & Results(0) & vbCr
    Msg = Msg & "Description: " & Results(1) & vbCr
    Msg = Msg & "Source: " & Results(2) & vbCr
    Msg = Msg & "Help File: " & Results(3) & vbCr
    Msg = Msg & "HelpContext: " & Results(4)
    MsgBox Msg, vbInformation

End Sub
```

After entering the code, select Run|Start. Then click each one of the buttons. Each function is called, the error information is returned to the calling procedure in an array inside the **Variant** variable, and the calling procedure reads the error codes that were returned and displays the message box in Figure 5.5.

The Class Library Error-Handling Scheme

Robust runtime error-handling and syntax checking is an essential feature of a class library written as an ActiveX component. There are several different schemes or approaches that you could use to implement a consistent error-handling scheme. Each of these approaches has some tradeoffs associated with it:

- One approach may be easier to implement than another but is less flexible and is less easily enhanced in the future.

- One approach may require more work on the part of the programmer who writes the ActiveX component, while another approach makes more demands on or constrains the programmer who writes the client application.

- An approach might be ideal for use by an in-process, ActiveX DLL component but would not be feasible at all if run on an out-of-process, ActiveX remote component.

The error-handling scheme outlined in the following sections implements all the general guidelines listed in the *Understanding The Principles Of Good Error-Handling Design* section earlier in this chapter. It also tries to maximize the flexibility of both kinds of Visual Basic programmers associated with the ActiveX component class library: the programmer responsible

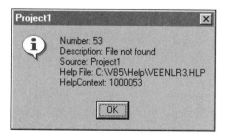

Figure 5.5 Elements of an array returned from a VB function.

for writing and maintaining it and the application programmer who wants to call and reuse its members.

Local ActiveX Components

An intuitive and easy-to-use set of exception-handling capabilities in a class library will do as much of the work for the client application's programmer as possible. If you want other Visual Basic programmers to reuse your class library code, you should provide clear and concise information about any type of error that occurs within a member. If a help topic exists for a runtime or syntax error message, make sure to include a Help button on the message box to signal this fact. Of course, clicking on the button should display the appropriate topic.

A good set of exception-handling capabilities will also prevent the client application from crashing when an error occurs, without requiring the client application programmer to enable an error handler every time a call to a class library's member is made. Imagine how unpleasant it would be to use VB5 if every time you made a call to an unfamiliar method you had to first set up elaborate error-handling code to find out what you were doing wrong. This same principle holds true for ActiveX components which, in a very real sense, are just extensions to Visual Basic's programming language.

SPECIFICATIONS FOR HANDLING SYNTAX ERRORS

The following items are the key specifications that govern the handling of syntax errors in the book's class library. These specs can serve as a template for the design of any local ActiveX component's error-handling scheme:

- At design time from within Visual Basic or at runtime, if the application incorrectly calls a member in the class library, the member should display a syntax error message. For example, a member that is passed the wrong kind of Visual Basic object should display a message like the one shown in Figure 5.6.

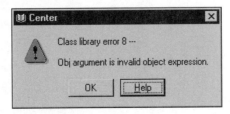

Figure 5.6 Example of a syntax error message.

- If the client application programmer or user needs more information to determine what is wrong with the object expression being passed to the member, clicking on the Help button in the message box should display an associated help topic like the one in Figure 5.7.

- When the client application programmer clears the message box, the member should return an array of syntax error codes that includes more data than what was displayed originally. It is up to the client application to decide whether or not to read the array. Most of the time, it will not be necessary to read the error codes. The information displayed in the message box should be sufficient.

SPECIFICATIONS FOR HANDLING RUNTIME ERRORS

The following items are the key specifications that govern the handling of runtime errors in the book's class library. Theses specs can serve as a template for the design of any local ActiveX component's error-handling scheme:

- At design time from within Visual Basic or at runtime, if a Visual Basic runtime error occurs while a member is executing, the member should handle it and display the runtime error message. For example, a member that requires the **Name** property or ordinal position of a **Field** object in a database may cause runtime error 3265 if it is passed a

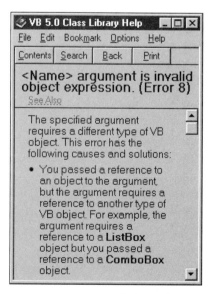

Figure 5.7   Example of a syntax error message help topic.

Figure 5.8 Example of a runtime error message.

reference to a nonexistent **Field** object. If this happens, the member should display a message like the one shown in Figure 5.8.

- If the client application programmer or user needs more information about the runtime error, clicking on the Help button in the message box should display a Visual Basic-associated help topic like the one shown in Figure 5.9.

- When the client application programmer clears the message box, the member should return an array of runtime error codes that includes more data than what was displayed originally. It is up to the application to decide whether or not to read the error codes.

Error-Handling By Remote ActiveX Components

Because an out-of-process, ActiveX EXE component can be used as a Remote Automation Object (RAO) class library on a server machine, it must be able to deal with syntax and runtime errors in a different way. An

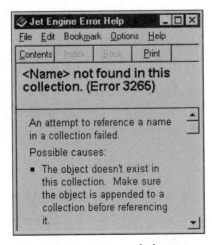

Figure 5.9 Example of the runtime error message help topic.

ActiveX EXE component should still handle any error and return the array with the associated error information, but it cannot display a message box or associated help topic. This is because those dialog boxes would be displayed modally on the server machine and this would, in turn, cause code execution to hang up within the method and confuse the programmer or user running the client application.

An out-of-process RAO ActiveX component should provide the following error-handling features:

- At design time from within Visual Basic or at runtime, if the client application programmer or user incorrectly calls a member in the class library, the member should handle the syntax error, return an array of error codes that includes all the data available about the error, and allow the client application to decide whether or not to read the error codes. For example, a member that is passed the wrong kind of Visual Basic object should return error codes that the client application can read, like those displayed in the message box in Figure 5.10.

- At design time from within Visual Basic or at runtime, if a Visual Basic runtime error occurs while the member is executing, the member should handle the runtime error, return an array of error codes that includes all the data available about the error, and allow the client application to decide whether or not to read the error codes. For example, a member that encounters runtime error 3265 while executing should return error codes that the client application can read, like those in the message box in Figure 5.11.

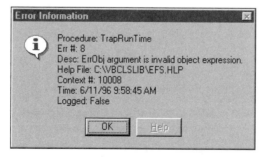

Figure 5.10 Example of syntax error codes read by a client application.

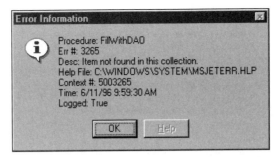

Figure 5.11   Example of runtime error codes read by a client application.

Checking an ActiveX EXE component

Because an out-of-process, ActiveX EXE component can be deployed either locally or remotely, the class library code itself should be able to determine whether it is being run as an RAO or not. If it is an RAO, then a flag should be turned on to prevent any error messages from being displayed. An example of how to do this is provided later in the book.

Examining The Pros And Cons Of The Class Library's Error-Handling Scheme

There are several advantages of the book's class library's scheme for handling errors. First, the amount of error information that can be returned from an ActiveX component to the client application is not fixed. If you want to add another item of information (for example, a more detailed description of the error), you just add another element to the returned array of error codes. Second, the client application programmer is not required to enable an error handler each time a call to an ActiveX component is made. Whether or not to do so is up to the programmer, just as when calling a Windows API function. Third, our approach puts the responsibility for syntax and runtime error-handling where it belongs: on the programmer who writes the ActiveX component. In this respect, it will encourage client application programmers to reuse the objects in your class library. Fourth, its implementation and functionality is consistent and automatically adapts itself to and handles the different kinds of ActiveX components.

The disadvantages of the book's class library scheme for handling errors are really quite minor. Because our scheme is a proprietary approach, it needs to be very well documented in the Help file for the ActiveX component. In addition, the design requires that every member in a class that can return a value be implemented as a **Function** procedure that returns a **Variant** array.

So much for Chapter 5 and our discussion of the elements of the public interface of an ActiveX component. Wow! Do you really have to worry about all these design features? Why not just jump to the fun part of the developer's job and start writing object-oriented code? Well, the more time you devote to the consideration of the design features of a good public interface at the beginning of your object-oriented development effort, the less hassle and rewrites you'll experience as you're actually writing the code. Take it from me: I've spent months developing the class library that comes with this book; if I had understood the elements of the public interface as well when I started this book as I do now after finishing it, the time I spent on programming and debugging would have been significantly less.

USING VB'S OBJECT BROWSER

6

Given the growing popularity of OLE Automation among Windows developers over the last couple of years, there are now many class libraries (that is, ActiveX components) whose public members are available for reuse in your projects. How does a VB client application programmer find out how to reuse the objects in these class libraries?

There are two ways to get the necessary information to reuse the objects in ActiveX components. First, you can go to the printed documentation or online Help file for the ActiveX component, search through the information, and try to determine how to call the objects' members. For ActiveX components created with some programming languages, like Delphi 2.0, this is the only way to do it. This is because, when Delphi creates an ActiveX component, it does not create a type library along with the ActiveX component.

Second, you can use Microsoft's Object Browser from VB to help you find out how to reuse an ActiveX component's objects. This assumes that the ActiveX component you are interested in was developed with a programming language like VB4 or VB5, which supports the creation of a type library that can be read by the Object Browser. VB's ability to automatically create a type library when it creates an ActiveX component is one of the major advantages it has over Delphi 2.0. In Chapter 6, you will take an in-depth look at how the new Object Browser that is included with VB5 works.

Using The References Dialog Box

Before you can view an ActiveX component's type library with the Object Browser, you need to set a reference to it, which you can do via the References dialog box. There are several reasons why you might want to set a reference to another class library in your VB client application:

- To view its members in the Object Browser window.
- To display any help topics related to its members.
- To copy and paste the example code to reuse one of its members into your client application.
- To enable your client application to instantiate a class through early binding. We covered early binding in detail in Chapter 4, so I won't go into more detail here.

To display the References dialog box, start VB5 and double click on the Standard EXE icon. Next, select Project | References. Visual Basic reads the Windows registration database, finds all references it might be able to use, and loads and displays the References dialog box, which is shown in Figure 6.1.

Depending on the speed of your PC and how many ActiveX components are registered on it, loading the References dialog box with the available references can take anywhere from 5 to 25 seconds. The References dialog box initially displays with several references selected. These preselected references are determined by Visual Basic's startup configuration. References will always be preset to three items: Visual Basic For Applications, Visual Basic objects and procedures, and OLE Automation. When the References dialog box first displays, the last preselected reference in the list is always selected.

The References dialog box has several important features that we need to discuss:

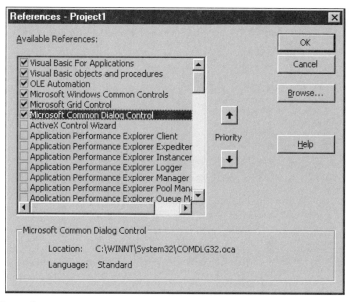

Figure 6.1 The References dialog box.

- **Available References**. This section lists the references available to your project. You add a reference to your project by selecting the checkbox next to its name; likewise, you remove a reference by clearing the checkbox next to its name. You cannot remove a reference for an item that is currently being used in your project. If you are not using any objects in a referenced library, you should clear the checkbox for that reference to minimize the number of object references Visual Basic must resolve, reducing the time it takes your project to compile.

- **Priority Buttons**. Clicking these buttons moves a reference up and down on the list. When you refer to an object in code, Visual Basic searches each application selected in the References dialog box in the order the applications are displayed. If two applications use the same name for an object, Visual Basic uses the definition provided by the application listed higher in the Available References box.

- **Result**. This frame, located at the bottom of the dialog box, displays the path of the reference selected in the Available References box, as well as the language version.

- **Browse**. Clicking on this button displays the Add Reference dialog box, which allows you to search other directories for the file types able to be listed as a reference.

The References dialog box can list four kinds of files as references: type/ class libraries (*.OLB, *.TLB), DLL files (*.DLL), executable files (*.EXE), and ActiveX controls (*.OCX).

Setting A Reference

To set a reference to a class library or ActiveX component (in this example, the book's class library) in your project, follow these steps:

1. Start VB5 and double click on the Standard EXE icon.

2. Select Project | References to display the References dialog box.

3. In the Available References list, select the item that you want to set a reference to.

4. Check the name of the ActiveX EXE version of the book's class library—Visual Basic 5.0 Class Library - EXE.

5. Click on the up arrow Priority button until the reference you selected moves up to the top of the Available References list box. Visual Basic will only permit you to move it up to the third item in the list, just below the references to Visual Basic For Applications and Visual Basic objects and procedures. These two references have the highest priority and cannot be superseded.

At this point, the References dialog box should appear as shown in Figure 6.2.

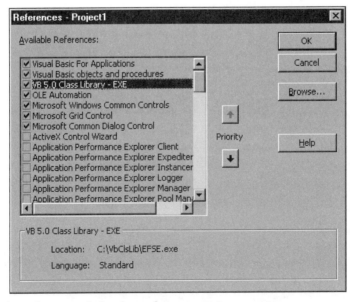

Figure 6.2 The References dialog box after prioritizing a setting.

Using The Object Browser

The Object Browser window displays the classes and members available from class libraries, and the modules and procedures in your Visual Basic project. Once you have set a reference in your Visual Basic project to an ActiveX component's class library, you can use the Object Browser to view the class library's reusable objects. We looked briefly at the Object Browser window in Chapter 3, but we will examine its functionality in more detail here.

The Object Browser window first appeared in a Microsoft application in January of 1994, when Excel 5 with VBA was released. It showed up a few months later in Project 4 with VBA. Following a year-and-a-half gap, the Object Browser made its debut in Visual Basic in November of 1995. There is a common thread that runs through these applications, which dictates that they have a feature like the Object Browser: They all contain programming languages that can call and reuse the objects in ActiveX components. In the cases of Excel and Project, the **CreateObject** function is available to do this. In the case of VB4 and VB5, you can use either the **CreateObject** function or the **As New** statement to instantiate a class in an ActiveX component.

As applications that were developed as OLE Automation servers (now ActiveX components) proliferated in 1995 and 1996, the need to be able to browse these applications quickly and easily in order to reuse their objects became clear. A third-party software vendor, Apex Software Corporation, even released a utility called VBA Companion, which it advertised as the ultimate Object Browser for OLE Automation and VBA programming.

With the release of VB5, Microsoft has upgraded its own Object Browser's functionality and flexibility with the addition of these features:

- The Object Browser is now a MDI child window instead of a dialog box, which allows you to move back and forth between your code module to the browser window, without having to reopen the browser each time.
- The window and its controls are resizable.
- The window has a toolbar and supports a right-button click pop-up menu to do the most common tasks quickly.
- You can sort and display the members of a class by alpha or by kind of member (that is, events, methods, and properties).
- You can do string searches and return a list of all the classes that contain the string.

- You can copy any item or text listed in the Object Browser and paste it into a code module or application.

To display the Object Browser window from VB5, select View | Object Browser or press F2. Figure 6.3 shows the window after you have selected a class library, class, and member.

Tables 6.1 and 6.2 describe the controls and pop-up menu commands that you can access from this window.

Running Example Code For A Member

If an ActiveX component's class library has a Help file, and the help topic for a member has example code in it, you can display the example code and run it to see how to call the member and handle the value(s) that it returns. To do so, use the example of the book's class library and follow these steps:

1. Start VB5 and double click on the Standard EXE icon.

2. Select Project | References to display the References dialog box.

3. In the Available References list, select the book's class library item—Visual Basic 5.0 Class Library.

4. Click on OK.

5. Press F2 to display the Object Browser and select EFSE from the Libraries/Projects list. Then select the **ClientApp** class and its **ShowMsg** member.

6. Click on the ? button to display its help topic.

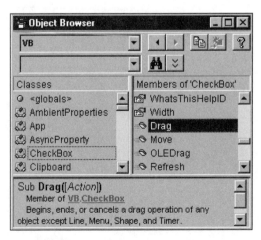

Figure 6.3 Object Browser window.

Table 6.1   The Object Browser window controls.

Control	Description
Libraries/Projects	This drop-down list in the upper-left corner of the window displays the libraries available to your project. Select from available libraries to view the classes, modules, procedures, methods, properties, and events you can use in code. When the Object Browser first appears during a Visual Basic session, the entry <All Libraries> is the selection (which actually displays the classes from Visual Basic itself). If you make another selection and then close the Object Browser, it restores your last selection the next time you display it. To add a class library to the Libraries/Projects list, use the References dialog box.
Search Text	This drop-down combo list allows you to enter a string that VB can use to search the class library. Clicking on the Search button starts the search. The Object Browser then expands its window to display a Search Results list, which contains all the classes containing that string.
Classes	If you select your own Visual Basic project in the Libraries/Projects list, the Classes list displays modules from your project, including any classes you defined in the current project. If you select a class library in the Libraries/Projects list, the Classes list displays the classes available in that library. If you select Show Hidden Members from the pop-up menu, the Classes list displays any hidden members of the library.
Members	If you select your own project in the Libraries/Projects box, the Members list displays procedures, properties, methods, and events you have defined. If you select a class library in the Libraries/Projects box, the Members list displays members for the class that is selected in the Classes list.
Toolbar Button	Displays the online help topic for the item selected in the Libraries, Classes, or Members list (if it has one). If the item does not have a help topic, it displays the Contents topic of the help file linked to the class library.
Item Description	A scrollable, read-only edit control that displays information about the currently selected item (its declaration and arguments, the class or library it belongs to, and a brief description of its purpose). It signifies that an argument is optional by enclosing it in brackets, or that an argument has been declared using the **ParamArray** keyword by displaying the declaration format; for example, ParamArray Properties() As Variant.

Table 6.2 The Object Browser window pop-up menu commands.

Menu Command	Description
Copy	Copies the selected item or text to the clipboard.
View Definition	Displays the code module or procedure for the currently selected item.
Find Whole Word Only	Qualifies a search to find only whole words; the default is to be not selected.
Group Members	Sorts and displays the members of a class by kind of member (that is, events, methods, and properties); the default is to be selected.
Show Hidden Members	Displays hidden members; the default is to be not selected.
References	Displays the References dialog box.
Properties	Displays the Member Options or Procedure Attributes dialog box, which enables you to specify help information for a member (Description, Help File, and Help Context ID); this item is enabled only for items in public classes of the current project.
Help	Displays the online help topic for the item selected in the Libraries, Classes, or Members list (if it has one); if the item does not have a help topic, it displays the Contents topic of the Help file linked to the class library.
Dockable	Positions the Object Browser window in the upper-left corner of the screen or in the last position you moved it to; the default is to be not selected.
Hide	Hides the Object Browser window; the default is to be not selected. To see the Object Browser again, select View	Object Browser or press F2.

7. Click the Example hotspot to display its Example code topic.

8. Select all the code below the heading COPY/PASTE INTO FORM1 and select Copy to place it on the clipboard.

9. Open the code window for Form1 and move to the bottom of the General Declarations section.

10. Paste the sample code from the clipboard into the code window. Visual Basic automatically assigns the sample code to the correct event procedures.

11. Select Run | Start, then double click on the **Form** object.

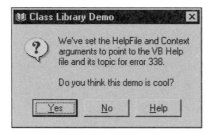

Figure 6.4   Form displayed by the **ShowMsg** method.

The **ShowMsg** method is called, it executes, and the encapsulated message box **Form** object shown in Figure 6.4 is displayed. Click on the Help button in the message box to display the specified help topic. Then click on Yes or No to close the message box. The calling procedure in the client application will then read the values returned by the **ShowMsg** method and display a message box of its own, as shown in Figure 6.5.

Linking A Help File To An ActiveX Component

As you have seen in this chapter and earlier in the book, the Object Browser's ability to display the correct help topic for any public member of a public class is an essential feature in object-oriented programming. Without such a feature, it would be much more difficult to know how to call members of reusable objects. In this last section, we'll create the various links that tell the Object Browser which help topic to display for any specific item in a class library. Of course, to establish these links at all, you must first write and compile the Windows Help file (a task that you will learn how to do later in the book). Meanwhile, you will learn the mechanics of how to establish the links now by using the book's class library in the following sections.

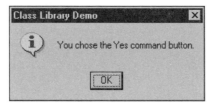

Figure 6.5   Message box displayed by the client application.

Specifying The Help File

To specify the Help file for an ActiveX component, follow these steps:

1. Start VB5 and double click on the Standard EXE icon.

2. Select File|Open Project, find the book's EFSE.VBP project, and click on Open.

3. Select Project|EFSE Properties to display the General tab of the Project Properties dialog box.

4. For the Help File Name entry, you can click the little button with the three dots to browse for the HLP file, or you can type the path and file name (in this example, C:\VBOOPEFS\VBCLSLIB\EFS.HLP).

5. For the Project Help Context ID entry, type the context number of the help topic to associate with the class library (in this example, 0 for the Contents topic).

6. Click on OK to store any changes you made to the General tab.

7. Open the Object Browser, select EFSE from the Libraries/Projects list, and click on the ? button on the toolbar to display the help topic for the class library. If the Contents topic is displayed, then the Help Context ID number you assigned it is correct.

Don't worry about the Help file path

You do not have to specify the path on which the ActiveX component's Help file is located. After the ActiveX component is installed on another PC, the path will probably not apply anyway. If a client application programmer tries to access the Help file from the Object Browser and the file is not located on the specified path, the Object Browser displays a dialog box, allowing the programmer to locate the Help file.

Specifying A Help Topic For A Class

Assuming that the book's ActiveX component's project is open within Visual Basic, follow these steps to specify a help topic for one of its classes:

1. Press F2 to display the Object Browser and select EFSE from the Libraries/Projects list.

2. Select the **ClientApp** class.

3. Right click on the **ClientApp** item to display the Object Browser's pop-up menu, and then select Properties. Visual Basic displays the Member Options dialog box.

4. For Description, type a brief statement of the purpose of the class (in this example, a description is already entered).

5. For Help Context ID, type the context number of the help topic you want to associate with the class (in this example, 2). This number is specified in the project (.HPJ) file used to compile the Help file.

6. Click on OK to save the changes you have made.

7. Click on the ? button on the Object Browser's toolbar to display the help topic for the class, and ensure that the Help Context ID number you assigned it is correct.

The Member Options dialog box for the **ClientApp** class is shown in Figure 6.6.

Specifying A Help Topic For A Member

Assuming that the book's ActiveX component's project is open within Visual Basic, follow these steps to specify a help topic for one of its members:

1. Press F2 to display the Object Browser and select EFSE from the Libraries/Projects list.

2. Select the **ClientApp** class and its **ShowMsg** member.

3. Right click on the **ShowMsg** item to display the Object Browser's pop-up menu and then select Properties. Visual Basic displays the Procedure Attributes dialog box.

4. For Description, type a brief statement of the purpose of the member (in this example, a description is already entered).

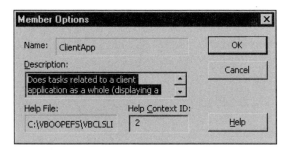

Figure 6.6   Member Options dialog box (**ClientApp** class).

5. For Help Context ID, type the context number of the help topic you want to associate with the member (in this example, 104). This number is specified in the project (.HPJ) file used to compile the Help file.

6. Click on OK to save the changes you have made.

7. Click on the ? button on the Object Browser's toolbar to display the help topic for the member, and ensure that the Help Context ID number you assigned it is correct.

The Procedure Attributes dialog box for the **ShowMsg** member is in Figure 6.7.

Features Of The Book's Help File

While we are on the topic of Help files, a good way to conclude this chapter is to discuss the general features of the book's class library Help file. Not every class library Help file needs to have all these features (for example, the New Syntax and Glossary sections are not necessary). However, when it comes time to design and create your own Help file for a class library, you could do far worse than use the Help file that comes with this book (EFS.HLP) as a template. The EFS.HLP file was modeled on and precisely imitates the Help file that comes with Visual Basic itself.

The Contents topic of EFS.HLP, shown in Figure 6.8, indicates the three major kinds of information contained in the book's class library Help file:

- Class Library Objects—A functional specification topic for each public class and public member of the class library, and an example code topic for each public member of the class library.

- A section containing all the new syntax that has been added to Visual Basic 4.0 and 5.0.

- A glossary of over 300 OOP and Windows terms.

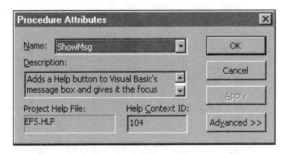

Figure 6.7　Procedure Attributes dialog box (**ShowMsg** Member).

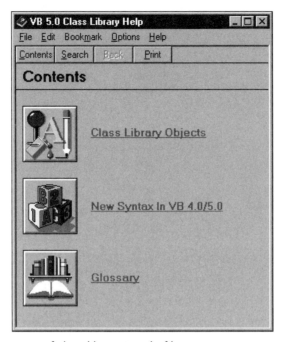

Figure 6.8 Contents topic of class library's Help file.

The other features included in EFS.HLP are the help topics for the syntax error messages of the class library and a comprehensive, cross-indexed set of keywords.

CREATING A MESSAGE BOX FOR AN ActiveX COMPONENT

Although VB4 enhanced its **MsgBox** function by adding the optional *HelpFile* and *Context* arguments, it did not allow you to display a Help button on the message box. This situation has not changed in Visual Basic 5.0. This missing feature seems peculiar, especially because:

- Many of the message boxes VB displays have a Help button.

- The **MsgBox** function in Excel 5's VBA, almost three years old, allows the display of a Help button.

- Methods in **ClassModule** objects require rigorous syntax checking and runtime error-handling, both of which would be enhanced by being able to display a message box with a Help button.

So, unless you put a prompt on a Visual Basic message box's title bar (for example, *Press F1 for Help*), the user has no way of knowing that there might be a Help file and topic associated with it.

Also, as you saw in Chapter 3, because an ActiveX EXE component runs in a different address space than that of the calling application, if code in the out-of-process component uses Visual Basic's **MsgBox** function, Windows will display the message box but will not give it the focus. Two scenarios can occur in this situation. First, if the calling application is displaying a **Form** object, the message box will be completely hidden behind the **Form** object; and so it will seem as if the message box has not been displayed. Second, if the calling application is not displaying a **Form** object, the message box will be displayed but will not have the focus.

Creating A Better Message Box

The **ShowMsg** method of the **ClientApp** class in the book's class library corrects the deficiencies of VB's **MsgBox** function by displaying a **Form** object that:

- Simulates the functionality of Visual Basic's normal message box in every way.
- Displays a Help button that is linked to a specified Help file and topic.
- Contains code in its **Resize** event procedure which ensures that it does get the focus, even when it is displayed by an out-of-process ActiveX component (as long as the out-of-process component is not running remotely, in which case no **Form** object of any kind should be displayed).

The **ShowMsg** method, its **Form** object, and its associated members in the **CL** class are used internally throughout the book's class library to display syntax and runtime error messages. This code is used more frequently than any other code in the class library.

The ShowMsg Method's Specifications

In Chapter 4, you learned how to create a relatively simple method (**Delete**), along with an associated **Form** object that it displayed modally. The basic techniques illustrated by the **Delete** method are used by several members of the book's class library, including the **ShowMsg** method, which is one of the more complex members in the class library. Most of this complexity is due to the need to validate the various optional arguments that it can take and to the sophisticated functionality of Visual Basic's **MsgBox** function it simulates. At this point in your exposure to VB5's object-oriented syntax and capabilities, you are about to swim into the deeper part of the pool.

As you learned in Chapter 5, the preferred way to specify and document the functionality of a member of a class library is in the form of a help topic. This help topic can then be viewed from the Object Browser by any client application programmer who wants to call and reuse the member. The topic in the class library's Help file (EFS.HLP) that specifies the detailed functionality of the **ShowMsg** method is shown in the sidebar.

ShowMsg method's specifications.

SYNTAX
```
Object.ShowMsg(Prompt, [Buttons], [Title], [HelpFile], [Context])
```

The **ShowMsg** method's syntax has the following object qualifier and named arguments:

- *Object*. Required. **Object** data type. An expression that evaluates to an object in the Applies To pop-up list.

- *Prompt*. Required. **String** data type. An expression displayed as the message in the dialog box. *Prompt* may have a maximum of 512 characters, excluding carriage return characters. Each line of the message, except the last one, must be terminated by a carriage return character, i.e., **Chr$(13)** or the VB intrinsic constant **vbCr**. Any single line may have a maximum of 50 characters.

- *Buttons*. Optional. **Variant** data type whose subtype is an **Integer** expression that is the sum of values specifying the number and type of command buttons to display, the icon to use, the default command button, and the modality of the message box. If omitted, the default setting for *Buttons* is zero. See *Settings* below for the valid settings of *Buttons*.

- *Title*. Optional. **Variant** data type whose subtype is a **String** expression that specifies the caption in the title bar of the message box. *Title* cannot exceed 40 characters. If omitted, the default setting for *Title* is the **EXEName** property of the class library.

- *HelpFile*. Optional. **Variant** data type whose subtype is a **String** expression that specifies the path and name of the

Help file to use to provide context-sensitive help for the message box. If *HelpFile* is provided, the *Context* argument must also be provided and the Help command button is enabled. If *HelpFile* is omitted, the Help command button is disabled.

- *Context*. Optional. **Variant** data type whose subtype is an **Integer** or **Long** expression that is the Help context number assigned to the context-sensitive help topic. If *Context* is provided, the *HelpFile* argument must also be provided and the Help command button is enabled. Valid settings are in the range from 1 to 2,147,483,647. If *Context* is omitted, the Help command button is disabled.

SETTINGS

The first group of values (0-5) describes the number and type of command buttons displayed in the dialog box; the second group (16, 32, 48, 64) describes the icon style; the third group (0, 256, 512) determines which command button is the default; and the fourth group (0, 4096) determines the modality of the message box. When adding numbers to create a final value for *Buttons*, use only one number from each group. See the Help topic titled *VB Constants: ShowMsg/TrapRunTime Methods* for the valid settings of the *Buttons* argument.

CALLED

From any procedure in the client application.

RETURNS

Upon success, two elements in a **Variant**. The elements contain these subtypes:

- 0 - MBR_SUCCESS. A **Boolean** (**True**) that specifies the member executed successfully.

- 1 - MBR_BUTTON. An **Integer** from one to seven that specifies the command button the user chooses. See the help topic titled *VB Constants: ShowMsg/TrapRunTime Methods* for the valid settings of the MBR_BUTTON element.

Upon failure, eight elements in a **Variant**. The elements contain the error codes that the class library returns when a runtime or syntax error occurs during the execution of one of its members.

REMARKS

- When both the *HelpFile* and *Context* arguments are provided, the user can choose the Help command button or press F1 to view the help topic associated with the context number.

- If the message box displays a Cancel, Abort or No command button, pressing the ESC key or choosing Close from the Control menu has the same effect as choosing one of those command buttons.

- Choosing the Help command button never closes the dialog box. The dialog box is not closed and no value is returned until the user chooses one of the other command buttons.

Creating The Message Box's GUI

Our task now is to create the message box's GUI. In this section, we'll begin by discussing the creation of the **Form** object and its controls. Then, we'll examine the code for each component.

Creating The Form And Its Controls

The layout of the **Form** object (frmShowMsg) and its controls is quite straightforward. The properties that need to be set for the **Form** are **BorderStyle**, **Icon**, and **KeyPreview**. **BorderStyle** is set to 3 - Fixed Dialog and **Icon** is set to BOOK02.ICO, which is loaded from VB's icon library. These property settings, along with some Windows API functions in the **Form_Load** event procedure of frmShowMsg, subclass the appearance of Visual Basic's message box. **KeyPreview** is set to **True** so that the **Click** event procedure of the Help button will be called to display the help topic when the user presses F1.

The differences between the appearance of VB5's message box and the class library's subclassed message box under the Windows 95 shell and 32-bit VB are subtle but meaningful. VB5's message box does not have a Control menu (which, if it did, you could easily double click to close the message box), and yet it has the little X button on the right of the title bar (which is harder to hit with the mouse). The class library's subclassed message box leaves both the X button and the control menu's icon visible (with only the Close item on the menu). The other major difference is that the class library's message box displays a Help button, which is disabled if values are not passed to the **ShowMsg** method's *HelpFile* and *Context* arguments. Figures 7.1 and 7.2 show the VB5 message box and the class library's message box, respectively.

There are five control objects used on the **Form** object: four **CommandButton** objects and a **PictureBox** object. The buttons are created as part of a control array so that their properties can be more easily set and returned and because, except for the Help button, their names/captions can change each time the **ShowMsg** method is called. To simulate the behavior of the icon on Visual Basic's message box, the **PictureBox** object needs the special property settings shown in Table 7.1.

The **AutoRedraw** and **Picture** settings are the only settings that need some explanation. At both design time and runtime, the **Picture** property remains set to (None) because Windows API functions are used to paint the appropriate message box icon from the Windows icon library onto the **PictureBox** object. Painting icons on a **PictureBox** object in this way requires that **AutoRedraw** be set to **True**.

> ### Use a PictureBox object for the icon
>
> *Because the message box's icon is painted with Windows API functions, you need to use a **PictureBox** object to hold the icon. An **Image** object does not have an **hDC** property (that is, it cannot be used as a device context), which the **DrawIcon** Windows API function requires.*

Figure 7.1　VB5's message box.

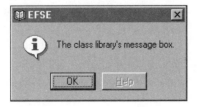

Figure 7.2　Class library's message box.

Table 7.1   Settings for the **PictureBox** object's properties.

Property	Setting
AutoRedraw	True
BorderStyle	0 - None
Picture	(None)
TabStop	False

There are two reasons for displaying the icons this way. First, it conserves system resources and minimizes the size of the ActiveX component by not requiring that all four icons be stored in the class library. Second, it enables the display of the correct set of icons, depending on which version of the Windows operating system is running. For example, when you are running the Windows 95 shell, the four icons appear as shown in Figure 7.3. When you are running Windows NT 3.51, the icons appear as shown in Figure 7.4.

It is good to remember that the Windows operating system itself is comprised of many reusable resources in the form of images, functions, objects, applications, and so on. Whenever possible, an experienced Visual Basic and Windows programmer reuses these to minimize the system resources required by an application and to provide a GUI for the user that is as consistent as possible with the current operating system.

Code For frmShowMsg And Its Controls

To help you better understand the code for the **Form** object and its controls, I've broken it down into several sections.

Figure 7.3   Windows 95-style message box icons.

Figure 7.4   Windows NT 3.51-style message box icons.

FORM-LEVEL DECLARATIONS AND PROPERTY PROCEDURES

The message box **Form** object uses three kinds of form-level variables. First, certain variables are required because we're using the **Property Let** and **Property Get** procedures to create custom properties. Although a custom property is set and returned with the **Property** procedures, it must be stored in a form-level variable. Second, one form-level flag is turned off and on in different event procedures. Third, there is a form-level object variable that is assigned an object instance of the **CL** class. There are also Windows API function declarations that are required.

Listing 7.1 shows the form-level declarations for frmShowMsg.

Listing 7.1   Form-level declarations for frmShowMsg.

```
' DLL functions:
#If Win32 Then

    Private Declare Function DeleteMenu& Lib "USER32" _
                            (ByVal hMenu&, ByVal IDItem&, _
                            ByVal Flags&)
    Private Declare Function DestroyIcon& Lib "USER32" _
                            (ByVal hIcon&)
    Private Declare Function DrawIcon& Lib "USER32" _
                            (ByVal hDC&, ByVal X&, _
                            ByVal Y&, ByVal hIcon&)
    Private Declare Function GetSystemMenu& Lib "USER32" _
                            (ByVal hWnd&, ByVal Revert&)
    Private Declare Function LoadIcon& Lib "USER32" _
                            Alias "LoadIconA" _
                            (ByVal hInst&, ByVal Icon&)
    Private Declare Function SetWindowPos& Lib "USER32" _
                            (ByVal hWnd&, _
                            ByVal hWndInsertAfter&, _
                            ByVal X&, ByVal Y&, ByVal Wid&, _
                            ByVal Hgt&, ByVal Flags&)
    Private Declare Function WinHelp& Lib "USER32" _
                            Alias "WinHelpA" _
                            (ByVal hWnd&, ByVal HelpFile$, _
                            ByVal Cmd&, ByVal Info As Any)

#Else

    Private Declare Function DeleteMenu% Lib "USER" _
                            (ByVal hMenu%, ByVal IDItem%, _
                            ByVal Flags%)
    Private Declare Function DestroyIcon% Lib "USER" _
                            (ByVal hIcon%)
    Private Declare Function DrawIcon% Lib "USER" _
                            (ByVal hDC%, ByVal X%, ByVal Y%, _
                            ByVal hIcon%)
```

```
Private Declare Function GetSystemMenu% Lib "USER" _
                          (ByVal hWnd%, ByVal Revert%)
Private Declare Function LoadIcon% Lib "USER" _
                          (ByVal hInst%, ByVal Icon&)
Private Declare Function SetWindowPos% Lib "USER" _
                          (ByVal hWnd%, _
                          ByVal hWndInsertAfter%, _
                          ByVal X%, ByVal Y%, ByVal Wid%, _
                          ByVal Hgt%, ByVal Flags%)
Private Declare Function WinHelp% Lib "USER" _
                          (ByVal hWnd%, ByVal HelpFile$, _
                          ByVal Cmd%, ByVal Info As Any)

#End If


' Form-level flag variables—
' · fLoaded flag that is turned on at end of Form_Load event
' procedure to signal to Form_Resize event procedure that it
' is now time to run its code.
Private fLoaded         As Boolean


' Form-level variables (set by Property Let procedures):
Private fHelpFile       As String
Private fCaption        As String
Private fKeyword        As String
Private fDefaultBtn     As Byte
Private fIconCL         As Byte
Private fNumMsgLines    As Byte
Private fButton         As Integer
Private fButtons        As Long
Private fContext        As Long
Private fHeight         As Long
Private fWidth          As Long
Private fMsg            As Variant


' Instantiate internal classes to reuse their members:
Private CL              As New CL
```

Name your variables carefully

It is a good Visual Basic programming practice to give the form-level variables associated with **Property** *procedures the same names as the* **Property** *procedures themselves, preceded by the* f *prefix to signify form-level scope.*

You will learn more about how VB5's **Property** procedure syntax works later in the book. For now, all you need to know is that the way it is used in the message box **Form** object is the simplest application of the syntax possible. A **Property Let** procedure assigns a value to its associated form-level variable. A **Property Get** procedure returns the value of its associated form-level variable in the same way that a **Function** procedure returns a value. The **Public** keyword, when used in front of a **Property** statement in a **Form** object, indicates that the custom property is accessible to all other procedures in all other forms and modules in the Visual Basic project. Listing 7.2 shows the code for a **Property Let** and a **Property Get** procedure in frmShowMsg.

Listing 7.2 Property Let/Get procedures for frmShowMsg.

```
Public Property Let Buttons(Setting As Long)

    fButtons = Setting

End Property

Public Property Get Button()

    Button = fButton

End Property
```

To call a **Property Let** procedure, you use this syntax:

```
frmShowMsg.Buttons = vbInformation
```

To call a **Property Get** procedure, you use this syntax:

```
' Variable.
Dim Result As Variant
Result = frmShowMsg.Choice
```

When Form_Load executes automatically

Returning or setting the value of a built-in property of a **Form** *object or one of its control objects causes the* **Form_Load** *event procedure of the* **Form** *object to execute. This can be a problem with certain kinds of code in* **Form_Load** *that you would not want to have run more than once. Setting a custom property with a* **Property Let** *procedure does not have this negative side effect.*

THE FORM OBJECT'S EVENT PROCEDURES

The essential code for the frmShowMsg **Form** object is in its **Load**, **Paint**, and **Resize** event procedures. Throughout the rest of the book, the only code that is explained in detail is code that exemplifies either new Visual Basic syntax or new object-oriented programming techniques. Syntax or techniques that have previously been discussed will not be explained again and usually will not be listed at all.

The code for the **Form_Load** event procedure is shown in Listing 7.3.

Listing 7.3   Form_Load event procedure for frmShowMsg.

```
Private Sub Form_Load()

    ' Constants for Windows API functions:
    Const MF_BYPOSITION = &H400

    ' Constants for elements in Cmd() control array:
    Const BTN_HELP = 0
    Const BTN_1 = 1
    Const BTN_2 = 2
    Const BTN_3 = 3

    ' Constants for literals:
    Const CM_MOVE = 1
    Const CM_SEPARATOR1 = 5
    Const CM_SEPARATOR2 = 7
    Const CM_SWITCHTO = 8
    Const ONE_HALF = 0.5
    Const LINE_HGT = 1.5
    Const SPACE_BTW_BTNS = 990

    ' Variables:
    Dim Button   As Integer
    Dim Ctl      As Control

    ' If custom Title property is not yet set, then Form_Load
    ' event is being triggered when hDC property of Form object
    ' is read in ParseMsg procedure. So exit procedure to speed
    ' up code and keep it from executing more than once.
    If fCaption = vbNullString Then Exit Sub

    ' Initialize—
    ' • Set properties of Form object.
    ' • Set properties of CommandButton objects.
    ' • Position icon's PictureBox object correctly.
    ' • Mimic behavior of Microsoft's dialog boxes.
    ' • Set flag to let Form_Resize event procedure run.
    Caption = fCaption
    Height = fHeight
    Width = fWidth

    Select Case fButtons
```

```
      Case vbOKOnly
          Cmd(BTN_1).Caption = "OK"
      Case vbOKCancel
          Cmd(BTN_1).Caption = "OK"
          Cmd(BTN_2).Caption = "Cancel"
      Case vbYesNo
          Cmd(BTN_1).Caption = "&Yes"
          Cmd(BTN_2).Caption = "&No"
      Case vbRetryCancel
          Cmd(BTN_1).Caption = "&Retry"
          Cmd(BTN_2).Caption = "Cancel"
      Case vbAbortRetryIgnore
          Cmd(BTN_1).Caption = "&Abort"
          Cmd(BTN_2).Caption = "&Retry"
          Cmd(BTN_3).Caption = "&Ignore"
      Case vbYesNoCancel
          Cmd(BTN_1).Caption = "&Yes"
          Cmd(BTN_2).Caption = "&No"
          Cmd(BTN_3).Caption = "Cancel"
  End Select

  Select Case fButtons
      Case vbOKOnly
          Cmd(BTN_1).Cancel = True
          Cmd(BTN_1).Default = True
          Cmd(BTN_1).Left = (ScaleWidth - 1860) * ONE_HALF
          Cmd(BTN_HELP).Left = Cmd(BTN_1).Left + SPACE_BTW_BTNS
      Case vbOKCancel, vbYesNo, vbRetryCancel
          Cmd(BTN_2).Cancel = True
          Cmd(fDefaultBtn).Default = True
          Cmd(BTN_1).Left = (ScaleWidth - 2850) * ONE_HALF
          Cmd(BTN_2).Left = Cmd(BTN_1).Left + SPACE_BTW_BTNS
          Cmd(BTN_HELP).Left = Cmd(BTN_2).Left + SPACE_BTW_BTNS
          Cmd(BTN_2).Visible = True
      Case vbAbortRetryIgnore, vbYesNoCancel
          Cmd(BTN_3).Cancel = True
          Cmd(fDefaultBtn).Default = True
          Cmd(BTN_1).Left = (ScaleWidth - 3860) * ONE_HALF
          Cmd(BTN_2).Left = Cmd(BTN_1).Left + SPACE_BTW_BTNS
          Cmd(BTN_3).Left = Cmd(BTN_2).Left + SPACE_BTW_BTNS
          Cmd(BTN_HELP).Left = Cmd(BTN_3).Left + SPACE_BTW_BTNS
          Cmd(BTN_2).Visible = True
          Cmd(BTN_3).Visible = True
  End Select

  If fHelpFile = "NA" Then Cmd(BTN_HELP).Enabled = False

  For Button = BTN_HELP To BTN_3
     Cmd(Button).Top = Height - 870
     Cmd(Button).TabIndex = Button
  Next Button

  picIcon.Top = 200 + ((fNumMsgLines) * LINE_HGT)
```

```
    If CL.IsWin95Shell Then
        DeleteMenu GetSystemMenu(hWnd, vbEmpty), _
                                CM_SEPARATOR1, MF_BYPOSITION
        DeleteMenu GetSystemMenu(hWnd, vbEmpty), _
                                CM_MOVE, MF_BYPOSITION
    Else
        DeleteMenu GetSystemMenu(hWnd, vbEmpty), _
                                CM_SWITCHTO, MF_BYPOSITION
        DeleteMenu GetSystemMenu(hWnd, vbEmpty), _
                                CM_SEPARATOR2, MF_BYPOSITION
        DeleteMenu GetSystemMenu(hWnd, vbEmpty), _
                                CM_SEPARATOR1, MF_BYPOSITION

        For Each Ctl In Controls
            Ctl.FontBold = True
        Next Ctl

        FontBold = True
    End If

    Move (Screen.Width - Width) • ONE_HALF, _
        (Screen.Height - Height) • ONE_HALF
    fLoaded = True

End Sub
```

There are several interesting things about the code in Listing 7.3. First, during the execution of the **ShowMsg** method's syntax checking and validation routines, it is necessary to read the **Form** object's **hDC** property in order to measure the widest line of the message. This is done in the **ParseMsg** method of the **CL** class, using Windows API functions (which we'll look at later in the book). However, as I mentioned a moment ago, reading any built-in property of a **Form** object (for example, **hDC**) triggers its **Load** event. To ensure that the **Form_Load** event procedure's code executes only once, this code is placed at the top of the procedure just below the declarations:

```
If fCaption = vbNullString Then Exit Sub
```

The custom **Caption** property is not set by the **ShowMsg** method until after the **ParseMsg** routine that reads the **hDC** property executes. So the variable **fCaption** will be a zero-length string at this point, and the rest of the **Form_Load** event procedure does not execute.

The second noteworthy feature of the code in the **Form_Load** event procedure is toward the bottom of the procedure and is related to the use of the **DeleteMenu** and **GetSystemMenu** Windows API functions. If the Windows 95 shell is being used, the **GetSystemMenu** and **DeleteMenu**

Windows API functions remove a separator bar and the Move item from the Control menu, leaving just the Close item. If the Windows NT 3.51 shell is being used, the same API functions delete other commands from the Control menu, leaving only the Move and Close items. If its second argument is zero (Null in C or **vbEmpty** in Visual Basic), **GetSystemMenu** returns the handle of the Control or System menu for the **Form** object whose handle is specified in its first argument. Then, **DeleteMenu** removes the specified menu item from the Control menu. In this example, each item is removed on the basis of its position or index value within the menu's array. The code then cycles through each member of Visual Basic's built-in **Controls** collection and sets each object's **FontBold** property to **False** for the Windows 95 shell or **True** for the Windows NT 3.51 shell.

The third aspect of the code in the **Form_Load** event procedure to note is the very last statement

```
fLoaded = True
```

which turns on a form-level flag that signals to the **Form_Resize** event procedure that it is now okay for it to execute. This form-level flag prevents the **Form_Resize** event procedure from executing two unnecessary times (when the **Width** and **Height** properties of frmShowMsg are set at the top of the **Form_Load** event procedure). The really important thing to note about this statement, however, is its form-level variable and the care with which it is documented. There is nothing more potentially confusing or obscure about Visual Basic code than how module-level variables/flags are used in the module's different procedures. In the case of **fLoaded**, the sequence in which the flag is turned on and off is documented in each place it is referenced (General Declarations section, **Form_Load** event procedure, and **Form_Resize** event procedure).

In object-oriented programming, module-level flag variables should be the exception rather than the rule (and, of course, public or global-level variables should never be used). In fact, with the exception of the module-level variables that are used to store values set by a **Property Let** procedure or to internally instantiate classes, the book's entire class library contains less than a half dozen module-level flag variables. The point is this: Use module-level variables sparingly to ease the task of documenting them correctly, which, as I just mentioned, is an absolute must.

The next event procedure we need to discuss is **Form_Paint**, which is shown in Listing 7.4.

Listing 7.4   Form_Paint event procedure for frmShowMsg.

```
Private Sub Form_Paint()

    ' Constants for Windows API functions:
    Const IDI_HAND = 32513&
    Const IDI_QUESTION = 32514&
    Const IDI_EXCLAMATION = 32515&
    Const IDI_ASTERISK = 32516&

    ' Constants for literals:
    Const X = 2
    Const Y = 2
    Const ONE_LINE = 1
    Const TWO_LINES = 2
    Const FIRST_LINE = 0

    ' Variables:
    Dim Lin         As Integer
    Dim IconNbr     As Long
    Dim HWndIcon    As Variant

    ' Specify text placement and type of icon and display them—
    ' • Set top margin for first line of message (margin
    '     varies depending on number of lines in message).
    ' • Set left margin and print each line of message (margin
    '     varies depending on whether or not icon is displayed).
    ' • Determine icon to display and associated WIN library ID.
    ' • Based on Windows library ID:
    '     a) Get handle in memory for icon and load it there.
    '     b) Draw copy on PictureBox.
    '     c) Destroy icon's handle to free memory it occupied.
    If fNumMsgLines = ONE_LINE Then
        CurrentY = 300
    ElseIf fNumMsgLines = TWO_LINES Then
        CurrentY = 250
    Else
        CurrentY = 200
    End If

    For Lin = FIRST_LINE To fNumMsgLines - 1

        If fIconCL = False Then
            CurrentX = 150
            picIcon.Visible = False
        Else
            CurrentX = 850
        End If

        Print fMsg(Lin)
    Next Lin

    If fIconCL <> False Then
```

```
        Select Case fIconCL
            Case vbCritical
                IconNbr = IDI_HAND
            Case vbQuestion
                IconNbr = IDI_QUESTION
            Case vbExclamation
                IconNbr = IDI_EXCLAMATION
            Case vbInformation
                IconNbr = IDI_ASTERISK
        End Select

        HWndIcon = LoadIcon(vbEmpty, IconNbr)

        If HWndIcon Then

            #If Win32 Then

                If DrawIcon(picIcon.hDC, X, Y, CLng(HWndIcon)) Then
                    DestroyIcon CLng(HWndIcon)
                End If

            #Else

                If DrawIcon(picIcon.hDC, X, Y, CInt(HWndIcon)) Then
                    DestroyIcon CInt(HWndIcon)
                End If

            #End If
        End If
    End If
End Sub
```

The **Form_Paint** event procedure's code uses Windows API functions (**LoadIcon**, **DrawIcon**, and **DestroyIcon**) to load the correct message box icon from the stock library of images that Windows contains and paint it on the **PictureBox** object. The four different icons in the library are identified by numeric values represented by Windows API constants. When you pass zero as its first argument (Null in C or **vbEmpty** in Visual Basic), **LoadIcon** loads the Windows stock library icon specified by its second argument into an area of memory identified by the handle it returns. **DrawIcon** draws the loaded icon on the device context (that is, the **PictureBox** object) specified by its first argument. The second and third arguments of **DrawIcon** specify the location (upper-left corner) on the device context to start drawing. You can read the value returned by **DrawIcon** to ensure that it succeeds. Once the icon is drawn successfully, **DestroyIcon** frees the memory where the icon was stored.

Visual Basic now allows you to load string literals, graphics, and data that are contained in a resource file at runtime, using the **LoadResString**,

LoadResPicture, and **LoadResData** functions. You could also use this approach to load the different icons for the two Windows shells, but, your class library DLL or EXE file would be slightly larger. In addition, you would need either the Enterprise Edition of Visual Basic, Visual C++, or some similar product to create the resource file itself.

The final event procedure is **Form_Resize**, which is shown in Listing 7.5.

Listing 7.5   Form_Resize event procedure for frmShowMsg.

```
Private Sub Form_Resize()

    ' Constants for Windows API function:
    Const HWND_TOPMOST = (-1)
    Const SWP_NOMOVE = &H2
    Const SWP_NOSIZE = &H1

    ' Constants for elements in Cmd() control array:
    Const BTN_1 = 1

    ' When Form_Load event procedure is done (that is, fLoaded
    ' flag has been turned on), set default button and prevent
    ' focus problem with out-of-process, OLE server.
    If fLoaded Then

        If Cmd(fDefaultBtn).Caption <> "&Help" Then
            Cmd(fDefaultBtn).SetFocus
        Else
            Cmd(BTN_1).SetFocus
        End If

        SetWindowPos hWnd, HWND_TOPMOST, _
                     vbEmpty, vbEmpty, vbEmpty, vbEmpty, _
                     SWP_NOMOVE Or SWP_NOSIZE

    End If

End Sub
```

The **Form_Resize** event procedure's code starts by reading the value of the form-level flag that signals whether the **Form_Load** event procedure is done executing. If it is not done, the flag is not yet turned on. If you do not use such a form-level flag, the **Form_Resize** event procedure executes several times because code at the top of the **Form_Load** event procedure sets the **Width** and **Height** properties of the **Form** object.

When the **Form_Resize** code finally executes, it does two things. First, it gives the focus to the first **CommandButton** object. This has to be done sometime anyway, and by doing it here, we avoid the focus problem that occurs when the class library is running as an ActiveX EXE component (see Chapter 3 for more details). Second, the **SetWindowPos** Windows API function ensures that if an ActiveX EXE component is running, the message box **Form** object stays on top of all other windows, remaining visible, even if the user clicks on a window in another application.

THE COMMANDBUTTON OBJECT'S CLICK PROCEDURE

Once the message box **Form** object is displayed modally, nothing happens until the user chooses one of the **CommandButton** objects. The functionality associated with these buttons is the same as for those on the message box created with Visual Basic's **MsgBox** function. The only difference is the display and behavior of the Help button. The code for the **Cmd_Click** event procedure is shown in Listing 7.6.

Listing 7.6   Cmd_Click event procedure for frmShowMsg.

```
Private Sub Cmd_Click(Index As Integer)

    ' Constants for Windows API functions:
    Const HELP_CONTEXT = &H1
    Const HELP_KEY = &H101

    ' Constants for elements in Cmd() control array:
    Const BTN_HELP = 0

    ' Constants for literals:
    Const CUSTOM_CTL_ERR = -1000000

    ' Depending on button user chooses—
    ' • If Help button:
    '    a) If VB custom control error message Help topic
    '        is needed, call by search/index keyword.
    '    b) If any other Help topic, call by context ID.
    ' • If any other button, return selection to ShowMsg
    '    method by:
    '    a) Setting Button property's variable to number of button.
    '    b) Hiding modal Form object so method's code resumes
    '        (ShowMsg, ShowRunTime or ShowSyntax method).
    If Index = BTN_HELP Then

        If fContext = CUSTOM_CTL_ERR Then
            WinHelp hWnd, fHelpFile, HELP_KEY, fKeyword
        Else
            WinHelp hWnd, fHelpFile, HELP_CONTEXT, fContext
        End If

    Else
```

```
    Select Case Cmd(Index).Caption
        Case "OK"
            fButton = 1
        Case "Cancel"
            fButton = 2
        Case "&Abort"
            fButton = 3
        Case "&Retry"
            fButton = 4
        Case "&Ignore"
            fButton = 5
        Case "&Yes"
            fButton = 6
        Case "&No"
            fButton = 7
    End Select

    Hide

  End If
End Sub
```

As you can see from the code in Listing 7.6, in all cases except the Help
button, clicking a **CommandButton** object sets the form-level variable
fButton to the number/constant specified for that button by Visual Basic's
MsgBox function. Next, the **Hide** method is applied to the **Form** object
and code execution returns to the **ShowMsg** method. The noteworthy code
in the **Cmd_Click** event procedure is related to the Help button. Normally,
when you want to display a topic from a Help file with Visual Basic, you use
the **HelpContextID** property (which is a **Long**) of a **Form** or control
object to specify the topic. In this case, the ability to display a help topic
needs to be more generic because **frmShowMsg** is also used by the
TrapRunTime method of the **Error** class.

Some Visual Basic runtime error messages do not have help topics associated with them (for example, those for certain custom control objects). In
such a case, the best approach is to display the generic *Trappable Errors*
topic from Visual Basic's Help file. Users can then jump to the specific help
topic for the custom control's runtime error. Because there is no way of
knowing whether there is a context ID number mapped to the *Trappable
Errors* topic or what that number might be, the only way to display the topic
is by its associated keyword, which is passed in to the form-level variable
fKeyword from the **ShowMsg** method.

In order to use this approach, however, you must run the Windows Help
engine by using the **WinHelp** Windows API function. Passing the constant
HELP_KEY as the third argument of **WinHelp** displays the first help topic

whose title is associated with the fourth argument. The fourth argument is a keyword in the list on Help's Search dialog box (Windows) or Help's Index dialog box tab (Windows 95). Passing the constant HELP_CONTEXT as the third argument of **WinHelp** displays the help topic specified by the fourth argument. In this case, the fourth argument is a Help context ID number.

The ShowMsg Method's Code

The code in the **ShowMsg** method is complex, and we will not look at all of its features in this chapter. Because some of its associated members in the **CL** class are also used by methods in the **Error** class, we'll be revisiting some of the code in Chapter 8.

The statement that declares the **ShowMsg** method is shown here:

```
Function ShowMsg(Prompt As String, _
                Optional Buttons, _
                Optional Title, _
                Optional HelpFile, _
                Optional Context)
```

The **ShowMsg** method is your first exposure to optional arguments. In our analysis of the **ShowMsg** method's code, we'll focus on the new syntax related to the use of optional arguments, the associated **ParseButtons** method of the **CL** class, and a couple other noteworthy features unique to this method in the class library. The syntactical elements related to optional arguments that we will examine here are:

- **Optional**. A keyword that allows the use of optional arguments when declaring a **Function**, **Sub**, **Property**, or **Event** procedure.
- **IsMissing**. A function that checks whether or not an optional argument is passed to a procedure.
- **VarType**. A function that determines the subtype of a **Variant** variable.

Optional arguments are variants

The data type of optional arguments defaults to and must be the ***Variant***. *In the interest of more concise code, we won't explicitly declare the* ***Variant*** *data type. Likewise, a* ***Function*** *procedure that is not explicitly declared as some other data type defaults to a* ***Variant***.

Syntax Associated With Optional Argument

When you declare an argument in a Visual Basic procedure with the **Optional** keyword, any code that you write in the procedure that uses that optional argument must first check to see if it was passed by using Visual Basic's **IsMissing** function. **IsMissing** returns **True** if the optional argument was not passed, or **False** if it was passed. **IsMissing** is typically preceded with the **Not** operator. For example, if you have an optional argument named **FailIfExists** in a procedure, you would write this kind of code to do something with the argument:

```
If Not IsMissing(FailIfExists) Then
    . . .
End If
```

These next three lines of code achieve the same effect:

```
If IsMissing(FailIfExists) = False Then
    . . .
End If
```

Speed things up with Not

Using the **Not** operator to determine if a **Boolean** is set to **False** (as in the first code snippet) is slightly faster and takes fewer bytes to store than explicitly testing to see if the **Boolean** is equal to **False**. See Visual Basic's Knowledge Base Help file for more information.

If an optional argument is passed, you then need to check what kind of variable or data the argument contains. Because an optional argument must be a **Variant** data type, it can contain almost anything. You can use Visual Basic's **VarType** function to check the subtype of the optional argument. Table 7.2 lists the possible values returned by **VarType**.

The **VarType** function never returns the value for **vbArray** by itself. It is always added to some other value to indicate an array of a particular type. For example, the value returned for an array of integers is calculated as **vbInteger** + **vbArray**, or 8194.

The portion of the **ShowMsg** code that follows in Listing 7.7 clearly illustrates the use of the **IsMissing** and **VarType** functions.

Table 7.2 Values returned by **VarType** function.

Value	Description
0 - vbEmpty	Empty (uninitialized)
1 - vbNull	Null (no valid data)
2 - vbInteger	Integer
3 - vbLong	Long
4 - vbSingle	Single
5 - vbDouble	Double
6 - vbCurrency	Currency
7 - vbDate	Date
8 - vbString	String
9 - vbObject	OLE Automation object
10 - vbError	Error
11 - vbBoolean	Boolean
12 - vbVariant	Variant (used only with arrays of Variants)
13 - vbDataObject	A data access object
14 - vbDecimal	Decimal
17 - vbByte	Byte
8192 - vbArray	Array

Listing 7.7 Syntax checking in ShowMsg method.

```
Function ShowMsg(Prompt As String, _
                Optional Buttons, _
                Optional Title, _
                Optional HelpFile, _
                Optional Context)

    . . .

    If Not IsMissing(HelpFile) And Not IsMissing(Context) Then

       If VarType(HelpFile) <> vbString Then
          E.TrapSyntax 4, PROC, "HelpFile", "String"
       Else
          CL.IsPath1 CStr(HelpFile), PROC, "HelpFile", SrcPath
          CL.IsFile CStr(HelpFile), SrcPath, PROC, _
                "HelpFile", "HLP"
       End If
```

```
    If VarType(Context) <> vbInteger And _
       VarType(Context) <> vbLong Then
          E.TrapSyntax 4, PROC, "Context", "Integer or Long"
    ElseIf Context < 0 Or Context > 2147483647 Then
          E.TrapSyntax 5, PROC, "Context"
    End If

  End If

End Function
```

If the optional **HelpFile** argument is not the correct subtype (that is, a **String**), then the **TrapSyntax** method of the **Error** class is called. If it is a **String**, the **IsPath1** and **IsFile** methods of the **CL** class check that it exists. The **Context** argument has to be either a positive **Integer** or **Long** or else **TrapSyntax** is called. These types of calls to the **TrapSyntax** method (and the error trap that is at the bottom of the **ShowMsg** method) are found in every member of the class library. You will learn the details of how the class library's error handling scheme is implemented in Chapters 8 and 9.

Parsing The Prompt Argument

The first argument of the **ShowMsg** method, **Prompt**, takes a string no longer than 500 characters, which is delimited by a carriage return character—**vbCr** or **Chr$(13)**—at least every 50 characters. This is different from Visual Basic's **MsgBox** function, which permits a message of about 1,024 characters and does not limit the length of a single line.

The **ShowMsg** method (and the **TrapRunTime** and **TrapSyntax** methods in the **Error** class) observes these constraints because programs that display Windows message boxes spread across the entire screen are ugly and inefficient. For example, although it is not documented, under Windows 95 and 640×480 VGA resolution, Visual Basic's **MsgBox** function allows a maximum message line length of 102 lowercase characters. Under higher, super-VGA resolutions, a message line can be even wider.

Once the 50 and 500 character parameters have been validated, **ShowMsg** calls **ParseMsg**, shown in Listing 7.8, which is an internal method in the **CL** class. **ParseMsg** is an interesting routine that uses two Windows API functions, **GetTextExtent** and **GetTextExtentPoint32**, to calculate the width of the longest message line. During these calculations, these API functions automatically factor in the effect of the current font (type, bold or normal, proportional or fixed pitch, and so on) to compute the precise width in pixels.

Listing 7.8   ParseMsg method of CL class.

```
Function ParseMsg(Prompt As String)

    ' _____
    ' Purpose: Parses Prompt argument by:
    '              • Separating it into lines.
    '              • Calculating width of longest line.
    '              • Calculating height of message box based on
    '                number of lines.
    '
    ' Called:  Internally from members of class library.
    '
    ' Accepts: Prompt: String expression containing message to be
    '                  parsed and displayed.
    '
    ' Returns: Upon success, at least 4 elements are returned in
    '          array contained in Variant variable:
    '
    '          Element #     Constant        Value
    '              0         PM_WID          Width of longest line
    '              1         PM_HGT          Height of message box
    '              2         PM_NUM_LINES    # of lines in message
    '              3...      PM_MSG_EL       Message lines (a)
    '
    ' Notes:   (a) Number of elements is dynamically resized to
    '              handle number of lines in message.
    ' _____


    ' Constants for elements in returned array:
    Const PM_WID = 0
    Const PM_HGT = 1
    Const PM_NUM_LINES = 2
    Const PM_MSG_EL = 3

    ' Constants for literals:
    Const RGT_MARGIN = 250
    Const TWIPS PER_PIXEL = 15
    Const ADJ_NBR = 4095
    Const LINE_HGT = 200
    Const ONE_LINE = 1
    Const TWO_LINES = 2
    Const FIRST_LINE = 3

    ' Variables:
    Dim Lin           As Integer
    Dim NumMsgLines   As Integer
    Dim Pos           As Integer
    Dim Wid           As Integer
    Dim MaxWid        As Integer
    Dim Hgt           As Integer
    Dim CurLine       As String
    Dim LastLine      As Integer
    Dim Msg()         As String
    Dim RetVals()     As Variant
```

```
#If Win32 Then
    Dim Dimens      As SIZE
#End If

' If not running WIN 95, turn Form object's bold on so
' call to device context below computes width correctly.
If Not IsWin95Shell Then frmShowMsg.FontBold = True

' Until all carriage returns are checked in Prompt
' argument, examine each line to find widest one—
' · Get position of next carriage return character.
' · Store part of string preceding it in array.
' · Find width of part/line in pixels and, if
'   it is widest line so far, store width.
' · Strip examined part of string and carriage return.
' · Increment line counter.
Do Until InStr(Prompt, vbCr) = False

    Pos = InStr(Prompt, vbCr)
    ReDim Preserve Msg(NumMsgLines) As String
    Msg(NumMsgLines) = Left$(Prompt, Pos - 1)
    CurLine = CStr(Msg(NumMsgLines))

    #If Win32 Then
        GetTextExtentPoint32 frmShowMsg.hDC, CurLine, _
                             Len(CurLine), Dimens
        Wid = Dimens.Wid
    #Else
        Wid = GetTextExtent(frmShowMsg.hDC, CurLine, _
                            Len(CurLine)) And ADJ_NBR
    #End If

    If Wid > MaxWid Then MaxWid = Wid

    Prompt = Mid$(Prompt, Pos + 1)
    NumMsgLines = NumMsgLines + 1

Loop

' Convert longest line from pixels to twips, add right margin,
' and unload message box form implicitly loaded above.
Wid = (MaxWid · Screen.TwipsPerPixelX) + RGT_MARGIN
Unload frmShowMsg

' Calculate height of message box form based on number of lines:
Select Case NumMsgLines
    Case 1
        Hgt = 1300 + (ONE_LINE · LINE_HGT) + 300
    Case 2
        Hgt = 1300 + (TWO_LINES · LINE_HGT) + 100
    Case 3
        Hgt = 1870
    Case Else
        Hgt = 1260 + ((NumMsgLines) · LINE_HGT)
End Select
```

```
' Fill array and return parameters:
ReDim RetVals(2) As Variant
RetVals(PM_WID) = Wid
RetVals(PM_HGT) = Hgt
RetVals(PM_NUM_LINES) = NumMsgLines
LastLine = NumMsgLines + 2

For Lin = FIRST_LINE To LastLine
   ReDim Preserve RetVals(Lin) As Variant
   RetVals(Lin) = Msg(Lin - PM_MSG_EL)
Next Lin

ParseMsg = RetVals

End Function
```

The **ParseMsg** method's code has several important items that we need to examine in more detail. First, before calculating the longest line, the font of the message box's **Form** object is set to normal (Windows 95 shell) or bold (Windows NT 3.51 shell), because this factor affects the calculation. Second, the widest message line, not the line with the greatest number of characters, is calculated. We use this approach because in a non-proportional font, the width of the line is affected by the width of each character in the font set. Figure 7.5 illustrates this concept.

The **GetTextExtent** (16-bit) and **GetTextExtentPoint32** (32-bit) Windows API functions compute the width and height of a line of text, using the current font of the device context specified in the first argument. The second and third arguments specify the line of text to be measured and its number of characters. In the case of **GetTextExtent**, you parse out the low-order word of the return value to get the width. For **GetTextExtentPoint32**, you pass the SIZE user-defined data type (represented by the variable **Dimens**) as its fourth argument and then read its width element. **GetTextExtentPoint32** is not supported by 16-bit Windows.

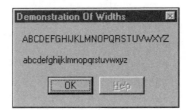

Figure 7.5 Varying line widths in a message box.

Setting The Form's Properties And Displaying The Form

If the values passed to the **ShowMsg** method's arguments are all valid, the method finishes up by setting the custom properties for the message box **Form** object. Then the method applies Visual Basic's **Show** method to the form modally, causing the code in the method to pause on that statement. When the user clicks on one of the buttons on the message box, code in its **Cmd_Click** event procedure applies the **Hide** method to the **Form** object, causing the code in the method to begin to execute again. The code that sets the **Form**'s properties, displays the form, and returns the number of the chosen button is shown in Listing 7.9.

Listing 7.9   Code that displays message box form.

```
Function ShowMsg(Prompt As String, _
               Optional Buttons, _
               Optional Title, _
               Optional HelpFile, _
               Optional Context)


    . . .


    With frmShowMsg

       Select Case Buttons
          Case vbOKOnly
             .DefaultBtn = BTN_1
          Case vbOKCancel, vbYesNo, vbRetryCancel

             Select Case DefaultBtn
                Case vbDefaultButton1
                   .DefaultBtn = BTN_1
                Case vbDefaultButton2
                   .DefaultBtn = BTN_2
             End Select

          Case vbAbortRetryIgnore, vbYesNoCancel

             Select Case DefaultBtn
                Case vbDefaultButton1
                   .DefaultBtn = BTN_1
                Case vbDefaultButton2
                   .DefaultBtn = BTN_2
                Case vbDefaultButton3
                   .DefaultBtn = BTN_3
             End Select

       End Select
```

```
    If Not IsMissing(HelpFile) And Not IsMissing(Context) Then
        .HelpFile = HelpFile
        .Context = Context
    ElseIf IsMissing(HelpFile) Or IsMissing(Context) Then
        .HelpFile = "NA"
    End If

    .Buttons = Buttons
    .HeightCL = Height
    .IconCL = Icon
    .Msg = Msg()
    .NumMsgLines = NumMsgLines
    .WidthCL = Width
    .CaptionCL = Title

End With

' Display method's Form object modally, so execution pauses
' until Hide method's applied in Cmd_Click event procedure.
#If Win32 Then
    frmShowMsg.Show vbModal
#Else

    If SystemModal Then
        frmShowMsg.Show vbSystemModal
    Else
        frmShowMsg.Show vbModal
    End If

#End If

' When Hide method's applied, return array and unload form.
ShowMsg = Array(True, frmShowMsg.Button)
Unload frmShowMsg
Exit Function

ET:

    If Err = SYNTAX Then ShowMsg = frmErrCodes.Codes
    If Err <> SYNTAX Then ShowMsg = CL.TrapErr(PROC)

End Function
```

Speed things up with With...End With

*Using the **With...End With** control structure to return or set properties is 5 percent faster than repeatedly referring to the object whose property you are returning or setting.*

Calling The ShowMsg Method Externally

In previous chapters, you have seen how to call a member of the book's class library externally from a client application. You also know that the help topic for any member in EFS.HLP has example code demonstrating how to call that member. To conclude this chapter, we will use the **ShowMsg** method to demonstrate how the design of its declaration and arguments makes it very easy to call the method by passing just the one required argument. If you want to customize the message box that **ShowMsg** displays, you can also avail yourself of the four optional arguments that it supports.

If you omit any registration-checking code, and if you are not concerned with the value that is returned, the basic call to the **ShowMsg** method can be made as easily as in the code in Listing 7.10. Just open a new project, enter the code in the **Form_DblClick** event procedure, run the project, and double click on the **Form** object.

Listing 7.10   Simple call to ShowMsg method.

```
Private Sub Form_DblClick()

    ' Declare object variable:
    Dim ClientApp As Object

    ' Instantiate class and assign it to object variable.
    Set ClientApp = CreateObject("EFSE.ClientApp")

    ' Call object's member using named argument.
    ClientApp.ShowMsg Prompt:="Just your basic message box—no frills attached!"

End Sub
```

8
HANDLING
RUNTIME ERRORS

I n developing the error-handling code and scheme for the book's class library, I had two high-level design objectives in mind. First, I wanted to meet all the requirements of a robust public interface for an ActiveX component. We discussed these requirements previously in Chapter 5, *Creating The Public Interface Of An ActiveX Component*. Second, I wanted the implementation to be in the form of a public **ClassModule** object, the **Error** class, which could also be reused by any client application.

More simply put, the objective of the **Error** class is to free the VB developer, either of ActiveX components or client applications, from ever having to write another error-trapping or syntax-checking routine. Because of Visual Basic's own underlying architecture, you will always have to enable error handlers with the **On Error** statement in a client application. But now those error handlers can call the **Error** class and let it do the rest of the work.

Design Of The Error Class

If something goes wrong while any public member of the book's class library is executing, that member will make a call to either the **TrapRunTime** or **TrapSyntax** method in the **Error** class. The **Error** class contains these public and private methods:

- **LogError**. A private member that fills an array with either runtime or syntax error information to return to the client application and logs the error in the appropriate file.

- **ShowRunTime**. A private member that simulates the behavior of Visual Basic's **MsgBox** function, adds a Help button to the message box, and displays a Visual Basic runtime error message. This is a simpler version of the routine that comprises the **ShowMsg** method of the **ClientApp** class.

- **ShowSyntax**. A private member that simulates the behavior of Visual Basic's **MsgBox** function, adds a Help button to the message box, and displays a class library syntax error message.

- **SplitMsg**. A private member that splits a Visual Basic runtime error message into separate lines that do not exceed the 50-character limit of the **ShowRunTime** method.

- **TrapRunTime**. A public member that traps any Visual Basic runtime error and displays its message and associated help topic (if it has one).

- **TrapSyntax**. Traps any syntax error that occurs in the class library and displays its message and associated help topic.

It would be possible to instantiate the **ClientApp** class and call its **ShowMsg** method to display the errors handled by the **TrapRunTime** and **TrapSyntax** methods. However, the **ShowRunTime** and **ShowSyntax** methods are called directly from within the **Error** class and, as a result, run faster because another class does not have to be instantiated. The way the **Error** class works, in its role as guardian of the class library's ActiveX component, is characterized by these specific attributes:

- Each public member of a public class in the class library contains an error handler to trap runtime errors.

- Each member implements data type mismatch and other syntax checking to the degree necessary to provide feedback to the client application programmer who is trying to call a member but is passing incorrect arguments. The class library safeguards the client application from unanticipated behavior caused by a member's execution. The golden rule, which I've mentioned before, but is certainly worth mentioning again is this: If there is any chance that a member could do the wrong thing—something not dictated by its functional specifications—then it does nothing.

- When handling a runtime or syntax error, the **Error** class follows these general steps. First, it displays an appropriate error message (unless it is being run as an RAO). Second, it creates a set of error codes that contain comprehensive information about the error. Third, it writes this error information to a file if the client application requests that service for a runtime error or if an unexpected runtime error occurs during the execution of a member. Fourth, it returns a **Variant** containing an array of error codes.

The TrapRunTime Method's Specifications

The **TrapRunTime** method handles any Visual Basic runtime error and displays its associated error message. If the error has a help topic in Visual Basic's Help file, that topic will also be able to be displayed. The topic in the class library's Help file (EFS.HLP) that specifies the detailed functionality of the **TrapRunTime** method is shown in the sidebar.

TrapRunTime method's specifications.

SYNTAX

```
Object.TrapRunTime(ErrObj, [Title], [Buttons], [Log], [IDClsLib])
```

The **TrapRunTime** method's syntax has the following object qualifier and named arguments:

- *Object.* Required. **Object** data type. An expression that evaluates to an object in the Applies To pop-up list.

- *ErrObj.* Required. **Object** data type. An expression that evaluates to VB's system-level **Err** object.

- *Title.* Optional. **Variant** data type whose subtype is a **String** expression that specifies the name of the procedure in which the runtime error occurred. *Title* appears in the title bar of the message box and cannot exceed 40 characters in length. If omitted, the default setting for *Title* is *Unknown Procedure*.

- *Buttons.* Optional. **Variant** data type whose subtype is an **Integer** expression that is the sum of values specifying the number and type of command buttons, icon (if any), default command button, and modality of the message box. If omitted, the default setting for *Buttons* is the Exclamation icon and the OK command button. See *Settings* below for the valid settings of *Buttons.*

- *Log.* Optional. **Variant** data type whose subtype is a **String** expression that specifies a valid path and ASCII text file to which an entry logging the runtime error is to be written. If the file does not yet exist, **TrapRunTime** creates it and writes the entry. If the file already exists, **TrapRunTime** opens it and appends the entry to the existing file. If *Log* is omitted, no entry is written.

- *IDClsLib.* Optional. **Variant** data type whose subtype is a **String** expression that specifies a security password. The correct password identifies the calling procedure as belonging to the class library. *IDClsLib* is only used internally; if you attempt to pass it when calling the method from a client application, a syntax error occurs.

SETTINGS

The first group of values (0 through 5) describes the number and type of command buttons displayed in the dialog box; the second group (16, 32, 48, 64) describes the icon style; the third group (0, 256, 512) determines which command button is the default; and the fourth group (0, 4096) determines the modality of the message box. When adding numbers to create a final value for *Buttons,* use only one number from each group. See the help topic titled *Visual Basic Constants: ShowMsg/TrapRunTime Methods* for the valid settings of the *Buttons* argument.

CALLED

From any procedure in a client application.

RETURNS

Upon success, eight elements in a **Variant**. The elements contain these subtypes:

- 0 - ERR_RESULT. An **Integer** from one to seven that specifies the command button the user chooses. See the help topic titled *Visual Basic Constants: ShowMsg/TrapRunTime Methods* for the valid settings of the ERR_RESULT element.

- 1 - ERR_SOURCE. A **String** that is the name of the method or property's procedure in which the runtime error occurred. If the *Title* argument was not passed, the default of *Unknown Procedure* is returned.

- 2 - ERR_NBR. An **Integer** that is the runtime error number.

- 3 - ERR_DESC. A **String** that is the description of the runtime error.

- 4 - ERR_HELPFILE. A **String** that specifies the path and name of the Help file containing the runtime error's help topic.

- 5 - ERR_CONTEXTID. An **Integer** that is the context ID number of the help topic for the runtime error.

- 6 - ERR_TIME. A **Date** that specifies the date and time of the runtime error.

- 7 - ERR_LOG. A **Boolean** that specifies whether information about the runtime error is written to a log file. It is **True** if a valid *Log* argument is passed, or **False** if the *Log* argument is not passed.

Upon failure, eight elements in a **Variant**. The elements contain these subtypes:

- 0 - ERR_RESULT. A **Boolean (False)** that specifies that a syntax or Visual Basic runtime error occurred while the **TrapRunTime** method itself was executing.

- 1 - ERR_SOURCE. A **String** that is "TrapRunTime".

- 2 - ERR_NBR. An **Integer** that is the error number.

- 3 - ERR_DESC. A **String** that is the description of the error.

- 4 - ERR_HELPFILE. A **String** that specifies the path and name of the help file containing the error's Help topic.

- 5 - ERR_CONTEXTID. An **Integer** that is the context ID number of the Help topic for the error.

- 6 - ERR_TIME. A **Date** that specifies the date and time of the error.

- 7 - ERR_LOG. A **Boolean** that specifies whether information about the error was written to the file ERRLOGRT.TXT, on the same path as the class library. **False** is returned if a syntax error occurs; **True** is returned if a runtime error occurs.

REMARKS

The **TrapRunTime** method does not relieve you of the need to enable an error-handling routine, with the **On Error** statement, in each procedure in the client application where a runtime error could occur.

Initialize/Terminate Events And Declarations

A **ClassModule** object has two events—**Initialize** and **Terminate**—that occur whenever it is instantiated and deinstantiated. These syntactical elements, which are described in detail here, were added to the language in VB4:

- **Initialize**. Occurs when an application creates an instance of a **Form**, **MDIForm**, **User** control, **Property Page**, or class. You write code in this event procedure to initialize any data used by the instance.

- **Terminate**. Occurs when all references to an instance of a **Form**, **MDIForm**, **User** control, **Property Page**, or class are removed from memory by setting all the variables that refer to the object to **Nothing** or when the last reference to the object falls out of scope. You write code in this event procedure to free any system resources used by an object reference, to close any files that were opened, and so on.

You can trigger the **Initialize** event of a **ClassModule** object in two ways. You use the **CreateObject** function to create an instance of a class, as in this code snippet:

```
' Declare a form-level object variable.
Dim Error As Object

' Instantiate Error class. Two parts of programmatic ID, delimited by dot, are:
' * EFSE (Project Name on General tab of Project Properties dialog box).
```

```
' * Error (Name property of ClassModule object).
Set Error = CreateObject("EFSE.Error")
```

Or, you can use the **As New** syntax to create an instance of a class, as in the following code snippet:

```
' Instantiate Error class to provide shared methods for Dialog class.
Private Error As New Error
```

Listing 8.1 shows the General Declarations section of ERROR.CLS.

Listing 8.1   General declarations in Error class.

```
' DLL functions:
#If Win32 Then

    Private Declare Function GetSystemDirectory& Lib "KERNEL32" _
                            Alias "GetSystemDirectoryA" _
                            (ByVal Buffer$, ByVal LenBuffer&)

#Else

    Private Declare Function GetSystemDirectory% Lib "KERNEL" _
                            (ByVal Buffer$, ByVal LenBuffer%)

#End If

' Class-level flags that are set in Initialize event
' procedure and are read by different members of class:
' * If cRAOServer is True, class is instantiated as RAO component.
' * If cEXEServer is True, class is instantiated as EXE component.
Private cRAOServer    As Boolean
Private cEXEServer    As Boolean

' Class-level variables:
Private cKeyword      As String

' Instantiate internal classes to reuse their members:
Private CL            As New CL
```

The two class-level **Boolean** variables are assigned their values in the **Initialize** event of the **Error** class:

```
' Check for RAO (Remote Automation Object) out-of-process
' component or local out-of-process, EXE component:
If Right$(App.Title, 1) = "R" Then cRAOServer = True
If Right$(App.Title, 1) = "E" Then cEXEServer = True
```

The code in the **Initialize** event works in this way: When you make the single set of Visual Basic source code that comprises the class library into the different kinds of ActiveX components, you signify the kind of component by adding a suffix (D, E, R, or 16 for DLL, EXE, RAO, or 16-bit, respectively) to the title of the project. You do this by setting the Title entry on the Make tab of the Project Properties dialog box when you make and register the ActiveX component, as shown in Figure 8.1.

If you use this naming scheme for the **Title** property of the ActiveX component, the class library can tell under what kind of component it is being run and, in the case of the **Error** class, turn on either the cRAOServer or cEXEServer class-level flag. If the class library is being run as an in-process DLL component, neither of these flags is turned on in the **Error** class.

The **Terminate** event of the **Error** class has this line of code:

```
' Free system resources associated with objects:
Set CL = Nothing
```

As I mentioned in Chapter 4, you should always explicitly free the system resources associated with any module-level object variables. There is one difference, however, between how you do this for a **ClassModule** object and how you do it for a **Form** object. In the case of a **Form** object, you should also explicitly set the **Name** property of the **Form** object to **Nothing**. You cannot do this with a **ClassModule** object. If you tried to add the statement

```
Set Error = Nothing
```

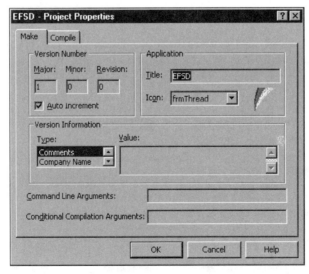

Figure 8.1   Signifying the type of ActiveX component.

to the **Terminate** event procedure, VB4 would display the syntax error message *Invalid use of property* when you tried to make the ActiveX component. It is unclear what this error message is trying to say because neither the object variable **Error** nor the keyword **Nothing** are properties. VB5 permits you to make the ActiveX component without raising a syntax error, but then it crashes when you attempt to reuse the **Error** object from a client application or internally. Simply put, neither VB4 nor VB5 will let you set the **Name** property of a **ClassModule** object to **Nothing** in its own **Terminate** event procedure.

The TrapRunTime Method's Code

The code for the **TrapRunTime** method and its related private members in the **Error** class is quite complex; we will not look at all of its features in this chapter. Our analysis of the **TrapRunTime** method's code in this section focuses on the new Visual Basic syntax that it uses, its associated methods, and a couple other noteworthy features unique to this method in the class library. The new syntactical elements we will tackle in this section are briefly described here:

- **Object**. An OLE Automation data type. If you want to pass a reference to a Visual Basic object to an argument in an ActiveX component's member, you must declare that argument as the data type **Object**.

- **TypeName**. A function that returns a string and provides information about a variable. In the book's class library, **TypeName** is used to determine what class or type of object is passed to an **Object** argument in a member.

- Returning an array. A **Function** procedure can return an array of values, if the values are first assigned to a **Variant**. For more information on this topic, see Chapter 5.

Parsing The Buttons Argument

We'll begin with the declaration of the **TrapRunTime** method:

```
Function TrapRunTime(ErrObj As Object, _
                Optional Title, _
                Optional Buttons, _
                Optional Log, _
                Optional IDClsLib)
```

The third argument of the **TrapRunTime** method, **Buttons**, is optional. It must be a **Variant** that contains an **Integer** or **Long** subtype. It has the same functionality as the second argument of the **ShowMsg** method of the **ClientApp** class (or Visual Basic's **MsgBox** function), and specifies the number and kind of buttons, icons (if any), default buttons, and modality of the error message box.

Because this argument can take any combination of 15 different values (as specified in Visual Basic's Help file, in the topic titled *MsgBox Function*) as a valid value, it is not feasible to syntax-check the argument with a brute force approach—there are just too many possible permutations to check. The class library's **CL** class contains a method called **ParseButtons**, shown in Listing 8.2, which is called by both the **ShowMsg** and **TrapRunTime** methods to validate their **Buttons** arguments.

Listing 8.2   ParseButtons method of CL class.

```
Function ParseButtons(Buttons, _
                    Member As String)

' _____

' Purpose: Parses Buttons argument of different members to
'           ensure valid value for creation of message box.
'
' Called:   Internally from members of class library.
'
' Accepts: Buttons: Variant whose subtype is Integer
'                   expression that specifies sum of values
'                   determining number and type of buttons to
'                   display, icon (if any), default button,
'                   and modality of message box.
'          Member:  String expression specifying name of
'                   member from which this method is called.
'
' Returns: Upon success, 5 elements in array contained in
'          Variant variable:
'
'          Element #    Constant        Value
'              0         PB_SUCCESS      True
'              1         PB_BTNS         Buttons setting
'              2         PB_ICON         Icon setting
'              3         PB_DEF_BTN      Default button setting
'              4         PB_SYS_MODAL    System modal setting
' _____

' Constants for elements in returned array:
Const PB_SUCCESS = 0
Const PB_BTNS = 1
Const PB_ICON = 2
Const PB_DEF_BTN = 3
Const PB_SYS_MODAL = 4
```

```
' Variables:
Dim RetVals(4) As Variant

If VarType(Buttons) <> vbInteger And _
   VarType(Buttons) <> vbLong Then
      E.TrapSyntax 4, Member, "Buttons", "Integer or Long"
End If

' Check system modal setting in Buttons argument and:
' * If it is 32-bit Windows, disallow it.
' * If it is 16-bit Windows, store Buttons
'   and strip it from Buttons argument.
If Buttons >= vbSystemModal Then

   #If Win32 Then
      E.TrapSyntax 7, Member, "Buttons"
   #Else
      RetVals(PB_SYS_MODAL) = True
      Buttons = Buttons - vbSystemModal
   #End If

End If

' Check default button setting in Buttons argument,
' store Buttons, and strip it from Buttons argument:
Select Case Buttons
   Case Is >= vbDefaultButton3
      RetVals(PB_DEF_BTN) = vbDefaultButton3
   Case Is >= vbDefaultButton2
      RetVals(PB_DEF_BTN) = vbDefaultButton2
   Case Else
      RetVals(PB_DEF_BTN) = vbDefaultButton1
End Select
Buttons = Buttons Mod 256

' Check icon setting in Buttons argument, store
' Buttons, and strip it from Buttons argument:
Select Case Buttons
   Case Is >= vbInformation
      RetVals(PB_ICON) = vbInformation
   Case Is >= vbExclamation
      RetVals(PB_ICON) = vbExclamation
   Case Is >= vbQuestion
      RetVals(PB_ICON) = vbQuestion
   Case Is >= vbCritical
      RetVals(PB_ICON) = vbCritical
End Select
Buttons = Buttons Mod 16

' Check buttons setting in Buttons argument and, if
' valid, store it and return all parameters, along
' with PB_SUCCESS = True to indicate success:
If Buttons < vbOKOnly Or Buttons > vbRetryCancel Then
   E.TrapSyntax 5, Member, "Buttons"
```

```
    Else
        RetVals(PB_SUCCESS) = True
        RetVals(PB_BTNS) = Buttons
        ParseButtons = RetVals
    End If

End Function
```

The **ParseButtons** method uses an algorithm that parses the value passed in to the **Buttons** argument, from the highest possible value (**vbSystemModal** or 4096) down to the lowest possible value (**vbOKOnly + vbApplication-Modal** or zero). As the algorithm works its way down through the four categories of possible values (modality, default button, kind of icon, and kinds of buttons), it subtracts, or parses out, the values associated with the first three categories. When it gets to the bottom of the parsing algorithm, all that can be left if **Buttons** is valid is a value from **vbOKOnly** (0) to **vbRetryCancel** (5).

The other important point that the **ParseButtons** method illustrates is a type of situation that calls for conditional compilation. Not all versions of Windows support the same set of features. The **ParseButtons** method's code checks whether or not the **Buttons** argument contains **vbSystemModal** (4096). If it does and the class library is running under 32-bit Windows, the syntax error message in Figure 8.2 appears.

Because the 32-bit version of Windows performs true multitasking, it does not permit a message box to be displayed as system modal. Visual Basic's **MsgBox** function permits you to set **Buttons** to **vbSystemModal** under 32-bit Windows, but this approach only makes the message box application modal. The constraint against system modality under 32-bit Windows is not documented in Visual Basic's Help file, but API32.HLP (which comes with Visual C++) indicates that the new input model for 32-bit Windows does not permit system modal windows.

Figure 8.2 Syntax error message related to system modality.

Using The Object And TypeName Syntaxes

The required **ErrObj** argument of the **TrapRunTime** method is declared as the OLE Automation data type **Object**. Remember, any ActiveX component's argument that takes an object reference can only be declared as the type **Object**.

The **TrapRunTime** method is designed to work with just the **ErrObj** argument, which must be passed Visual Basic's built-in **Err** object. The **TypeName** function is used to check what kind of an object reference has been passed to the OLE Automation **Object** data type. It returns a string corresponding to the class or type name of the object reference. VB5's class name for the **Err** object is ErrObject, so these initial lines of code in the **TrapRunTime** method syntax-check the **ErrObj** argument:

```
If TypeName(ErrObj) <> "ErrObject" Then
    On Error GoTo ET
    TrapSyntax 8, PROC, "ErrObj"
ElseIf ErrObj.Number < 1 Or ErrObj.Number > 65534 Then
    On Error GoTo ET
    TrapSyntax 5, PROC, "Number property of Err"
End If
```

For a list of the class or type names in Visual Basic's object hierarchy, select Language Reference | Objects on the Contents tab of Visual Basic's Help file. If you are using control objects on a form, their class or type names appear in the drop-down combo box at the top of the Properties window (to the right of the **Name** property of each control object).

The Error Message's Help Topic

Once **TrapRunTime** has validated its **ErrObj** argument and its four optional arguments, the method determines the path of Visual Basic's error Help file (VEENLR3.HLP in VB5 or VB.HLP in VB4) or MSJETERR.HLP (for Jet DAO errors) for the runtime error that occurred. Listing 8.3 shows the code to accomplish this task.

Listing 8.3   Code to find runtime error's Help file.

```
Function TrapRunTime(ErrObj As Object, _
                Optional Title, _
                Optional Buttons, _
                Optional Log, _
                Optional IDClsLib)

    . . .

    Select Case HelpFile
```

```
Case "MSJETERR.HLP"

    NumChars = GetSystemDirectory(WindowsPath, _
                                Len(WindowsPath))
    HelpFile = Left$(WindowsPath, CInt(NumChars)) & _
                "\" & HelpFile

    If Dir$(HelpFile) = NONE Then HelpFile = "NA"

    ErrHeader = "DAO error " & ErrNbr & " —" & vbCr & vbCr

Case "CMDLG96.HLP"

    NumChars = GetWindowsDirectory(WindowsPath, _
                                Len(WindowsPath))
    HelpFile = Left$(WindowsPath, CInt(NumChars)) & _
                "\HELP\" & HelpFile

    If Dir$(HelpFile) = NONE Then HelpFile = "NA"

    ErrHeader = "CommonDialog error " & _
        ErrNbr & " —" & vbCr & vbCr

Case Else

    If Dir$(HelpFile) = NONE Then HelpFile = "NA"

    ErrHeader = "VB error " & ErrNbr & " —" & vbCr & vbCr

    If Right$(HelpFile, 6) = "VB.HLP" Then
        cKeyword = "errors,errors,trappable"
    Else
        cKeyword = "trappable errors"
    End If

End Select

    . . .


End Function
```

By default, Microsoft Access installs the Help file MSJETERR.HLP on the Windows system path. If the runtime error is a Jet DAO error, the code in Listing 8.3 uses the Windows API function **GetSystemDirectory** to find the system directory. When you call it, you must first declare a fixed-length string variable (that is, **SystemPath**). **GetSystemDirectory** copies to the variable **SystemPath** the Windows system path (leaving any trailing null characters still in place in the fixed-length string) and returns the length, in characters, of the Windows system path. You then use Visual Basic's **Left$** function to parse out the path. The Jet DAO error message Help file, titled

Jet Error Help, is not included with VB5. If the current system does not have Microsoft Access or Microsoft Office Professional installed on it, then the Help file will not be found and the Help button will not be enabled on the error message box.

TrapRunTime also determines the help topic associated with the runtime error (from the *HelpFile* and *HelpContext* property settings of the **Err** object). VB displays three general kinds of runtime error messages and help topics when you use the **Raise** method of the **Err** object to artificially generate an error. First, it can display a specific message that matches the VBA runtime error that occurred. For example, the code in Listing 8.4 results in the error information displayed in Figure 8.3.

Listing 8.4 Code to display VBA error codes.

```
Private Sub Form_DblClick()

    ' Variable.
    Dim Msg As String

    ' Enable error handler and artificially generate runtime error:
    On Error Resume Next
    Err.Raise 3

    ' Display settings of Err object's properties and its help topic:
    Msg = "Err #: " & Err & vbCr
    Msg = Msg & "Desc: " & Err.Description & vbCr
    Msg = Msg & "Help File: " & Err.HelpFile & vbCr
    Msg = Msg & "Help #: " & Err.HelpContext
    MsgBox Prompt:=Msg, _
            Buttons:=vbInformation, _
            Title:="VBA Runtime Error", _
            HelpFile:=Err.HelpFile, _
            Context:=Err.HelpContext

End Sub
```

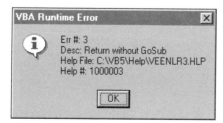

Figure 8.3 The **Err** object's settings for VBA errors.

Second, Visual Basic can display the generic runtime error 95 (Application-defined or object-defined error) for non-VBA errors that are generated artificially with the **Raise** method. Application-defined or object-defined errors occur when an error is generated using the **Err** object's **Raise** method or the **Error** statement, but the number does not correspond to an error defined by VBA. Such errors may be defined by the host application (for example, Excel or Visual Basic), but if you want to generate them from code, you must use the **Raise** method and fill in all relevant arguments. The **TrapRunTime** method maps a non-VBA error generated by the **Raise** method to its correct help topic number, but it still displays the generic runtime error 95 message. For example, the code in Listing 8.5 results in the error information displayed in Figure 8.4.

Listing 8.5   Code to display artificially generated, non-VBA error codes.

```
Private Sub Form_DblClick()

    ' Variable.
    Dim Msg As String

    ' Enable error handler and artificially generate runtime error:
    On Error Resume Next
    Err.Raise 400

    ' Display settings of Err object's properties and its help topic:
    Msg = "Err #: " & Err & vbCr
    Msg = Msg & "Desc: " & Err.Description & vbCr
    Msg = Msg & "Help File: " & Err.HelpFile & vbCr
    Msg = Msg & "Help #: " & Err.HelpContext
    MsgBox Prompt:=Msg, _
           Buttons:=vbInformation, _
           Title:="Artificially-Generated, Non-VBA Error Codes", _
           HelpFile:=Err.HelpFile, _
           Context:=Err.HelpContext

End Sub
```

Figure 8.4   The **Err** object's settings for artificially generated, non-VBA errors.

Figure 8.5 The VB help topic for artificially generated, non-VBA errors.

If you press F1 to see the help topic associated with the error message, the topic shown in Figure 8.5 is displayed.

Third, if a non-VBA runtime error actually occurs in an application (as opposed to artificially generating it), then the specific error message and help topic is displayed. For example, the code in Listing 8.6 results in the error information displayed in Figure 8.6.

Listing 8.6   Code to display runtime, non-VBA error codes.

```
Private Sub Form_DblClick()

    ' Variable.
    Dim Msg As String

    ' Enable error handler and cause actual runtime error:
    On Error Resume Next
    Show vbModal

    ' Display settings of Err object's properties and its help topic:
    Msg = "Err #: " & Err & vbCr
    Msg = Msg & "Desc: " & Err.Description & vbCr
    Msg = Msg & "Help File: " & Err.HelpFile & vbCr
    Msg = Msg & "Help #: " & Err.HelpContext
    MsgBox Prompt:=Msg, _
        Buttons:=vbInformation, _
        Title:="Runtime, Non-VBA Error Codes", _
        HelpFile:=Err.HelpFile, _
        Context:=Err.HelpContext

End Sub
```

Figure 8.6 The **Err** object's settings for runtime, non-VBA errors.

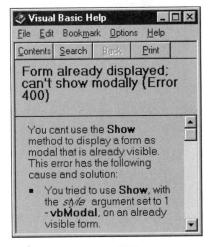

Figure 8.7 The VB help topic for runtime, non-VBA errors.

If you press F1 to see the help topic associated with the error message, the topic shown in Figure 8.7 is displayed.

I must also point out a bug in VB5 in regard to error messages and help topics for the three built-in ActiveX control objects. The runtime errors related to the **CommonDialog**, **Grid**, and **OLE Container** ActiveX controls are mapped by Visual Basic to non-existent help topics. For example, if you put a **CommonDialog** ActiveX control on a **Form** object, the code in Listing 8.7 results in the error information displayed in Figure 8.8 (if you click on Cancel from the Color dialog box).

Listing 8.7 Code to demonstrate missing help topics for CommonDialog errors.

```
Private Sub Form_DblClick()

    ' Variable.
    Dim Msg As String
```

```
' Enable error handler.
On Error Resume Next

' Set common dialog's CancelError property
' and display Color dialog box:
CommonDialog1.CancelError = True
CommonDialog1.ShowColor

' After user chooses Cancel (which causes runtime error 32,755),
' display settings of Err object's properties and its help topic:
Msg = "Err #: " & Err & vbCr
Msg = Msg & "Desc: " & Err.Description & vbCr
Msg = Msg & "Help File: " & Err.HelpFile & vbCr
Msg = Msg & "Help #: " & Err.HelpContext
MsgBox Prompt:=Msg, _
       Buttons:=vbInformation, _
       Title:="CommonDialog Error", _
       HelpFile:=Err.HelpFile, _
       Context:=Err.HelpContext

End Sub
```

If you press F1 to see the help topic associated with the error message, either the topic shown in Figure 8.9 is displayed or nothing happens at all.

Because of this bug, the **TrapRunTime** method remaps runtime errors for Visual Basic's built-in ActiveX control objects to different topics. In this example, **TrapRunTime** finds CMDLG96.HLP (it's located on the WINDOWS\HELP path) and remaps the error to the help topic titled

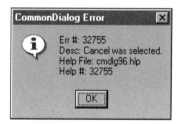

Figure 8.8   The **Err** object's settings for CommonDialog, non-VBA errors.

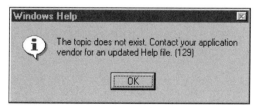

Figure 8.9   The Windows Help message (no topic found).

CommonDialog Error Constants. In other cases, when there is no specific help topic, it remaps the error to the generic help topic titled *Trappable Errors.*

So, if you put a **CommonDialog** control on a **Form** object in VB5, run the code in Listing 8.8, and click the Help button on the error message box, **TrapRunTime** displays the help topic shown in Figure 8.10. If you run the code in Listing 8.8 under VB4 and click the Help button, **TrapRunTime** displays the help topic shown in Figure 8.11.

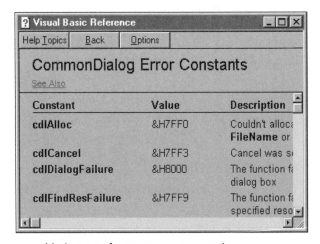

Figure 8.10 Remapped help topic for VB5 CommonDialog error.

Figure 8.11 Remapped help topic for VB4 CommonDialog error.

Listing 8.8   Code to demonstrate the remapped help topic for a CommonDialog error.

```
Private Sub Form_DblClick()

    ' Variable.
    Dim Error As Object

    ' Instantiate Error class:
    #If Win32 Then
        Set Error = CreateObject("EFSE.Error")
    #Else
        Set Error = CreateObject("EFS16.Error")
    #End If

    ' Enable error handler.
    On Error Resume Next

    ' Set common dialog's CancelError property
    ' and display Color dialog box:
    CommonDialog1.CancelError = True
    CommonDialog1.ShowColor

    ' After user chooses Cancel (which causes runtime error 32,755),
    ' handle it with TrapRunTime method of Error class:
    Error.TrapRunTime Err, "Form_DblClick"

End Sub
```

Splitting The Error Message

After the **TrapRunTime** method remaps a runtime error's help topic, if the error message (from the **Description** property of the **Err** object) is longer than 50 characters, the method runs the message through a private method in the **Error** class called **SplitMsg**. Because the **TrapRunTime** method uses the same routine to display an error message as the **ShowMsg** method does, no single line in the runtime error message can be longer than 50 characters (a specification of the *Prompt* argument of **ShowMsg**). The code for the **SplitMsg** method is shown in Listing 8.9.

Listing 8.9   Code for the private SplitMsg method.

```
Private Function SplitMsg(VBErrMsg As String) As String

    ' _____

    ' Purpose: Splits VB runtime error message into separate
    '          lines that do not exceed 50-character limit of
    '          ShowRunTime method.
    '
```

```
' Called:  Internally from TrapRunTime method.
'
' Accepts: VBErrMsg: String expression that is Description
'                    property of Err object.
'
' Returns: Reformatted error message.
' _____


' Constants for literals:
Const MAX_CHARS = 40

' Variables:
Dim TmpStr     As String
Dim NewMsg     As String
Dim Pos        As Byte
Dim LastPos    As Byte
Dim CharNbr    As Integer

' Initialize:
CharNbr = 1
TmpStr = VBErrMsg


' Until entire message has been examined—
' * Get position of next space in message line being parsed.
' * If space is more than 40 characters from start of line:
'    a) If it is last space, use position of previous space.
'    b) Replace space with carriage return character.
'    c) Add corrected line to other corrected lines.
'    d) Strip corrected line from message.
'    e) Reset character counter.
' * If no space is found and we've reached end of message:
'    a) Add last corrected line to other corrected lines.
'    b) Set exit condition for Do Until loop.
' * If space is found, but it is less than 40 characters from
'    start of line, update character counter and keep looking.
Do Until CharNbr = Len(VBErrMsg)

   Pos = InStr(CharNbr, TmpStr, Chr$(vbKeySpace))

   If CharNbr > MAX_CHARS Then

      If Pos = False Then Pos = LastPos

      NewMsg = NewMsg & Left$(TmpStr, Pos - 1) & vbCr
      TmpStr = Mid$(TmpStr, Pos + 1)
      CharNbr = 1
   ElseIf Pos = False Then
      NewMsg = NewMsg & TmpStr
      CharNbr = Len(VBErrMsg)
   Else
      CharNbr = Pos + 1
   End If
```

```
        LastPos = Pos

    Loop

    SplitMsg = NewMsg

End Function
```

Using the keyword Private

*The **Private** keyword, when used to declare a procedure, indicates that it is accessible only to other procedures in the module where it is declared. If procedures in a standard or class module are not explicitly declared using either the **Public** or **Private** keyword, they are public by default.*

The best that can be said for the algorithm that splits the runtime error message is that it works. It's not the most elegant code, but it does the job. The most important thing to note about the **SplitMsg** method (and all the other internal methods in the **CL** and **Error** classes) is that it does not enable an error handler. Instead, an error handler is enabled in the public member (in this example, **TrapRunTime**) that calls the internal, supporting method. Because of the way Visual Basic's own error-handling architecture works, if a runtime error occurs in a procedure that does not have an enabled error handler, Visual Basic works its way back down the stack of live procedures looking for an enabled error handler. The first enabled error handler that it finds is the one it uses to trap the error.

Not enabling error handlers in private, internal methods has three advantages:

- This approach minimizes the number of error handlers that have to be enabled throughout the ActiveX component.
- When a member fails and returns error codes to the client application, the ERR_SOURCE (1) element in the returned array always identifies the public member as the source of the error, not an internal member (whose name, of course, is unknown to the client application programmer and would just be confusing).
- This technique permits the **TrapSyntax** method to implement its own validation scheme in a similar and elegant way.

Logging And Returning Error Codes

The last thing the **TrapRunTime** method does is call a private method in the **Error** class called **LogError** to fill a **Variant** array with error codes, write them to a text file (if specified to do so), and return them to the client application. The **LogError** method performs these functions for both the **TrapRunTime** and **TrapSyntax** public methods because, although the error information itself is different, the number of elements in the array of error codes that each public method returns is the same. The code for the **LogError** method is shown in Listing 8.10.

Listing 8.10   Code for the private LogError method.

```
Private Function LogError(ErrNbr As Long, _
                          Procedure As String, _
                          ErrMsg As String, _
                          HelpFile As String, _
                          Context As Long, _
                          Log As String, _
                          Button As Byte)


' _____

' Purpose: Fills array with either runtime or syntax error
'          information to return to client application and
'          logs error in appropriate file.
'
' Called:  Internally from TrapRunTime or TrapSyntax members.
'
' Accepts: ErrNbr:    Long expression that specifies error #.
'          Procedure: String expression that specifies name of
'                     procedure in which error occurred.
'          ErrMsg:    String expression that specifies error
'                     message.
'          HelpFile:  String expression that specifies path
'                     and name of Help file containing error's
'                     help topic.
'          Context:   Long expression that specifies Help
'                     context number assigned to error's help
'                     topic.
'          Log:       String expression that specifies path
'                     and file to which to write log entry.
'                     If vbNullString is passed, no entry is
'                     made.
'          Button:    Byte expression that specifies either
'                     number of button user chose on runtime
'                     error message box or False.
'
' Returns: 8 elements in Variant.
'
'          El #  Constant           Value
'           0    ERR_RESULT         Number of button or False
```

```
'            1      ERR_SOURCE        Procedure containing error
'            2      ERR_NBR           Number of error
'            3      ERR_DESC          Description of error
'            4      ERR_HELPFILE      Help file with error topic
'            5      ERR_CONTEXTID     Context number of topic
'            6      ERR_TIME          Date/time error occurs
'            7      ERR_LOG           Logged to file (True/False)
' _____


' Constants for literals:
Const NO_LOG_FILE = vbNullString

' Variables:
Dim FileName     As String
Dim LogRetVal    As Boolean
Dim FileNbr      As Integer
Dim RetVals      As Variant

' * Specify error log file.
' * If error is to be logged to file:
'    a) Get next available file number and open log file.
'    b) Write blank separator line and 5 entry lines.
'    c) Close log file.
' * Set Codes custom property in ERRCODES.FRM for members
'    to read from their error handlers. Codes are stored
'    in FRM module because, if they are stored in Error
'    class, they go out of scope (when Terminate event
'    occurs) before their values can be read.
' * Return error information.
If Right(HelpFile, 6) = "VB.HLP" Or _
   Right(HelpFile, 12) = "MSJETERR.HLP" Then
      FileName = Log
Else
      FileName = App.Path & "\ERRLOGST.TXT"
End If

If Log <> NO_LOG_FILE Then
   FileNbr = FreeFile
   Open FileName For Append As FileNbr
   Print #FileNbr,
   Print #FileNbr, "- Entry for " & Now & " -"
   Print #FileNbr, "Source: " & Procedure
   Print #FileNbr, "Number: " & ErrNbr
   Print #FileNbr, "Description: " & ErrMsg
   Print #FileNbr, "HelpFile: " & HelpFile
   Print #FileNbr, "HelpContext: " & Context
   Close FileNbr
   LogRetVal = True
End If

RetVals = Array(Button, Procedure, ErrNbr, ErrMsg, _
            HelpFile, Context, Now, LogRetVal)
```

```
If Right$(FileName, 12) = "ERRLOGST.TXT" Then
    frmErrCodes.Codes = RetVals
End If

LogError = RetVals

End Function
```

The first five arguments of the **LogError** method replicate and are derived from properties of the **Err** object. The value of the sixth argument, **Log**, can either specify the path and file name to write the error information to or be **vbNullString** (that is, a zero-length string). The value of the seventh argument, **Button**, can vary, depending on the type of error. The possible combinations are:

- Syntax error. **False**. The only button the client application's programmer or user can choose from the error message box is OK, so there is no need to return a specific value for **Button**.

- Runtime error. **vbOK** (1) through **vbNo** (7). If the client application does not pass the optional *Buttons* argument to the **TrapRunTime** method, the *Button* argument of **LogError** is always **vbOK** (1). If the client application passes the optional *Buttons* argument, the *Button* argument for **LogError** depends on the button chosen from the error message box.

- Runtime error. **False**. If an unexpected runtime error occurs during the execution of a member of the class library, the only button the client application's programmer or user can choose from the error message box is OK, so there is no need to return a specific value for **Button**.

For syntax errors only, the **LogError** method temporarily stores the error codes in the **Codes** custom property of the frmErrCodes **Form** object of the class library. The codes are immediately read from there by the **TrapSyntax** method and returned to the client application. The reason why I take this approach, which technically violates the encapsulation of the **Error** class, is explained in detail in Chapter 9.

9
HANDLING SYNTAX ERRORS

As I mentioned earlier in the book, the general objective of the syntax checking method **TrapSyntax** in the **Error** class is to mimic Visual Basic's own handling of syntax errors. A class library written as an ActiveX component is, in a very real sense, an extension to Visual Basic's integrated development environment. So, when a client application programmer tries to use one of the methods of a class library, the class library's response when it is passed an invalid argument should simulate Visual Basic's response when a call to one of its methods uses incorrect syntax or an invalid argument.

If, for example, a client application programmer calls the **ShowMsg** method from the class library and passes it an invalid argument, the class library should respond in the same general way as Visual Basic itself does when you pass an invalid argument to its **MsgBox** function. The code in Listing 9.1 instantiates the class library's **ClientApp** class, calls its **ShowMsg** method, and passes an invalid value to the optional **HelpFile** argument (**HelpFile** is dependent on the **Context** argument and cannot be passed by itself). The class library handles the syntax error and responds by displaying the message box shown in Figure 9.1.

Listing 9.1   Sample syntax error handling with the class library.

```
Private Sub Form_DblClick()

    ' Declare object variable:
    Dim ClientApp As Object

    ' Instantiate class:
    #If Win32 Then
        Set ClientApp = CreateObject("EFSE.ClientApp")
    #Else
        Set ClientApp = CreateObject("EFS16.ClientApp")
    #End If

    ' Call object's member using named arguments,
    ' but pass invalid value to Buttons argument:
    ClientApp.ShowMsg Prompt:="Message", _
                      HelpFile:="C:\VBCLSLIB\EFS.HLP"

End Sub
```

The code in Listing 9.2 calls Visual Basic's **MsgBox** function and passes the same invalid value to the optional **HelpFile** argument (the dependent **Context** argument is not passed). Visual Basic handles the syntax error and responds by displaying the message box in Figure 9.2. Note that although the message box Visual Basic displays terms it a runtime error, what occurs is really more in the nature of a syntax error.

Listing 9.2   Sample syntax error-handling with VB.

```
Private Sub Form_DblClick()

    MsgBox Prompt:="Message", _
           HelpFile:="C:\VB5\VB.HLP"

End Sub
```

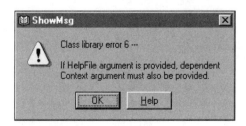

Figure 9.1   Syntax error message from the class library.

You should note several things about this comparison. As I mentioned a moment ago, the message box Visual Basic displays in Figure 9.2 calls the error a runtime error, when what occurs is really more in the nature of a syntax error. The next thing you should notice is that neither case requires that an error handler be enabled for a client application programmer to be told there is a syntax error. In addition, both approaches allow the client application programmer to get further information by clicking on the Help button the message box provides. Finally, you should note that the degree to which you provide specific feedback is arbitrary. In the case of Visual Basic, everyone knows that the syntax error messages are not as focused and precise as they could be. In the case of a class library, it is up to you to decide how specific you want the syntax error message to be; the syntax error messages in the book's class library provide very detailed feedback.

The TrapSyntax Method's Specifications

The **TrapSyntax** method handles any syntax error that occurs in the class library and displays its message and, if the client application programmer chooses Help or presses F1, its associated help topic. The topic in the class library's Help file (EFS.HLP) that specifies the detailed functionality of the **TrapSyntax** method is duplicated in the sidebar.

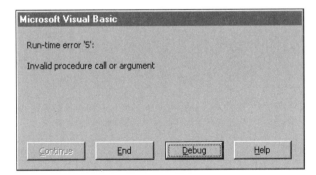

Figure 9.2 Syntax error message from Visual Basic.

The TrapSyntax method's specifications.

SYNTAX

```
Object.TrapSyntax(ErrNbr, Title, [IDStrs( )])
```

The **TrapSyntax** method's syntax has the following object qualifier and arguments:

- *Object*. Required. **Object** data type. An expression that evaluates to an object in the Applies To pop-up list.

- *ErrNbr*. Required. **Long** data type. A numeric expression that specifies the syntax error number.

- *Title*. Required. **String** data type. A **String** expression that specifies the name of the procedure in which the syntax error occurred. *Title* appears in the title bar of the message box and cannot exceed 40 characters in length.

- *IDStrs( )*. Optional. **Variant** data type. A **ParamArray** array of expressions that customize and identify the error message. The expressions must be passed individually, and there cannot be more than five expressions. When **TrapSyntax** is called internally, only **String** expressions are passed. If **TrapSyntax** is called from outside the class library, the first expression must be **True** and the other expressions must be **Strings**; if **True** is not passed when **TrapSyntax** is called externally, an untrapped OLE Automation runtime error occurs and the error codes are not returned.

CALLED

From any procedure in the class library or client application.

RETURNS

Upon success, eight elements in a **Variant**. The elements contain these subtypes:

- 0 - ERR_RESULT. A **Boolean** (**False**) that specifies that the public member of the class library (or a procedure in a client application) which was called failed to execute correctly.

- 1 - ERR_SOURCE. A **String** that is the name of the method or property's procedure in which the syntax error occurred.

- 2 - ERR_NBR. An **Integer** that is the syntax error number.

- 3 - ERR_DESC. A **String** that is the description of the syntax error.

- 4 - ERR_HELPFILE. A **String** that specifies the path and name of the Help file containing the syntax error's help topic.

- 5 - ERR_CONTEXTID. An **Integer** that is the context ID number of the help topic for the syntax error.

- 6 - ERR_TIME. A **Date** that specifies the date and time of the syntax error.

- 7 - ERR_LOG. A **Boolean** that specifies whether information about the syntax error was written to an error log. **False** is always returned for syntax error messages because the assumption is that the developer or tester of the class library will fix calls resulting in syntax errors at design time and not experience them at runtime.

Upon failure, eight elements in a **Variant**. The elements contain these subtypes:

- 0 - ERR_RESULT. A **Boolean** (**False**) that specifies that a syntax or Visual Basic runtime error occurred while the **TrapSyntax** method itself was executing.

- 1 - ERR_SOURCE. A **String** that is "TrapSyntax".

- 2 - ERR_NBR. An **Integer** that is the error number.

- 3 - ERR_DESC. A **String** that is the description of the error.

- 4 - ERR_HELPFILE. A **String** that specifies the path and name of the Help file containing the error's help topic.

- 5 - ERR_CONTEXTID. An **Integer** that is the context ID number of the help topic for the error.

- 6 - ERR_TIME. A **Date** that specifies the date and time of the error.

- 7 - ERR_LOG. A **Boolean** (**True**) that specifies that information about the error was written to a log file on the same path as the class library. Runtime errors are logged in ERRLOGRT.TXT and syntax errors in ERRLOGST.TXT.

REMARKS

- The **TrapSyntax** method and the error messages it supports can be called by external procedures not contained in the class library.

- Because the **TrapSyntax** method has a **ParamArray** optional argument, it cannot take named arguments. If you try to call the member using named arguments, Visual Basic displays OLE Automation runtime error 446 ("Object doesn't support named arguments") or 448 ("Named argument not found").

The TrapSyntax Method's Code

The code for the **TrapSyntax** method in the **Error** class is quite straightforward. Because we have studied the **TrapRunTime** method (and its related private methods) in Chapter 8, understanding how **TrapSyntax** works will not be too difficult. The only new syntactical element in the **TrapSyntax** method is the **ParamArray** keyword. The **ParamArray** keyword, which is the most complex piece of syntax in VB5, allows the use of an optional argument that is a **Variant** array. The argument's **Variant** array can contain any number of elements and each element can be any data type except a user-defined data type.

The flow of the **TrapSyntax** method's code and execution is a little more complex than that of the **TrapRunTime** method. Assuming that the method is being called from within the class library, the basic flow of **TrapSyntax** is detailed here:

- The method is passed required and optional arguments from any public member that detects a syntax error.
- The method enables its own error handler at the beginning of itself.
- The method syntax-checks the values passed to its arguments (this is primarily to check calls from procedures in a client application and to assist in debugging the class library).

- Based on the required **ErrNbr** argument and the optional **IDStrs( )** array of customizing strings, the method constructs the appropriate error message.

- The method calls the private **ShowSyntax** method to display the error message.

- The method calls the private **LogError** method to write the error information to a file (only if some runtime or syntax error occurred during its own execution) and to temporarily store the error codes (via a **Property Let** procedure in the frmErrCodes **Form** object).

- The method disables its own error handler with an **On Error GoTo 0** statement.

- The method uses VB's **Raise** method to set the **Number** property of the **Err** object to **True** (-1). This does two things. First, it sets **Number** to a predefined value that tells the calling member that a syntax error has occurred. Second, it reroutes code execution back to the error handler in the calling public member.

- The public member reads the value of the **Number** property of the **Err** object, sees that it is **True** (Const SYNTAX = TRUE), reads the error codes that were stored in the frmErrCodes **Form** object (via a **Property Get** procedure), and returns them to the client application.

Validating The ParamArray IDStrs( ) Argument

Let's begin by examining the declaration of the **TrapSyntax** method, which is shown here:

```
Function TrapSyntax(ErrNbr As Long, _
                    Title As String, _
                    ParamArray IDStrs())
```

The third argument of the **TrapSyntax** method, **IDStrs( )**, is a **ParamArray** optional argument that must be a **Variant** array. If passed, the subtype of the first element of the zero-based **Variant** array is normally a **String** that customizes the syntax error message. However, if **TrapSyntax** is called externally from a client application, **IDStrs( )** is no longer optional; it must be passed and the subtype of the first element must be a **Boolean** that evaluates to **True**.

Whether called internally from a public member of the class library or externally from a client application, the **IDStrs( )** argument can accept from one to four strings to customize a syntax error message. The customization scheme, if used, is a function of the given error message. For example, the message for syntax error 4 takes two customization strings (<Name> argument must be <kind> expression). There are currently 48 different syntax error messages in the class library. You can find a list of them in the class library's Help file (EFS.HLP) under the search words *error numbers*. Each syntax error message's help topic specifies its customization scheme (if any).

The code to validate the **Title** and **IDStrs( )** arguments is shown in Listing 9.3.

Listing 9.3 Validation code in the TrapSyntax method.

```
Function TrapSyntax(ErrNbr As Long, _
                    Title As String, _
                    ParamArray IDStrs())

    ' Constants for literals:
    Const SYNTAX = True
    Const ERR_LOG = 7
    Const MAX_CHARS = 40
    Const MAX_ITEMS = 5
    Const FIRST_IDSTR = 0
    Const NO_LOG_FILE = vbNullString
    Const NO_TITLE = vbNullString
    Const NO_ARG_NM = vbNullString
    Const CONTEXT_BASE_NBR = 10000
    Const IE_TITLE = -1001
    Const IE_IDSTRS1 = -1002
    Const IE_IDSTRS2 = -1003
    Const IE_ERR_NBR = -1004
    Const IE_EXTERNAL = -1005
    Const ID = "I believe in the resurrection of the body"


    ' Variables:
    Dim Msg          As String
    Dim ErrMsg       As String
    Dim HelpClassLib As String
    Dim LogFile      As String
    Dim External     As Boolean
    Dim Str          As Integer
    Dim FirstIDStr   As Integer
    Dim InternalErr  As Integer
    Dim Strs(1 To 5) As String

    ' Enable error handler and do syntax checking:
    On Error GoTo ET
```

```
    If Title = NO_TITLE Then
        Title = "TrapSyntax"
    ElseIf VarType(Title) <> vbString Then
        InternalErr = IE_TITLE
        GoTo ET
    ElseIf Len(Title) > MAX_CHARS Then
        InternalErr = IE_TITLE
        GoTo ET
    End If


    ' If IDStrs() argument is passed, check it for:
    ' * Invalid upper bound.
    ' * Invalid first element (if called externally).
    ' * Elements to customize message that are not strings.
    ' Read customization strings and assign them to variables.
    If Not IsMissing(IDStrs) Then

        If UBound(IDStrs) > MAX_ITEMS - 1 Then
            InternalErr = IE_IDSTRS1
            GoTo ET
        ElseIf VarType(IDStrs(FIRST_IDSTR)) <> vbString Then

            If IDStrs(FIRST_IDSTR) <> True Then
                InternalErr = IE_EXTERNAL
                GoTo ET
            Else
                External = True
                FirstIDStr = 1
            End If

        End If

        For Str = FirstIDStr To UBound(IDStrs)

            If VarType(IDStrs(Str)) <> vbString Then
                InternalErr = IE_IDSTRS2
                GoTo ET
            Else

                If FirstIDStr = 1 Then
                    Strs(Str) = IDStrs(Str)
                Else
                    Strs(Str + 1) = IDStrs(Str)
                End If

            End If

        Next Str

    End If

    . . .

End Function
```

If any validation check of the **Title** and **IDStrs( )** arguments fails, the relevant internal syntax error number is set and the **TrapSyntax** method is aborted. Execution is rerouted to the enabled error handler at the bottom of the method, where the internal error number is read and the internal syntax error message is displayed.

Constructing The Syntax Error Message

Now that you understand the validation check, we need to examine the code that constructs the syntax error message. Listing 9.4 shows the code to accomplish this task.

Listing 9.4   Code to construct message in TrapSyntax method.

```
Function TrapSyntax(ErrNbr As Long, _
                    Title As String, _
                    ParamArray IDStrs())

    . . .

    ' Construct message related to syntax error number (Case
    ' Else below traps for invalid ErrNbr argument):
    If External Then
        ErrMsg = "Error " & ErrNbr & " ---" & vbCr
    Else
        ErrMsg = "Class library error " & ErrNbr & " ---" & vbCr
    End If

    Select Case ErrNbr

        Case 1
            Msg = "Member cannot run under " & Strs(1)

        Case 2
            Msg = Strs(1) & " argument is invalid." & vbCr
            Msg = Msg & "It cannot exceed " & Strs(2)
            Msg = Msg & " characters."

        Case 3
            Msg = "Prompt argument is invalid." & vbCr
            Msg = Msg & "A line exceeds 50 characters."

        Case 4
            Msg = Strs(1) & " argument must be "
            Msg = Msg & Strs(2) & " expression."

        . . .

        Case 48
            Msg = "File " & Strs(1) & " is not found." & vbCr
```

```
    Case Else
        InternalErr = IE_ERR_NBR
        GoTo ET

  End Select

End Function
```

There are a few things I'd like to discuss in regard to this code. First, if you can use either the **If...Then...Else** statement or the **Select Case** statement in a given situation, then you should use **Select Case**, which runs anywhere from 30 to 400 percent faster than the **If...Then...Else** statement. The farther down in the selection levels the **True** condition is encountered, the greater the performance benefit. In addition, because of the way the **Error** class and its **TrapSyntax** method are designed, you can easily add new syntax error messages to the class library by writing additional **Case** statements and their messages above the **Case Else** statement (Case 49, Case 50, and so on). The last **Case Else** statement syntax-checks the **ErrNbr** argument. If **ErrNbr** is not one of the existing syntax error numbers, execution is rerouted to the enabled error handler at the bottom of the method.

To understand how the customizing strings of the **IDStrs( )** argument work with a specific error message, you can look at the help topic for that error message in EFS.HLP. For example, syntax error 4 takes two customizing strings. If you look under the search words *error numbers* in EFS.HLP, you can display the help topic for error 4, as in Figure 9.3.

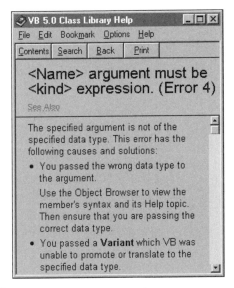

Figure 9.3   Help topic for syntax error message 4.

Displaying The Message And Returning The Codes

Moving right along, the code that displays the syntax error message and stores the error codes is in Listing 9.5.

Listing 9.5   Code to display message and return codes in the TrapSyntax method.

```
Function TrapSyntax(ErrNbr As Long, _
                    Title As String, _
                    ParamArray IDStrs())

    . . .

    ErrMsg = ErrMsg & vbCr & Msg & vbCr

    If Not cRAOServer Then
        ShowSyntax Prompt:=ErrMsg, _
                Title:=CStr(Title), _
                Context:=ErrNbr + CONTEXT_BASE_NBR
    End If

    HelpClassLib = App.Path & "\EFS.HLP"
    LogError ErrNbr:=ErrNbr, _
            Procedure:=CStr(Title), _
            ErrMsg:=Msg, _
            HelpFile:=HelpClassLib, _
            Context:=ErrNbr + CONTEXT_BASE_NBR, _
            Log:=NO_LOG_FILE, _
            Button:=False

    If External Then
        TrapSyntax = frmErrCodes.Codes
    Else
        On Error GoTo 0
        Err.Raise Number:=SYNTAX
    End If

    . . .

End Function
```

A few points of interest in this code: The syntax error message is not displayed by the class library if it is running as an out-of-process ActiveX RAO component. Notice also that the private **LogError** method is called to store the error codes. We worked through this procedure in Chapter 8, so I won't go into any more detail here. Finally, if **TrapSyntax** was called externally (that is, the **Boolean** variable External is **True**), the method immediately returns the error codes to the client application. However, if the method was called internally, it disables its own error handler and generates a runtime error whose **Number** property is set to **True**. This signals to the calling member of the class library that a syntax error has occurred and reroutes code execution back to the error handler in the calling member.

Stepping Through The Syntax-Checking Algorithm

As you are aware by now, the algorithm that the book's class library uses to handle syntax checking is not confined to the **TrapSyntax** method. Rather, it begins in the public member whose services are being used. At this point, the algorithm may call related internal methods in the **CL** class, then call the **TrapSyntax** method to construct and display the error message, and so on.

The best way to ensure that you understand how the class library handles syntax checking is to step through this example:

1. Open the class library's project EFSE.VBP in 32-bit Visual Basic.

2. Select the **Error** class, select the statement **On Error GoTo 0** (toward the bottom of the **TrapSyntax** method), and then select Debug | Toggle Breakpoint (or click the toolbar's shortcut button).

3. Select the **ClientApp** class, select the statement **If Err = SYNTAX Then ShowMsg = frmErrCodes.Codes** (toward the bottom of the **ShowMsg** method), then select Debug | Toggle Breakpoint.

4. Select Tools | Options to display the Options dialog box.

5. Display the General tab and select the Error Trapping - Break on Unhandled Errors option button. When internally testing the syntax-checking capabilities of the class library, the Break on Unhandled Errors setting must be selected to simulate the behavior of the class library when it is called externally.

6. Enter the code in Listing 9.6 in the **Form_DblClick** event procedure of a code-free Form1.

Listing 9.6   Tracing syntax error-handling within the class library.

```
Private Sub Form_DblClick()

    ' Declare object variable:
    Dim ClientApp As Object
```

```
' Instantiate class:
#If Win32 Then
    Set ClientApp = CreateObject("EFSE.ClientApp")
#Else
    Set ClientApp = CreateObject("EFS16.ClientApp")
#End If

' Call object's member using named arguments,
' but pass invalid value to Buttons argument:
ClientApp.ShowMsg Prompt:="Message", _
                  HelpFile:="C:\VBCLSLIB\EFS.HLP"

End Sub
```

Select Run | Start and double click on the **Form** object. The **TrapSyntax** method displays syntax error message 6; when you close the message box, code execution breaks on the statement **On Error GoTo 0** as in Figure 9.4.

This is the point where the flow of the syntax-checking algorithm in the class library gets a little tricky. When you select Run | Continue, **TrapSyntax** disables its own error handler (with the **On Error GoTo 0** statement) and generates a runtime error whose **Number** property is set to **True** (with the **Err.Raise Number:=SYNTAX** statement, where SYNTAX is a constant whose value is -1). The reason this is done is to force code execution to reroute back to the error handler (that is, the line label ET) in the calling member. At that point, code execution breaks on the statement **If Err = SYNTAX Then ShowMsg = frmErrCodes.Codes** as in Figure 9.5.

Now you can single-step through the remainder of the code to see how the **ShowMsg** method completes the following tasks. You should be able to see where **ShowMsg**:

- Reads that the **Number** property of the **Err** object equals **True** (that is, **Err = SYNTAX**, where SYNTAX is a constant that equals **True**).

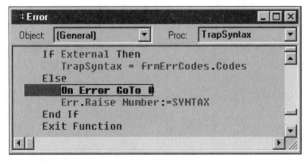

Figure 9.4　The **TrapSyntax** method's code paused.

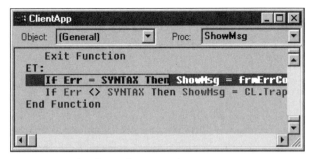

Figure 9.5   The **ShowMsg** method's code paused.

- Goes to the **Property Get** procedure named **Codes** in the frmErrCodes **Form** object.

- Reads the values of the error codes that were previously set by the **LogError** method.

- Returns the error codes in the **Variant** that is passed back to the client application.

Making The Error Class Stand Alone

The **Error** class is one of the most useful objects in the book's class library. If you were to decide that you want to pull it out of the book's class library and put it in a standalone ActiveX component, simply follow these steps:

1.   Copy the members of the **CL** class used by the **Error** class and its associated **Form** object to the appropriate modules. Table 9.1 lists the members whose code you should copy to the clipboard and the modules to paste the code into. Remember to copy the beginning and ending stubs of each member. After you copy these five members, change their declarations by prefixing them with the **Private** keyword.

2.   In ERROR.CLS, remove the declaration **Private CL As New CL** from the General Declarations section, remove the existing code from the **Initialize** and **Terminate** events, and replace all instances of the string "CL." with an empty string (set the find-and-replace dialog box to Current Module and Match Case). Four instances should be replaced.

3. In SHOWMSG.FRM, remove the declaration **Private CL As New CL** from the General Declarations section, remove the statement **Set CL = Nothing** from the **Form_Unload** event, and replace all instances of the string "CL." with an empty string (set the find-and-replace dialog box to Current Module and Match Case). Two instances should be replaced.

4. Copy the Windows API function declarations listed in Table 9.2 from the General Declarations section of the **CL** class to the General Declarations sections of ERROR.CLS and SHOWMSG.FRM.

5. Copy the user-defined data types listed in Table 9.3 from the General Declarations section of the **CL** class to the General Declarations sections of ERROR.CLS and SHOWMSG.FRM.

6. In ERROR.CLS, replace all instances of the string "E." with an empty string (set the find-and-replace dialog box to Current Module and Match Case). Six instances should be replaced.

7. Select the file STARTUP.BAS and remove the general declarations and the code in **Sub Main**, but leave the **Sub Main** procedure's stubs intact.

8. Save the files ERRCODES.FRM, ERROR.CLS, SHOWMSG.FRM, and STARTUP.BAS to the directory where you will create the VB project that is to become the new ActiveX component.

9. Start a new Visual Basic ActiveX DLL or EXE project and remove Class1 from it. Next, select Project | Add File and add the four files you saved to the new project.

10. Select Project | Properties and make the necessary entries to the General tab of the Project Properties dialog box (Project Type, StartUp Object, and so on). Ensure that the Startup Object is **Sub Main**.

11. Select File | Make Project to make and register the ActiveX component, and then save the Visual Basic project. For a reminder of the details involved in Steps 8 and 9, see Chapter 3.

12. Test the **TrapRunTime** and **TrapSyntax** methods of the new ActiveX component that contains the revised **Error** class.

If you religiously followed the preceding sequence of steps, you should have ended up with a standalone error-handling class in the form of an ActiveX component. You also will have learned the hard way the value of adhering as strictly as possible to the OOP attribute of encapsulation. Even though I only violate encapsulation in the book's class library in one

Table 9.1 Members to copy from **CL** class.

Member To Copy	Modules To Paste Into
IsTitle	ERROR.CLS
IsUnloadFromApp	SHOWMSG.FRM
IsWin95Shell	SHOWMSG.FRM & ERROR.CLS
ParseButtons	ERROR.CLS
ParseMsg	ERROR.CLS

Table 9.2 Windows API function declarations to copy from **CL** class.

API Function To Copy	Modules To Paste Into
FindWindow (16/32-bit)	SHOWMSG.FRM & ERROR.CLS
GetTextExtent (16-bit)	ERROR.CLS
GetTextExtentPoint32 (32-bit)	ERROR.CLS

Table 9.3 User-defined data types to copy from **CL** class.

Data Type To Copy	Modules To Paste Into
SIZE (32-bit)	ERROR.CLS

general way (placing procedures called by more than one module into the private **CL** class), you can see what a hassle it is to pull together the necessary members and declarations for a standalone class. Just in case you couldn't get the standalone error class to work, you can find a copy of all the files needed to make it into an ActiveX component on the path C:\VBOOPEFS\ERRORCLS. The project name is ERRCLS.VBP. Just open it in VB5 and select File|Make ERRCLS.DLL and you'll have a robust, commercial-quality error handler.

10
SUBCLASSING VISUAL
BASIC OBJECTS

I n object-oriented programming, a *subclass* is a class that is created from another class, called the *superclass*. In the purest sense of the term, a language that supports subclassing permits you to do several things to a superclass. First, a subclass inherits all the members (that is, methods, properties, and events) of its superclass. Second, you can create new members for the subclass to enhance its functionality and improve upon the superclass. Third, you can override the behavior of existing members of the superclass by modifying their behavior or restricting access to them.

VB5 still does not really support inheritance, at least in the sense that the term is used in conjunction with pure OOP languages like Smalltalk and Eiffel. There were rumors at one point that support for simple inheritance would be added to VB5; but, as of the Beta2 release and based on material in VB's Help file and Visual Basic Books Online, that is not the case. There is a new VB Add-In called the Class Builder Utility, which can help a developer to implement a kind of inheritance called *containment*. However, this is not what most OOP developers have in mind when they use the term inheritance.

In Chapter 10, we examine how you can use Visual Basic to create classes that, in an effective way, subclass its own **Form** and control objects but without using inheritance. The book's class library includes the **Dialog**, **Graphic**, **List**, and **Text** classes, which contain members that subclass **ComboBox**, **DBCombo**, **DBList**, **Form**, **Image**, **ListBox**, **PictureBox**, **RichTextBox**, and **TextBox** objects. In addition, the **File** class contains some members that subclass the appearance and behavior of the **CommonDialog** ActiveX control. In this chapter, we'll focus on the members of the **List**, **Graphic**, and **Dialog** classes; we'll save the members of the **File** and **Text** classes for a later chapter.

As you will see, we'll often be using Windows API functions when subclassing Visual Basic controls. We take this approach for two reasons. First, most types of functionality omitted by the developers of Visual Basic, which you would want to add to a control object, are governed by what the Windows operating system and its API permit you to do. Second, performance is always an issue in this type of work; adding additional features to a control object is self-defeating if the perceived response time of the control is no longer acceptable.

Subclassing VB's List Controls

We'll begin our discussion on subclassing the list controls with an introduction to the **List** class. The **List** class is composed of seven public members that subclass Visual Basic's **ComboBox**, **DBCombo**, **DBList**, or **ListBox** objects. The name of each public member and a description of its purpose are shown in Table 10.1.

Of the methods in the **List** class, the ones that best illustrate VB5's ability to subclass its own control objects in a non-polymorphic way are the **FillWithDAO**, **CopyItems**, and **FindItem** methods. We'll be examining these methods in this chapter. The other methods are designed and work in a similar way. You can examine the code for them in the class library and view their help topics in EFS.HLP.

Listing 10.1 shows the class-level declarations of the **List** class.

Table 10.1 The public members of the **List** class.

Member	Description
Center	Centers certain VB objects, including list-related ones, within the client area of their parent or container objects.
CopyItems	Copies selected item(s) from one ListBox control object to another.
DeleteItems	Deletes selected item(s) from a list-related control object.
FillWithDAO	Fills a list-related control object with items from a database, using Jet Data Access Objects syntax.
FillWithDataCtl	Fills a list-related control object with items from a database accessed by a Data object.
Load	Loads a specified file into certain VB control objects, including list-related ones.
Save	Saves the contents of certain VB control objects, including list-related ones, to a specified file.

Listing 10.1 Class-level declarations of List class.

```
' User-defined data types:
#If Win32 Then

    Private Type RECT
        Lft As Long
        Top As Long
        Rgt As Long
        Bot As Long
    End Type

#Else

    Private Type RECT
        Lft As Integer
        Top As Integer
        Rgt As Integer
        Bot As Integer
    End Type

#End If

' DLL functions:
#If Win32 Then

    Private Declare Function GetClientRect& Lib "USER32" _
                    (ByVal hWnd&, Rct As RECT)
    Private Declare Function SendMessage& Lib "USER32" _
                    Alias "SendMessageA" _
                    (ByVal hWnd&, ByVal Msg&, _
                    ByVal Param&, Param As Any)
```

```
        Private Declare Function SendMsg& Lib "USER32" _
                              Alias "SendMessageA" _
                              (ByVal hWnd&, ByVal Msg&, _
                              ByVal Param&, ByVal Param$)

    #Else

        Private Declare Function GetClientRect% Lib "USER" _
                              (ByVal hWnd%, Rct As RECT)
        Private Declare Function SendMessage& Lib "USER" _
                              (ByVal hWnd%, ByVal Msg%, _
                              ByVal Param%, Param As Any)
        Private Declare Function SendMsg& Lib "USER" _
                              Alias "SendMessage" _
                              (ByVal hWnd%, ByVal Msg%, _
                              ByVal Param%, ByVal Param$)

    #End If

    ' Instantiate internal classes to reuse their members:
    Private CL   As New CL
    Private E    As New Error
```

The **Terminate** event of the **List** class has this code:

```
' Free system resources associated with objects:
Set CL = Nothing
Set E = Nothing
```

At this point in the book, the preceding code should be second nature to you. However, you might wonder why there is no code in the **Initialize** event of the **List** class. All the members of the **List** class are able to be run under all types of ActiveX components (in-process, out-of-process local, and out-of-process remote), so there is no reason to use the **Initialize** event to determine the kind of ActiveX component being run.

Filling A List From A Database

Although Visual Basic provides a data-bound list box (the **DBList** object), it is part of an ActiveX control file (DBLIST32.OCX or DBLIST16.OCX) that is about 150 K in size. One reason this file is so large is that it supports both the **DBList** object and the **DBCombo** object. In many situations, you will not want to include such a large ActiveX control in your project. Instead, you could write code to fill the **ComboBox** object or **ListBox** object with data from a **Database** object created with DAO (Data Access Objects) syntax. The **FillWithDAO** method does this. The topic in the class library's Help file (EFS.HLP) that specifies the detailed functionality of the **FillWithDAO** method is shown in the sidebar.

The FillWithDAO method's specifications.

SYNTAX

```
Object.FillWithDAO(CboOrLst, Dbs, Rst, Field, [Order])
```

The **FillWithDAO** method's syntax has the following object qualifier and named arguments:

- *Object*. Required. **Object** data type. An expression that evaluates to an object in the Applies To pop-up list.

- *CboOrLst*. Required. **Object** data type. An expression that evaluates to the **Name** property of a Visual Basic control object in the Applies To pop-up list (**ComboBox** or **ListBox**).

- *Dbs*. Required. **Object** data type. An expression that evaluates to the **Name** property of a **Database** object.

- *Rst*. Required. **Object** data type. An expression that evaluates to the **Name** property of a **Recordset** object.

- *Field*. Required. **Variant** data type whose subtype is a **String** or numeric expression that specifies a **Field** object in a **Recordset** object which contains the items to fill the list with. **Field** can be passed either as an index value (zero, one, two, and so on) or as the **Name** property of the **Field** object.

- *Order*. Optional. **Variant** data type whose subtype is a numeric expression that must evaluate to zero (for an ascending sort) or to one (for a descending sort). If a value other than zero or one is passed to **Order**, it defaults to zero.

CALLED

From any procedure in a client application.

RETURNS

Upon success, one element in a **Variant**. It contains a **Boolean** (**True**) that specifies the member executed successfully.

Upon failure, eight elements in a **Variant**. The elements contain the error codes that the class library returns when a runtime or syntax error occurs during the execution of one of its members.

> ## REMARKS
>
> - If the **Sorted** property of the **CboOrLst** argument's object reference is **True**, the **Sorted** property's setting sorts the items even if the **Order** argument is not passed.
>
> - If the **Sorted** property of the **CboOrLst** argument's object reference is **True**, setting the **Order** argument to 1 (descending) results in a conflict and a class library syntax error.

PASSING ARGUMENTS BYREF VS. BYVAL

It is important to understand some points about the difference between passing a value to an argument in an ActiveX component's member by reference or by value. The VB Help file, in the help topic titled *Function Statement*, describes these two ways of passing an argument:

- Passing a value to an argument declared **ByRef** in a procedure is Visual Basic's default approach. In this case, Visual Basic passes a pointer to the address of the value, rather than a copy of the value, to the argument of the procedure. This allows the procedure to access the actual variable and, as a result, change it.

- Passing a value to an argument declared **ByVal** in a procedure is Visual Basic's other possible approach. In this case, Visual Basic passes a copy of the value, rather than its address, to the argument of the procedure. The variable itself cannot be accessed by the procedure and, as a result, its value cannot be changed.

However, this distinction between declaring and passing arguments **ByVal** and **ByRef** is not true for all Visual Basic data types. It is true for the traditional data types such as **String**, **Integer**, **Long**, and so on, but it is not true when you declare and pass an **Object** data type, which is effectively always passed by reference. Even if you declare an object argument **ByVal**, after VB performs the method's operation on the copy of the object, it will replace the original object in the client application with the modified copy of the object.

If you want to modify an object within a procedure, while leaving the original object intact, you must make a new instance or copy of the object with the **As New** statement. All the public members of the book's class library that take arguments of the **Object** data type are designed to operate on the object in the client application, not on a new instance or copy of it.

The **CboOrLst** argument of the **FillWithDAO** method is declared as the generic OLE Automation **Object** data type. An ActiveX component's argument, to which an object reference is to be passed, can only be declared as this kind of object data type. The sample code for the **FillWithDAO** method in EFS.HLP fills a **ListBox** object with items from the sample database that comes with Visual Basic (BIBLIO.MDB) as shown in Figure 10.1.

Speeding things up with ByRef

*Passing variables as Visual Basic's default of **ByRef** is 3 to 4 percent faster than passing them **ByVal**.*

INABILITY TO OVERRIDE VB OBJECT'S PROPERTY SETTING

Your ability to subclass a Visual Basic control object is constrained in one way. If the property of a Visual Basic control object is read-only at runtime, you may or may not be able to override its setting when you subclass it. For example, the **ComboBox** and **ListBox** objects have the **Sorted** property, which can only be set at design time in Visual Basic's Properties window.

In VB4, you could, for a **Form** object with a **ListBox** control object, write the statement

```
List1.Sorted = True
```

and try to compile it. However, the executable will not compile, and the error message in Figure 10.2 will be displayed.

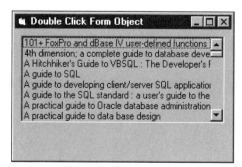

Figure 10.1 Example of the **FillWithDAO** method.

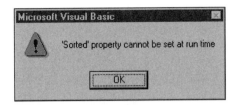

Figure 10.2 VB4 error message—property read-only at runtime.

In VB5, if you write the same statement

```
List1.Sorted = True
```

and try to run it, the syntax error message in Figure 10.3 will be displayed.

So it is clear that the **FillWithDAO** method cannot set the **Sorted** property of a **ListBox** or **ComboBox** object passed to its **CboOrLst** argument. If **Sorted** is **False**, however, the **FillWithDAO** method can use the **Sort** method of the **CL** class to presort, in an array variable, the items from the specified database's field. Then it fills the **ListBox** or **ComboBox** object with the presorted items from the array. But, if the **Sorted** property is **True** and a client application programmer calls the **FillWithDAO** method and specifies its **Order** argument as 1 (for a descending sort), **FillWithDAO** cannot override the **Sorted** property's setting. In this case, syntax-checking code catches the conflict between the settings of the **Sorted** property and the **Order** argument, as shown in Listing 10.2. The syntax error message that the class library displays is shown in Figure 10.4.

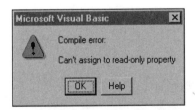

Figure 10.3 VB5 error message—property read-only at runtime.

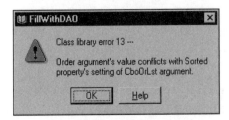

Figure 10.4 Syntax error message from **FillWithDAO** method.

Listing 10.2   Code to syntax check the setting of the Sorted property.

```
Function FillWithDAO(CboOrLst As Object, _
                     Dbs As Object, _
                     Rst As Object, _
                     Field, _
                     Optional Order)

    . . .

    ElseIf Not IsMissing(Order) Then

        If Order = SORT_DSC And CboOrLst.Sorted = True Then
            E.TrapSyntax 13, PROC, "Order", "Sorted", "CboOrLst"
        End If

    End If

    . . .

End Function
```

If you write a method in an ActiveX component to subclass a Visual Basic control object and there is any possibility of the type of override problem we have been discussing, you should syntax-check the argument whose setting might create the conflict.

CATCHING A SYNTAX ERROR BY FORCING A RUNTIME ERROR

The **Field** argument of the **FillWithDAO** method is declared as a **Variant** data type, which allows it to accept either an integer (signifying the ordinal position of the **Field** object of the **Recordset** object) or a string (signifying the **Name** property of the **Field** object). Because it can accept these different kinds of values, syntax-checking it could be laborious.

In situations like this, another approach may be easier to implement. The **FillWithDAO** method uses just two lines of code to validate its **Field** argument, as shown in Listing 10.3.

Listing 10.3   Code to catch syntax error by causing a runtime error.

```
Function FillWithDAO(CboOrLst As Object, _
                     Dbs As Object, _
                     Rst As Object, _
                     Field, _
                     Optional Sort)

    . . .
```

```
ReDim Items(FIRST_REC) As Variant
Items(FIRST_REC) = Rst(Field)

. . .

End Function
```

When the statement

```
Items(FIRST_REC) = Rst(Field)
```

tries to read the first record of a DAO recordset's field and the specified field (whether by ordinal position or name) does not exist, at least two different runtime errors can occur:

- **Error 91**. The object variable cannot be set (for example, because the **Field** object's design table is open in Access).
- **Error 3265**. The item does not exist in collection.

The two lines of code in Listing 10.3, in conjunction with the error handler at the bottom of the method, serve to validate the **Field** argument. To the client application programmer, it does not matter whether the invalid argument is flagged by a syntax or a runtime error message, just that it is caught at all. Figure 10.5 shows the typical error message that the **FillWithDAO** method displays.

SORTING ALGORITHMS IN VISUAL BASIC

There have been many articles published on the various sorting algorithms and how you can implement them in Visual Basic. In addition, there are two VB books that are good sources for these kinds of generic algorithms. One is *Visual Basic Algorithms: A Developer's Sourcebook Of Ready-To-Run Code*, Rod Stephens, ISBN 0-471-13418-X. The other is *Mathematical Algorithms In Visual Basic For Scientists And Engineers*, Namir Shammas, ISBN 0-07-912003-2.

Figure 10.5   Runtime error message from **FillWithDAO** method.

The **Sort** method of the **CL** class uses the bubble sort algorithm to sort an array of items in ascending or descending order. The algorithm itself is commonplace, and you can study it if you wish. However, there are several general points to note about any sorting algorithms you may implement with Visual Basic code:

- Sorting algorithms may not result in precisely the same sort order as implemented by the **Sorted** property of Visual Basic's **ComboBox** or **ListBox** object. For example, some sorting algorithms result in a true ASCII sort that is case sensitive; but the **Sorted** property implements an ascending sort that is not case sensitive. However, the **Sort** method of the **CL** class (when the sort is an ascending one) results in the same order as the **Sorted** property of the **ComboBox** or **ListBox** object.

- Sorting algorithms written in VB are always much slower than their counterparts written in the C or Assembly languages.

- The more items there are in the array, the greater the difference in speed between the native VB code sort and a C or Assembly-language sort.

Third-party Windows DLLs that implement sorts in C and Assembly are readily available. Crescent Software's QuickPak Professional is one that jumps to mind. Just as a class library can call API functions from Windows, own DLLs, it can also call routines that are performance-sensitive (like sorts) from third-party DLLs.

Batch-Copying Items In A List

The **CopyItems** method copies selected items from a source **ListBox** object to a destination **ListBox** object. This method subclasses Visual Basic's **ListBox** object so you can easily implement one of the most commonly used Windows GUI metaphors. The GUI often appears as shown in Figure 10.6. The user selects the items to copy or transfer from one list to another, chooses the appropriate button, and a call to the **CopyItems** method of the **List** class of the book's class library does the rest.

The topic in the class library's Help file (EFS.HLP) that specifies the detailed functionality of the **CopyItems** method is shown in the sidebar.

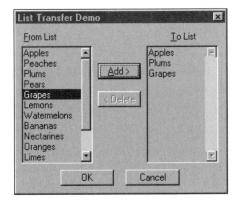

Figure 10.6 Windows GUI for copying items in a list.

The CopyItems method's specifications.

SYNTAX

```
Object.CopyItems(LstSrc, LstDst, [DeleteSrc])
```

The **CopyItems** method's syntax has the following object qualifier and named arguments:

- *Object*. Required. **Object** data type. An expression that evaluates to an object in the Applies To pop-up list.

- *LstSrc*. Required. **Object** data type. An expression that evaluates to the **Name** property of a Visual Basic **ListBox** control object from which the items are copied.

- *LstDst*. Required. **Object** data type. An expression that evaluates to the **Name** property of a Visual Basic **ListBox** control object to which the items are copied.

- *DeleteSrc*. Required. Optional. **Variant** data type whose subtype is a numeric expression that evaluates to **True**. If **DeleteSrc** is passed, the **CopyItems** method, after copying the selected items, deletes them from the source **ListBox** object.

CALLED

From any procedure in the client application.

RETURNS

Upon success, one element in a **Variant**. It contains a **Boolean** (**True**) that specifies the member executed successfully.

Upon failure, eight elements in a **Variant**. The elements contain the error codes that the class library returns when a runtime or syntax error occurs during the execution of one of its members.

DECLARING WINDOWS API CONSTANTS CONDITIONALLY

You have already seen that declarations of Windows API functions and their associated user-defined data types must be conditionally compiled in order to run under both 32-bit and 16-bit Visual Basic and Windows. Microsoft's Windows developers also changed the values of some of the existing 16-bit Windows API constants when they wrote 32-bit Windows.

This fact is not documented anywhere in API32.HLP, nor is there a handy list of the constants that have dual values. The only way to be sure that you declare Windows API constants with the correct values is to use Visual Basic's Text API Viewer (or some other similar utility) to get the constants. The Text API Viewer comes in two versions, one for 16-bit Visual Basic (with VB4) and one for 32-bit Visual Basic (with VB4 and VB5). Each one loads the correct constant values for its version of Windows. The **CopyItems** method uses Windows API function constants that must be conditionally declared. This process is done at the beginning of the method, as shown in Listing 10.4.

Listing 10.4   Conditional declaration of constants.

```
Function CopyItems(LstSrc As Object, _
                   LstDst As Object, _
                   Optional DeleteSrc)

    ' Constants for Windows API functions
    ' (allow for conditional compilation):
#If Win32 Then

    Const LB_ADDSTRING = &H180
    Const LB_DELETESTRING = &H182
    Const LB_GETSELCOUNT = &H190
    Const LB_GETSELITEMS = &H191

#Else

    Const WM_USER = &H400
```

```
      Const LB_ADDSTRING = (WM_USER + 1)
      Const LB_DELETESTRING = (WM_USER + 3)
      Const LB_GETSELCOUNT = (WM_USER + 17)
      Const LB_GETSELITEMS = (WM_USER + 18)

  #End If

  . . .

End Function
```

SUSPENDING REPAINTING OF A CONTROL

One of the easiest ways to improve the performance of certain GUI-related Visual Basic algorithms is to temporarily suspend the repainting of the control object whose display is affected by the algorithm. For example, the **CopyItems** method can be called to fill a **ListBox** object with many items and, if its **DeleteSrc** argument is passed, to also delete those items from the source **ListBox** object. Each time one of these actions (adding or deleting an item) takes place, Windows repaints the **ListBox** object's display. This continual repainting is unnecessary and can slow down certain algorithms by 100 percent or more.

In such a situation, you could temporarily set the control's **Visible** property to **False** until the algorithm is done and then reset **Visible** to **True** to update the display of the control. However, this approach is clumsy and visually confuses the user. A better alternative is to call the Windows API function **SendMessage** to suspend painting of the control object before the algorithm begins, and to call it again after the algorithm is done to refresh the display of the control.

In the **CopyItems** method, these two lines of code suspend repainting of the **ListBox** objects:

```
SendMessage LstSrc.hWnd, WM_SETREDRAW, False, vbEmpty
SendMessage LstDst.hWnd, WM_SETREDRAW, False, vbEmpty
```

After the method has copied the items, these two lines of code refresh the **ListBox** objects:

```
SendMessage LstSrc.hWnd, WM_SETREDRAW, True, vbEmpty
SendMessage LstDst.hWnd, WM_SETREDRAW, True, vbEmpty
```

When **SendMessage** is called with its second argument set to the constant WM_SETREDRAW and its third argument set to **False**, Windows suspends repainting the object specified by the handle of the first argument. When you want to refresh the object, pass **True** as the third argument. In both cases, the fourth argument is set to zero (**Null** in C or **vbEmpty** in Visual Basic).

MANIPULATING SELECTED ITEMS WITH SENDMESSAGE

Listing 10.5 shows the typical native Visual Basic code to copy selected items from one **ListBox** object to another and then delete them from the source.

Listing 10.5   Manipulating selected items.

```
' Variable.
Dim SelItem As Integer

' Copy selected items to second ListBox object:
For SelItem = 0 To List1.ListCount - 1

   If List1.Selected(SelItem) Then
      List2.AddItem List1.List(SelItem)
   End If

Next SelItem

' Delete selected items from source LIstBox object:
For SelItem = List1.ListCount - 1 To 0 Step -1

   If List1.Selected(SelItem) Then
      List1.RemoveItem SelItem
   End If

Next SelItem
```

There is nothing wrong with these Visual Basic routines, except that they run from 200 to 300 percent slower than the same algorithms implemented using the **SendMessage** Windows API function. When you encapsulate this algorithm as a method in a class library (with its call-processing overhead and syntax-checking already slowing performance) and handle potentially large numbers of selected items, you need all the speed you can muster.

To use the **SendMessage** function in the **CopyItems** method, you need to first get the number of selected items by using the native Visual Basic statement:

```
NumSel = LstSrc.SelCount
```

Then you dynamically size a **Long** (32-bit) or **Integer** (16-bit) array variable to the same number of elements as there are selected items using the following declarations:

```
ReDim ListIndexesLng(FIRST_SEL To LastSel) As Long
ReDim ListIndexesInt(FIRST_SEL To LastSel) As Integer
```

The code block in Listing 10.6 fills the arrays with the index values of the selected items. This approach, coupled with the suspension of the repainting of the **ListBox** objects, are the major factors in the increase in speed of the algorithm.

Listing 10.6 Filling an array with index values.

```
Function CopyItems(LstSrc As Object, _
                   LstDst As Object, _
                   Optional DeleteSrc)

    . . .

    #If Win32 Then
        ReDim ListIndexesLng(FIRST_SEL To LastSel) As Long
        SendMessage LstSrc.hWnd, LB_GETSELITEMS, _
                NumSel, ListIndexesLng(vbEmpty)
    #Else
        ReDim ListIndexesInt(FIRST_SEL To LastSel) As Integer
        SendMessage LstSrc.hWnd, LB_GETSELITEMS, _
                NumSel, ListIndexesInt(vbEmpty)
    #End If

    #If Win32 Then

        For Sel = FIRST_SEL To LastSel
            SendMsg LstDst.hWnd, LB_ADDSTRING, _
                    vbEmpty, LstSrc.List(ListIndexesLng(Sel))
        Next Sel

    #Else

        For Sel = FIRST_SEL To LastSel
            SendMsg LstDst.hWnd, LB_ADDSTRING, _
                    vbEmpty, LstSrc.List(ListIndexesInt(Sel))
        Next Sel

    #End If

    If NumSel <> LstSrc.ListCount Then

        If Not IsMissing(DeleteSrc) Then

            #If Win32 Then

                For Sel = LastSel To FIRST_SEL Step -1
                    SendMessage LstSrc.hWnd, LB_DELETESTRING, _
                            ListIndexesLng(Sel), vbEmpty
                Next Sel

            #Else
```

```
            For Sel = LastSel To FIRST_SEL Step -1
                SendMessage LstSrc.hWnd, LB_DELETESTRING, _
                            ListIndexesInt(Sel), vbEmpty
            Next Sel
        #End If
    End If

  Else

    If Not IsMissing(DeleteSrc) Then LstSrc.Clear

  End If

  . . .
```

There are three main points to note about the code in Listing 10.6. First, when the Windows API function **SendMessage** is used with the constant LB_GETSELITEMS, it fills a **Long** array (32-bit) or **Integer** array (16-bit) with the index values of the selected items in a **ListBox** object. Using this technique, you are able to loop through only the selected items (not every item in the **ListBox**, as you must if you use the native Visual Basic code solutions) to copy them to the destination list and, if the **DeleteSrc** argument is passed, to delete them from the source list.

Passing array variables to API functions

*For Windows API functions, an array variable has to be passed with the 0 element specified (that is, **vbEmpty**). This is different than passing an array variable to a **Function** or **Sub** procedure in Visual Basic (where the array is passed without specifying an element).*

Second, when the Windows API function **SendMsg** is used (**SendMsg** being a **String** data type-safe alias for **SendMessage**), it copies each selected item from the source **ListBox** object to the destination one. The third argument must be set to zero (**Null** in C or **vbEmpty** in Visual Basic). This is slightly faster than using Visual Basic's **AddItem** method.

Third, when the Windows API function **SendMessage** is used with the constant LB_DELETESTRING, it deletes the selected items in a **ListBox** object. The fourth argument must be set to zero.

The **CopyItems** method, like all the code in the book's class library, takes advantage of Visual Basic's support for conditional compilation. However, as you might imagine from the code in Listing 10.6, there is a significant amount of work involved to add comprehensive conditional compilation to a complex Visual Basic project. You should budget an additional 10 to 25 percent in coding and debugging time to implement conditional compilation with VB5. The lower percentage applies to projects that use few or no Windows API functions. The higher percentage applies to projects like the book's class library, which uses a large number of Windows API functions.

Searching For An Item In A List

The **FindItem** method subclasses Visual Basic's **ListBox** object and adds a method to execute the conventional Windows search algorithm for lists, as implemented in Help's Search dialog box (Windows 3.x) or on the Index tab of the Help Topics dialog box (Windows 95 and Windows NT 4). The algorithm is generally used in conjunction with a **TextBox** object, which is used to find an item in the list.

When you enter the initial letters of an item, the **FindItem** method (called from the **Change** event procedure of the **TextBox** object) selects the first item in the **ListBox** object that has those letters and places it at the top of the list, as shown in Figure 10.7. If the user presses Backspace repeatedly and clears the **TextBox** object, the method selects the first item in the list, as shown in Figure 10.8.

The topic in the class library's Help file (EFS.HLP) that specifies the detailed functionality of the **FindItem** method is shown in the sidebar.

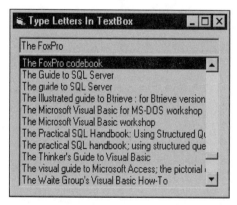

Figure 10.7 Windows GUI for finding an item in a list (1).

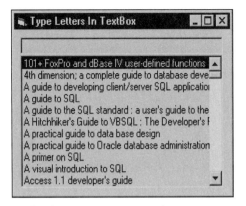

Figure 10.8   Windows GUI for finding an item in a list (2).

The FindItem method's specifications.

SYNTAX

```
Object.FindItem(Lst, Item, [ExactMatch])
```

The **FindItem** method's syntax has the following object qualifier and named arguments:

- *Object*. Required. **Object** data type. An expression that evaluates to an object in the Applies To pop-up list.

- *Lst*. Required. **Object** data type. An expression that evaluates to the **Name** property of a **ListBox** object, which contains the items to be searched. The **MultiSelect** property of *Lst* must be set to 0 - None.

- *Item*. Required. **String** data type. An expression that specifies the item to find in *Lst*.

- *ExactMatch*. Optional. **Variant** data type whose subtype is a numeric expression that evaluates to **True**. If **ExactMatch** is passed, it specifies that the item to be found and the item in **Lst** must match exactly.

CALLED

From any procedure in the client application but often from the **Change** event procedure of a **TextBox** object.

RETURNS

Upon success, one element in a **Variant**. It contains a **Boolean** (**True**) that specifies the member executed successfully.

Upon failure, eight elements in a **Variant**. The elements contain the error codes that the class library returns when a runtime or syntax error occurs during the execution of one of its members.

THE FINDITEM METHOD'S CODE

Listing 10.7 shows the code for the **FindItem** method.

Listing 10.7 The FindItem method's code.

```
Function FindItem(Lst As Object, _
                  Item As String, _
                  Optional ExactMatch)

    ' Constants for Windows API functions
    ' (allow for conditional compilation):
    #If Win32 Then
        Const LB_FINDSTRINGEXACT = &H1A2
        Const LB_SELECTSTRING = &H18C
    #Else
        Const WM_USER = &H400
        Const LB_FINDSTRINGEXACT = (WM_USER + 35)
        Const LB_SELECTSTRING = (WM_USER + 13)
    #End If

    ' Constants for literals:
    Const PROC = "FindItem"
    Const SYNTAX = True
    Const FIRST_ITEM = 0
    Const NO_SELECTION = -1

    ' Variables:
    Dim LstIndex As Long

    ' Enable error handler and do syntax checking:
    On Error GoTo ET
    If TypeName(Lst) <> "ListBox" Then
        E.TrapSyntax 8, PROC, "Lst"
    ElseIf Lst.MultiSelect <> vbMultiSelectNone Then
        E.TrapSyntax 18, PROC, "MultiSelect", "Lst", "0 - None"
    ElseIf VarType(Item) <> vbString Then
        E.TrapSyntax 4, PROC, "Item", "String"
    ElseIf Not IsMissing(ExactMatch) Then

        If ExactMatch <> True Then
            E.TrapSyntax 5, PROC, "ExactMatch"
        End If
```

```
End If

' Execute member's algorithm—
' * If Item argument is zero-length string:
'    a) If no item was previously selected, keep first item
'       at top but do not select it.
'    b) If some item was previously selected, select first
'       item.
' * If Item argument is not zero-length string:
'    a) If looking for exact match, try to find it and select
'       that item. Then put item in topmost position in
'       ListBox object.
'    b) If not looking for exact match, try to find item
'       containing first occurrence of search string and
'       select that item.
'    c) If item returned is second item, check if first item
'       also has search string; if it does, select that item.
'       This adjusts for peculiarity of SendMsg API function,
'       which never returns ListIndex value of zero.
'    d) Then put item in topmost position in ListBox object.
If Item = vbNullString Then

    If Lst.ListIndex = NO_SELECTION Then
        Lst.TopIndex = FIRST_ITEM
    Else
        Lst.ListIndex = FIRST_ITEM
    End If

Else

    If Not IsMissing(ExactMatch) Then
        LstIndex = SendMsg(Lst.hWnd, LB_FINDSTRINGEXACT, _
                        vbEmpty, Item)
        Lst.ListIndex = LstIndex
    Else
        LstIndex = SendMsg(Lst.hWnd, LB_SELECTSTRING, _
                        vbEmpty, Item)

        If LstIndex = 1 Then

            If InStr(Lst.List(FIRST_ITEM), Item) Then
                LstIndex = FIRST_ITEM
            End If

        End If
    End If

    If LstIndex <> NO_SELECTION Then Lst.TopIndex = LstIndex

End If

FindItem = Array(True)
Exit Function
```

```
ET:

   If Err = SYNTAX Then FindItem = frmErrCodes.Codes
   If Err <> SYNTAX Then FindItem = CL.TrapErr(PROC)
End Function
```

The code that implements the **FindItem** method uses the Windows API function **SendMsg**. Although it is possible to write this algorithm with native Visual Basic code, its execution would be pitifully slow. When called with the constant LB_FINDSTRINGEXACT or LB_SELECTSTRING, **SendMsg** searches a **ListBox** object for an item that either exactly matches the string or whose initial characters match the string specified by its fourth argument. Its third argument must be set to zero (**Null** in C or **vbEmpty** in Visual Basic).

Subclassing VB's Graphics Controls

We'll begin our discussion on subclassing the graphics controls with an introduction to the **Graphic** class. The **Graphic** class is comprised of members that subclass Visual Basic's **Form**, **Image**, or **PictureBox** objects. It currently contains the four public members described in Table 10.2.

The method that we'll examine is the **Stretch** method, which subclasses Visual Basic control objects in a non-polymorphic way.

Stretching A Graphic Image

One of the interesting differences between the **Image** and **PictureBox** control objects is the way the Visual Basic development team chose to

Table 10.2 The public members of the **Graphic** class.

Member	Description
Center	Centers certain VB objects, including graphics-related ones, within the client area of their parent or container objects.
Load	Loads a specified file into certain VB control objects, including graphics-related ones.
Save	Saves the contents of certain VB control objects, including list-related ones, to a specified file.
Stretch	Copies a graphic image from a source object to a destination object, sizing it to fit the destination object (32-bit only).

implement the ability to stretch or resize a graphic image. The **Image** object has the **Stretch** property, which you can set to either **True** or **False**. If **True**, the graphic image is resized to fit the **Image** object's dimensions; if **False** (the default), the **Image** object resizes itself to fit the dimensions of the graphic image.

In the case of the **PictureBox** object, however, there is no **Stretch** property. Instead, it has the **AutoSize** property, which you can set to either **True** or **False**. If **True**, the **PictureBox** object is resized to display the entire graphic image; if **False** (the default), the dimensions of both the **PictureBox** object and the graphic image remain constant. If the graphic image is smaller than the **PictureBox** object, the background color of the **PictureBox** is displayed in the unoccupied portion of the control. If the graphic image is larger than the **PictureBox** object, the portion of the image that exceeds the size of the **PictureBox** object is clipped and not displayed.

In some circumstances, it would be nice if the **PictureBox** object also had a **Stretch** property, so it would emulate the behavior of the **Image** object when the graphic image is smaller or larger than itself. The **Stretch** method of the **Graphic** class subclasses the **Form**, **PictureBox**, and **Printer** objects of 32-bit VB to add this capability to them.

The topic in the class library's Help file (EFS.HLP) that specifies the detailed functionality of the **Stretch** method is shown in the sidebar.

The Stretch method's specifications.

SYNTAX

```
Object.Stretch(ObjSrc, ObjDst)
```

The **Stretch** method's syntax has the following object qualifier and named arguments:

- *Object*. Required. **Object** data type. An expression that evaluates to an object in the Applies To pop-up list.

- *ObjSrc*. Required. **Object** data type. An object expression that evaluates to the **Name** property of a **Form** or **PictureBox** object, whose **AutoRedraw** property is set to **True** and whose **Picture** property is set to a valid graphic image.

- *ObjDst*. Required. **Object** data type. An object expression that evaluates to the **Name** property of a **Form**, **PictureBox**, or **Printer** object. If it is a **Form** or **PictureBox** object, its **AutoRedraw** property must be set to **True**.

CALLED

From any procedure in the client application.

RETURNS

Upon success, one element in a **Variant**. It contains a **Boolean** (**True**) that specifies the member executed successfully.

Upon failure, eight elements in a **Variant**. The elements contain the error codes that the class library returns when a runtime or syntax error occurs during the execution of one of its members.

REMARKS

- The **Stretch** method only works with 32-bit Visual Basic. The way its code behaves is a good example of the subtle differences that exist between the different versions of Windows and Visual Basic. It runs under either 32-bit Windows 95 or Windows NT 4.0. The method's code, if run directly from within an application, also runs under 16-bit VB4; but it will not run from within an ActiveX component.

- The **Stretch** method will accept the same object reference for both its *ObjSrc* and *ObjDst* arguments; but, if you do this, the **Picture** property of the object gets set to **False** (that is, no graphic).

- The source image can be copied/stretched to a **Printer** object only if the image is a Windows metafile (.WMF).

THE STRETCH METHOD'S CODE

The **Stretch** method, shown in Listing 10.8, uses Visual Basic's own **PaintPicture** method (added to VB4) to perform its functionality. The nice thing about the **Stretch** method is that it is a subset of the features of the **PaintPicture** method, which can take as many as 10 required and optional arguments. If all you want to do is resize the graphic image to fit a container control object, you will find it much easier to call the **Stretch** method of the book's class library and just pass the two required object references as arguments.

Listing 10.8 The Stretch method's code.

```
Function Stretch(ObjSrc As Object, _
                ObjDst As Object)

    ' Constants for literals:
    Const PROC = "Stretch"
    Const SYNTAX = True

    ' Variables:
    Dim DstIsForm     As Boolean
    Dim SrcIsForm     As Boolean
    Dim SrcDstSame    As Boolean

    ' Enable error handler and do syntax checking:
    On Error GoTo ET

#If Win16 Then
    E.TrapSyntax 1, PROC, "16-bit VB"
#End If

    If Not CL.IsForm(ObjSrc) Then

        If TypeName(ObjSrc) <> "PictureBox" Then
            Error.TrapSyntax 8, PROC, "ObjSrc"
        End If

    Else
        SrcIsForm = True
    End If

    If ObjSrc.Picture = False Then
        E.TrapSyntax 18, PROC, "Picture", "ObjSrc", "valid graphic"
    ElseIf ObjSrc.AutoRedraw = False Then
        E.TrapSyntax 18, PROC, "AutoRedraw", "ObjSrc", "True"
    End If

    If Not CL.IsForm(ObjDst) Then

        If TypeName(ObjDst) <> "PictureBox" And _
           TypeName(ObjDst) <> "Printer" Then
            Error.TrapSyntax 8, PROC, "ObjDst"
        End If

    Else
        DstIsForm = True
    End If

    If DstIsForm Or TypeName(ObjDst) = "PictureBox" Then
```

```
        If ObjDst.AutoRedraw = False Then
            E.TrapSyntax 18, PROC, "AutoRedraw", "ObjDst", "True"
        End If

    End If


    ' Execute member's algorithm—
    ' * Check if ObjSrc and ObjDst arguments are same object
    '   (elements in control array, with Index property set
    '   zero or greater, are not same object).
    ' * If ObjDst is not Printer object and arguments are
    '   different objects, set Picture property to False
    '   (that is, no graphic image).
    ' * If source and destination objects are same, stretch
    '   graphic by first using PictureBox object on method's
    '   associated Form object as interim container object.
    '   Then use PaintPicture method.
    ' * If source and destination objects are different, just
    '   use PaintPicture method to stretch graphic.
    ' * NOTE: Using PaintPicture method is not equivalent to
    '   setting Picture property of destination object.
    If VarType(ObjSrc) = VarType(ObjDst) Then
        On Error Resume Next

        If ObjSrc.Index >= 0 Then
            If Err = 438 Then SrcDstSame = True
        End If

        On Error GoTo ET
    End If

    If TypeName(ObjDst) <> "Printer" And Not SrcDstSame Then

        #If Win32 Then
            ObjDst.Picture = LoadPicture()
        #End If

    End If

    If SrcDstSame Then

        #If Win32 Then
            frmStretch.picStretch.Picture = ObjSrc.Picture
            ObjSrc.Picture = LoadPicture()
            ObjDst.PaintPicture frmStretch.picStretch.Picture, _
                            vbEmpty, vbEmpty, _
                                ObjDst.ScaleWidth, ObjDst.ScaleHeight
            Unload frmStretch
        #End If

    Else
        ObjDst.PaintPicture ObjSrc.Picture, vbEmpty, vbEmpty, _
                        ObjDst.ScaleWidth, ObjDst.ScaleHeight
```

```
    End If

    Stretch = Array(True)
    Exit Function

ET:

    If Err = SYNTAX Then Stretch = frmErrCodes.Codes
    If Err <> SYNTAX Then Stretch = CL.TrapErr(PROC)

End Function
```

The **Stretch** method has several important features. Using Visual Basic's **PaintPicture** method to paint a graphic image on a control object is not the same as setting the control object's **Picture** property. Because of this, if the **ObjSrc** or **ObjDst** argument's object reference is a **Form** or **PictureBox** object, the **AutoRedraw** property of the object reference must be set to **True**. Otherwise, the graphic image that the **Stretch** method creates will not be persistent and the method will display the syntax error message shown in Figure 10.9. If the **Picture** property of the source object equals **False** (that is, zero or no graphic), the method will display the syntax error message shown in Figure 10.10.

The **Stretch** method will accept the same object reference for both its **ObjSrc** and **ObjDst** arguments, but, if you do this, the **Picture** property of the object gets set to **False** (that is, no graphic). Then, if you were to apply the **Stretch** method again to the same control object, the method would display the syntax error message in Figure 10.10. Finally, the **Stretch** method always sets the **Picture** property of the **ObjDst** argument's object reference to zero, except if **ObjDst** refers to the **Printer** object.

Ideas For Subclassing VB Graphic Objects

The **Graphic** class is a work-in-progress. The three Visual Basic books I listed at the beginning of this chapter are filled with good ideas for subclassing

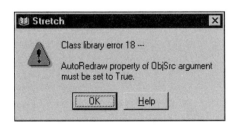

Figure 10.9   **Stretch** method's syntax error message (1).

Figure 10.10 Stretch method's syntax error message (2).

the graphics capabilities of the **Form**, **Image**, **PictureBox**, and **Printer** objects. Most of them rely on the large number of Windows API functions available in the Graphics Device Interface DLL file (GDI32.DLL for the 32-bit API and GDI.EXE for the 16-bit API).

Here, in no particular order, is a baker's dozen of subclassing ideas to add to the **Graphic** class:

- Draw a focus band around a **PictureBox** object that gets the focus.
- Draw a picture on a minimized **Form** object's icon.
- Draw a transparent bitmap or icon on a **Form** object.
- Gradate a **Form** object's background color.
- Scroll a graphic image in a **PictureBox** object.
- Scroll the client area of a **Form** object.
- Tile a bitmap as wallpaper on a **Form** object's background.
- Clip/restrict the cursor's movement to a **Form** or **PictureBox** object.
- Clip/restrict a graphic image on a **Form** object.
- Display a color palette in a **PictureBox** object.
- Flash the title bar on a **Form** object.
- Make an exploding **Form** object.
- Make a **PictureBox** object into a progress bar.

If you want to see how to implement these subclassing ideas, I suggest you pick up a copy of the Windows API Browser utility. This utility, which I developed, is a cheap and comprehensive source of information. For more information on this gem—what it does and how you can get it—see *The Windows API Browser Utility* section in Chapter 1.

Table 10.3   The public members of the **Dialog** class.

Member	Description
CancelStyle	Displays either just the client area of a Form object or the client area surrounded only by the border.
Center	Centers certain VB objects, including Form and MDIForm objects, within the client area of their parent or container objects.
ShowCL	Changes the attributes of a dialog-style Form object and its control objects to display the customized appearance of dialog boxes in the book's class library.

Subclassing VB's Form Object

We'll begin our discussion on subclassing the VB **Form** object with an introduction to the **Dialog** class. Table 10.3 describes the three public methods currently in the **Dialog** class.

In this section, we'll be focusing on the two methods that subclass the Visual Basic **Form** object in a non-polymorphic way: **CancelStyle** and **ShowCL**.

The CancelStyle Method's Specifications

The topic in the class library's Help file (EFS.HLP) that specifies the detailed functionality of the **CancelStyle** method is shown in the sidebar.

The CancelStyle method's specifications.

SYNTAX

`Object.CancelStyle(Frm, [Border])`

The **CancelStyle** method's syntax has the following object qualifier and named arguments:

- *Object*. Required. **Object** data type. An expression that evaluates to an object in the Applies To pop-up list.

- *Frm*. Required. **Object** data type. An object that evaluates to the **Name** property of a **Form** object.

- *Border*. Optional. **Variant** data type whose subtype is a numeric expression that evaluates to **True** and specifies that the client area is to retain its border. If **Border** is omitted, the client area's border is removed.

CALLED

Only from the **Form_Load** event procedure of a client application.

RETURNS

Upon success, one element in a **Variant**. It contains a **Boolean** (**True**) that specifies the member executed successfully.

Upon failure, eight elements in a **Variant**. The elements contain the error codes that the class library returns when a runtime or syntax error occurs during the execution of one of its members.

REMARKS

- Setting the **BorderStyle** property of a **Form** object to 0 - None achieves a similar effect, but it does not provide the option of retaining the border around the client area. You might want to keep the border to display a **Form** object as a tooltip. There are other subtle differences in the way a **Form** object and the control objects on it behave, depending on whether its style attributes have been removed with the **CancelStyle** method or by setting the **BorderStyle** property to 0 - None.

- The **CancelStyle** method negates any design time **BorderStyle** setting of a **Form** object, effectively setting **BorderStyle** to 0 - None. You cannot directly change **BorderStyle** to 0 - None at runtime because this property is read-only at runtime.

The CancelStyle Method's Code

Listing 10.9 shows the code for the **CancelStyle** method.

Listing 10.9   The CancelStyle method's code.

```
Function CancelStyle(Frm As Object, _
                    Optional Border)

    ' Constants for Windows API functions:
    Const GWL_STYLE = (-16)
    Const WS_DLGFRAME = &H400000
    Const WS_SYSMENU = &H80000
```

```
        Const WS_MINIMIZEBOX = &H20000
        Const WS_MAXIMIZEBOX = &H10000
        Const WS_THICKFRAME = &H40000
        Const WS_BORDER = &H800000

        ' Constants for literals:
        Const PROC = "CancelStyle"
        Const SYNTAX = True
        Const ADJ = 10

        ' Variables:
        Dim Style As Long

        ' Enable error handler and do syntax checking:
        On Error GoTo ET

        If Not CL.IsForm(Frm) Then
            E.TrapSyntax 8, PROC, "Frm"
        ElseIf Not IsMissing(Border) Then
            If Border <> True Then E.TrapSyntax 5, PROC, "Border"
        End If

        ' Execute member's algorithm—
        ' * Get attributes of current window style.
        ' * Remove attributes for frames, control-menu, minimize
        '   and maximize buttons (creating new style).
        ' * If Border argument is missing, remove it too.
        ' * Set new style of Form object.
        ' * Change/reset Height of Form object so Paint event of
        '   Form object does not result in visual distortion.
        Style = GetWindowLong(Frm.hWnd, GWL_STYLE)
        Style = Style And Not WS_THICKFRAME _
                    And Not WS_DLGFRAME _
                    And Not WS_MINIMIZEBOX _
                    And Not WS_MAXIMIZEBOX _
                    And Not WS_SYSMENU

        If IsMissing(Border) Then Style = Style And Not WS_BORDER

        SetWindowLong Frm.hWnd, GWL_STYLE, Style
        Frm.Height = Frm.Height + ADJ
        Frm.Height = Frm.Height - ADJ
        CancelStyle = Array(True)
        Exit Function

ET:

    If Err = SYNTAX Then CancelStyle = frmErrCodes.Codes
    If Err <> SYNTAX Then CancelStyle = CL.TrapErr(PROC)

End Function
```

I'd like to point out a few things about the **CancelStyle** method's code. Notice that it uses the Windows API function **GetWindowLong** to retrieve information about the **Form** object specified in its first argument. The second argument, the constant GWL_STYLE, specifies the kind of information to retrieve and returns it as a **Long** that is stored in the **Style** variable. Also notice that Visual Basic's **And** and **Not** operators are used to identify the style attributes to remove. Finally, the Windows API function **SetWindowLong** changes the **Form** object's attributes to the new ones stored in the **Style** variable. If you run the example code from the help topic for the **CancelStyle** method, it displays the **Form** object shown in Figure 10.11.

The ShowCL Method's Specifications

In addition to the **CancelStyle** method, we'll be examining how the **ShowCL** method subclasses VB's **Form** object. The topic in the class library's Help file (EFS.HLP) that specifies the detailed functionality of the **ShowCL** method is shown in the sidebar.

Figure 10.11 CancelStyle method's effect on **Form** object.

The ShowCL method's specifications.

SYNTAX

```
Object.ShowCL(Frm, Properties( ))
```

The **ShowCL** method's syntax has the following object qualifier and named arguments:

- *Object*. Required. **Object** data type. An expression that evaluates to an object in the Applies To pop-up list.

- *Frm*. Required. **Object** data type. An object that evaluates to the **Name** property of a **Form** object.

- *Properties( )*. Required. **Boolean** data type. The array's lower bound can be any non-negative number, and the array can contain from one to three elements. To specify any element, you must also specify all the elements preceding it in the array. The expression in each element must evaluate to **True** or **False**. If **True**, see *Settings* for the specifications of the three elements. If **False**, the design time settings of the **Form** object are used.

SETTINGS

The settings of the elements of *Properties( )* are:

- First; CL_BOLD. Turns on the **FontBold** property of the **Form** object and its control objects (if running under the old Windows NT 3.51-style shell) or turns it off (if running under the new Windows 95-style shell).

- Second; CL_DLG. Retains only the Close and Move items on the control menu of the **Form** object and removes the Minimize and Maximize buttons from the title bar.

- Third; CL_DLG. Displays the **Form** object on top of all other windows.

CALLED

Only from the **Form_Load** event procedure of a client application.

> **RETURNS**
>
> Upon success, one element in a **Variant**. It contains a **Boolean** (**True**) that specifies the member executed successfully.
>
> Upon failure, eight elements in a **Variant**. The elements contain the error codes that the class library returns when a runtime or syntax error occurs during the execution of one of its members.

The ShowCL Method's Code

The **ShowCL** method changes the attributes of a dialog-style **Form** object and its control objects to display the customized appearance of dialog boxes in the book's class library. Listing 10.10 shows the code for the **ShowCL** method.

Listing 10.10   The ShowCL method's code.

```
Function ShowCL(Frm As Object, _
                Properties() As Boolean)

    ' Constants for Windows API function:
    Const MF_BYPOSITION = &H400
    Const HWND_TOPMOST = (-1)
    Const SWP_NOMOVE = &H2
    Const SWP_NOSIZE = &H1
    Const NUM_PROPS = 3
    Const GWL_STYLE = (-16)
    Const WS_MINIMIZEBOX = &H20000
    Const WS_MAXIMIZEBOX = &H10000

    ' Constants for elements in Properties argument:
    Const CL_DLG = 1
    Const CL_ONTOP = 2

    ' Constants for literals:
    Const PROC = "ShowCL"
    Const SYNTAX = True
    Const ADJ = 1
    Const CM_SIZE = 2
    Const CM_MAXIMIZE = 4
    Const CM_SEPARATOR1 = 5
    Const CM_SEPARATOR2 = 7
    Const CM_SWITCHTO = 8

    ' Variables:
    Dim Win95Shell   As Boolean
    Dim PropIsTrue   As Boolean
    Dim Item         As Byte
    Dim Style        As Long
```

```
Dim Prop        As Variant
Dim FirstProp   As Variant
Dim LastProp    As Variant
Dim Ctl         As Control

' Enable error handler and do syntax checking:
On Error GoTo ET

If Not CL.IsForm(Frm) Then
    E.TrapSyntax 8, PROC, "Frm"
ElseIf Not CL.IsSized(Properties) Then
    E.TrapSyntax 41, PROC, "Properties()"
End If

FirstProp = LBound(Properties)
LastProp = UBound(Properties)

If LastProp - FirstProp + ADJ > NUM_PROPS Then
    E.TrapSyntax 12, PROC, _
                 "Properties()", CStr(NUM_PROPS)
End If

' Execute member's algorithm—
' * Check if member is running under Windows 95 shell.
'   If each element has been passed and is True:
'   a) Set normal or bold font.
'   b) Customize control menu to class library's style.
'   c) Keep Form object on top.
If CL.IsWin95Shell Then Win95Shell = True

For Prop = FirstProp To LastProp
   PropIsTrue = Properties(Prop)

   If Prop = FirstProp Then
      On Error Resume Next

      If PropIsTrue Then

         If Win95Shell Then

            For Each Ctl In Frm.Controls
               Ctl.FontBold = False
            Next Ctl

            Frm.FontBold = False
         Else

            For Each Ctl In Frm.Controls
               Ctl.FontBold = True
            Next Ctl

            Frm.FontBold = True
         End If
      End If
```

```
        On Error GoTo ET

    ElseIf Prop = FirstProp + CL_DLG Then

        If PropIsTrue Then

            If Not Win95Shell Then
                DeleteMenu GetSystemMenu(Frm.hWnd, False), _
                                    CM_SWITCHTO, _
                                    MF_BYPOSITION
                DeleteMenu GetSystemMenu(Frm.hWnd, False), _
                                    CM_SEPARATOR2, _
                                    MF_BYPOSITION
            End If

            Style = GetWindowLong(Frm.hWnd, GWL_STYLE)
            Style = Style And Not WS_MINIMIZEBOX _
                        And Not WS_MAXIMIZEBOX
            SetWindowLong Frm.hWnd, GWL_STYLE, Style
            DeleteMenu GetSystemMenu(Frm.hWnd, vbEmpty), _
                                CM_SEPARATOR1, _
                                MF_BYPOSITION

            For Item = CM_MAXIMIZE To CM_SIZE
                DeleteMenu GetSystemMenu(Frm.hWnd, vbEmpty), _
                                    Item, _
                                    MF_BYPOSITION
            Next Item
        End If

    ElseIf Prop = FirstProp + CL_ONTOP Then

        If PropIsTrue Then
            SetWindowPos Frm.hWnd, HWND_TOPMOST, _
                            vbEmpty, vbEmpty, vbEmpty, vbEmpty, _
                            SWP_NOMOVE Or SWP_NOSIZE
        End If
    End If
Next Prop

ShowCL = Array(True)
Exit Function

ET:

If Err = SYNTAX Then ShowCL = frmErrCodes.Codes
If Err <> SYNTAX Then ShowCL = CL.TrapErr(PROC)

End Function
```

If you run the example code from the help topic for the **ShowCL** method under the Windows 95-style shell, with all three elements of its **Properties()** argument set to **True**, it displays the **Form** object shown in Figure 10.12.

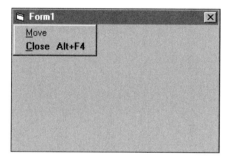

Figure 10.12 **ShowCL** method's effect on **Form** object.

CUSTOM PROPERTIES AND THE PARAMARRAY KEYWORD

11

One of the new syntactical features in VB4 and VB5, for the lack of which VB3 programmers had to use workarounds of various kinds, are **Property** procedures. **Property** procedures allow you to add custom properties to any kind of module, and to execute code when the property is set or returned. For example, you could add an **Inverted** property to a form. When **Inverted** is set to **True**, the code in the associated **Property** procedure would call a Windows API function to invert a bitmap on the form.

When you coded with VB3, you were always forced to use module-level or project-level variables to store the value of a variable like **Inverted** in the preceding example. And, because VB3's syntax did not require that **Inverted** be linked to any consistent kind of control structure in order to set or return its value, it was easy to end up with a project that was hard to debug and maintain. The new **Property** procedures in VB4 and VB5 provide a solution to these kinds of problems.

An Introduction To Property Procedures

VB5 supports three kinds of **Property** procedures:

- **Property Get**. Returns the value of a custom property of a module.
- **Property Let**. Assigns a value to a custom property of a module.
- **Property Set**. Sets a reference to an object for the custom property of a module.

Property procedures provide several advantages over public variables. Public variables can be assigned a new value at any point in the code of a project. **Property** procedures, on the other hand, provide a consistent and disciplined interface for setting or returning the value of a property, which facilitates good programming practices. Unlike public variables, **Property** procedures can have a help topic associated with them in the Object Browser. Also, if the value of a property requires formatting, data validation, or other processing, the code to do so can be encapsulated in its **Property** procedure. Finally, the internal code of a **Property** procedure can be modified without modifying any of the code that calls the **Property** procedure. For example, if you formatted percentages to two decimal places, this formatting can be changed in the **Property** procedure; the new format will then automatically be provided to any code calling the **Property** procedure.

Let's take a moment to briefly review the characteristics of each type of **Property** procedure.

The Property Get Procedure's Attributes

A **Property Get** procedure has these characteristics:

- The name and data type of each argument in a **Property Get** procedure must be the same as the corresponding arguments in a **Property Let** procedure (if one exists).
- The return type of a **Property Get** procedure must be the same data type as the last (or most times the only) argument in a corresponding **Property Let** procedure (if one exists) that defines the value assigned to the property on the right-hand side of an expression.
- Unlike a **Sub** or **Property Let** procedure, you can use a **Property Get** procedure on the right-hand side of an expression in the same way you

use a function or a property name when you want to return the value of a property.

- A **Property Get** procedure is read-only in nature.

The Property Let Procedure's Attributes

A **Property Let** procedure has these characteristics:

- Every **Property Let** statement must define at least one argument for the procedure it defines. That argument (or the last argument if there is more than one) contains the actual value to be assigned to the property when the procedure defined by the **Property Let** statement is invoked.
- The name and data type of each argument in a **Property Let** procedure (except the last argument) must be the same as the corresponding arguments in a **Property Get** procedure (if one exists).
- The last argument is the value assigned to the property on the right-hand side of an expression.
- The data type of the last (or most times the only) argument must be the same as the return type of the corresponding **Property Get** procedure.
- Unlike a function and a **Property Get** procedure, both of which return a value, you can only use a **Property Let** procedure on the left-hand side of a property assignment expression or **Let** statement.
- A **Property Let** procedure is write-only in nature.

The Property Set Procedure's Attributes

A **Property Set** procedure has these characteristics:

- Every **Property Set** statement must define at least one argument for the procedure it defines. That argument (or the last argument if there is more than one) contains the actual object reference for the property when the procedure defined by the **Property Set** statement is invoked.
- The last argument is the object reference used on the right-hand side of an object reference assignment.
- Unlike a function and a **Property Get** procedure, both of which return a value, you can only use a **Property Set** procedure on the left-hand side of an object reference assignment (**Set** statement).
- A **Property Set** procedure is write-only in nature.

Using Property Procedures

In Chapter 7, we looked briefly at **Property Get** and **Property Let** procedures. These two procedures are straightforward, so we'll begin with them. As I pointed out at the beginning of the chapter, a **Property Let** procedure assigns a value to its associated module-level variable, and a **Property Get** procedure returns the value of its associated module-level variable. The setting of the custom property has to be stored in a module-level variable so that it does not go out of scope and can later be read. Declaring and writing a **Property Let** procedure is really quite simple, as shown in this code snippet from the **frmThread Form** object of the book's class library:

```
Public Property Let AsynchDone(Setting)
    fAsynchDone = True
End Property
```

Declaring and writing the associated **Property Get** procedure is done like this:

```
Public Property Get AsynchDone()
    AsynchDone = fAsynchDone
End Property
```

To call a **Property Let** procedure, you use this syntax:

```
frmThread.AsynchDone = True
```

To call a **Property Get** procedure, you use this syntax:

```
' Variable.
Dim Result As Variant

Result = frmThread.AsynchDone
```

The syntax and use of the **Property Set** procedure is a little more complex. A **Property Set** procedure sets a reference to an object and writes or assigns that reference to a module-level **Object** variable. A **Property Get** procedure is used to read the object reference most recently assigned by the **Property Set** procedure. These two object-related procedures can be used to store (and later read) the **Name** property of an object that is not known in advance.

There are no public **Property Set** or **Property Get** procedures in the book's class library, although it does use all three kinds of **Property** procedures internally. We will discuss the reasons why the book's class library does not use public **Property** procedures later. For now, the best way to understand how these procedures are used is to work through the following steps:

1. Start Visual Basic and open a Standard EXE project.

2. Add two **CommandButton** objects and three **PictureBox** objects to Form1.

3. Align the **PictureBox** objects horizontally across the top of the **Form** object and align the **CommandButton** objects below the **PictureBox** objects.

4. Enter the code shown in Listing 11.1 in the appropriate procedures.

Listing 11.1   Sample Property Get and Set procedures.

```
' General Declarations section:
' Form-level variable.
Dim Obj As Object

Public Property Get PicBox()
   Set PicBox = Obj
End Property

Public Property Set PicBox(Setting As Object)

   ' Ensure object reference passed is to PictureBox
   If TypeName(Setting) = "PictureBox" Then
     Set Obj = Setting
   Else
     MsgBox "Can only assign PictureBox to PicBox property."
   End If

End Property

Private Sub Command1_Click()

   ' Variables:
   Dim RndNbr     As Integer
   Dim LowBound   As Integer
   Dim UpBound    As Integer

   ' Initialize:
   LowBound = 1
   UpBound = 3
   Randomize

   ' Restore original BackColor setting of picture boxes:
   Picture1.BackColor = &H8000000F
   Picture2.BackColor = &H8000000F
   Picture3.BackColor = &H8000000F
```

```
' Randomly select one of three picture boxes.
RndNbr = Int((UpBound - LowBound + 1) * Rnd + LowBound)

' Store reference to selected picture box
' by calling Set Property procedure:
Select Case RndNbr
   Case 1
      Set PicBox = Picture1
   Case 2
      Set PicBox = Picture2
   Case 3
      Set PicBox = Picture3
End Select

' Toggle buttons off and on:
Command1.Enabled = False
Command2.Enabled = True

End Sub

Private Sub Command2_Click()

   ' Variables:
   Dim RndNbr     As Integer
   Dim LowBound   As Integer
   Dim UpBound    As Integer
   Dim Obj        As Object

   ' Initialize:
   LowBound = 0
   UpBound = 15
   Randomize

   ' Get reference to previously selected picture
   ' box by calling Get Property procedure:
   Set Obj = PicBox

   ' Randomly select color value and use it to set Backcolor
   ' property of previously selected picture box:
   RndNbr = Int((UpBound - LowBound + 1) * Rnd + LowBound)
   Obj.BackColor = QBColor(RndNbr)

   ' Toggle buttons off and on:
   Command2.Enabled = False
   Command1.Enabled = True

End Sub

Private Sub Form_Load()
   Command1.Caption = "&Select PicBox"
   Command2.Caption = "&Color PicBox"
End Sub
```

After you have entered the code, select Run | Start. Choose the Select PicBox button to randomly assign the **Name** property of one of the three **PictureBox** objects to an **Object** variable with the **Property Set** procedure. Choose the Color PicBox button to read the **Name** property of the randomly assigned **PictureBox** object with the **Property Get** procedure and then randomly change its **BackColor** property. Note the validation code in the **Property Set PicBox** procedure, which checks whether the object reference passed to it is a **PictureBox** object or not. This example illustrates one of the advantages of using **Property** procedures as opposed to just setting and reading public variables.

Understanding The ParamArray Keyword

The **ParamArray** keyword, which is used with an argument in a **Declare**, **Sub**, or **Function** statement, is probably the most complex syntactical element in Visual Basic. Although it enables the creation of very flexible and powerful methods, it requires a great deal of syntax-checking code in order to ensure its correct use. The following list describes the **ParamArray** keyword's attributes:

- It can only be used only as the last argument.
- It indicates that the argument is an **Optional** array of **Variant** elements.
- It allows you to handle an arbitrary or indeterminate number of arguments.
- No other argument in the statement can be specified as **Optional**.
- It may not be used with **ByVal**, **ByRef**, or **Optional**.

Advantages Of ParamArray Argument

You can use a **ParamArray** argument to create an optional argument that accepts:

- Only discrete, individual parameters.
- Only an array of values.
- An indeterminate number of elements of the same data type.
- An arbitrary number of elements, which you specify when you develop the method, of the same data type.

- An indeterminate number of elements, each of which can be a different data type.

- An arbitrary number of elements, which you specify when you develop the method, each of which can be a different data type.

Some other advantages of using a **ParamArray** argument, besides its obvious flexibility, include:

- The ability to limit the number of arguments that comprise the public interface of a method, making it easier to understand how to call it.

- An easier way for the client application programmer to call the method and make the calling statement more readable, because you can pass all the elements required inside a single array.

- The ability to easily create **Properties( )** arguments for methods, which bind up several settings and different data types in one array. A call using this approach in a method executes significantly faster (especially over a network) than setting several different custom properties, one at a time.

ParamArray Argument In CheckSecurity Member

The **CheckSecurity** method of the **ClientApp** class takes a **ParamArray** argument called **Properties( )**, which illustrates the flexibility and power of the **ParamArray** keyword. The topic in the class library's Help file (EFS.HLP) that specifies the detailed functionality of the **CheckSecurity** method is shown in the sidebar.

CheckSecurity method's specifications.

SYNTAX

```
Object.CheckSecurity(Properties( )...)
```

The **CheckSecurity** method's syntax has the following object qualifier and argument:

- *Object*. Required. **Object** data type. An expression that evaluates to an object in the Applies To pop-up list.

- *Properties( )*. Optional. **Variant** data type. A **ParamArray** array containing one element that is passed in as a **Variant** array. This **Variant** array's lower bound can be any value and the array can contain from one to eight elements, which specify the customizable properties of the security dialog box. To specify any element, you must also specify all the elements preceding it in the array. If you pass more than eight elements, the extraneous elements are ignored. To specify the default value of a string element, pass **vbNullString** (a zero-length string); to specify the default value of a numeric element, pass **vbEmpty** (that is, zero). See *Settings* below for the subtypes and valid settings of the eight elements.

SETTINGS

The **Properties( )** argument's settings are:

- 1st element: SEC_MINLEN_LOG. An **Integer** expression that specifies the minimum length of the login ID. Valid settings are four, five, or six. The default is five.

- 2nd element: SEC_MAXLEN_LOG. An **Integer** expression that specifies the maximum length of the login ID. Valid settings are seven, eight, or nine. The default is eight.

- 3rd element: SEC_MINLEN_PASS. An **Integer** expression that specifies the minimum length of the password. Valid settings are five, six, or seven. The default is six.

- 4th element: SEC_MAXLEN_PASS. An **Integer** expression that specifies the maximum length of the password. Valid settings are seven, eight, or nine. The default is eight.

- 5th element: SEC_ALPHA_LOG. An **Integer** expression that specifies the number of alpha characters the login ID must contain. Valid settings are zero, one, or two. The default is zero.

- 6th element: SEC_NUMERIC_PASS. An **Integer** expression that specifies the number of numeric characters the password must contain. Valid settings are zero, one, or two. The default is zero.

- 7th element: SEC_TITLE. A **String** expression that specifies the caption to display in the title bar of the Security dialog box. May be no longer than 40 characters. The default is *Security*.

- 8th element: SEC_ICON. A **String** expression that specifies the path and name of the icon file displayed in the **Image** object on the Security dialog box. The default is SECUR08.ICO from Visual Basic's stock library of icons.

CALLED
From any procedure in a client application.

RETURNS
Upon success, two elements in a **Variant**. The elements contain these subtypes:

- 0 - MBR_SUCCESS. A **Boolean** (**True**) that specifies the member executed successfully.

- 1 - MBR_ENTRIES. A **String** that specifies the login ID and password (delimited by a carriage return character) or, if the user chooses Cancel, **vbNullString** (a zero-length string).

Upon failure, eight elements in a **Variant**. The elements contain the error codes that the class library returns when a runtime or syntax error occurs during the execution of one of its members.

REMARKS
It would be possible to create the same functionality that the **CheckSecurity** method provides by creating and setting eight separate properties instead of using the **ParamArray** array approach. However, calling one method is significantly faster (especially over a network) than setting eight separate property values.

Because the **CheckSecurity** method has a **ParamArray** optional argument, it cannot take named arguments. If you try to call the member using a named argument, Visual Basic displays OLE Automation runtime error 446 ("Object doesn't support named arguments") or 448 ("Named argument not found").

Different Ways To Call CheckSecurity

Because of the flexibility of the **ParamArray** keyword and the way the **CheckSecurity** method is designed, it is possible to call the method in five different ways:

- You can call **CheckSecurity** and not pass the optional **Properties( )** argument.
- You can call **CheckSecurity** and pass the optional **Properties( )** argument, with all eight elements passed in the **Variant** array.
- You can call **CheckSecurity** and pass the optional **Properties( )** argument, but with fewer than eight elements passed in the **Variant** array.
- You can call **CheckSecurity** and pass the optional **Properties( )** argument, with from one to eight elements passed in the **Variant** array; however, one or more of the elements is set to **vbEmpty/vbNullString** so that the method uses the default value for the element(s).
- You can call **CheckSecurity** and pass the optional **Properties( )** argument, and set the lower bound of the array to any value.

Let's take a look at each of these techniques (plus a few others) in greater detail.

CALLING CHECKSECURITY—NO ARGUMENT

To call the **CheckSecurity** method without passing the **Properties( )** argument, open a Standard EXE project in Visual Basic and use the code in Listing 11.2.

Listing 11.2   Code to call CheckSecurity—no argument.

```
Private Sub Form_DblClick()

    ' Declare object variable.
    Dim ClientApp As Object

    ' Instantiate ClientApp class.
    Set ClientApp = CreateObject("EFSE.ClientApp")

    ' Call member (no argument passed).
    ClientApp.CheckSecurity

End Sub
```

In the case of the call in Listing 11.2, the **CheckSecurity** method uses the default values of the eight properties/elements to display the Security dialog box shown in Figure 11.1.

Figure 11.1 CheckSecurity dialog box—no argument.

CALLING CHECKSECURITY—ALL ELEMENTS PASSED

To call the **CheckSecurity** method and pass all eight elements to the **Properties( )** argument, open a Standard EXE project in Visual Basic and use the code in Listing 11.3.

Listing 11.3   Code to call CheckSecurity—all elements passed.

```
Private Sub Form_DblClick()

    ' Variables:
    Dim VBPath          As String
    Dim ClientApp       As Object
    Dim Properties(7)   As Variant

    ' Constants for different properties:
    Const SEC_MINLEN_LOG = 0
    Const SEC_MAXLEN_LOG = 1
    Const SEC_MINLEN_PASS = 2
    Const SEC_MAXLEN_PASS = 3
    Const SEC_ALPHA_LOG = 4
    Const SEC_NUMERIC_PASS = 5
    Const SEC_TITLE = 6
    Const SEC_ICON = 7

    ' Instantiate ClientApp class.
    Set ClientApp = CreateObject("EFSE.ClientApp")

    ' Generate error to find VB's path (this finds
    ' it without using Windows API functions):
    On Error Resume Next
    Err.Raise Number:=3
    VBPath = Err.HelpFile
    If Right$(VBPath, 6) = "VB.HLP" Then
        VBPath = Mid$(Err.HelpFile, 1, Len(Err.HelpFile) - 6)
    ElseIf Right$(VBPath, 11) = "VEENLR3.HLP" Then
        VBPath = Mid$(Err.HelpFile, 1, Len(Err.HelpFile) - 16) _
                    & "GRAPHICS\"
    End If

    ' Assign ParamArray argument settings to variables
    ' and call object's member (all elements passed):
    Properties(SEC_MINLEN_LOG) = 4
```

```
Properties(SEC_MAXLEN_LOG) = 7
Properties(SEC_MINLEN_PASS) = 5
Properties(SEC_MAXLEN_PASS) = 8
Properties(SEC_ALPHA_LOG) = 1
Properties(SEC_NUMERIC_PASS) = 1
Properties(SEC_TITLE) = "My Own Private Security Dialog"
Properties(SEC_ICON) = VBPath & "ICONS\MISC\SECURO3.ICO"
ClientApp.CheckSecurity Properties()
```

End Sub

In the case of the call in Listing 11.3, the **CheckSecurity** method syntax
checks and then uses the eight values passed to the **Properties( )** argument
to display the Security dialog box shown in Figure 11.2.

CALLING CHECKSECURITY—ONLY SEVEN ELEMENTS PASSED

To call the **CheckSecurity** method and pass only the first seven elements to
the **Properties( )** argument, open a Standard EXE project in Visual Basic
and use the code in Listing 11.4.

Listing 11.4 Code to call CheckSecurity.

```
Private Sub Form_DblClick()

    ' Variables:
    Dim ClientApp       As Object
    Dim Properties(6)   As Variant

    ' Constants for different properties:
    Const SEC_MINLEN_LOG = 0
    Const SEC_MAXLEN_LOG = 1
    Const SEC_MINLEN_PASS = 2
    Const SEC_MAXLEN_PASS = 3
    Const SEC_ALPHA_LOG = 4
    Const SEC_NUMERIC_PASS = 5
    Const SEC_TITLE = 6

    ' Instantiate ClientApp class.
    Set ClientApp = CreateObject("EFSE.ClientApp")

    ' Assign ParamArray argument settings to variables and
    ' call object's member (only seven elements passed):
    Properties(SEC_MINLEN_LOG) = 4
    Properties(SEC_MAXLEN_LOG) = 7
    Properties(SEC_MINLEN_PASS) = 5
    Properties(SEC_MAXLEN_PASS) = 8
    Properties(SEC_ALPHA_LOG) = 1
    Properties(SEC_NUMERIC_PASS) = 1
    Properties(SEC_TITLE) = "My Own Private Security Dialog"
    ClientApp.CheckSecurity Properties()

End Sub
```

Figure 11.2 CheckSecurity dialog box—all elements passed.

Figure 11.3 CheckSecurity dialog box—only seven elements passed.

In the case of the call in Listing 11.4, the **CheckSecurity** method syntax checks and then uses the seven values passed to the **Properties( )** argument to display the Security dialog box shown in Figure 11.3.

CALLING CHECKSECURITY—ELEMENT SET TO NO VALUE

To call the **CheckSecurity** method and pass all eight elements to the **Properties( )** argument, while setting the seventh element to **vbNullstring** (no value) so **CheckSecurity** will ignore its setting and use the default, open a Standard EXE project in Visual Basic and use the code in Listing 11.5.

Listing 11.5 Code to call CheckSecurity—element set to no value.

```
Private Sub Form_DblClick()

    ' Variables:
    Dim VBPath          As String
    Dim ClientApp       As Object
    Dim Properties(7)   As Variant

    ' Constants for different properties:
    Const SEC_MINLEN_LOG = 0
    Const SEC_MAXLEN_LOG = 1
    Const SEC_MINLEN_PASS = 2
    Const SEC_MAXLEN_PASS = 3
    Const SEC_ALPHA_LOG = 4
    Const SEC_NUMERIC_PASS = 5
    Const SEC_TITLE = 6
    Const SEC_ICON = 7
```

```
' Instantiate ClientApp class.
Set ClientApp = CreateObject("EFSE.ClientApp")

' Generate error to find VB's path (this finds
' it without using Windows API functions):
On Error Resume Next
Err.Raise Number:=3
VBPath = Err.HelpFile
If Right$(VBPath, 6) = "VB.HLP" Then
   VBPath = Mid$(Err.HelpFile, 1, Len(Err.HelpFile) - 6)
ElseIf Right$(VBPath, 11) = "VEENLR3.HLP" Then
   VBPath = Mid$(Err.HelpFile, 1, Len(Err.HelpFile) - 16) _
                 & "GRAPHICS\"
End If

' Assign ParamArray argument settings to variables and
' call object's member (seventh element set to vbNullString):
Properties(SEC_MINLEN_LOG) = 4
Properties(SEC_MAXLEN_LOG) = 7
Properties(SEC_MINLEN_PASS) = 5
Properties(SEC_MAXLEN_PASS) = 8
Properties(SEC_ALPHA_LOG) = 1
Properties(SEC_NUMERIC_PASS) = 1
Properties(SEC_TITLE) = vbNullString
Properties(SEC_ICON) = VBPath & "ICONS\MISC\SECUR03.ICO"
ClientApp.CheckSecurity Properties()

End Sub
```

In the case of the call in Listing 11.5, the **CheckSecurity** method syntax checks the eight values passed to the **Properties( )** argument. When it finds that the seventh element is set to **vbNullString** (or, for elements that take a numeric expression, to **vbEmpty**), it ignores that element's value and uses the default. When you use a **ParamArray Properties( )** argument in a method, it is imperative that it provide a way for the client application programmer to skip over an element or elements that he or she does not want to set. The technique of passing **vbEmpty/vbNullString** for such an element, which the book's class library uses, is effective and easy to implement. The call in Listing 11.5 displays the Security dialog box shown in Figure 11.4.

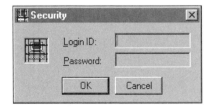

Figure 11.4 CheckSecurity dialog box—seventh element set to no value.

CALLING CHECKSECURITY—LOWER BOUND ANY VALUE

To call the **CheckSecurity** method and pass all eight elements to the **Properties( )** argument, while using any lower bound for the initial element of the array, open a Standard EXE project in Visual Basic and use the code in Listing 11.6.

Listing 11.6   Code to call CheckSecurity—lower bound any value.

```
Private Sub Form_DblClick()

    ' Variables:
    Dim VBPath              As String
    Dim ClientApp           As Object
    Dim Properties(-4 To 3)  As Variant

    ' Constants for different properties:
    Const SEC_MINLEN_LOG = -4
    Const SEC_MAXLEN_LOG = -3
    Const SEC_MINLEN_PASS = -2
    Const SEC_MAXLEN_PASS = -1
    Const SEC_ALPHA_LOG = 0
    Const SEC_NUMERIC_PASS = 1
    Const SEC_TITLE = 2
    Const SEC_ICON = 3

    ' Instantiate ClientApp class.
    Set ClientApp = CreateObject("EFSE.ClientApp")

    ' Generate error to find VB's path (this finds
    ' it without using Windows API functions):
    On Error Resume Next
    Err.Raise Number:=3
    VBPath = Err.HelpFile
    If Right$(VBPath, 6) = "VB.HLP" Then
        VBPath = Mid$(Err.HelpFile, 1, Len(Err.HelpFile) - 6)
    ElseIf Right$(VBPath, 11) = "VEENLR3.HLP" Then
        VBPath = Mid$(Err.HelpFile, 1, Len(Err.HelpFile) - 16) _
                    & "GRAPHICS\"
    End If

    ' Assign ParamArray argument settings to variables and
    ' call object's member (lower bound of array  is -4):
    Properties(SEC_MINLEN_LOG) = 4
    Properties(SEC_MAXLEN_LOG) = 7
    Properties(SEC_MINLEN_PASS) = 5
    Properties(SEC_MAXLEN_PASS) = 8
    Properties(SEC_ALPHA_LOG) = 1
    Properties(SEC_NUMERIC_PASS) = 1
    Properties(SEC_TITLE) = "My Own Private Security Dialog"
    Properties(SEC_ICON) = VBPath & "ICONS\MISC\SECURO3.ICO"
    ClientApp.CheckSecurity Properties()

End Sub
```

The call in Listing 11.6 demonstrates that the **CheckSecurity** method gives the client application programmer complete freedom to declare the lower bound of the array as any value (in this example, -4). You might be wondering why anyone would want to do this. The point is that the class library should impose as few constraints as possible. Although very few programmers notice it, Visual Basic itself permits you to declare an array whose lower bound is a negative value. A class library that is designed to be an application framework and an extension of Visual Basic itself should not impose any limits on the client application programmer other than those of the language itself. The dialog box that **CheckSecurity** displays in this case is the same as the one shown in Figure 11.2.

CALLING CHECKSECURITY—PASSING MORE THAN EIGHT ELEMENTS

If you call the **CheckSecurity** method and pass more than eight elements to the **Properties( )** argument, the method ignores the extraneous elements and displays the dialog box based on the settings of the initial eight elements.

CALLING CHECKSECURITY—PASSING INDIVIDUAL PARAMETERS

If you call the **CheckSecurity** method and try to pass individual parameters to the **Properties( )** argument, as in Listing 11.7, instead of passing them in an array, the **Security** method's code displays the syntax error message shown in Figure 11.5.

Listing 11.7 Code to trigger ParamArray error (must be array).

```
Private Sub Form_DblClick()

    ' Variables:
    Dim ClientApp    As Object
    Dim MinLenLog    As Integer
    Dim MaxLenLog    As Integer

    ' Assign variables:
    MinLenLog = 4
    MaxLenLog = 7

    ' Instantiate ClientApp class.
    Set ClientApp = CreateObject("EFSE.ClientApp")

    ' Call object's member passing invalid, individual value.
    ClientApp.CheckSecurity MinLenLog, MaxLenLog

End Sub
```

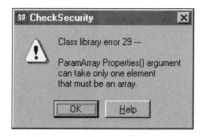

Figure 11.5 Message for ParamArray error (must be array).

CALLING CHECKSECURITY—PASSING AN INVALID ELEMENT

If you call the **CheckSecurity** method and try to pass an element that is not the specified subtype to the **Properties( )** argument, as in Listing 11.8, the **Security** method's code displays the syntax error message shown in Figure 11.6. The subtype of the **Properties( )** argument's third element must be an **Integer**, but the code in Listing 11.8 tries to pass it a **String**.

Listing 11.8   Code to trigger ParamArray error (invalid subtype).

```
Private Sub Form_DblClick()

    ' Variables:
    Dim VBPath          As String
    Dim ClientApp       As Object
    Dim Properties(7)   As Variant

    ' Constants for different properties:
    Const SEC_MINLEN_LOG = 0
    Const SEC_MAXLEN_LOG = 1
    Const SEC_MINLEN_PASS = 2
    Const SEC_MAXLEN_PASS = 3
    Const SEC_ALPHA_LOG = 4
    Const SEC_NUMERIC_PASS = 5
    Const SEC_TITLE = 6
    Const SEC_ICON = 7

    ' Instantiate ClientApp class.
    Set ClientApp = CreateObject("EFSE.ClientApp")

    ' Generate error to find VB's path (this finds
    ' it without using Windows API functions):
    On Error Resume Next
    Err.Raise Number:=3
    VBPath = Err.HelpFile
    If Right$(VBPath, 6) = "VB.HLP" Then
        VBPath = Mid$(Err.HelpFile, 1, Len(Err.HelpFile) - 6)
    ElseIf Right$(VBPath, 11) = "VEENLR3.HLP" Then
        VBPath = Mid$(Err.HelpFile, 1, Len(Err.HelpFile) - 16) _
                    & "GRAPHICS\"
```

```
End If

' Assign ParamArray argument settings to variables and call
' object's member (element number 2 is invalid/a string):
Properties(SEC_MINLEN_LOG) = 4
Properties(SEC_MAXLEN_LOG) = 7
Properties(SEC_MINLEN_PASS) = "abc"
Properties(SEC_MAXLEN_PASS) = 8
Properties(SEC_ALPHA_LOG) = 1
Properties(SEC_NUMERIC_PASS) = 1
Properties(SEC_TITLE) = "My Own Private Security Dialog"
Properties(SEC_ICON) = VBPath & "ICONS\MISC\SECUR03.ICO"
ClientApp.CheckSecurity Properties()

End Sub
```

CALLING CHECKSECURITY—PASSING AN UNINITIALIZED ELEMENT

If you call the **CheckSecurity** method and try to pass an uninitialized element (the fifth one) to the **Properties( )** argument, as in Listing 11.9, the **Security** method's code displays the syntax error message shown in Figure 11.7.

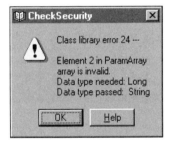

Figure 11.6 Message for ParamArray error (invalid subtype).

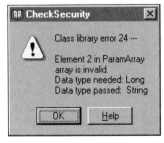

Figure 11.7 Message for ParamArray error (element uninitialized).

Listing 11.9   Code to trigger ParamArray error (element uninitialized).

```
Private Sub Form_DblClick()

    ' Variables:
    Dim VBPath          As String
    Dim ClientApp       As Object
    Dim Properties(7)   As Variant

    ' Constants for different properties:
    Const SEC_MINLEN_LOG = 0
    Const SEC_MAXLEN_LOG = 1
    Const SEC_MINLEN_PASS = 2
    Const SEC_MAXLEN_PASS = 3
    Const SEC_ALPHA_LOG = 4
    Const SEC_NUMERIC_PASS = 5
    Const SEC_TITLE = 6
    Const SEC_ICON = 7

    ' Instantiate ClientApp class.
    Set ClientApp = CreateObject("EFSE.ClientApp")

    ' Generate error to find VB's path (this finds
    ' it without using Windows API functions):
    On Error Resume Next
    Err.Raise Number:=3
    VBPath = Err.HelpFile
    If Right$(VBPath, 6) = "VB.HLP" Then
        VBPath = Mid$(Err.HelpFile, 1, Len(Err.HelpFile) - 6)
    ElseIf Right$(VBPath, 11) = "VEENLR3.HLP" Then
        VBPath = Mid$(Err.HelpFile, 1, Len(Err.HelpFile) - 16) _
                    & "GRAPHICS\"
    End If

    ' Assign ParamArray argument settings to variables and call
    ' object's member (element number 4 is uninitialized):
    Properties(SEC_MINLEN_LOG) = 4
    Properties(SEC_MAXLEN_LOG) = 7
    Properties(SEC_MINLEN_PASS) = 5
    Properties(SEC_MAXLEN_PASS) = 8
    ' The fifth element is left uninitialized.
    Properties(SEC_NUMERIC_PASS) = 1
    Properties(SEC_TITLE) = "My Own Private Security Dialog"
    Properties(SEC_ICON) = VBPath & "ICONS\MISC\SECURO3.ICO"
    ClientApp.CheckSecurity Properties()

End Sub
```

CALLING CHECKSECURITY—PASSING AN UNSIZED ARRAY

If you call the **CheckSecurity** method and try to pass an array that has not been dimensioned to the **Properties( )** argument, as in Listing 11.10, the **Security** method's code displays the syntax error message shown in Figure 11.8.

Listing 11.10 Code to trigger ParamArray error (array not sized).

```
Private Sub Form_DblClick()

    ' Variables:
    Dim ClientApp      As Object
    Dim Properties()   As Variant

    ' Instantiate ClientApp class.
    Set ClientApp = CreateObject("EFSE.ClientApp")

    ' Call object's member passing invalid, unsized array.
    ClientApp.CheckSecurity Properties()

End Sub
```

The CheckSecurity Method's Code

The degree of flexibility demonstrated in the previous sections, regarding the **Properties( )** argument of the **CheckSecurity** method, is due to three factors. First, the declaration of the **Properties( )** argument with the **ParamArray** keyword provides, in a manner of speaking, the superclass of flexibility. Second, the **CheckSecurity** method's code is written in such a way that it applies certain constraints to the **ParamArray** keyword's flexibility and, again in a manner of speaking, subclasses it. Third, the **IsParamArray** method of the **CL** class is called by **CheckSecurity** (and other members of the class library) to do some of the syntax checking of the **ParamArray** argument. This same type of code appears in several mem-

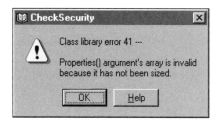

Figure 11.8 Message for ParamArray error (array not sized).

bers of the class library. We will analyze it in depth for the **CheckSecurity** method and then only refer to it later on in the book. The code for the **CheckSecurity** method is in Listing 11.11.

Listing 11.11   The CheckSecurity method's code.

```
Function CheckSecurity(ParamArray Properties())

    ' Constants for elements in Props array:
    Const SEC_MAXLEN_LOG = 1
    Const SEC_MINLEN_PASS = 2
    Const SEC_MAXLEN_PASS = 3
    Const SEC_ALPHA_LOG = 4
    Const SEC_NUMERIC_PASS = 5
    Const SEC_TITLE = 6
    Const SEC_ICON = 7

    ' Constants for literals:
    Const PROC = "CheckSecurity"
    Const SYNTAX = True
    Const ADJ = 1
    Const LOW_BOUND = 0
    Const MAX_PROPS = 8
    Const NO_VAL1 = vbEmpty
    Const NO_VAL2 = vbNullString
    Const ARG_NM = "Properties()"

    ' Variables:
    Dim SrcPath        As String
    Dim TmpStr         As String
    Dim El             As Variant
    Dim Prop           As Variant
    Dim Props          As Variant
    Dim ValidTypes(7)  As Variant

    ' Enable error handler and do syntax checking:
    On Error GoTo ET
    If cRAOServer Then
        E.TrapSyntax 1, PROC, "ActiveX RAO component"
    End If

    ' Check ParamArray Properties() argument--
    ' * Ensure it is Variant array.
    ' * Assign Properties() array to Variant Props. Passing as
    '   Properties() causes "Invalid ParamArray use" error.
    ' * Ensure array is dimensioned.
    ' * Specify valid data types for elements.
    ' * Call IsParamArray method to check argument for:
    '   a) Uninitialized element.
    '   b) Element with invalid data type.
    ' * Ensure valid value for each property.
    If Not IsMissing(Properties()) Then
      Props = Properties(LOW_BOUND)
```

```
If VarType(Props) <> vbVariant + vbArray Then
    E.TrapSyntax 29, PROC, ARG_NM
ElseIf Not CL.IsSized(Props) Then
    E.TrapSyntax 41, PROC, ARG_NM
End If

For El = LOW_BOUND To SEC_NUMERIC_PASS
    ValidTypes(El) = vbLong
Next El

ValidTypes(SEC_TITLE) = vbString
ValidTypes(SEC_ICON) = vbString

CL.IsParamArray PROC, ValidTypes(), Props, MAX_PROPS

El = LBound(Props)

For Each Prop In Props

    If Prop <> CVar(NO_VAL1) And Prop <> CVar(NO_VAL2) Then

        If El = LBound(Props) Then

            If Prop <> 4 And Prop <> 5 And Prop <> 6 Then
                E.TrapSyntax 26, PROC, "Minimum", _
                            "login ID", ARG_NM, "4, 5 or 6"
            End If
            frmCheckSecurity.MinLoginID = Prop

        ElseIf El = LBound(Props) + SEC_MAXLEN_LOG Then

            If Prop <> 7 And Prop <> 8 And Prop <> 9 Then
                E.TrapSyntax 26, PROC, "Maximum", _
                            "login ID", ARG_NM, "7, 8 or 9"
            End If
            frmCheckSecurity.MaxLoginID = Prop

        ElseIf El = LBound(Props) + SEC_MINLEN_PASS Then

            If Prop <> 5 And Prop <> 6 And Prop <> 7 Then
                E.TrapSyntax 26, PROC, "Minimum", _
                            "password", ARG_NM, "5, 6 or 7"
            End If
            frmCheckSecurity.MinPassword = Prop

        ElseIf El = LBound(Props) + SEC_MAXLEN_PASS Then

            If Prop <> 7 And Prop <> 8 And Prop <> 9 Then
                E.TrapSyntax 26, PROC, "Maximum", _
                            "password", ARG_NM, "7, 8 or 9"
            End If
            frmCheckSecurity.MaxPassword = Prop

        ElseIf El = LBound(Props) + SEC_ALPHA_LOG Then
```

```
           If Prop <> 0 And Prop <> 1 And Prop <> 2 Then
               E.TrapSyntax 27, PROC, "alpha", _
                            "login ID", ARG_NM, "0, 1 or 2"
           End If
           frmCheckSecurity.NumAlphaChars = Prop

       ElseIf El = LBound(Props) + SEC_NUMERIC_PASS Then

           If Prop <> 0 And Prop <> 1 And Prop <> 2 Then
               E.TrapSyntax 27, PROC, "numeric", _
                            "password", ARG_NM, "0, 1 or 2"
           End If
           frmCheckSecurity.NumNumericChars = Prop

       ElseIf El = LBound(Props) + SEC_TITLE Then
           CL.IsTitle Prop, PROC
           frmCheckSecurity.CaptionCL = Prop

       ElseIf El = LBound(Props) + SEC_ICON Then
           TmpStr = "SEC_ICON element of Properties()"
           CL.IsPath1 CStr(Prop), PROC, TmpStr, SrcPath
           CL.IsFile CStr(Prop), SrcPath, PROC, TmpStr, "ICO"
           frmCheckSecurity.IconCL = Prop
       End If
    End If

    El = El + 1

  Next Prop
End If

' Display method's Form object modally, so execution pauses
' until Hide method's applied in Cmd_Click event procedure.
frmCheckSecurity.Show vbModal

' When Hide method's applied, return array and unload form.
CheckSecurity = Array(True, frmCheckSecurity.Tag)
Unload frmCheckSecurity
Exit Function

ET:

  If Err = SYNTAX Then CheckSecurity = frmErrCodes.Codes
  If Err <> SYNTAX Then CheckSecurity = CL.TrapErr(PROC)

End Function
```

ACCEPTING ONLY AN ARRAY

The code in the **CheckSecurity** method that syntax-checks the **Properties( )** argument to accept only an array is shown here:

```
Function CheckSecurity(ParamArray Properties())
   . . .

      Props = Properties(LOW_BOUND)

      If VarType(Props) <> vbVariant + vbArray Then
         E.TrapSyntax 29, PROC, ARG_NM
      ElseIf Not CL.IsSized(Props) Then
         E.TrapSyntax 41, PROC, ARG_NM
      End If
   . . .

End Function
```

Several things happen in this code snippet. First, the initial or lower-bound element of the **Properties( )** argument is assigned to the **Variant Props**. Second, the subtype of **Props** is checked to ensure that it is an array (that is, equal to **vbVariant + vbArray**); if it is not, syntax error message 29 is displayed. Third, if it is an array, the **IsSized** method of the **CL** class is called to check that **Props** has been dimensioned; if it has not, syntax error message 41 is displayed.

SPECIFYING VALID SUBTYPES OF ELEMENTS

The code in the **CheckSecurity** method that specifies the valid subtypes of the elements of the **Properties( )** argument is shown here:

```
Function CheckSecurity(ParamArray Properties())
   . . .

      For El = LOW_BOUND To SEC_NUMERIC_PASS
         ValidTypes(El) = vbInteger
      Next El

      ValidTypes(SEC_TITLE) = vbString
      ValidTypes(SEC_ICON) = vbString
   . . .

End Function
```

The valid subtypes are specified in the method's help topic (**Integer** for the initial six elements, **String** for the last two). The code snippet assigns the valid subtypes (in the form of the Visual Basic intrinsic constants **vbInteger** - 2 and **vbString** - 8) to the array **ValidTypes(7)** declared at the top of the **CheckSecurity** method.

IsParamArray Method's Code

The code in the **CheckSecurity** method that validates the rest of the specified attributes of the **Properties( ) ParamArray** argument is in the generic **IsParamArray** method of the **CL** class. **IsParamArray** is called from the **CheckSecurity** method by this statement:

```
CL.IsParamArray PROC, ValidTypes(), Props, MAX_PROPS
```

IsParamArray takes the following four arguments:

- *PROC* is a **String** constant that equals the name of the method (in this case, "CheckSecurity").
- *ValidTypes( )* is the array containing the valid types for the elements in the **Properties( )** argument (in this case, six **Integers** and two **Strings**).
- *Props* is the surrogate **Variant** that contains the values passed to the **Properties( )** argument.
- *MAX_PROPS* is a constant specifying the maximum number of elements to be processed from the **Properties( )** argument (in this case, eight).

The code for the **IsParamArray** method is shown in Listing 11.12.

Listing 11.12   The IsParamArray method's code.

```
Sub IsParamArray(Member As String, _
                 ValidTypes(), _
                 Params, _
                 MaxParams As Integer)


' _____

' Purpose: Checks for two kinds of syntax errors in any
'          ParamArray argument:
'             * An uninitialized element in ParamArray array.
'             * Elements in ParamArray array with invalid
'               subtypes.
'
' Called:  Internally from members of class library.
'
' Accepts: Member:       String expression specifying name of
'                        member from which ParamArray array is
'                        being passed.
'          ValidTypes(): Variant. Each element in array
'                        specifies valid subtype of
'                        corresponding element in ParamArray
'                        argument. Scheme for specifying type
'                        is one used by VB's VarType function.
'          Params:       Variant that contains array holding
'                        contents of ParamArray argument being
'                        validated.
```

```
'           MaxParams:    Integer expression specifying
'                         maximum number of elements to be
'                         processed in ParamArray argument.
' _____

' Constants for literals:
Const FIRST_TYPE_STR = 0
Const LAST_TYPE_STR = 18
Const OFFSET = 1

' Variables:
Dim IDStr1        As String
Dim IDStr2        As String
Dim IDStr3        As String
Dim TypeStr       As Byte
Dim NumEls        As Variant
Dim ElAdj         As Variant
Dim Param         As Variant
Dim FirstParam    As Variant
Dim LastParam     As Variant
Dim TypeStrs(18)  As String

' Initialize by assigning types of values VarType function can return:
TypeStrs(0) = "Uninitialized"
TypeStrs(1) = "Contains no valid data"
TypeStrs(2) = "Integer"
TypeStrs(3) = "Long"
TypeStrs(4) = "Single"
TypeStrs(5) = "Double"
TypeStrs(6) = "Currency"
TypeStrs(7) = "Date"
TypeStrs(8) = "String"
TypeStrs(9) = "OLE Automation object"
TypeStrs(10) = "Error"
TypeStrs(11) = "Boolean"
TypeStrs(12) = "Variant (only for arrays)"
TypeStrs(13) = "Non-OLE Automation object"
TypeStrs(14) = "Decimal"
TypeStrs(15) = vbNullString
TypeStrs(16) = vbNullString
TypeStrs(17) = "Byte"
TypeStrs(18) = "Array"

' Execute member's algorithm—
' * Compute number of elements in array.
' * Compute last element to check. It can be based on:
'   a) Maximum number of elements allowed, if same number of
'      elements were passed in.
'   b) Number of elements passed in, if that number is less
'      than maximum number of elements.
'   c) Maximum number of elements allowed, if number of
'      elements passed in is greater than maximum allowed.
' * Check for uninitialized element among those to be checked.
' * Check for invalid subtype among those elements to be
```

```
'    checked and display message specifying valid subtype
'    and invalid subtype passed.

NumEls = UBound(Params) + OFFSET - LBound(Params)
FirstParam = LBound(Params)

If NumEls = MaxParams Then
    LastParam = UBound(Params)
ElseIf NumEls < MaxParams Then
    LastParam = FirstParam + NumEls - OFFSET
ElseIf NumEls > MaxParams Then
    LastParam = UBound(Params) - (NumEls - MaxParams)
End If

For Param = FirstParam To LastParam

    If VarType(Params(Param)) = vbEmpty Then
        E.TrapSyntax 23, Member, CStr(Param)
    End If

Next Param

ElAdj = LBound(Params)

For Param = FirstParam To LastParam
    IDStr1 = "Element " & Param

    If VarType(Params(Param)) <> ValidTypes(Param - ElAdj) Then

        For TypeStr = FIRST_TYPE_STR To LAST_TYPE_STR
            If ValidTypes(Param - ElAdj) = TypeStr Then
                IDStr2 = TypeStrs(TypeStr)
                Exit For
            End If

        Next TypeStr

        For TypeStr = FIRST_TYPE_STR To LAST_TYPE_STR

            If VarType(Params(Param)) = TypeStr Then
                IDStr3 = TypeStrs(TypeStr)
                E.TrapSyntax 24, Member, IDStr1, _
                                IDStr2, IDStr3
                Exit For
            End If

        Next TypeStr
    End If
Next Param
End Sub
```

There are several major points to note about the code in the **IsParamArray** method. Each element of the **TypeStrs( )** array is assigned a **String** description that corresponds to a description of a value returned by Visual Basic's **VarType** function. For example, element 2 of **TypeStrs( )** is assigned the string "Integer" and element 8 is assigned the string "String" because these are the descriptions of the values 2 and 8 returned by **VarType** (see the help topic in Visual Basic's Help file titled *VarType Function* for a list of these descriptions). The strings assigned to the **TypeStrs( )** array are used in the syntax error messages to describe the valid subtype for each element. Another significant point is that the variables **FirstParam** and **LastParam** hold the element numbers of the lower and upper bounds of the *Params* argument, which is a surrogate for the **Properties( )** argument. Because the lower bound of the array can be any value (including a negative one), and because more elements than the maximum allowed may have been passed, the value of the upper bound has to be carefully calculated. Finally, the code in the two loops headed by the statement

```
For TypeStr = FIRST_TYPE_STR To LAST_TYPE_STR
```

determines the customized strings to be passed to syntax error message 24. In the example shown in Listing 11.8, **IDStr2** was "Integer" and **IDStr3** was "String".

As with almost all methods in the **CL** class, there is no error handler enabled in the **IsParamArray** method. So if a syntax error is found, after the **TrapSyntax** method displays the message and raises the artificial runtime error of **True**, code execution reverts back to the enabled error handler in the public method that called the **IsParamArray** method. That public method then returns the error codes.

Cautionary Notes About The ParamArray Keyword

Obviously, the kind of power and flexibility demonstrated in the examples of the **ParamArray** argument does not just happen. The Visual Basic programmer who writes a class library with methods that use a **ParamArray** argument must ensure that the client application programmer who calls those methods does not unwittingly shoot himself or herself in the foot.

As a Visual Basic class library developer, you can take two big steps to ensure that methods with **ParamArray** arguments are used correctly:

- Document any restrictions on the use of the **ParamArray** argument in the help topic for its member.

- Use a generic private method to automate as much of the syntax checking required by a **ParamArray** argument as possible. Syntax checking the contents of a **ParamArray** optional argument is a complex and tedious task. It is definitely something you only want to write the code for once, if at all possible.

Custom Properties Vs. ParamArray Properties( ) Argument

As I stated earlier in this chapter, the book's class library does not contain any public custom properties. One reason for this is that this class library, which is essentially an application framework for Visual Basic, does not require any public custom properties. However, the book's class library does use many **Property Get**, **Property Let**, and **Property Set** procedures internally. Internal custom properties in a class library are especially useful for three purposes. First, unlike the case with built-in properties of a **Form** object, you can set an encapsulated form's custom properties without causing its **Form_Load** event to occur. Second, a custom property is the easiest way of passing an object reference to a module and storing it there. Third, because of the way the **Error** class is designed and the way in which its public and private members interact with the other classes in the class library, the custom property Codes in the frmErrCodes **Form** object is the easiest way of storing and retrieving error information after the **Error** class goes out of scope.

In comparison to the use of a **ParamArray Properties( )** argument, the performance and size-of-file penalties incurred if you were to use a corresponding number of public custom properties makes them an unattractive alternative. These penalties would be especially high if you were to use public custom properties in a Remote Automation Object's ActiveX component. Once you have learned the techniques required to effectively use **ParamArray** arguments, you will find little need to use public custom properties under most circumstances.

12 POLYMORPHIC METHODS

I f two or more classes have methods that share the same name, take the same arguments, and have the same basic purpose, but are implemented differently, the methods are said to be *polymorphic*. Polymorphism is the ability to hide the implementation details of a method behind a common public interface. A client application programmer can call and apply a polymorphic method to different objects without knowing anything about how the method is implemented. Polymorphism enables the object-oriented programmer to simplify the public interface to a class library by minimizing the number of different methods. For example, instead of having a **CenterForm** method, a **CenterPictureBox** method, and so on, there is just the **Center** method. Polymorphism makes the maintenance of legacy code easier and promotes reuse of the objects in a class library by client application programmers.

Polymorphism hides the complexity of the method from the client application programmer. For example, there are obviously major differences between the code you would write to center a **Form** object on the screen, a MDI child form on a

MDIForm object, or an **Image** object on a **PictureBox** object. But the client application programmer does not need to know anything about these differences to use the **Center** method.

In the book's class library, there are three polymorphic methods: **Center**, **Load**, and **Save**. The **Center** method is a member of the **Dialog**, **Graphic**, and **List** classes. The **Load** and **Save** methods are members of the **Graphic**, **List**, and **Text** classes. In this chapter, we will focus on these three methods as they apply to the **Dialog**, **List**, and **Graphic** classes. We will look at how the **Load** and **Save** methods work in the **Text** class in a later chapter.

The Center Method

The **Center** method centers certain Visual Basic objects within the client area of their parent/container objects. The topic in the class library's Help file (EFS.HLP) that specifies the detailed functionality of the **Center** method is shown in the sidebar.

Center method's specifications.

SYNTAX

```
Object.Center(Obj)
```

The **Center** method's syntax has the following object qualifier and named arguments:

- *Object*. Required. **Object** data type. An expression that evaluates to an object in the Applies To pop-up list.

- *Obj*. Required. **Object** data type. An expression that evaluates to the **Name** property of a Visual Basic object in the Applies To pop-up list. The supported objects are **Form**, **MDIForm**, **ComboBox**, **DBCombo**, **DBList**, **ListBox**, **Image**, and **PictureBox**.

CALLED

From any procedure in a client application; but, for a **Form** or **MDIForm** object, normally from its **Load** event procedure.

RETURNS

Upon success, one element in a **Variant**. It contains a **Boolean** (**True**) that specifies the member executed successfully.

Upon failure, eight elements in a **Variant**. The elements contain the error codes that the class library returns when a runtime or syntax error occurs during the execution of one of its members.

REMARKS

The **Center** method can produce unexpected results when a large form, designed at a high resolution (for example, 1024×768), is displayed on a lower-resolution monitor at runtime:

- If the design time **ScaleHeight** property of the form is greater than the height of the **Screen** object, Visual Basic sets the **ScaleHeight** of the form to the height of the **Screen** object so the form will fit. But Visual Basic will not display any controls on the form whose **Top** property is greater than the height of the **Screen** object.

- If the design time **ScaleWidth** property of the form is greater than the width of the **Screen** object, Visual Basic sets the **ScaleWidth** of the form to the width of the **Screen** object so the form will fit. But Visual Basic will not display any controls on the form whose **Left** property is greater than the width of the **Screen** object.

- If both the **ScaleHeight** and **ScaleWidth** properties of the form at design time are greater than the height and width of the **Screen** object, Visual Basic maximizes the form. But Visual Basic will not display any controls on the form whose **Top** property is greater than the height of the **Screen** object or whose **Left** property is greater than the width of the **Screen** object.

The Center Method's Code— Graphic/List Classes

Except for the syntax checking code, which validates that one of the supported Visual Basic objects has been passed to its **Obj** argument, the code for the **Center** method of the **Graphic** and **List** classes is functionally the same. The code for the implementation in the **Graphic** class is shown in Listing 12.1.

Listing 12.1 The Center method's code—Graphic class.

```
Function Center(Obj As Object)

    ' Constant for literals:
    Const PROC = "Center"
    Const SYNTAX = True
    Const ONE_HALF = 0.5

    ' Variables:
    Dim OrigScaleMode   As Byte
    Dim ParWid          As Long
    Dim ParHgt          As Long
    Dim Rct             As RECT

    ' Enable error handler and do syntax checking:
    On Error GoTo ET

    If TypeName(Obj) <> "Image" And _
       TypeName(Obj) <> "PictureBox" Then
         Error.TrapSyntax 8, PROC, "Obj"
    End If

    ' Execute member's algorithm—
    ' * Store original ScaleMode setting and temporarily
    '   convert to twips.
    ' * Get client coordinates of control object's parent.
    ' * Compute height and width of client portion of parent
    '   and convert pixels to twips (15 twips per pixel).
    ' * Compute X and Y coordinates of control to center.
    ' * Restore original ScaleMode setting.
    OrigScaleMode = Obj.Container.ScaleMode
    Obj.Container.ScaleMode = vbTwips
    GetClientRect Obj.Container.hWnd, Rct
    ParWid = (Rct.Rgt - Rct.Lft) * Screen.TwipsPerPixelY
    ParHgt = (Rct.Bot - Rct.Top) * Screen.TwipsPerPixelX
    Obj.Left = (ParWid - Obj.Width) * ONE_HALF
    Obj.Top = (ParHgt - Obj.Height) * ONE_HALF
    Obj.Container.ScaleMode = OrigScaleMode

    Center = Array(True)
    Exit Function

ET:

    If Err = SYNTAX Then Center = frmErrCodes.Codes
    If Err <> SYNTAX Then Center = CL.TrapErr(PROC)

End Function
```

The Center Method's Code—Dialog Class

The code for the **Center** method of the **Dialog** class, shown in Listing 12.2, is functionally quite different from that of the **Center** method of the **Graphic** and **List** classes. As you would expect, it is pretty much the same code used in the **CenterForm** procedure you wrote in Chapter 2.

Listing 12.2   The Center method's code—Dialog class.

```
Function Center(Obj As Object)

    ' Constants for literals:
    Const PROC = "Center"
    Const SYNTAX = True
    Const ONE_HALF = 0.5

    ' Variables:
    Dim ChildFrm    As Boolean
    Dim ParWid      As Long
    Dim ParHgt      As Long
    Dim Rct         As RECT

    ' Enable error handler and do syntax checking:
    On Error GoTo ET

    If Not CL.IsForm(Obj) And Not _
          CL.IsMDIForm(Obj) Then
              E.TrapSyntax 8, PROC, "Obj"
    End If

    ' * If Frm argument is MDI child:
    '   a) Get handle of MDIForm object and client coordinates.
    '   b) Compute height and width of client portion of MDIForm
    '      and convert pixels to twips.
    '   c) Compute X and Y coordinates of MDI child to center.
    ' * If Frm argument is not MDI child, compute against Screen.
    ' * Center Form object using Left (X) and Top (Y) properties.
    On Error Resume Next

    If Obj.MDIChild Then

        If Err = False Then
            ChildFrm = True
            GetClientRect GetParent(Obj.hWnd), Rct
            ParWid = (Rct.Rgt - Rct.Lft) * Screen.TwipsPerPixelY
            ParHgt = (Rct.Bot - Rct.Top) * Screen.TwipsPerPixelX
            Obj.Left = (ParWid - Obj.Width) * ONE_HALF
            Obj.Top = (ParHgt - Obj.Height) * ONE_HALF
        End If

    End If
```

```
If Not ChildFrm Then
    Obj.Left = (Screen.Width - Obj.Width) * ONE_HALF
    Obj.Top = (Screen.Height - Obj.Height) * ONE_HALF
End If

Center = Array(True)
Exit Function

ET:
    If Err = SYNTAX Then Center = frmErrCodes.Codes
    If Err <> SYNTAX Then Center = CL.TrapErr(PROC)

End Function
```

If you examined the code for the **Center** method in the **Graphic** and **List** classes and saw how similar it is, you might wonder whether there would be any advantage in consolidating all the code of the various implementations in one member in the **CL** class. It is possible to do this and to then call the **Center** method of the **CL** class from the three public classes that contain the **Center** method.

In the case of the **Center** method, the number of lines of redundant code is so small that the possible reduction in size of the ActiveX component's file (DLL or EXE) is immaterial. Likewise, maintenance of the class library's code base would not be made significantly easier. However, for another polymorphic method, which might apply to many different classes and be much more complex in its implementation, it might make sense to implement the details of the different algorithms in a method of the **CL** class. In that case, the many instances of the polymorphic method in the public classes would function essentially as wrapper procedures. The only code that the wrapper procedures would include would do syntax checking, make the call to the member of the **CL** class, and return the result of the method to the client application.

Before you consider implementing an approach that uses wrapper methods in the public classes and a single, one-holds-all functionality class in a private class like **CL**, you should consider the potential benefits. First, there is no improvement in performance to be realized; if anything, performance will degrade slightly. Second, whatever reduction in the size of the ActiveX component's file(s) you achieve is essentially immaterial, given an era when hard drives are incredibly large and cheap (and getting larger and cheaper all the time). Third, any reduction in the amount of RAM required to handle the instantiated classes of the ActiveX component is also immaterial. The Intel Pentium or Pentium Pro hardware platforms that will be typical of the desktop or workstation machine within a couple years will make almost all questions regarding available RAM obsolete. In short, when you are tempted to violate the OOP attribute of encapsulation to save a little RAM or hard drive space, think long and hard before doing so.

The Load Method

The **Load** method loads a file into certain Visual Basic objects. The topic in the class library's Help file (EFS.HLP) that specifies the detailed functionality of the **Load** method is shown in the sidebar.

Load method's specifications.

SYNTAX

```
Object.Load(Obj, File, [LockFile])
```

The **Load** method's syntax has the following object qualifier and named arguments:

- *Object*. Required. **Object** data type. An expression that evaluates to an object in the Applies To pop-up list.

- *Obj*. Required. **Object** data type. An expression that evaluates to the **Name** property of a Visual Basic object in the Applies To pop-up list. The supported objects are **Form**, **Image**, **PictureBox**, **ComboBox**, **ListBox**, **RichTextBox**, and **TextBox**.

- *File*. Required. **String** data type. An expression that specifies the path and name of a file to load into *Obj*.

- *LockFile*. Optional. **Variant** data type whose subtype is a numeric expression that evaluates to **True**. If *LockWrite* is passed, no another application can open the loaded file until it is closed by the client application.

CALLED

From any procedure in a client application.

RETURNS

Upon success, two elements in a **Variant**. The elements contain these subtypes:

- 0 - MBR_SUCCESS. A **Boolean** (**True**) that specifies the member executed successfully.

- 1 - MBR_FILENBR. An **Integer** that specifies the file number of the loaded file. If the *LockFile* argument is omitted, **vbEmpty** (that is, uninitialized).

Upon failure, eight elements in a **Variant**. The elements contain the error codes that the class library returns when a runtime or syntax error occurs during the execution of one of its members.

REMARKS

- The **Load** method applies to the class library's **Graphic** object only under 32-bit Visual Basic.

- You can use the **OpenCL** method of the **File** object to provide the user with a common dialog box to specify the path and name of the file to pass to the *File* argument of the **Load** method.

- If you pass the *LockFile* argument, you must store the file number returned by the **Load** method if you want to later replace the original file with the **Save** method.

- When you use the **Load** method with a **ComboBox** or **ListBox** object, the plain ASCII text file that you load must delimit the items of the list with a carriage return character (that is, **vbCr**). If the **Save** method of the **List** class was used to create the text file, the delimiters are automatically added.

- When you use the **Load** method with a **RichTextBox** object, you have the option of loading a Rich Text Format (RTF) file either as rich text or as plain ASCII text.

The Load Method's Code—Graphic Class

The code for the implementation of the **Load** method in the **Graphic** class is shown in Listing 12.3.

Listing 12.3   The Load method's code—Graphic class.

```
Function Load(Obj As Object, _
              File As String, _
              Optional LockWrite)

    ' Constants for literals:
    Const PROC = "Load"
    Const SYNTAX = True
    Const VALID_FILE_EXTS = "(.BMP or .ICO or .WMP)."

    ' Variables:
    Dim Msg        As String
    Dim SrcPath    As String
    Dim FileExt    As String
    Dim LockFile   As Boolean
    Dim FileNbr    As Integer

    ' Enable error handler and do syntax checking:
    On Error GoTo ET

    #If Win16 Then
        E.TrapSyntax 1, PROC, "16-bit VB"
    #End If

    If Not CL.IsForm(Obj) Then

        If TypeName(Obj) <> "Image" And _
           TypeName(Obj) <> "PictureBox" Then
              E.TrapSyntax 8, PROC, "Obj"
        End If

    End If

    CL.IsPath1 File, PROC, "File", SrcPath
    CL.IsFile File, SrcPath, PROC, "File"
    FileExt = UCase$(Right$(File, 4))

    Select Case FileExt
        Case ".BMP", ".ICO", ".WMF"
        Case Else
            E.TrapSyntax 19, PROC, "File", VALID_FILE_EXTS
    End Select

    ' Execute member's algorithm—
    ' * If LockWrite argument is passed, turn on flag.
    ' * Load graphic file into object.
    ' * If LockFile flag is on, open file in Lock Write
    '   mode.
    ' * NOTE: This opening of file to lock it is "kludge"
    '   required by fact that VB's LoadPicture method does
    '   not provide file-locking option.
    ' * If any runtime error occurs, substitute generic
    '   error message "Can't perform requested operation" and
```

```
'    add a little information to it. This is better than
'    displaying many possible runtime errors that can
'    occur when opening/loading file.
If Not IsMissing(LockWrite) Then LockFile = True

CL.SetHourglass True
Obj.Picture = LoadPicture(File)

If LockFile Then
    FileNbr = FreeFile
    Open File For Input Lock Write As FileNbr
End If

CL.SetHourglass False
Load = Array(True, FileNbr)
Exit Function

ET:

CL.SetHourglass False

If Err = SYNTAX Then Load = frmErrCodes.Codes
If Err <> SYNTAX Then
    Err.Number = 17
    Msg = "Can't perform requested operation. "
    Msg = Msg & "Can't load file into "

    If CL.IsForm(Obj) Then
        Msg = "Form."
    Else

        If TypeName(Obj) = "Image" Then
            Msg = Msg & "Image control."
        Else
            Msg = Msg & "PictureBox control."
        End If

    End If

    Err.Description = Msg
    Err.HelpContext = 1000017
    Load = CL.TrapErr(PROC)
End If

End Function
```

There are three points to note about the code of the **Load** method of the
Graphic class. First, the syntax-checking code checks the extension of the
File argument to determine if the file contains a bitmap, icon, or metafile.
However, the determination is made strictly on the basis of the nominal
extension; if someone renames a graphics file and, in the process, changes
the extension from .ICO to something besides .BMP or .WMF, the **Load**

method will reject the **File** argument as invalid. Second, because the **Load** method uses Visual Basic's **LoadPicture** function, which does not provide a file-locking option, we resort to using the **FreeFile** function and **Open** statement to obtain a file number for a dummy file that has been opened as write-locked. This file number is then returned from the **Load** method to the client application. Third, several different runtime errors can occur in the process of using Visual Basic's **LoadPicture** function and **Open** statement. Rather than confuse the client application's user by displaying different runtime error messages at different times, the **Load** method substitutes the generic runtime error 17 (*Can't perform requested operation*) and appends the string "Can't load file into '*kind*' control." to the error message, where *kind* can be either a **Form**, **Image**, or **PictureBox** object.

The Load Method's Code—List Class

The code for the implementation of the **Load** method in the **List** class is shown in Listing 12.4.

Listing 12.4   The Load method's code—List class.

```
Function Load(Obj As Object, _
              File As String, _
              Optional LockWrite)

   ' Constants for literals:
   Const PROC = "Load"
   Const SYNTAX = True
   Const ADJ = 1
   Const VALID_FILE_EXT = ".TXT"

   ' Variables:
   Dim Msg        As String
   Dim SrcPath    As String
   Dim FileText   As String
   Dim LockFile   As Boolean
   Dim FileNbr    As Integer
   Dim Pos        As Long
   Dim Item       As Long

   ' Enable error handler and do syntax checking:
   On Error GoTo ET

   If TypeName(Obj) <> "ComboBox" And _
      TypeName(Obj) <> "ListBox" Then
         E.TrapSyntax 8, PROC, "Obj"
   End If

   CL.IsPath1 File, PROC, "File", SrcPath
   CL.IsFile File, SrcPath, PROC, "File"
```

```
            If UCase$(Right$(File, 4)) <> VALID_FILE_EXT Then
                E.TrapSyntax 11, PROC, "File", VALID_FILE_EXT
            End If

            ' Execute member's algorithm-
            ' * If LockWrite argument is passed, turn on flag.
            ' * Depending on flag's setting, open file in correct
            '   mode and assign file's contents to variable.
            ' * Assuming that text file was saved with Save method
            '   (that is, for each line delimited by carriage return):
            '   a) Add line to list.
            '   b) Strip that line and carriage return.
            '   c) Increment counter.
            '   d) Repeat until end of file.
            ' * If LockFile flag is not on, close file.
            ' * If any runtime error occurs, substitute generic
            '   error message "Can't perform requested operation" and
            '   add a little information to it. This is better than
            '   displaying many possible runtime errors that can
            '   occur when opening/loading file.
            CL.SetHourglass True

            If Not IsMissing(LockWrite) Then LockFile = True

            FileNbr = FreeFile

            If LockFile Then
                Open File For Input Lock Write As FileNbr
            Else
                Open File For Input As FileNbr
            End If

            Do Until EOF(FileNbr)
                FileText = Input$(LOF(FileNbr), FileNbr)
            Loop

            Obj.Clear
            Pos = ADJ

            Do Until Pos = False Or FileText = vbNullString
                Pos = InStr(FileText, vbCr)
                Obj.AddItem Left$(FileText, Pos - ADJ)
                FileText = Mid$(FileText, Pos + ADJ + ADJ)
                Item = Item + 1
            Loop

            If Not LockFile Then Close FileNbr

            CL.SetHourglass False
            Load = Array(True, FileNbr)
            Exit Function

ET:

            CL.SetHourglass False
```

```
    If Err = SYNTAX Then Load = frmErrCodes.Codes
    If Err <> SYNTAX Then
        Err.Number = 17
        Msg = "Can't perform requested operation. "
        Msg = Msg & "Can't load file into "

        If TypeName(Obj) = "ComboBox" Then
            Msg = Msg & "ComboBox control."
        Else
            Msg = Msg & "ListBox control."
        End If

        Err.Description = Msg
        Err.HelpContext = 1000017
        Load = CL.TrapErr(PROC)
    End If

End Function
```

Besides the points noted previously regarding the **Load** method of the **Graphic** class, I'd like to mention one additional point about the **Load** method of the **List** class. The syntax checking code checks the extension of the **File** argument to determine if the file contains ASCII text. However, the determination is made strictly on the basis of the nominal extension of .TXT; if someone renames text file and, in the process, changes the extension from .TXT to something else, the **Load** method will reject the **File** argument as invalid.

The Save Method

The **Save** method saves the contents of certain Visual Basic objects to a file. The topic in the class library's Help file (EFS.HLP) that specifies the detailed functionality of the **Save** method is shown in the sidebar.

The Save method's specifications.

SYNTAX

```
Object.Save(Obj, File, [FileNumber])
```

The **Save** method's syntax has the following object qualifier and named arguments:

- *Object.* Required. **Object** data type. An expression that evaluates to an object in the Applies To pop-up list.

- *Obj*. Required. **Object** data type. An expression that evaluates to the **Name** property of a Visual Basic object in the Applies To pop-up list. The supported objects are **Form**, **Image**, **PictureBox**, **ComboBox**, **ListBox**, **RichTextBox**, and **TextBox**.

- *File*. Required. **String** data type. An expression that specifies the path and name of a file to load into *Obj*.

- *FileNumber*. Optional. **Variant** data type whose subtype is a numeric expression that evaluates to a number from 1 to 511. If you use the **Load** method to open a file as locked, you must store the returned file number in the client application in order to later pass it to the *FileNumber* argument of the **Save** method.

CALLED

From any procedure in a client application.

RETURNS

Upon success, one element in a **Variant**. It contains a **Boolean** (**True**) that specifies the member executed successfully.

Upon failure, eight elements in a **Variant**. The elements contain the error codes that the class library returns when a runtime or syntax error occurs during the execution of one of its members.

REMARKS

- The **Save** method applies to the class library's **Graphic** object only under 32-bit Visual Basic.

- You can use the **SaveAs** method of the **File** object to provide the user with a common dialog box to specify the path and name of the file to pass to the *File* argument of the **Save** method.

- When you use the **Save** method with Visual Basic's **RichTextBox** object, you have the option of saving a Rich Text Format (RTF) file either as rich text or as plain ASCII text. If you save it as plain text and the *File* argument's file extension is .RTF, the **Save** method changes the file extension to .TXT and does not write over the rich text version of the file.

- When you save a file as rich text with the **Save** method, the format that it is saved under is not the same as the RTF file format of Word For Windows. This limitation is a function of Visual Basic's own **SaveFile** method (which is what the **Save** method uses).

The Save Method's Code—Graphic Class

The code for the implementation of the **Save** method in the **Graphic** class is shown in Listing 12.5.

Listing 12.5   The Save method's code—Graphic class.

```
Function Save(Obj As Object, _
              File As String, _
              Optional FileNumber)

    ' Constants for literals:
    Const PROC = "Save"
    Const SYNTAX = True
    Const VALID_FILE_EXTS = "(.BMP or .ICO or .WMP)."

    ' Variables:
    Dim Msg        As String
    Dim SrcPath    As String
    Dim FileExt    As String
    Dim FileNbr    As Integer

    ' Enable error handler and do syntax checking:
    On Error GoTo ET

    #If Win16 Then
        E.TrapSyntax 1, PROC, "16-bit VB"
    #End If

    If Not CL.IsForm(Obj) Then

        If TypeName(Obj) <> "Image" And _
           TypeName(Obj) <> "PictureBox" Then
               E.TrapSyntax 8, PROC, "Obj"
        End If

    End If

    CL.IsPath1 File, PROC, "File", SrcPath
    FileExt = Right$(File, 4)

    Select Case UCase$(FileExt)
        Case ".BMP", ".ICO", ".WMF"
        Case Else
            E.TrapSyntax 19, PROC, "File", VALID_FILE_EXTS
```

```
    End Select

    ' Execute member's algorithm--
    ' * If FileNumber argument is passed, close file previously
    '   opened in Lock Write mode with Load method.
    ' * Save graphic from object.
    ' * If any runtime error occurs, substitute generic
    '   error message "Can't perform requested operation" and
    '   add a little information to it. This is better than
    '   displaying many possible runtime errors that can
    '   occur when opening/writing to file.

    If Not IsMissing(FileNumber) Then Close FileNumber

    CL.SetHourglass True
    SavePicture Obj.Picture, File
    CL.SetHourglass False
    Save = Array(True)
    Exit Function

ET:

    CL.SetHourglass False

    If Err = SYNTAX Then Save = frmErrCodes.Codes
    If Err <> SYNTAX Then
        Err.Number = 17
        Msg = "Can't perform requested operation. "
        Msg = Msg & "Can't save graphic from "

        If CL.IsForm(Obj) Then
            Msg = "Form."
        Else
            If TypeName(Obj) = "Image" Then
                Msg = Msg & "Image control."
            Else
                Msg = Msg & "PictureBox control."
            End If
        End If

        Err.Description = Msg
        Err.HelpContext = 1000017
        Save = CL.TrapErr(PROC)
    End If

End Function
```

There is little to note about this method. Like the **Load** method, if any runtime error occurs during its execution, it substitutes the generic runtime error 17 (*Can't perform requested operation*). However, the **Save** method appends the string "Can't save graphic from '*kind*' control." to the error message, where *kind* can be either a **Form**, **Image**, or **PictureBox** object.

The Save Method's Code—List Class

The code for the implementation of the **Save** method in the **List** class is shown in Listing 12.6.

Listing 12.6   The Save method's code—List class.

```
Function Save(Obj As Object, _
              File As String, _
              Optional FileNumber)

    ' Constants for literals:
    Const PROC = "Save"
    Const SYNTAX = True
    Const VALID_FILE_EXT = ".TXT"
    Const FIRST_ITEM = 0

    ' Variables:
    Dim Msg       As String
    Dim SrcPath   As String
    Dim FileNbr   As Integer
    Dim Item      As Long

    ' Enable error handler and do syntax checking:
    On Error GoTo ET

    If TypeName(Obj) <> "ComboBox" And _
       TypeName(Obj) <> "ListBox" Then
           E.TrapSyntax 8, PROC, "Obj"
    End If

    CL.IsPath1 File, PROC, "File", SrcPath

    If UCase$(Right$(File, 4)) <> VALID_FILE_EXT Then
        E.TrapSyntax 11, PROC, "File", VALID_FILE_EXT
    End If

    ' Execute member's algorithm—
    ' * If FileNumber argument is passed, close file previously
    '   opened in Lock Write mode with Load method.
    ' * Open sequential file and write each item in list as
    '   new line in text file.
    ' * If any runtime error occurs, substitute generic
    '   error message "Can't perform requested operation" and
    '   add a little information to it. This is better than
    '   displaying many possible runtime errors that can
    '   occur when opening/writing to file.
    If Not IsMissing(FileNumber) Then Close FileNumber

    CL.SetHourglass True
    FileNbr = FreeFile
    Open File For Output As FileNbr

    For Item = FIRST_ITEM To Obj.ListCount - 1
```

```
      Print #FileNbr, Obj.List(Item)
   Next Item

   Close FileNbr
   CL.SetHourglass False
   Save = Array(True)
   Exit Function

ET:

   CL.SetHourglass False

   If Err = SYNTAX Then Save = frmErrCodes.Codes
   If Err <> SYNTAX Then
      Err.Number = 17
      Msg = "Can't perform requested operation. "
      Msg = Msg & "Can't save items from "

      If TypeName(Obj) = "ComboBox" Then
         Msg = Msg & "ComboBox control."
      Else
         Msg = Msg & "ListBox control."
      End If

      Err.Description = Msg
      Err.HelpContext = 1000017
      Save = CL.TrapErr(PROC)
   End If

End Function
```

There is little to note about this method. Like the **Load** method, if any
runtime error occurs during its execution, it substitutes the generic runtime
error 17 (*Can't perform requested operation*). However, the **Save** method
appends the string "Can't save items from '*kind*' control." to the error
message, where *kind* can be either a **ComboBox** or **ListBox** object.

Calling The Load And Save Methods

The best way to demonstrate the **Load** and **Save** methods is to use the
example code in the help topic for either method in the class library's Help
file (EFS.HLP). To do so, follow these steps:

1. Select File | New Project and open a Standard EXE project.

2. Add a **CommandButton** object, **Image** object, **ListBox** object, and
    TextBox object to Form1.

3. Set the **MultiLine** property of Text1 to **True** and the **Index** property
    of Command1 to zero.

4. From the secondary Help window containing the example code, copy and paste the code from under the heading COPY/PASTE INTO FORM1 into the General Declarations section of Form1.

5. Run the project. The dialog box in Figure 12.1 is displayed. Click on the various buttons and watch as the **Load** and **Save** methods perform their functions.

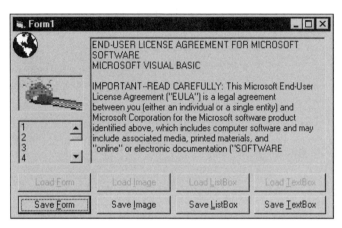

Figure 12.1 Demonstration of **Load** and **Save** methods.

13
Context-Sensitive Help And Collections

In the never-ending quest to make software easier to use by the non-programmer, context-sensitive help is clearly the direction in which the Windows operating system is headed. Windows 95 and Windows NT 4 both support context-sensitive Help buttons on most of their dialog boxes. They also support tooltips for all their toolbar buttons and for the buttons displayed on the Windows 95-style shell's taskbar.

The availability of context-sensitive Help is signified by a question mark button on the right side of the title bar of a dialog box. When you click this button, the cursor changes to the arrow and question mark mouse pointer and the application is prepared to display context-sensitive Help on the object the user next clicks. The Visual Basic Help file refers to this kind of Help as Whats This help and to the arrow and question mark cursor as the Whats This pointer.

The ubiquitous pop-up tooltips are another form of context-sensitive Help. A tooltip is a word or short phrase that describes the function of a toolbar button or other control, and it appears as a pop-up when you pause the mouse pointer over an object. Microsoft first used tooltips with the toolbar buttons of Excel 5.0, released in January of 1994. It is clear that VB programmers who want to write client applications with a GUI that is consistent with the 32-bit Windows operating systems will have to provide context-sensitive Help in one or both of these formats.

Visual Basic's Context-Sensitive Help Syntax

In contrast to VB3, VB4 and VB5 make it easy to implement context-sensitive Help. The syntactical elements that exist for implementing Windows 95-style context-sensitive Help are listed here:

- **WhatsThisButton**. A property that returns or sets a value that determines whether the What's This button appears in the title bar of a **Form** object.

- **WhatsThisHelp**. A property that returns or sets a value that determines whether context-sensitive Help uses the What's This pop-up provided by Windows 95 Help or the main Help window.

- **WhatsThisHelpID**. A property that returns or sets an associated Help context ID number for an object.

- **ToolTipText**. A property (new to VB5) that returns or sets a tooltip for a control object.

- **WhatsThisMode**. A method that causes the mouse pointer to change into the What's This pointer and prepares the application to display What's This Help on the selected object.

- **ShowWhatsThis**. A method that displays a specified topic in a Help file using the What's This pop-up provided by Windows 95 Help.

The WhatsThisButton Property's Attributes

The **WhatsThisButton** property has these characteristics:

- It returns or sets a value that determines whether the What's This button appears on the title bar of a **Form** object. It is read-only at run time and applies only to the **Form** object.

- It requires the Microsoft Windows 95 or Microsoft Windows NT 3.51 operating systems.

- The **WhatsThisHelp** property of a **Form** object must be **True** for the **WhatsThisButton** property to be **True**. These two properties are codependent and toggle from **True** to **False** together.
- If the **WhatsThisButton** and the **WhatsThisHelp** properties are **True**, either the **BorderStyle** property of the **Form** object must be set to 3 - Fixed Dialog or the properties of the **Form** object must be set as indicated in Table 13.1 for the What's This button to be displayed on the title bar of the form.

The WhatsThisHelp Property's Attributes

The **WhatsThisHelp** property has these characteristics:

- It returns or sets a value that determines whether the form uses one of the What's This access techniques to start Windows Help and load the context-sensitive topic identified by the **WhatsThisHelpID** property of a control. It is read-only at runtime and applies only to the **Form** and **MDIForm** objects.
- It requires the Microsoft Windows 95 or Microsoft Windows NT (versions 3.51 or 4) operating systems.

There are three access techniques for providing context-sensitive What's This Help in an application. First, you can use a What's This button in the title bar of the form by setting the form's **WhatsThisButton** property to **True**. Clicking on the What's This button changes the mouse pointer to the "arrow-and-question" cursor. Then left-clicking on a control displays the context-sensitive help topic specified by the control's **WhatsThisHelpID** property. Second, you can call the **WhatsThisMode** method of a form. This produces the same behavior as clicking on the What's This button without using a button. For example, you can invoke this method from a command on a menu in the menu bar of your application. Third, you can call the

Table 13.1   Settings of **Form** object's properties to display What's This button.

Property	Setting
BorderStyle	1 - Fixed Single or 2 - Sizable
ControlBox	True
MinButton	False
MaxButton	False

ShowWhatsThis method for a particular control. The context-sensitive help topic displayed is specified by the **WhatsThisHelpID** property of the control.

The WhatsThisHelpID Property's Attributes

The **WhatsThisHelpID** property has these characteristics:

- It returns or sets an associated Help context ID number for an object and provides, in conjunction with the use of one of the three access techniques for What's This Help, context-sensitive Help for the object.
- To refer to a valid help topic, the Help context ID number must be a **Long** value greater than zero.
- It requires the Microsoft Windows 95 or Microsoft Windows NT (versions 3.51 or 4) operating systems.

The Windows 3.x model uses the F1 key to start Windows Help and load the topic identified by the **HelpContextID** property. The Windows 95 model typically uses the What's This button in the upper-right corner of the window to start Windows Help and load a topic identified by the **WhatsThisHelpID** property.

The ToolTipText Property's Attributes

The **ToolTipText** property has these characteristics:

- It returns or sets a tooltip for a control object.
- The tooltip appears when you pause the mouse pointer over a control object.

Unlike the tooltips for most toolbar buttons, which are automatically hidden after a few seconds, the **ToolTipText** property's tip remains on the screen until you move the mouse pointer off of the control object or click/select it.

The WhatsThisMode Method's Attributes

The **WhatsThisMode** method has these characteristics:

- It is used to invoke Help from a menu in the menu bar of your application.
- It has the same effect as when the user clicks on the What's This button in the title bar of the form (that is, changes the mouse pointer to the What's This pointer).

- For the **WhatsThisMode** method to work, the **WhatsThisHelp** property of the **Form** object must be set to **True** at design time.

WhatsThisMode only works if ...

Although it does not say so in Visual Basic's Help file in the topic titled WhatsThisMode Method, *this method only works if called from the **Click** event procedure of a **Menu** control object or from a **UserForm** object. If you call it from any other procedure, the What's This mouse pointer flickers on and then immediately resets itself to the default pointer.*

The ShowWhatsThis Method's Attributes

The **ShowWhatsThis** method has these characteristics:

- It is used to provide context-sensitive Help from a pop-up context menu in your application.
- It applies to most of the standard Visual Basic control objects.

Pros And Cons Of The What's This Help Approach

There are two major advantages to using the What's This Help approach. It is consistent with the "look-and-feel" of context-sensitive Help in the Windows 95 and Windows NT operating systems, and no code is required to implement it.

However, there are several disadvantages associated with relying exclusively on the What's This Help approach. First, it only runs under the Microsoft Windows 95 or Microsoft Windows NT (versions 3.51 or 4) operating systems. If you are writing Visual Basic code that you want to conditionally compile to run under a Windows 3.x operating system, the What's This Help approach will not work. Second, in its What's This button access mode, the approach is restricted to **Form** objects whose style is equivalent to that of a dialog box. Third, the context-sensitive help topics that you specify for each object must have been specified and compiled in the Help file as pop-up topics. If they were not specified as pop-up topics, only the title of the help topic will be displayed. Fourth, most of the large-scale

Windows applications that Microsoft sells (like Word, Excel, and so on) do not rely on it exclusively. Instead, they allow you to enable context-sensitive Help by clicking the context-sensitive Help button on the toolbar or by pressing Shift+F1.

Demonstrating The What's This Help Properties

Follow these steps to see Visual Basic's new context-sensitive Help properties:

1. Select File | New Project and open a Standard EXE project.
2. Add three **CommandButton** objects to Form1.
3. Set Form1's **BorderStyle** property to 3 - Fixed Dialog and its **WhatsThisButton** property to **True**.
4. Enter the code shown in Listing 13.1.

Listing 13.1 Code to demonstrate What's This Help properties.

```
Private Sub Form_Load()

    ' Generate error to find Visual Basic Help file path (this
    ' finds it without using Windows API functions):
    On Error Resume Next
    Err.Raise 3
    App.HelpFile = Err.HelpFile

    ' Set HelpContextID properties to different values
    ' (that is, Visual Basic error message Help topics):
    Command1.WhatsThisHelpID = 335
    Command2.WhatsThisHelpID = 336
    Command3.WhatsThisHelpID = 337

End Sub
```

Start the project and click on the Whats This button on the title bar of the **Form** object. The mouse pointer changes to the arrow-and-question cursor and context-sensitive Help is enabled, as shown in Figure 13.1.

Next, click on the Command2 button and VB4 and Windows will display the help topic specified by the **WhatsThisHelpID** property of Command2, as shown in Figure 13.2. VB5 and Windows either display the generic message *No Help topic is associated with this item* or an empty pop-up.

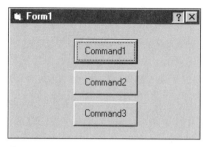

Figure 13.1 What's This Help enabled.

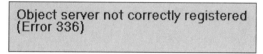

Figure 13.2 Non-pop-up help topic displayed as pop-up.

Because the Visual Basic error message help topic in Figure 13.2 was not created and compiled as a pop-up topic in Visual Basic's Help file, only the title of the topic is displayed. As you can see, one of the disadvantages of using Visual Basic's context-sensitive Help properties, in conjunction with Windows 95 or NT, is that the associated topic can only be displayed as a pop-up.

Understanding Visual Basic's Collection Object

In Visual Basic, a **Collection** is an object that contains a related set of objects. Visual Basic itself has many **Collection** objects in its object hierarchy. Visual Basic's built-in **Collection** objects have no methods and only one property, **Count**. Two of the most commonly used of the built-in **Collection** objects are the **Controls** collection and the **Forms** collection.

The **Controls** collection is an object whose items represent each control object on a **Form** object, including elements of control arrays. You can use the **Controls** collection object to iterate through all loaded control objects on a **Form** object. The **Forms** collection is an object whose items represent each loaded form (that is, the **MDIForm** object, MDI child **Form** objects, and non-MDI **Form** objects) in an application. You can use the **Forms** collection object to iterate through all loaded forms.

Creating Your Own Collection Object

You can instantiate your own **Collection** objects from Visual Basic's **Collection** class. Those that you create, in addition to having the **Count** property, have the **Add**, **Item**, and **Remove** methods.

Because a **Collection** object stores its items as **Variant** data types, it can store data of almost any type, including the **Object** data type. You can even have a **Collection** object that stores other **Collection** objects, allowing you to create very complex and powerful data structures.

Demonstrating The Collection Object

The code example in Listing 13.2 illustrates how powerful and flexible Visual Basic's **Collection** object can be. The example uses two **Form** objects, each of which has two different types of control objects on it. When the project is run:

- A new **Collection** object named **AllCtls** is created.
- Two members are added to **AllCtls**: the **Controls** collection on **Form1** and the **Controls** collection on **Form2**.
- Various properties of the objects contained in the two members of **AllCtls** are read and displayed on a message box.
- Then the **Caption** properties of the control objects on **Form2** are changed, by changing them in the **Collection** object, and their new settings are redisplayed.

Follow these steps to run the example code:

1. Select File|New Project and open a Standard EXE project.
2. Select Project|Add Form and double click on the Form icon.
3. Add a **PictureBox** object and **CommandButton** object to Form1.
4. Add a **Label** object and **CheckBox** object to Form2.
5. Enter the code shown in Listing 13.2.

Listing 13.2   Code to demonstrate the Collection object.

```
' General Declarations section of Form1:
' Create instance of Visual Basic's Collection class.
Dim AllCtls As New Collection

Private Sub Command1_Click()
```

```
' Variables:
Dim Msg          As String
Dim Ctl          As Object
Static Counter   As Integer

' Read 1st member of Collection object (that is, controls
' on Form1) and construct property information to display:
Msg = "Properties of 1st member of AllCtls collection:"
Msg = Msg & vbCr & vbCr
Msg = Msg & "Name --" & vbCr

For Each Ctl In AllCtls(1)
   Msg = Msg & "    " & Ctl.Name & vbCr
Next

Msg = Msg & vbCr & "Enabled --" & vbCr

For Each Ctl In AllCtls(1)
   Msg = Msg & "    " & Ctl.Enabled & vbCr
Next

' Read 2nd member of Collection object (that is, controls
' on Form2) and construct property information to display:
Msg = Msg & vbCr
Msg = Msg & "Properties of 2nd member of AllCtls collection:"
Msg = Msg & vbCr & vbCr
Msg = Msg & "Caption --" & vbCr

For Each Ctl In AllCtls(2)
   Msg = Msg & "    " & Ctl.Caption & vbCr
Next

Msg = Msg & vbCr & "TabIndex --" & vbCr

For Each Ctl In AllCtls(2)
   Msg = Msg & "    " & Ctl.TabIndex & vbCr
Next

MsgBox Msg, vbInformation

' Actually change captions of objects on Form2 by
' changing them in 2nd member of Collection object:
If Counter = 0 Then
   Counter = Counter + 1
End If

For Each Ctl In AllCtls(2)
   Ctl.Caption = "Caption" & Counter
   Counter = Counter + 1
Next

' Display new Caption properties:
Msg = "Captions of 2nd member of AllCtls" & vbCr
Msg = Msg & "collection have changed. They are now:" & vbCr & vbCr
```

```
    For Each Ctl In AllCtls(2)
        Msg = Msg & Ctl.Caption & vbCr
    Next

    MsgBox Msg, vbInformation
    Command1.Caption = "&Demo Again"

End Sub

Private Sub Form_Load()

    ' Add two members to Collection object which was
    ' created in General Declarations section:
    ' * Controls collection on Form1.
    ' * Controls collection on Form2.
    AllCtls.Add Form1.Controls
    AllCtls.Add Form2.Controls

    ' Set properties of Form objects:
    Form1.Left = 440
    Form1.Top = 2640
    Form1.Height = 1695
    Form1.Width = 1910
    Form2.Left = 440
    Form2.Top = 1245
    Form2.Height = 1170
    Form2.Width = 1910

    ' Set properties of control objects on Form1:
    Picture1.Enabled = False
    Picture1.Left = 180
    Picture1.Top = 120
    Picture1.Height = 495
    Picture1.Width = 1215
    Command1.Left = 180
    Command1.Top = 720
    Command1.Height = 495
    Command1.Width = 1215
    Command1.Caption = "&Demo"

    ' Set properties of control objects on Form2:
    Form2.Label1.Left = 120
    Form2.Label1.Top = 120
    Form2.Label1.Height = 195
    Form2.Label1.Width = 1215
    Form2.Check1.Left = 120
    Form2.Check1.Top = 420
    Form2.Check1.Height = 255
    Form2.Check1.Width = 1215

    ' Display Form2 to see its controls' captions change.
    Form2.Show

End Sub
```

Start the project and click on the Demo button on **Form1**. Visual Basic displays the message box in Figure 13.3, which shows the initial settings of some properties of the controls in the **AllCtls** collection (that is, the **Controls** collections on **Form1** and **Form2**).

After you clear the message box in Figure 13.3, Visual Basic displays a second message box, shown in Figure 13.4, which indicates that the **Caption** properties of two of the controls in the **AllCtls** collection (the **CheckBox** and **Label** objects) have been changed. If you look at these two controls on **Form2**, you can see that they have indeed changed. To iterate through this demonstration again, click on the Demo Again button.

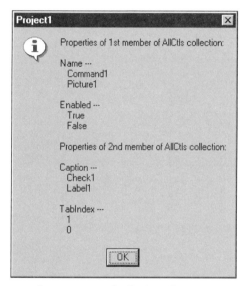

Figure 13.3   Initial settings of properties of **AllCtls** collection.

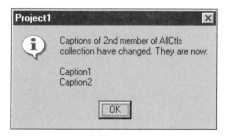

Figure 13.4   Changed settings of properties of **AllCtls** collection.

This demonstration shows that you can set any properties available at runtime of any control objects on a **Form** object by referencing the members of the **Form** object's **Controls** collection. You can even do this after you have created your own **Collection** object and filled it with clone **Controls** collections from several **Form** objects.

The **ShowCS** method of the **Help** class that is explained in the following section uses the same techniques demonstrated in this example, but in a far more sophisticated and useful way.

The Help Class

The **Help** class is composed of members that provide the various kinds of Windows Help for a client application. It currently contains the five public members described in Table 13.2.

In this chapter, we will focus on the **ShowCS** method.

The ShowCS Method

As you saw earlier in the chapter, the What's This Help approach to providing context-sensitive Help has certain limitations. The **ShowCS** method corrects these deficiencies. The method will:

- Run under all Windows operating systems.
- Work with any **Form** object, regardless of its **BorderStyle** property setting.

Table 13.2   The public members of the **Help** class.

Member	Description
RunMisc	Sets the contents topic for, sets an index for, runs a Help macro for, or closes the specified Windows Help file.
ShowAbout	Displays the conventional Windows About dialog box.
ShowCS	Displays context-sensitive Help for a Form or MDIForm object and its control objects.
ShowDlg	Displays various Help dialog boxes (Contents, Search, Find, and Help on Help) for a specified Help file.
ShowTopic	Displays the Contents Help topic, a jump topic, a pop-up topic, or a topic associated with a keyword for a specified Help file.

- Allow you to specify any help topic as context-sensitive for an object, regardless of whether the topic was specified and compiled in the Help file as a pop-up topic or as a jump topic.

- Emulate the large-scale Windows applications that Microsoft sells. (You will be able to start context-sensitive Help by either clicking on the context-sensitive Help button or by pressing Shift+F1.)

The topic in the class library's Help file (EFS.HLP) that specifies the detailed functionality of the **ShowCS** method is shown in the sidebar.

The ShowCS method's specifications.

SYNTAX

```
Object.ShowCS(Frm, Action, [HelpFile])
```

The **ShowCS** method's syntax has the following object qualifier and named arguments:

- *Object.* Required. **Object** data type. An expression that evaluates to an object in the Applies To pop-up list.

- *Frm.* Required. **Object** data type. An expression that evaluates to the **Name** property of a **Form** or **MDIForm** object.

- *Action.* Required. **Byte** data type. A value or constant which determines whether to enable context-sensitive Help, to display the context-sensitive help topic, or to cancel context-sensitive Help. See *Settings* below for the valid settings of *Action.*

- *HelpFile.* Optional. **Variant** data type whose subtype is a **String** expression specifying the Help file to use to provide context-sensitive Help. If the *Action* argument is set to 2 - CS_SHOW_TOPIC or 3 - CS_SHOW_POPUP, then the *HelpFile* argument is required. Otherwise, *HelpFile* is optional.

SETTINGS

The *Action* argument's settings are:

- 0 - CS_CANCEL. Cancels context-sensitive Help.

- 1 - CS_ACTIVATE. Enables context-sensitive Help.

- 3 - CS_SHOW_TOPIC. Displays context-sensitive help topic.

- 4 - CS_SHOW_POPUP. Displays context-sensitive help pop-up.

If you use these constants, you must declare them yourself. They are not intrinsic to Visual Basic and are not listed in the Object Browser.

CALLED

Normally from the **Click** event procedure of an **Image** object or **PictureBox** object whose **Picture** property is set to the Windows conventional context-sensitive Help icon (arrow and question). It can also be called from the **KeyDown** event procedure of a **Form** object whose **KeyPreview** property is set to **True** with code that executes when the user presses Shift+F1.

RETURNS

Upon success, one element in a **Variant**. It contains a **Boolean** (**True**) that specifies the member executed successfully.

Upon failure, eight elements in a **Variant**. The elements contain the error codes that the class library returns when a runtime or syntax error occurs during the execution of one of its members.

REMARKS

- If there is a **CommandButton** object on the form whose **Cancel** property is set to **True**, the **ShowCS** method detects this and temporarily sets it to **False** when the *Action* argument is 1 - CS_ACTIVATE. This allows the user to press Esc to cancel the **ShowCS** method. When its *Action* argument is set to 0 - CS_CANCEL, 2 - CS_SHOW_TOPIC, or 3 - CS_SHOW_POPUP, the **ShowCS** method restores the **Cancel** property of the **CommandButton** object to **True**.

- If there is a **Label** object on the form whose **Name** property or **Tag** property includes the string *StatusBar* or *Status Bar*, the **ShowCS** method detects this and temporarily sets that label's caption to *Right click object for Help or press Esc to cancel* when the *Action* argument is 0 - CS_ACTIVATE. When *Action* is set to 0 - CS_CANCEL, 2 - CS_SHOW_TOPIC, or 3 - CS_SHOW_POPUP, the **ShowCS** method restores the

> **Caption** property or the **Name** property of the label to its original value.

The ShowCS Method's Code

To help you better understand the **ShowCS** method, I have split the code into several sections.

READING/SETTING PROPERTIES OF A CONTROLS COLLECTION

As you saw earlier in this chapter, every **Form** object with controls on it has Visual Basic's built-in **Controls** collection encapsulated within it. So, when you pass the **Name** property of a **Form** object (or the identifier **Me**) to a method in a class library, you are also passing its **Controls** collection by reference. As a result, the method's code can return the values of any property of any control on that **Form** object, which can be read at runtime. Also, you can change the setting of any property that can be set at runtime.

ShowCS reads and changes the following control properties:

- **MousePointer** property of a **Form** object and all control objects.
- **Cancel** property of a **CommandButton** object (if it is set to **True**).
- **Caption** property of a **Label** object (if its **Tag** or **Name** property contains the string "StatusBar" or "Status Bar").

Listing 13.3 shows the code that reads and sets the properties of the **Controls** collection of the **Form** object.

Listing 13.3   ShowCS method's code to read/set properties.

```
Function ShowCS(Frm As Object, _
             Action As Byte, _
             Optional HelpFile)

    . . .

    If Action = CS_ACTIVATE Then
       Activated = True
       Prompt = "Right-click object for Help" & _
             " or press ESC to cancel"
       CancelPos = NO_CANCEL_BUTTON
       SBarPos = NO_STATUSBAR_LABEL

       #If Win32 Then
          OrigPointer = Frm.MousePointer
```

```
#Else
   OrigPointer = GetClassWord(Frm.hWnd, GCW_HCURSOR)
   HWndInst = LoadLibrary(CURSOR_DLL)

   If HWndInst >= HINSTANCE_ERROR Then
      HWndPointer = LoadCursor(HWndInst, IDC_CONTEXTHELP)
   End If

#End If

#If Win32 Then
   Frm.MousePointer = vbArrowQuestion
#Else
   SetClassWord Frm.hWnd, GCW_HCURSOR, HWndPointer
#End If

For Each Ctl In Frm.Controls
   On Error Resume Next

   #If Win32 Then
      Ctl.MousePointer = vbArrowQuestion
   #Else
      SetClassWord Ctl.hWnd, GCW_HCURSOR, HWndPointer
   #End If

   On Error GoTo ET

   If TypeName(Ctl) = "CommandButton" Then

      If Ctl.Cancel = True Then
         CancelPos = El
         Ctl.Cancel = False
      End If

   ElseIf TypeName(Ctl) = "Label" Then

      If InStr(Ctl.Name, SB_ID2) <> False Then
         StatusBar = True
      ElseIf InStr(Ctl.Name, SB_ID1) <> False Then
         StatusBar = True
      ElseIf InStr(Ctl.Tag, SB_ID2) <> False Then
         StatusBar = True
      ElseIf InStr(Ctl.Tag, SB_ID1) <> False Then
         StatusBar = True
      End If

      If StatusBar Then
         OrigCaption = Ctl.Caption
         Ctl.Caption = Prompt
         SBarPos = El
      End If
   End If

   El = El + 1
```

```
    Next Ctl

    GetCursorPos Pt
    SetCursorPos Pt.X, Pt.Y

  . . .

End If

End Function
```

There are several important points to note about the code in Listing 13.3. First, under 16-bit Visual Basic, the **ShowCS** method uses Windows API functions to read the setting of the **MousePointer** property for each control. The **GetClassWord** Windows API function retrieves the information specified by its second argument (the current mouse pointer) about the class to which the control object specified by its first argument belongs. The mouse pointer setting is returned as a **Long**. The **LoadLibrary** Windows API function then loads the library module BTTNCUR.DLL and returns an instance handle to the area in memory where the module is loaded. Finally, the **LoadCursor** Windows API function retrieves the specified cursor resource from the specified library module and assigns it to the handle in memory.

Second, under 16-bit Visual Basic, the **ShowCS** method uses Windows API functions to change the setting of the **MousePointer** property for each control. The **SetClassWord** Windows API function sets the parameter specified by its second argument (the context-sensitive Help mouse pointer) for the class to which the control object specified by its first argument belongs. The mouse pointer to be changed is specified by the third argument (the handle of the original pointer).

Third, when you cycle through the **Controls** collection or any **Collection** object and set the same property for every member of the collection, it is better to be safe than sorry. Enable an inline error handler so that if one of the members of the collection does not have the property, you can avoid runtime error 438 ("Object doesn't support this property or method") and just skip over that member. Be sure, though, to disable the inline error handler and re-enable your normal error handler when you are done cycling through the collection.

Fourth, if there is a **Label** object in the **Controls** collection whose **Caption** or **Tag** property is set to the string "StatusBar" or "Status Bar", that **Label** object's **Caption** property is temporarily set to the string "Right click object for Help or press Esc to cancel". This is done to let the user know that context-sensitive Help has been enabled. Likewise, if there is a **CommandButton** object in the **Controls** collection whose **Cancel** property is set to **True**, that **CommandButton** object's setting is temporarily set to **False**. This is done so that pressing Esc will not cause the **Click** event procedure of that button to execute.

Using third-party DLLs

A class library can make calls to and use the routines or resources in any third-party DLL file. The book's class library calls BTTNCUR.DLL to get a context-sensitive Help cursor for 16-bit Windows. Remember, however, if you do make calls to third-party DLLs from a class library, those DLLs have to be included on the ActiveX component's distribution disks.

DETERMINING WHAT OBJECT A USER CLICKED

Often in Visual Basic and Windows programming, it is necessary to determine which object the user clicked on the **Screen** or on a **Form**. The **ShowCS** method demonstrates a generic way to do this, as shown in Listing 13.4. After the client application calls the method the first time (with the **Action** argument set to 1 - CS_ACTIVATE), a single line of code from the **Click** event procedure of each control object for which there is a context-sensitive Help topic calls the **ShowCS** method again (with the **Action** argument set this time to 2 - CS_SHOW_TOPIC, or 3 - CS_SHOW_POPUP).

Listing 13.4   ShowCS method's code to read object clicked.

```
Function ShowCS(Frm As Object, _
            Action As Byte, _
            Optional HelpFile)

    . . .

    If Action = CS_SHOW_TOPIC And Activated Or _
       Action = CS_SHOW_POPUP And Activated Then

        GetCursorPos Pt

        #If Win32 Then
            HWndObjHelp = WindowFromPoint(Pt.X, Pt.Y)
        #Else
            HWndObjHelp = WindowFromPoint(agPOINTAPItoLong(Pt))
        #End If
```

```
        If Frm.hWnd = HWndObjHelp Then
            HelpTopicID = Frm.HelpContextID

            If Action = CS_SHOW_TOPIC Then
                WinHelp Frm.hWnd, HelpFile, _
                        HELP_CONTEXT, HelpTopicID
            ElseIf Action = CS_SHOW_POPUP Then
                WinHelp Frm.hWnd, HelpFile, _
                        HELP_CONTEXTPOPUP, HelpTopicID
            End If

        ElseIf Frm.hWnd <> HWndObjHelp Then

            For Each Ctl In Frm.Controls

                If CL.HasHandle(Ctl) = "True" Then

                    If Ctl.hWnd = HWndObjHelp Then

                        If Ctl.HelpContextID <> False Then

                            HelpTopicID = Ctl.HelpContextID

                            If Action = CS_SHOW_TOPIC Then
                                WinHelp Frm.hWnd, HelpFile, _
                                        HELP_CONTEXT, HelpTopicID
                            ElseIf Action = CS_SHOW_POPUP Then
                                WinHelp Frm.hWnd, HelpFile, _
                                        HELP_CONTEXTPOPUP, HelpTopicID
                            End If

                            Exit For
                        ElseIf Ctl.HelpContextID = False Then
                            HelpTopicID = Frm.HelpContextID

                            If Action = CS_SHOW_TOPIC Then
                                WinHelp Frm.hWnd, HelpFile, _
                                        HELP_CONTEXT, HelpTopicID
                            ElseIf Action = CS_SHOW_POPUP Then
                                WinHelp Frm.hWnd, HelpFile, _
                                        HELP_CONTEXTPOPUP, HelpTopicID
                            End If

                            Exit For
                        End If
                    End If
                End If
            Next Ctl
        End If
    End If

    . . .


End Function
```

There are several important points to note about the code in Listing 13.4. First, the **GetCursorPos** Windows API function retrieves the screen coordinates of the mouse pointer's current position and stores them in the user-defined data type POINTAPI (represented by the variable **Pt**).

Second, the **WindowFromPoint** Windows API function retrieves the handle of the window (that is, **Form** or control object) that contains the specified point (that is, where the mouse pointer was when the user clicked the right mouse button). In C and Windows SDK terminology, any Visual Basic object that has the **hWnd** property is considered a window.

Third, only Visual Basic control objects that have an **hWnd** property also have a **HelpContextID** property and, so, can be assigned a context-sensitive Help topic number. For example, a **Label** object does not have either property. For such a control object, the code in Listing 13.4 looks to the **Form** object, reads its **HelpContextID** property setting, and displays the **Form** object's help topic. You could write this routine in another way and read the **Container** property of such a control object, and then examine the container object to see if it has a **HelpContextID** property.

RESTORING ORIGINAL SETTINGS AND CLEANING UP

The **ShowCS** method, in the course of its execution, creates several handles to areas in memory. It is important, that when the method is done executing, you destroy the handles and clean up the system resources that were used to avoid memory leaks.

Visual Basic normally takes care of this kind of housekeeping chore for you automatically. But, when you call Windows API functions that use system resources, you must do your own clean-up work. Listing 13.5 shows the code that restores the original settings of the properties of the **Controls** collection and prevents memory leaks.

Listing 13.5   ShowCS method's code to clean up.

```
Function ShowCS(Frm As Object, _
                Action As Byte, _
                Optional HelpFile)

    . . .

    #If Win32 Then
        Frm.MousePointer = OrigPointer
    #Else
        SetClassWord Frm.hWnd, GCW_HCURSOR, OrigPointer
    #End If
```

```
On Error Resume Next

For Each Ctl In Frm.Controls

    #If Win16 Then
        SetClassWord Ctl.hWnd, _
                    GCW_HCURSOR, OrigPointer
    #ElseIf Win32 Then
        Ctl.MousePointer = OrigPointer
    #End If

Next Ctl

On Error GoTo ET

GetCursorPos Pt
SetCursorPos Pt.X, Pt.Y

If CancelPos <> NO_CANCEL_BUTTON Then
    Frm.Controls(CancelPos).Cancel = True
End If

If SBarPos <> NO_STATUSBAR_LABEL Then
    Frm.Controls(SBarPos).Caption = OrigCaption
End If

#If Win16 Then
    DestroyCursor HWndPointer
    FreeLibrary HWndInst
#End If

    . . .

End Function
```

There are three points to note about the code in Listing 13.5. First, under 16-bit Visual Basic, the **SetCursorPos** Windows API function sets the position, in screen coordinates, of the mouse pointer. In this situation, **SetCursorPos** is being called to refresh the mouse pointer image and make it visible after it has been restored to its original setting. The position itself does not change. This situation is typical of the many little quirks in Windows programming that you learn about when you work with the Windows API.

Second, the **DestroyCursor** Windows API function destroys the cursor that was previously loaded by the **LoadCursor** function (Listing 13.3) and then frees the memory that it occupied. The **FreeLibrary** Windows API function decrements the reference count of the specified module previously loaded by **LoadLibrary**. When the reference count reaches zero, the memory occupied by the module is freed.

Third, if there was a **CommandButton** object in the **Controls** collection whose **Cancel** property was originally set to **True**, that **CommandButton** object's setting is restored. Likewise, if there was a **Label** object in the **Controls** collection whose **Caption** or **Tag** property was set to the string "StatusBar" or "Status Bar", that **Label** object's **Caption** property is restored to its original setting.

Calling The ShowCS Method

The best way to demonstrate the **ShowCS** method is to use the example code in its help topic in the class library's Help file (EFS.HLP). To do so, follow these steps:

1. Select File | New Project and open a Standard EXE project.
2. Add a **CommandButton** object and a **Label** object to Form1.
3. Set the **Index** property of Command1 to **True**.
4. From the secondary Help window containing the example code, copy and paste the code from under the heading COPY/PASTE INTO FORM1 into the General Declarations section of Form1.
5. Run the project. The dialog box shown in Figure 13.5 is displayed.
6. Press Shift+F1. The **Form_KeyDown** event occurs, the **ShowCS** method is called, and context-sensitive Help is enabled, as shown in Figure 13.6.

Figure 13.5 ShowCS method demo—initial dialog box.

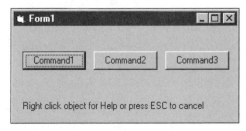

Figure 13.6 ShowCS method demo—context-sensitive Help enabled.

7. Right click on the Command1 button to display the Help jump topic shown in Figure 13.7. Right click on the **Form** object to display the Help pop-up topic in Figure 13.8.

The context ID numbers of these help topics (and the other topics that would be displayed if you click on other control objects on the dialog box) were assigned to the control object in the **Form_Load** event procedure.

Notes About Other Methods Of The Help Class

If you are interested in seeing how the other methods of the **Help** class work, you can run the example code in their help topics in the class library's Help file (EFS.HLP). We will look at the **ShowAbout** method in

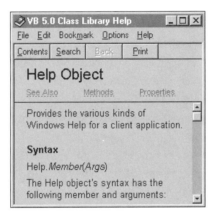

Figure 13.7   ShowCS method demo—jump topic.

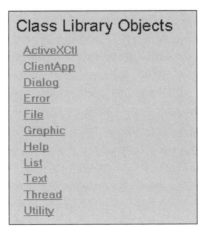

Figure 13.8   ShowCS method demo—pop-up topic.

detail later in the book. Before we move onto the next chapter though, I would like to mention a few miscellaneous points about the **RunMisc**, **ShowDlg**, and **ShowTopic** methods:

- It is a conventional Windows programming practice to check to see if the associated Help file for a terminated application is displayed and, if so, close it. Visual Basic itself behaves this way. If you call the **RunMisc** method and pass its **Kind** argument the value HELP_QUIT (&H2), it will close the specified Help file.

- The **RunMisc** method also executes Help macros. Although most Visual Basic and Windows programmers are unaware of it, the Windows Help application (WINHLP32.EXE for 32-bit Windows and WINHELP.EXE for 16-bit Windows) has a mini-programming language of its own, implemented with macro functions. For example, the example code for the **RunMisc** method calls the **CreateButton** and **ExecProgram** macros. **CreateButton** adds a button with the caption *PBrush* to the Visual Basic Help file's button bar. **ExecProgram** specifies that the Windows Paint accessory program will start up when you click the PBrush button. Of course, these macros are in effect only for the current instance of the Help file.

- The **ShowDlg** method addresses a bug in VB5 (and in most of Microsoft's other applications). Assume that you are running Windows 95 or Windows NT 3.51 or 4. If you start Visual Basic and select Help | Search For Help On, VB displays the Help Topics dialog box with the focus on the Index tab. Now, if you close the Help Topics dialog box and select Help | Microsoft Visual Basic Help Topics, the dialog box is redisplayed, but the Index tab still has the focus (instead of the Contents tab, which is what is specified). There are Help macros in WINHLP32.EXE that are supposed to display the Contents, Index, and Find tabs of the Help Topics dialog box, but they do not consistently work correctly. The only one that works correctly all the time is the Search macro, which displays the dialog box with the Index tab having the focus. The **ShowDlg** method corrects this bug and consistently gives the specified tab of the dialog box the focus.

- The **ShowTopic** method can display a jump topic or a pop-up topic. However, like the **ShowCS** method of the class library and the What's This Help feature set of Visual Basic, a topic is displayed correctly as a pop-up only if it has been specified and compiled in the Help file as a pop-up. If it was not specified as a pop-up topic, only the title of the help topic is displayed.

14

ACTIVEX COMPONENTS AND MODELESS FORMS

In Chapter 3, we learned that Visual Basic can create two general kinds of ActiveX components: in-process DLL components and out-of-process EXE components. As I pointed out in that chapter, each kind of component has some unique features. The DLL version runs significantly faster than the EXE version, but it can only be created with 32-bit Visual Basic and can only be run on a 32-bit Windows operating system.

Also, under VB4, the DLL version could not display a modeless **Form** object. This has been changed in VB5; but, because I wanted the source code for this book's class library to also run under VB4, the book's class library continues to display modeless forms only from its out-of-process ActiveX component.

The EXE version of an ActiveX component runs in a thread (or process) within the system's memory that is separate from the memory thread under which the client application that calls it is running (therefore, the name *out-of-process*). Because it does run in a separate thread, the EXE version, although slower, can do certain things that the DLL version cannot:

- It can run under both Windows 3.x (16-bit) and Windows 95 and NT (32-bit) operating systems.

- It can display modeless forms under VB4.

- It can have a **Form** object specified as its Startup Object on the General tab of the Project Properties dialog box, which means that it does not require a **Sub Main** procedure in a standard module. Just because you can do this does not mean that you should. In order to maintain a single set of source code for both in-process and out-of-process versions of an ActiveX component, you should keep the Startup Object set to **Sub Main**.

- An out-of-process ActiveX component can execute asynchronous or batch-processing methods under VB4 and VB5. A client application can call this kind of method, passing it the arguments it requires, and the method can execute its code in another thread of memory. This code may take hours to run, but, before the lengthy task is begun, the method returns a value to the client application. This return value signals that everything is fine and that the out-of-process ActiveX component is executing the batch-processing operation. The client application, having received this return value from the out-of-process component, regains control over itself and is able to perform other tasks.

- An RAO (Remote Automation Object) can only be implemented as an out-of-process ActiveX component. An RAO extends the asynchronous or threaded capability already described. You can only create an RAO component with the Enterprise Edition of Visual Basic; but, using this technology, you can call and run a batch-processing type of operation on a remote machine thousands of miles away from the client's machine.

- Many kinds of Visual Basic add-ins are created as an out-of-process ActiveX component.

- An out-of-process ActiveX component can be run in two different modes. If it is started by a client application that wants to reuse one of its objects, its **StartMode** property is set to **vbSModeAutomation** (1). If it is run as an executable (for example, by starting it with Visual Basic's **Shell** function), its **StartMode** property is set to **vbSModeStandalone** (0). Code in the **Sub Main** procedure of an out-of-process ActiveX component can read the setting of its **StartMode** property and react accordingly.

Until now, we have been dealing almost entirely with members of the book's class library, which run the same (except for the speed factor) under both in-process and out-of-process ActiveX components. In this chapter, we will focus on members that run under VB4 and VB5 only under out-of-process ActiveX components and that display associated modeless **Form** objects. Table 14.1 briefly describes each of these members. We will look at all of them in this chapter except for the **ShowToolTip** and **Edit** methods, which are addressed in later chapters.

Table 14.1   Members of the class library that display modeless forms.

Method	Class	Description
ShowSplash	ClientApp	Displays a splash screen while a client application is loading (ActiveX EXE component only).
CancelSplash	ClientApp	Unloads the splash screen previously displayed by the ShowSplash method (ActiveX EXE component only).
ShowToolTip	ClientApp	Displays a tooltip for the control object beneath the mouse pointer, based on the control's Tag property (ActiveX EXE component only).
Edit	Text	Does the conventional operations of the Windows Edit menu (Undo, Redo, Cut, Copy, Paste, Find, Replace, and so on). 32-bit only. ActiveX EXE component only when the Kind argument is set to 10 - ED_FIND, 11 - ED_REPL, or 12 - ED_GOTO.
BrowseWinAPI	Utility	Runs the Windows API Browser utility (ActiveX EXE component only).
WatchRAM	Utility	Displays a RAM monitor (32-bit and ActiveX EXE component only).
GetWindowInfo	Utility	Displays information for the window (handle, class name, caption, and so on) currently under the mouse pointer (ActiveX EXE component only).

Identifying Kinds Of ActiveX Components

The different kinds of ActiveX components (in-process, out-of-process local, and out-of-process remote) support different features, and their members behave differently. A class library that is created with a single set of Visual Basic source code needs to be able to determine, when one of its classes is instantiated, from what kind of component it is being run.

Using The Initialize Event To ID A Component

You can use several approaches to code a class library to identify from what kind of component it is being run. The way the book's class library does it, for those classes where the kind of component makes a difference, is to run a routine in the **Initialize** event of the class that is instantiated. The typical code for this routine is shown in Listing 14.1.

Listing 14.1 Code in the Initialize event of classes.

```
Private Sub Class_Initialize()

    ' Turn on class-level flag specifying kind of ActiveX
    ' component being run. Kind is identified by last
    ' character of Title property of component's App object,
    ' which is set on Make tab of Properties dialog box.
    ' Variables:
    Dim KindOfComponent As String

    KindOfComponent = Right$(App.Title, 1)

    Select Case KindOfComponent
       Case "D"
          cDLLServer = True
       Case "E", "6"
          cDLLServer = False
       Case "R"
          cRAOServer = True
    End Select

End Sub
```

This code works because, when you make the class library's single set of Visual Basic source code into the different kinds of ActiveX components, you signify the kind of component by adding a suffix (D, E, R, or 16 for DLL, EXE, RAO, or 16-bit) to the **Title** property of the **App** object. You make this setting on the Make tab of the Project Properties dialog box as

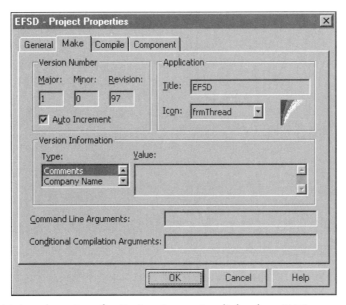

Figure 14.1   Make tab settings for Project Properties dialog box (DLL).

shown in Figure 14.1. In the naming scheme that I use, I also use this setting for the Project Name entry on the General tab.

In conjunction with this naming scheme, the code in the **Initialize** event can determine under which of these four conditions the ActiveX component is being run:

- As an in-process component. The module-level flag variable **cDLLServer** is set to **True**.

- As a local, out-of-process component. The module-level flag variable **cDLLServer** is set to **False**.

- As a remote, out-of-process component. The module-level flag variable **cRAOServer** is set to **True**.

- As the 16-bit version of the component (which can only be a local, out-of-process component). The module-level flag variable **cDLLServer** is set to **False**.

Although it is only a simulation, the **cRAOServer** flag setting would work with an actual Remote Automation Object ActiveX component. In the book's class library, it is used to demonstrate the fact that a remote ActiveX component should not expose a member that displays a dialog box of any kind. This is because any dialog box displayed by an RAO's member would appear on the remote machine's monitor, not on the client application machine's monitor.

In some classes, for whose members it is not necessary to distinguish between all of the different kinds of components, the following statements in the **Initialize** event are sufficient:

```
If Right$(App.Title, 1) = "R" Then cRAOServer = True
If Right$(App.Title, 1) = "E" Then cEXEServer = True
```

In these cases, just one or two module-level flag variables are used (**cRAOServer** and **cEXEServer**).

Simulating Identification Of An RAO Component

Follow these steps to see how the identification scheme for an RAO ActiveX server works:

1. Ensure that the EFSR.EXE version of the book's class library is registered. Follow the setup instructions in the book's Introduction to register EFSR.VBP's ActiveX component

2. Select File | New Project and open a Standard EXE project.

3. Enter the code in Listing 14.2.

4. Run the project and double click on the **Form** object to initialize the RAO version of the class library's server.

Syntax checking code in the **ShowMsg** method of the **ClientApp** class checks whether the class is being called from a RAO server. If so, the **ShowMsg** method returns **False** and a set of syntax error codes. The client application reads the error codes and displays the message in Figure 14.2.

Listing 14.2   Code to demonstrate identification of an RAO server.

```
' General Declarations Section:
' Form-level variable.
Dim ClientApp As Object

Private Sub Form_DblClick()

    ' Constants for elements in returned array:
    Const MBR_CHOICE = 0
    Const ERR_SOURCE = 1
    Const ERR_NBR = 2
```

```
        Const ERR_DESC = 3
        Const ERR_HELP_FILE = 4
        Const ERR_HELP_CONTEXT = 5
        Const ERR_TIME = 6
        Const ERR_LOG = 7

        ' Variables:
        Dim Msg        As String
        Dim Results    As Variant

        ' Call object's unsupported member, using named argument
        ' and reading returned value to display error codes.
        Results = ClientApp.ShowMsg(Prompt:="Test")

        If Not Results(MBR_CHOICE) Then
            Msg = "Client application reads the error codes returned" & vbCr
            Msg = Msg & "from the RAO simulation and displays them--" & vbCr
            Msg = Msg & vbCr & "Member: " & Results(ERR_SOURCE) & vbCr
            Msg = Msg & "Err #: " & Results(ERR_NBR) & vbCr
            Msg = Msg & "Desc: " & Results(ERR_DESC) & vbCr
            Msg = Msg & "Help File: " & Results(ERR_HELP_FILE) & vbCr
            Msg = Msg & "Help #: " & Results(ERR_HELP_CONTEXT) & vbCr
            Msg = Msg & "Time: " & Results(ERR_TIME) & vbCr
            Msg = Msg & "Logged: " & Results(ERR_LOG)
            MsgBox Msg, vbInformation
        End If

End Sub

Private Sub Form_Load()

    ' Instantiate class. Programmatic ID has two parts delimited by dot:
    ' * Project name on General tab of Project Properties dialog box.
    ' * Name property of ClassModule object.
    Set ClientApp = CreateObject("EFSR.ClientApp")

End Sub

Private Sub Form_Unload(Cancel As Integer)

    ' Free system resources associated with object variable.
    Set ClientApp = Nothing

End Sub
```

The cRAOServer flag also ...

The **cRAOServer** flag setting also governs whether the **TrapSyntax** and **TrapRunTime** methods of the **Error** class display dialog boxes. In this simulation, in which the **cRAOServer** flag is turned on, **TrapSyntax** executes and returns the appropriate error codes, but it does not display the error message from inside the class library.

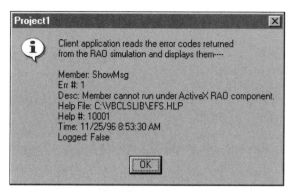

Figure 14.2   Syntax error codes returned from the RAO version of class library.

Displaying A Splash Screen

Most Windows applications that take any time at all to initialize their data structures first display some kind of splash screen. Once the data is initialized and loaded, the splash screen is unloaded and the first window that the user interacts with is displayed.

Until this point in the book, all the methods that we have studied display **Form** objects modally; that is, the user must take some action before the dialog box can be closed and the client application's program can continue to execute. Most Windows and Visual Basic applications display the great majority of their **Form** objects as modal dialog boxes.

However, if you were to display a splash screen modally, no further code execution could occur until the splash screen was unloaded. This would, of course, defeat the purpose of the splash screen in the first place, which is to allow startup processing to be done while the splash screen is displayed. Obviously, a splash screen must be displayed modelessly. This is the case whether you display it from a normal Visual Basic project or from inside a class library.

The ShowSplash Method's Specifications

As we discussed earlier in this chapter, only an out-of-process ActiveX component can display a **Form** object modelessly under both VB4 and VB5. The **ShowSplash** method of the **ClientApp** class is written to syntax check the kind of ActiveX component that it is being run under and to abort its execution if it is not an out-of-process component. The topic in the class library's Help file (EFS.HLP) that specifies the detailed functionality of the **ShowSplash** method is duplicated in the sidebar.

ShowSplash method's specifications.

SYNTAX

`Object.ShowSplash(Graphic, Captions( ))`

The **ShowSplash** method's syntax has the following object quali-fier and named arguments:

- *Object*. Required. **Object** data type. An expression that evalu-ates to an object in the Applies To pop-up list.

- *Graphic*. Required. **String** data type. An expression that speci-fies the path and name of a bitmap, icon, or Windows metafile to be displayed on the splash screen.

- *Captions( )*. Required. **String** data type. The array's lower bound can be any value and the array must contain three elements. The expression in each element specifies a different label to display on the splash screen. None of the labels can be longer than 40 characters. See *Settings* for a description of the three elements.

SETTINGS

The **Captions( )** argument's settings are:

- 1st element: SS_APP_NAME. The name of the client application.

- 2nd element: SS_VER_NBR. The version number of the client application.

- 3rd element: SS_COPYRIGHT. The copyright notice of the client application.

CALLED

From the **Sub Main** general procedure or **Form_Load** event procedure of the startup module in a client application.

RETURNS

Upon success, one element in a **Variant**. It contains a **Boolean** (**True**) that specifies the member executed successfully.

Upon failure, eight elements in a **Variant**. The elements contain the error codes that the class library returns when a runtime or syntax error occurs during the execution of one of its members.

REMARKS

- The **ShowSplash** method can only be called when the **ClientApp** class is instantiated from an out-of-process EXE component. This is because the splash screen itself is displayed modelessly and an in-process DLL component cannot display a modeless **Form** object under VB4.

- **ShowSplash** displays the splash screen. To unload the splash screen, call the **CancelSplash** method of the **ClientApp** object.

The ShowSplash Method's Code

The majority of the **ShowSplash** method's code, which is shown in Listing 14.3, is devoted to syntax checking. By now, you have seen a lot of this kind of code. However, note the new statements that identify the kind of ActiveX component that is running.

Listing 14.3   ShowSplash method's syntax-checking code.

```
Function ShowSplash(Graphic As String, _
                    Captions() As String)
    . . .

    ' Enable error handler and do syntax checking:
    On Error GoTo ET

    If cDLLServer Then
        E.TrapSyntax 1, PROC, "ActiveX DLL component"
    ElseIf cRAOServer Then
        E.TrapSyntax 1, PROC, "ActiveX RAO component"
    End If

    . . .

End Function
```

There are two kinds of components under which **ShowSplash** cannot run. First, an in-process DLL component is forbidden because such a component can only display a modal dialog box under VB4. Second, an out-of-process, remote EXE component is forbidden because a remote component should not display any kind of dialog box.

Once the **ShowSplash** method has validated the type of component and the values passed in to its arguments, it executes the code in Listing 14.4. This code modelessly displays the splash screen and returns control to the client application that called it.

Listing 14.4   The ShowSplash method's code to display modeless form.

```
Function ShowSplash(Graphic As String, _
                 Captions() As String)
    . . .

    ' Set custom properties of Form object and display modelessly.
    ' Method returns control to client application, which must
    ' later call CancelSplash method to unload splash screen.

    El = LBound(Captions)

    With frmShowSplash
        .Graphic = Graphic
        .AppName = Captions(El)
        .Version = Captions(El + 1)
        .Copyright = Captions(El + 2)
        .Show
    End With

    ShowSplash = Array(True)

    . . .

End Function
```

After the statement **ShowSplash = Array(True)** executes, program execution has split into two processes or threads. In one thread, the client application has received the returned value from the class library and is executing its initialization routines. In the out-of-process component's thread, the class library loads its frmShowSplash **Form** object and executes the code in Listing 14.5.

Listing 14.5   Code in splash screen's Form object.

```
Private Sub Form_Load()

    ' Constants for literals:
    Const ONE_HALF = 0.5

    CL.SetHourglass True

    ' Center splash screen and set its properties:
    Move (Screen.Width - Width) * ONE_HALF, _
```

```
        (Screen.Height - Height) * ONE_HALF
    Caption = vbNullString
    imgPlaque.Picture = LoadPicture(fGraphic)
    lblAppName = fAppName
    lblVersion = lblVersion & fVersion
    lblCopyright = lblCopyright & fCopyright

End Sub

Public Property Let Quit(Setting)

    ' CancelSplash method sets this custom
    ' property to unload Form object:
    CL.SetHourglass False
    Unload Me

End Property

Private Sub Form_Unload(Cancel As Integer)

    ' Free system resources associated with objects:
    Set CL = Nothing
    Set frmShowSplash = Nothing

End Sub
```

There is one important point to note about the code in the frmShowSplash **Form** object. The client application somehow has to signal to the class library when it is time to remove the splash screen. There are several different ways to do this. You could pass an argument to the **ShowSplash** method that specifies the duration in milliseconds that the splash screen should be displayed. However, the easiest and most flexible way is to give the frmShowSplash **Form** object the write-only custom property named **Quit**, which is set by a simple **CancelSplash** method that the client application calls at the end of its initialization routine. The **CancelSplash** method does not require any arguments and runs the code in Listing 14.6.

Listing 14.6   The CancelSplash method's code.

```
Function CancelSplash()

    ' Constants for literals:
    Const PROC = "CancelSplash"
    Const SYNTAX = True

    ' Enable error handler and do syntax checking:
    On Error GoTo ET

    If cDLLServer Then
        E.TrapSyntax 1, PROC, "ActiveX DLL component"
    ElseIf cRAOServer Then
```

```
        E.TrapSyntax 1, PROC, "ActiveX RAO component"
    End If

    ' Set custom property in splash screen Form object.
    ' Unload statement there triggers Unload event.
    frmShowSplash.Quit = True
    CancelSplash = Array(True)
    Exit Function

ET:

    If Err = SYNTAX Then CancelSplash = frmErrCodes.Codes
    If Err <> SYNTAX Then CancelSplash = CL.TrapErr(PROC)

End Function
```

When the **Quit** custom property flag of frmShowSplash is turned on, the **Unload** statement in the property **LetQuit** procedure executes, the splash screen disappears, and the **ClientApp** class is deinstantiated. The sample code in the class library's Help file (EFS.HLP) demonstrates the **ShowSplash** and **CancelSplash** methods with the settings that are displayed in Figure 14.3.

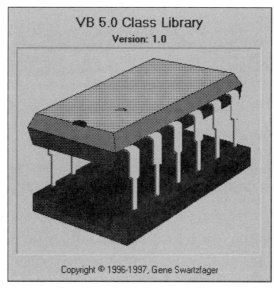

Figure 14.3 Splash screen displayed by **ShowSplash** method.

Using the Graphic argument

*The **Graphic** argument of the **ShowSplash** method accepts the BMP, ICO, or WMF Windows graphic formats in any size or resolution. This is because the control used to display the graphic on the splash screen is an **Image** object whose **Stretch** property is set to **True**.*

Running An App From An ActiveX Component

It is possible to write mini applications and encapsulate their functionality inside an out-of-process ActiveX component. Often, a useful utility application requires only one **Form** object as its GUI. If you write a method in an out-of-process component to modelessly display a utility's GUI, there is no need to make that utility into a separate executable file.

In fact, there are good reasons not to make every little utility that you might write with Visual Basic into a separate executable. If you adopt an object-oriented strategy instead and write and encapsulate them within a single **Utility** class, you gain the following advantages:

- The source code for all your utilities is in one place, making maintenance easier.

- Revisions or enhancements to the source code can be made for the entire suite of mini-utilities at one time, making redistribution of the suite easier.

- ActiveX components can be installed as shared components on a 32-bit Windows system. This means that, in the case of Visual Basic's Setup Wizard and Windows 95 or NT 4 for example, all such shared components are placed on the same directory (that is, \PROGRAM FILES\COMMON FILES\OLESVR).

- The public interface to all such utilities is readily available to anyone who wants to use them via the Object Browser.

In the rest of this chapter, we'll be taking a look at three utilities in the book's class library, each with its own associated GUI **Form** object. The first utility is a RAM monitor for 32-bit Windows systems, which constantly updates and displays the amount of the system's available RAM and virtual memory. The second utility displays information about the window object (its handle, caption, class name, parent, grandparent, and so on) over which the mouse pointer is currently moving. The third utility is a demo version of my Windows API browser. These three utilities have these features in common:

- Their GUIs are displayed modelessly from out-of-process ActiveX components.
- Once a client application calls and displays them from the book's class library, you can close the client application and the utilities continue to run in their own threads.
- Their windows are always kept on top of any other application's window.

Creating Copies Of The Same Instance Of A Class

Imagine that you have a client application with a **Form** object that looks like Figure 14.4. Let's assume that you have instantiated the **Utility** class of the book's class library in Form1. Then, if you click on WatchRAM to call the **WatchRAM** method of the **Utility** class, the **Form** object in Figure 14.5 appears.

Figure 14.4 Client application running utilities from a component.

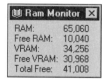

Figure 14.5 RAM Monitor utility from class library.

If you display the Windows task list, it shows the out-of-process ActiveX component (EFSE.EXE) as one of the current tasks, as shown in Figure 14.6. If you now click the **GetWindowInfo** button on Form1 to call that method of the **Utility** class, it displays the **Form** object in Figure 14.7.

If you display the Windows task list once again, it still shows just the one out-of-process component as a current task. The reason why only one out-of-process component is listed as a current task is because Windows has created a copy of the previously instantiated class. This occurs because of the setting of the **Instancing** property of the **Utility** class. It is set to 5 - MultiUse. As we learned in Chapter 3, when **Instancing** is set to 5 - MultiUse, requests by a client application for an instance of the class will

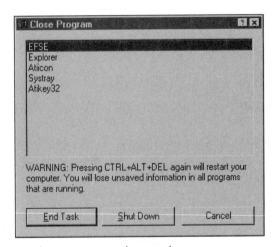

Figure 14.6   List of currently running Windows tasks.

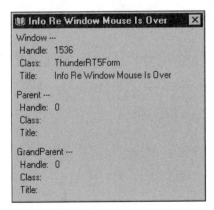

Figure 14.7   Window Info utility from class library.

be supplied by an already running copy of the out-of-process ActiveX component, if one exists. Creating a copy of the same instantiated class uses system resources more efficiently. In this scenario, the RAM Monitor's value for total free memory only decreases by about 50 K when a copy of the instance is created to run the Window Information utility.

CreateObject vs. GetObject

For most ActiveX components (for example, Microsoft's Excel and Word), you use Visual Basic's **CreateObject** *function when the component is not already running and Visual Basic's* **GetObject** *function to get a reference to and make a copy of an already-instantiated object. However, as mentioned in Visual Basic's Help file in the topic titled* GetObject Function, *you cannot use* **GetObject** *to obtain a reference to a class in an ActiveX component created with Visual Basic.*

Creating New Instances Of A Class

If you now open the book's out-of-process class library project (EFSE.VBP or EFS16.VBP), change the **Instancing** property of the **Utility** class to 3 - SingleUse, and remake the ActiveX component, the component will behave differently. If you run the same client application as before and display the RAM Monitor utility, the Windows task list shows one instance of EFSE.EXE running, as in the scenario examined in the previous section. But, if you now click **GetWindowInfo** to display that utility, two things change from the previous scenario:

- The Windows task list shows that two separate instances of the out-of-process ActiveX component are running, as shown in Figure 14.8.
- The amount of free memory that the RAM Monitor displays has decreased by over 500 K, compared to the approximately 50 K under the previous scenario.

Given the obvious inefficiency of creating a new instance of a class, why would you ever set the **Instancing** property of a class to 3 - SingleUse? One important situation that comes to mind is when the ActiveX component is being run as an RAO (Remote Automation Object). In this case, a setting of 3 - SingleUse ensures that each new client has immediate access to the services provided by the members of the class in question. This improves perceived response time, which is already degraded somewhat by network transmission overhead, network traffic, and so on.

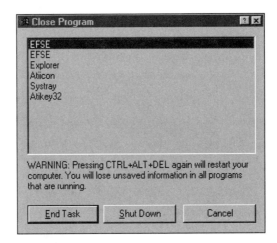

Figure 14.8 Two ActiveX instances.

Now let's take a look at the methods that drive these utilities.

The WatchRAM Method's Specifications

The **WatchRAM** method displays a 32-bit RAM monitor. The topic in the class library's Help file (EFS.HLP) that specifies the detailed functionality of the **WatchRAM** method is duplicated in the sidebar.

The WatchRAM method's specifications.

SYNTAX

```
Object.WatchRAM
```

The **WatchRAM** method's syntax has the following object qualifier:

- *Object*. Required. **Object** data type. An expression that evaluates to an object in the Applies To pop-up list.

CALLED

From any procedure in a client application.

RETURNS

Upon success, one element in a **Variant**. It contains a **Boolean** (**True**) that specifies the member executed successfully.

Upon failure, eight elements in a **Variant**. The elements contain the error codes that the class library returns when a runtime or syntax error occurs during the execution of one of its members.

REMARKS

- The **WatchRAM** method can only be called when the **Utility** class is instantiated from an out-of-process EXE component. This is because the RAM Monitor window is displayed modelessly and an in-process DLL component cannot display a modeless **Form** object under Visual Basic 4.0.

- The RAM Monitor window is kept on top of all other windows.

- It only runs under 32-bit Visual Basic because it uses a Windows API function (**GlobalMemoryStatus**) not found in the 16-bit Windows API.

The RAM Monitor Utility

The **WatchRAM** method's code is elementary. It takes no arguments and, after syntax checking the kind of component it is being run from (in-process, out-of-process remote, and 16-bit components are forbidden), it uses Visual Basic's **Show** method to display the frmWatchRAM **Form** object modelessly. It then immediately returns the usual indicator of success to the client application. The code for the **WatchRAM** method is in Listing 14.7.

Listing 14.7   WatchRAM method's code.

```
Function WatchRAM()

    ' Constants for literals:
    Const PROC = "WatchRAM"
    Const SYNTAX = True

    ' Enable error handler and do syntax checking:
    On Error GoTo ET

#If Win16 Then
    E.TrapSyntax 1, PROC, "16-bit VB"
#Else

    If cDLLServer Then
        E.TrapSyntax 1, PROC, "ActiveX DLL component"
    ElseIf cRAOServer Then
```

```
      E.TrapSyntax 1, PROC, "ActiveX RAO component"
  End If

  ' Display RAM monitor Form object modelessly
  ' and return True to indicate success:
  frmWatchRAM.Show
  WatchRAM = Array(True)

#End If

Exit Function

ET:

  If Err = SYNTAX Then WatchRAM = frmErrCodes.Codes
  If Err <> SYNTAX Then WatchRAM = CL.TrapErr(PROC)

End Function
```

The interesting code related to the **WatchRAM** method is in its associated **Form** object. There is a **Timer** object on frmWatchRAM that has a design-time **Interval** property setting of 1 millisecond and has the code in Listing 14.8 in its **Timer** event procedure.

Listing 14.8 WatchRAM Timer object's code.

```
Private Sub tmrWatchRAM_Timer()

  #If Win32 Then

    ' Constants for literals:
    Const LBL1 = "  RAM:"
    Const LBL2 = "  Free RAM: "
    Const LBL3 = "  VRAM:"
    Const LBL4 = "  Free VRAM:"
    Const LBL5 = "  Total Free:"
    Const ONE_SEC = 1000
    Const BYTE_ADJ = 0.0009765625
    Const COMMA = "###,###"
    Const NONE = vbNullString

    ' Variables:
    Dim Mem As MEMORYSTATUS

    ' Until Form object is unloaded via Control menu's Close
    ' item, read/display current memory statistics every second:
    Mem.TypeSize = Len(Mem)
    GlobalMemoryStatus Mem
    Cls
    CurrentY = 50
    Print LBL1, Format$((Mem.PhysTot * BYTE_ADJ), COMMA)
```

```
      If Format$((Mem.PhysFree * BYTE_ADJ), COMMA) = NONE Then
         Print LBL2, "0"
      Else
         Print LBL2, Format$((Mem.PhysFree * BYTE_ADJ), COMMA)
      End If

      Print LBL3, Format$((Mem.PageFileTot * BYTE_ADJ), COMMA)
      Print LBL4, Format$((Mem.PageFileFree * BYTE_ADJ), COMMA)
      Print LBL5, Format$((Mem.PhysFree * BYTE_ADJ + _
                          Mem.PageFileFree * BYTE_ADJ), COMMA)

      tmrWatchRAM.Interval = ONE_SEC

   #End If

End Sub
```

You should note three points about the code in Listing 14.8. First, the code is conditionally compiled only under 32-bit Visual Basic because it uses a Windows API function that does not exist in the 16-bit Windows API. Second, the Windows API function **GlobalMemoryStatus** fills the user-defined data type MEMORYSTATUS (represented here by the variable **Mem**) with information about current memory availability. MEMORYSTATUS contains these eight **Long** members:

- **TypeSize**
- **MemLoad**
- **PhysTotal**
- **PhysFree**
- **PageFileTot**
- **PageFileFree**
- **VirtualTot**
- **VirtualFree**

Before calling **GlobalMemoryStatus**, API32.HLP says that you should set the **TypeSize** member of MEMORYSTATUS. You can do this with the generic statement **Mem.TypeSize = Len(Mem)**. Some books suggest that you hard-code it with the statement **Mem.TypeSize = 32** (each of the eight **Long** members takes four bytes of storage). However, it is better to get in the habit of using the generic statement.

Third, once the initial read of the memory values is done and displayed, the code sets the **Interval** property of the **Timer** object to 1000 milliseconds (that is, ONE_SEC). This is done to prevent the display from constantly flickering. It is set to 1 millisecond at design-time in the Properties window so that the initial calculation and display occurs immediately.

The GetWindowInfo Method's Specifications

The **GetWindowInfo** method displays information for the window (handle, class name, caption, and so on) currently under the mouse pointer. The topic in the class library's Help file (EFS.HLP) that specifies the detailed functionality of the **GetWindowInfo** method is shown in the sidebar.

GetWindowInfo method's specifications.

SYNTAX

```
Object.GetWindowInfo
```

The **GetWindowInfo** method's syntax has the following object qualifier:

- *Object*. Required. **Object** data type. An expression that evaluates to an object in the Applies To pop-up list.

CALLED

From any procedure in a client application.

RETURNS

Upon success, one element in a **Variant**. It contains a **Boolean** (**True**) that specifies the member executed successfully.

Upon failure, eight elements in a **Variant**. The elements contain the error codes that the class library returns when a runtime or syntax error occurs during the execution of one of its members.

REMARKS

- The **GetWindowInfo** method can only be called when the **Utility** class is instantiated from an out-of-process ActiveX component. This is because the utility's window is displayed modelessly and an in-process ActiveX component cannot display a modeless **Form** object under Visual Basic 4.0.

- The information display window is kept on top of all other windows.

The Window Info Utility

As far as its algorithm is concerned, the **GetWindowInfo** method is a mirror image of the **WatchRAM** method. The only difference is that it does not forbid a 16-bit component. The interesting code related to the **GetWindowInfo** method is in its associated **Form** object. There is a **Timer** object on frmGetWindowInfo that has a design-time **Interval** property setting of 1 millisecond and has the code in Listing 14.9 in its **Timer** event procedure.

Listing 14.9   GetWindowInfo Timer object's code.

```
Private Sub tmrGetWindowInfo_Timer()

    ' Variables:
    Dim HWndWindow     As Variant
    Dim HWndParent     As Variant
    Dim HWndGrandPar   As Variant
    Dim Buffer         As String * 256
    Dim Pt             As POINTAPI

    ' Steps in algorithm are:
    ' * Get current mouse position.
    ' * Get handle of object mouse is over and display it.
    ' * Get class name of object, strip Nulls from buffer, and display it.
    ' * Get caption of object and display it.
    ' * If object has parent, get same three pieces
    '   of information for parent and display them.
    ' * If parent object has parent, get same three pieces
    '   of information for grandparent and display them.
    GetCursorPos Pt

    #If Win32 Then
        HWndWindow = WindowFromPoint(Pt.X, Pt.Y)
    #Else
        HWndWindow = WindowFromPoint(agPOINTAPItoLong(Pt))
    #End If

    lblWndHWnd = HWndWindow
    GetClassName HWndWindow, Buffer, Len(Buffer)
    lblWndCls = Left$(Buffer, InStr(Buffer, vbNullChar) - 1)
    GetWindowText HWndWindow, Buffer, Len(Buffer)
    lblWndTtl = Trim(Left$(Buffer, InStr(Buffer, vbNullChar) - 1))
    HWndParent = GetParent(HWndWindow)
    lblParHWnd = HWndParent
    GetWindowText HWndParent, Buffer, Len(Buffer)
    lblParTtl = Trim(Trim(Left$(Buffer, InStr(Buffer, vbNullChar) - 1)))

    If HWndParent Then
        GetClassName HWndParent, Buffer, Len(Buffer)
        lblParCls = Left$(Buffer, InStr(Buffer, vbNullChar) - 1)
    Else
```

```
      lblParCls = vbNullString
   End If

   HWndGrandPar = HWndParent

   Do While HWndParent
      HWndGrandPar = HWndParent
      HWndParent = GetParent(HWndGrandPar)
   Loop

   lblGrpHWnd = HWndGrandPar
   GetWindowText HWndGrandPar, Buffer, Len(Buffer)
   lblGrpTtl = Trim(Left$(Buffer, InStr(Buffer, vbNullChar) - 1))

   If HWndGrandPar Then
      GetClassName HWndGrandPar, Buffer, Len(Buffer)
      lblGrpCls = Left$(Buffer, InStr(Buffer, vbNullChar) - 1)
   Else
      lblGrpCls = vbNullString
   End If

End Sub
```

You should note three points about the code in Listing 14.9. First, the Windows API function **GetCursorPos** retrieves the X and Y coordinates of the mouse pointer's current position and places them in the user-defined data type POINTAPI (represented in the code by the variable **Pt**). Second, the Windows API function **WindowFromPoint** retrieves the handle of the window or control object that contains the specified point (that is, where the mouse pointer currently is on the screen). When running under 16-bit Visual Basic, the code uses a function from APIGUIDE.DLL (created by Daniel Appleman) to convert the user-defined data type structure to a **Long**.

Third, once you have the handle of a Windows object, you can get any information about it that the Windows operating system can provide. A series of Windows API functions is used to retrieve the object's class name, caption, parent's handle, and so on. **GetClassName** retrieves the class name of the window specified by its first argument (the window's handle). The second argument points to a fixed-string buffer that is filled with the class name. The third argument specifies the length, in characters, of the fixed-string buffer. **GetWindowText** works exactly like **GetClassName**, except that it retrieves the text of the specified window's title bar. **GetParent** retrieves the handle of the specified window's parent window. If the window has no parent window, the return value is zero (Null in C or **vbEmpty** in Visual Basic).

The Windows API Browser Utility

The **BrowseWinAPI** method runs a free demo version of the Windows API Browser utility. When you ran the book's setup routine in the Introduction, it installed this utility on the path C:\VBOOPEFS\VBADDINS\BRWSAPIS. The topic in the class library's Help file (EFS.HLP) that specifies the detailed functionality of the **BrowseWinAPI** method is shown in the sidebar.

BrowseWinAPI method's specifications.

SYNTAX

```
Object.BrowseWinAPI
```

The **BrowseWinAPI** method's syntax has the following object qualifier:

- *Object.* Required. **Object** data type. An expression that evaluates to an object in the Applies To pop-up list.

CALLED

From any procedure in a client application.

RETURNS

Upon success, one element in a **Variant**. It contains a **Boolean** (**True**) that specifies the member executed successfully.

Upon failure, eight elements in a **Variant**. The elements contain the error codes that the class library returns when a runtime or syntax error occurs during the execution of one of its members.

REMARKS

- The **BrowseWinAPI** method can only be called when the **Utility** class is instantiated from an out-of-process ActiveX component. This is because the Windows API Browser utility is displayed modelessly and an in-process ActiveX component cannot display a modeless **Form** object under Visual Basic 4.0.

- The Windows API Browser utility included with the book's class library is a free demo version, which includes only the 16-bit Windows API set. To see an order form for the 32-bit/ 16-bit Windows API Browser ($9.99 + $5.00 S/H), start the

Help file BRWSAPIS.HLP, choose the Support button, and click the Order Form hotspot. To print the order form, from the File menu of this Help file, choose Print or, under Windows 95, choose the Print command button. You can also copy and paste the order form into an e-mail message, fill it out, and send it to one of the e-mail addresses listed on the order form.

When you call the **BrowseWinAPI** method from a client application, it displays the Windows API Browser utility window in Figure 14.9.

Figure 14.9 Windows API Browser utility window.

15

ACTIVEX COMPONENTS AND HIDDEN FORMS

A powerful and flexible technique that an ActiveX component supports is the ability to display a control object that is layered on an encapsulated **Form** object, which itself is hidden. The **Form** object is hidden or covered over because these two things are done to it before it is displayed:

- It is subclassed to strip it of all its window-style attributes.

- Its client area is sized either to nothing or to precisely the same dimensions as the control that is layered on it.

From a class library, you can use one of three techniques to display a control on a hidden **Form** object and make it appear as if the control belongs to the client application's **Form** object:

- You can set the **BorderStyle** and **ScaleHeight** properties of the **Form** object so that it is hidden when it is displayed. This approach enables a client application to call a method from a class library that displays a **CommonDialog** control object which is layered on the hidden **Form** object. To the client application, it appears as if it is displaying its own **CommonDialog** control.

- You can use a Windows API function to keep the hidden **Form** object on top of all other windows, and you can set its **Left** and **Top** properties to position it above the client application's **Form** object. This approach enables a client application to call a method from a class library that displays a control object that is layered on the hidden **Form** object. To the client application, it appears as if it is displaying its own control.

- You can return an object reference from a method of a class library to the client application that called it. This object reference is the **Name** property of an ActiveX control object on the hidden **Form** object. This approach enables a client application to use a Windows API function to change the ActiveX control's parent window from the hidden **Form** object in the class library to its own **Form** object. To the client application, it appears as if it is displaying its own ActiveX control.

In this chapter, you will study three members in the book's class library. Each member illustrates one of the preceding techniques for displaying a control object that is layered on a hidden **Form** object. Table 15.1 describes each of these members.

Table 15.1   Methods to display a control on a hidden **Form** object.

Method	Class	Description
SelectFont	Text	Enables a client application to display the Font dialog box of the CommonDialog control. The class library's Form object, which contains this CommonDialog control, has its properties set in such a way that it does not become visible when its Load event occurs. Code in its Form_Resize event procedure then modally displays the Font dialog box.
ShowToolTip	ClientApp	Enables a client application to display a conventional Windows tooltip for any of its control objects. The Windows API function SetWindowPos displays the class library's hidden Form object, which has a tooltip Label object, sized to precisely the dimensions of the style-stripped Form object, layered on top of it.

continued

Table 15.1   Methods to display a control on a hidden **Form** object (continued).

Method	Class	Description
LoadStatusBar	ActiveXCtl	Enables a client application to display Microsoft's 32-bit StatusBar ActiveX control object. The method returns a reference to the StatusBar control to the client application, which then uses the Windows API function SetParent to gain control over it and position it on one of its Form objects.

Displaying A Common Dialog Box

We'll begin with the **SelectFont** method, which displays the Font common dialog box and returns information about the user's selection. This information can include the font's name and size, whether it should be normal/bold/italicized, what color it should be, and so on.

What The SelectFont Method Does

Before we analyze the specifications of the **SelectFont** method, it helps to see what it does first. To demonstrate the **SelectFont** method, follow these steps:

1. Select File | New Project and open a Standard EXE project.

2. Enter the code shown in Listing 15.1.

3. Run the project and double click on the **Form** object. The **SelectFont** method displays the Font dialog box shown in Figure 15.1.

Listing 15.1   Code to call SelectFont method.

```
' General Declarations Section:
' Form-level variable.
Dim Text As Object

Private Sub Form_Load()

    ' Instantiate class. Programmatic ID has two parts delimited by dot:
    ' * Project Name on General tab of Project Properties dialog box.
    ' * Name property of ClassModule object.
    #If Win32 Then
        Set Text = CreateObject("EFSE.Text")
    #ElseIf Win16 Then
        Set Text = CreateObject("EFS16.Text")
    #End If

End Sub
```

```
Private Sub Form_DblClick()

    ' Constants for values returned from members:
    Const MBR_SUCCESS = 0
    Const SF_NAME = 1
    Const SF_SIZE = 2
    Const SF_BOLD = 3
    Const SF_ITALIC = 4
    Const SF_STRIKE = 5
    Const SF_UNDER = 6

    ' Variables:
    Dim Msg        As String
    Dim Results    As Variant
    Hide

    ' Call object's member.
    Results = Text.SelectFont(cdlCFBoth)

    ' If method executes successfully, read whether user chose
    ' Cancel or some font and display appropriate message:
    If Results(MBR_SUCCESS) Then

        If Results(SF_NAME) = vbNullString Then
            Msg = "User chose Cancel."
        Else
            Msg = "User chose this font--" & vbCr
            Msg = Msg & "Name: " & Results(SF_NAME) & vbCr & vbCr
            Msg = Msg & "Size: " & Results(SF_SIZE) & vbCr
            Msg = Msg & "Bold: " & Results(SF_BOLD) & vbCr
            Msg = Msg & "Italic: " & Results(SF_ITALIC) & vbCr
            Msg = Msg & "Strikethru: " & Results(SF_STRIKE) & vbCr
            Msg = Msg & "Underline: " & Results(SF_UNDER)
        End If

    Else
        Msg = "Member failed."
    End If

    MsgBox Prompt:=Msg, Buttons:=vbInformation, Title:="Class Library Demo"
    Show

End Sub

Private Sub Form_Unload(Cancel As Integer)

    ' Free system resources associated with objects:
    Set Text = Nothing
    Set Form1 = Nothing

End Sub
```

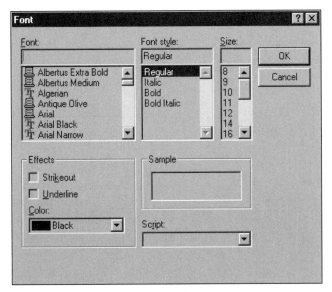

Figure 15.1 The **SelectFont** method's common dialog box.

In the Font dialog box, select a font and some attributes (font style, size, and so on) and then click on OK. The **SelectFont** method returns your selections to the client application, which in this demonstration reads and displays them in a message box, as shown in Figure 15.2.

The SelectFont Method's Specifications

The detailed functionality of the **SelectFont** method is shown in the sidebar that follows.

Figure 15.2 The selections returned from **SelectFont** method.

The SelectFont method's specifications.

SYNTAX

```
Object.SelectFont([Flags], [Min], [Max])
```

The **SelectFont** method's syntax has the following object qualifier and named arguments:

- *Object.* Required. **Object** data type. An expression that evaluates to an object in the Applies To pop-up list.

- *Flags.* Optional. **Variant** data type whose subtype is an **Integer** or **Long** constant or value that specifies the options for the Font dialog box. You can set more than one flag by either using the **Or** operator or by adding together the desired constant values. If omitted, the default setting for *Flags* is zero. See the help topic titled *VB Constants: SelectFont Method* for a description of the possible settings of the *Flags* argument.

- *Min.* Optional. **Variant** data type whose subtype is a numeric expression that specifies the minimum font size able to be selected. The smallest and largest values allowed are 8 and 72 respectively. If omitted, the default setting for *Min* is 8.

- *Max.* **Variant** data type whose subtype is a numeric expression that specifies the maximum font size able to be selected. The smallest and largest values allowed are 8 and 72 respectively. If omitted, the default setting for *Max* is 8.

CALLED

From any procedure in a client application.

RETURNS

Upon success, eight elements in a **Variant**. The elements contain these subtypes:

- 0- CF_SUCCESS. A **Boolean** (**True**) that specifies the member executed successfully.

- 1- CF_NAME. A **String** that specifies the selected font or, if the user clicks on Cancel, **vbNullString** (that is, a zero-length string).

- 2 - CF_SIZE. An **Integer** that specifies the size of the font selected or, if the user clicks on Cancel, the subtype of **vbEmpty** (that is, uninitialized).

- 3 - CF_BOLD. A **Boolean** that specifies whether the style of the selected font is bold (**True**) or not (**False**); or, if the user clicks on Cancel, the subtype of **vbEmpty** (that is, uninitialized).

- 4 - CF_ITALIC. A **Boolean** that specifies whether the style of the selected font is italic (**True**) or not (**False**); or, if the user clicks on Cancel, the subtype of **vbEmpty** (that is, uninitialized).

- 5 - CF_STRIKE. A **Boolean** that specifies whether the style of the selected font is strikethru (**True**) or not (**False**); or, if the user clicks on Cancel, the subtype of **vbEmpty** (that is, uninitialized).

- 6 - CF_UNDER. A **Boolean** that specifies whether the style of the selected font is underline (**True**) or not (**False**); or, if the user clicks on Cancel, the subtype of **vbEmpty** (that is, uninitialized).

- 7 - CF_COLOR. A **Long** that specifies the color of the selected font or, if the user clicks on Cancel, the subtype of **vbEmpty** (that is, uninitialized).

Upon failure, eight elements in a **Variant**. The elements contain the error codes that the class library returns when a runtime or syntax error occurs during the execution of one of its members.

REMARKS

Although the **CommonDialog** control's Font dialog box permits you to set most of its properties prior to displaying it, the **SelectFont** method subclasses it so you can only set its **Flags**, **Min**, and **Max** properties.

The SelectFont Method's Code

The **SelectFont** method's code, shown in Listing 15.2, works the way it does because its associated frmComDlg **Form** object has its **BorderStyle** property set to 0 - None and its **ScaleHeight** property set to zero. The **BorderStyle** property must be set at design time in the Properties window.

Listing 15.2   The SelectFont method's code.

```
Function SelectFont(Optional Flags, _
                    Optional Min, _
                    Optional Max)

    ' Constants for literals:
    Const PROC = "SelectFont"
    Const SYNTAX = True
    Const NO_FONT = " "
    Const CD_FONT = 4
    Const MIN_SIZE = 8
    Const MAX_SIZE = 72

    ' Constants for elements returned from member:
    Const CF_SUCCESS = 0
    Const CF_NAME = 1
    Const CF_SIZE = 2
    Const CF_BOLD = 3
    Const CF_ITALIC = 4
    Const CF_STRIKE = 5
    Const CF_UNDER = 6
    Const CF_COLOR = 7

    ' Variables:
    Dim TmpFlags      As Long
    Dim DBox          As CommonDialog
    Dim RetVals(7)    As Variant
    Dim Font(1 To 2)  As Byte

    ' Enable error handler and do syntax checking:
    On Error GoTo ET
    If cRAOServer Then E.TrapSyntax 1, PROC

    If Not IsMissing(Min) Then
        If Min < MIN_SIZE Or Min > MAX_SIZE Then
            E.TrapSyntax 5, PROC, "Min"
        End If
    End If

    If Not IsMissing(Max) Then
        If Max < MIN_SIZE Or Max > MAX_SIZE Then
            E.TrapSyntax 5, PROC, "Max"
        End If
    End If

    If Not IsMissing(Flags) Then
        If VarType(Flags) <> vbInteger And _
           VarType(Flags) <> vbLong Then
            E.TrapSyntax 4, PROC, "Flags", "Integer or Long"
```

```
            ElseIf Flags < vbEmpty Then
                    E.TrapSyntax 5, PROC, "Flags"
        End If
End If

' Execute member's algorithm—
' * If type of font has not been specified, set flag.
' * Ensure cdlCFLimitSize flag is set if Min or Max
'     argument is passed.
' * Set properties of CommonDialog's container Form object.
If Not IsMissing(Flags) Then
    Font(cdlCFScreenFonts) = Flags And cdlCFScreenFonts
    Font(cdlCFPrinterFonts) = Flags And cdlCFPrinterFonts

    If Font(cdlCFScreenFonts) Or Font(cdlCFPrinterFonts) Then
        TmpFlags = Flags
    ElseIf Not Font(cdlCFScreenFonts) And _
            Not Font(cdlCFPrinterFonts) Then
        TmpFlags = Flags + cdlCFBoth
    End If

    If Not Flags And cdlCFEffects Then
        TmpFlags = TmpFlags + cdlCFEffects
    End If

Else
    TmpFlags = cdlCFBoth + cdlCFEffects
End If

If Not IsMissing(Min) Or Not IsMissing(Max) Then
    If Not TmpFlags And cdlCFLimitSize Then
        TmpFlags = TmpFlags + cdlCFLimitSize
    End If
End If

Set DBox = frmComDlg.Cdl

With DBox

    If Not IsMissing(Min) And IsMissing(Max) Then
        .FontSize = Min
        .Min = Min
        .Max = MAX_SIZE
    ElseIf IsMissing(Min) And Not IsMissing(Max) Then
        .FontSize = MIN_SIZE
        .Min = MIN_SIZE
        .Max = Max
    ElseIf Not IsMissing(Min) And Not IsMissing(Max) Then
        .FontSize = Min
        .Min = Min
        .Max = Max
    End If

    .Flags = TmpFlags
```

```
End With

' Display method's Form object modally, so execution pauses
' until Hide method's applied in Form_Resize event procedure.
frmComDlg.Dialog = CD_FONT
frmComDlg.Show vbModal

' When Hide method is applied:
' * Assign values to elements to be returned from method.
' * Unload associated Form object.
' * Return array from method.
RetVals(CF_SUCCESS) = True

With DBox

    If .FontName <> NO_FONT Then
        RetVals(CF_NAME) = .FontName
        RetVals(CF_SIZE) = .FontSize
        RetVals(CF_BOLD) = .FontBold
        RetVals(CF_ITALIC) = .FontItalic
        RetVals(CF_STRIKE) = .FontStrikethru
        RetVals(CF_UNDER) = .FontUnderline
        RetVals(CF_COLOR) = .Color
    End If

End With

Set DBox = Nothing
Unload frmComDlg
SelectFont = RetVals
Exit Function

ET:

    If Err = SYNTAX Then SelectFont = frmErrCodes.Codes
    If Err <> SYNTAX Then
        Unload frmComDlg
        SelectFont = CL.TrapErr(PROC)
    End If

End Function
```

There are three important points to note about the **SelectFont** method's code. First, the **CommonDialog** ActiveX control on the **Form** object has its **Name** property set to just the three-letter prefix Cdl. Then, to reduce the number of object references separated by a dot delimiter, we assign the object variable **DBox** the reference frmComDlg.Cdl and use the **With...End With** statement.

Avoid using the dot delimiter

When returning or setting properties of objects, you should avoid using the dot delimiter whenever possible. The code runs slightly faster for each dot delimiter that you eliminate.

Second, the **Form** object's custom property **Dialog** is set to CD_FONT (4) to signal to code in its **Form_Resize** event procedure which common dialog box to display. Then the **Form** object is displayed modally with the statement

```
frmComDlg.Show vbModal
```

so that code execution in the method pauses after the **Form_Load** event is triggered.

Third, after the user clicks on OK to select a font or on Cancel to close the dialog box, the method, in addition to returning **True** in the first element (CF_SUCCESS) of the array, returns either **vbNullString** or the values of the various properties of the **CommonDialog** control selected by the user. The **Form** object that contains the **CommonDialog** control is only unloaded after the properties have been read.

No vbNullString for FontName

*When the user clicks on Cancel in the Font common dialog box, its **FontName** property is assigned a string containing a space, not **vbNullString**. This is inconsistent with the behavior of the Open and Save As common dialog boxes, which do return **vbNullString** in the **FileName** property when Cancel is selected.*

The code in the **SelectFont** method's associated frmComDlg **Form** object is shown in Listing 15.3.

Listing 15.3   Code in SelectFont method's associated form.

```
Private Sub Form_Resize()

    ' Constants for common dialog container
    ' Form object's Tag property:
    Const CD_OPEN = 1
    Const CD_SAVE = 2
```

```
            Const CD_COLOR = 3
            Const CD_FONT = 4
            Const CD_PRINTER = 5

            ' Constants for literals:
            Const ONE_HALF = 0.5

            ' Variables:
            Dim KindOfDlg As Byte

            ' Display common dialog:
            ' * Prevent focus problem associated with out-of-process,
            '   ActiveX component.
            ' * Center common dialog box (different for 16/32-bit).
            ' * Custom property fDialog, set by method, specifies dialog
            '   box to show (code execution pauses until user closes
            '   dialog box).
            ' * Hide modal Form object so method's code resumes.
            '   (OpenCL, PrintCL, SaveAs, SelectColor or SelectFont).
            SetFocus

        #If Win32 Then

            Select Case fDialog
                Case CD_OPEN, CD_SAVE
                    Left = ((Screen.Width - 4700) * ONE_HALF) - 900
                    Top = ((Screen.Height - 3150) * ONE_HALF) - 600
                Case CD_PRINTER
                    Left = ((Screen.Width - 6250) * ONE_HALF) - 920
                    Top = ((Screen.Height - 3950) * ONE_HALF) - 1280
                Case CD_COLOR
                    Left = ((Screen.Width - 3650) * ONE_HALF)
                    Top = ((Screen.Height - 4900) * ONE_HALF)
                Case CD_FONT
                    Left = ((Screen.Width - 6200) * ONE_HALF) - 300
                    Top = ((Screen.Height - 5150) * ONE_HALF) - 1350

        #Else

            Select Case fDialog
                Case CD_OPEN, CD_SAVE
                    Left = ((Screen.Width - 7150) * ONE_HALF) - 900
                    Top = ((Screen.Height - 3630) * ONE_HALF) - 600
                Case CD_PRINTER
                    Left = ((Screen.Width - 6000) * ONE_HALF) - 920
                    Top = ((Screen.Height - 3530) * ONE_HALF) - 1280
                Case CD_COLOR
                    Left = ((Screen.Width - 4000) * ONE_HALF)
                    Top = ((Screen.Height - 4800) * ONE_HALF)
                Case CD_FONT
                    Left = ((Screen.Width - 7000) * ONE_HALF) - 300
                    Top = ((Screen.Height - 5100) * ONE_HALF) - 1350
```

```
#End If

End Select

For KindOfDlg = CD_OPEN To CD_PRINTER

    If KindOfDlg = fDialog Then
        On Error Resume Next
        Cdl.Action = fDialog
        Exit For
    End If

Next KindOfDlg

Hide

End Sub
```

The essential point to understand about the code in the **Form_Resize** event procedure is why it is written in that particular event procedure. As we discussed earlier in the chapter, the **Form** object that contains the **CommonDialog** control is never actually displayed, so the code that displays the Font dialog box has to be automatically executed by some operating system event. This system event needs to be one from whose event procedure Visual Basic's **SetFocus** method can be applied to frmComDlg without causing runtime error 5 (Invalid procedure call), which rules out the **Form_Load** event procedure. The **SetFocus** statement is used to ensure that the common dialog box that will be displayed avoids the focus problem associated with an out-of-process ActiveX component. Either the **Form_Resize** or the **Form_Activate** event procedure fulfills these requirements; however, because **Form_Resize** fires before **Form_Activate**, I placed the code in the **Form_Resize** event procedure.

There are two other points to note about the code in Listing 15.3. First, most of the code is conditionally compiled and sets the **Left** and **Top** properties of frmComDlg. Why is this done and why are all of these odd and different coordinates used? The short answer is that this code centers the common dialog box on the screen. The long answer is a little more complicated. The help topic in Visual Basic's Help file titled *CommonDialog Control* states that you cannot specify where a dialog box is displayed; however, this statement does not mean that the various dialog boxes are not positioned in a consistent manner.

The way it works is that each one of the common dialog boxes is positioned in relation to the top-left corner of the **Form** object that contains the

CommonDialog control. The X and Y coordinates of each dialog box, in relation to the **Form** object's X and Y coordinates, are different but consistent. Once you know this, it is easy enough to use a ruler, measure where each dialog box is displayed on the screen, and adjust the code that sets the **Left** and **Top** properties of frmComDlg until each common dialog box is centered on the screen. There also happens to be a different set of coordinates for the 32-bit and 16-bit versions of the common dialog boxes, which the conditionally compiled code takes into account. So, although VB's Help file is correct when it says that you cannot directly control the position of the common dialog boxes, the book's class library demonstrates that you can indirectly control and center them.

The second point to note is that setting the **CommonDialog** control's **Action** property is what actually displays the appropriate dialog box. VB5 still supports the **Action** property (along with the newer **ShowFont** method). It takes fewer lines of code from within the **For...Next** loop to use the **Action** property, so I use it. It displays the common dialog box modally; and, so, code execution pauses on the statement **Cdl.Action = fDialog** until the user closes the common dialog box. At that point, code execution resumes in the **SelectFont** method, which returns the user's selection(s) to the client application.

Other Methods That Display Common Dialog Boxes

The **SelectFont** method is one of five members in the book's class library that display the various Windows common dialog boxes. Table 15.2 describes the other four members. We will examine the methods that display the Open and Save As common dialog boxes later in the book because they utilize techniques common to the **File** class (discussed in Chapter 18). The **PrintCL** and **SelectColor** methods conceptually work in the same way as the **SelectFont** method and, so, we will not analyze their code.

Keeping A Form/Control On Top

In this section, we'll examine the **ShowToolTip** method, which enables a client application to display a conventional Windows tooltip for any of its control objects. You looked at the topics of context-sensitive Help and tooltips in Chapter 13. There you saw that VB5 has a new **ToolTipText**

Table 15.2 Other methods that display the Windows common dialog boxes.

Method	Class	Description
OpenCL	File	Enables a client application to display the Open common dialog box. The method returns either vbNullString or the path and name of the selected file(s). The OpenCL method subclasses the behavior of the Open dialog box, by changing the caption of its default button (for the 16-bit version) and permitting the use of wildcards.
PrintCL	File	Enables a client application to display the Print common dialog box. The method returns either vbNullString or the values of various properties of the dialog box set by the user.
SaveAs	File	Enables a client application to display the Save As common dialog box. The method returns either vbNullString or the path and name of the selected file(s). The SaveAs method subclasses the behavior of the Save As dialog box, by changing the caption of its default button (for the 16-bit version) and permitting the use of wildcards.
SelectColor	ClientApp	Enables a client application to display the Color common dialog box. The method returns either vbNullString or the Long value of the selected color.

property, which enables you to easily display a tooltip for almost any VB control object. But the **ToolTipText** property has some limitations (it can't specify the color of the tip, or how much of a delay before it is displayed, or how long it is displayed before it is hidden). The **ShowToolTip** method of the book's ActiveX component addresses these limitations.

What The ShowToolTip Method Does

Before we analyze the specifications of the **ShowToolTip** method, it helps to see what it does first. To demonstrate the **ShowToolTip** method, follow these steps:

1. Select File|New Project and open a Standard EXE project. Add a **CommandButton** object and a **TextBox** object to Form1.

2. Set the **Index** property of Command1 to zero and the **Index** property of Text1 to zero.

3. Open the class library's Help file (EFS.HLP), find the help topic for the **ShowToolTip** method, click on its Example hotspot, and copy and paste the example code into the General Declarations section of Form1.

4. Run the project. The dialog box in Figure 15.3 is displayed.

5. Move the mouse pointer over a control object and a tooltip is displayed like the one shown in Figure 15.4.

The ShowToolTip Method's Specifications

The **ShowToolTip** method displays a tooltip for the control object beneath the mouse pointer, based on the control's **Tag** property. The detailed functionality of the **ShowToolTip** method is shown in the sidebar.

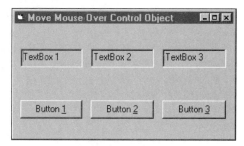

Figure 15.3 Dialog box to demo **ShowToolTip** method.

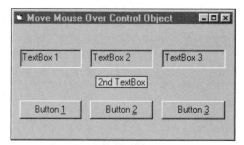

Figure 15.4 Tooltip displayed by **ShowToolTip** method.

The ShowToolTip method's specifications.

SYNTAX

`Object.ShowToolTip(Obj, [Cancel], [Color], [Delay], [Hide])`

The **ShowToolTip** method's syntax has the following object qualifier and named arguments:

- *Object.* Required. **Object** data type. An expression that evaluates to an object in the Applies To pop-up list.

- *Obj.* Required. **Object** data type. An expression that evaluates to any Visual Basic object that has a **Tag** property.

- *Cancel.* Optional. **Variant** data type whose subtype is a numeric expression that must evaluate to **True**. When *Cancel* is passed, the tooltip's container **Form** object in the class library is unloaded. To unload the container **Form** object, you must call the **ShowToolTip** method from the **Form_Unload** event procedure of the client application.

- *Color.* Optional. **Variant** data type whose subtype is a numeric expression that specifies the background color of the tooltip. Valid settings are Visual Basic's color constants (eight colors under 16-bit Visual Basic and nine colors under 32-bit). If omitted, the default setting for *Color* is **vbInfoBackground** (that is, the Windows system background color for tooltips) for 32-bit or **vbYellow** for 16-bit. See the help topic titled *VB Constants: ShowToolTip Method* for the valid settings of the *Color* argument.

- *Delay.* **Variant** data type whose subtype is a numeric expression that specifies the length of the delay in seconds before the tooltip is displayed. Valid settings are zero, one, two, or three. If omitted, the default setting for *Delay* is one. This emulates the Windows 95 operating system's tooltip algorithm for its taskbar.

- *Hide.* Optional. **Variant** data type whose subtype is a numeric expression that specifies the length of time in seconds before the tooltip that was displayed is hidden. Valid settings are from three to seven. If omitted, the default setting for *Hide* is five. This emulates the Windows 95 operating system's tooltip algorithm for its taskbar.

CALLED

From a general procedure in a module of a client application. This general procedure is called from the **MouseMove** event procedure of:

- Any control object with a **Tag** property that needs a tooltip displayed.

- Any **Form** object, whose **Tag** property should be set to a zero-length string (that is, "" or **vbNullString**).

- Any **PictureBox** object on which **Image** objects are layered as toolbar buttons. The **PictureBox** object's **Tag** property should be set to a zero-length string.

RETURNS

Upon success, one element in a **Variant**. It contains a **Boolean** (**True**) that specifies the member executed successfully.

Upon failure, eight elements in a **Variant**. The elements contain the error codes that the class library returns when a runtime or syntax error occurs during the execution of one of its members.

REMARKS

- The **ShowToolTip** method displays a **Form** object that never gets the focus. It can only be called when the **ClientApp** class is instantiated from an out-of-process EXE component. This is because the tooltip must be displayed modelessly and an in-process DLL component cannot display a modeless **Form** object under VB4.

- To unload the tooltip's container **Form** object, you must call the **ShowToolTip** method in the **Form_Unload** event procedure of the client application and pass the optional *Cancel* argument. If you do not explicitly unload it, its **Terminate** event does not occur and the tooltip still appears on the screen.

- **Image** objects used as toolbar buttons and layered inside a **PictureBox** object must be part of a control array.

The ShowToolTip Method's Code

The **ShowToolTip** method is one of the three most complex members of the book's class library (along with the **ShowCS** and **LoadStatusBar** methods). To understand its code, you need to first understand the design of its associated GUI elements. The tooltip that is displayed is actually a **Label** object, layered on the frmShowTip **Form** object in the class library. The two GUI elements have these attributes:

- The **Form** object is stripped of its style attributes and border by the **CancelStyle** method, which is called from its **Form_Load** event procedure. Just setting the **BorderStyle** property of frmShowTip to 0 - None does not result in the desired appearance of the tooltip.

- The **Label** object's **BorderStyle** property is set to 0 - None, and its **Left**, **Top**, **Height**, and **Width** properties are set so that it is sized the same as, and positioned on top of, the client area of the style-stripped **Form** object. Factors that allow for the display of the form's thin black border and some space before and after the tooltip's string are taken into account.

- The **ShowToolTip** method then displays the tooltip (that is, form/label) modelessly, on top of all other windows, and without the focus.

Before analyzing its code, it is also important for you to understand how the **ShowToolTip** method is called. It takes only one required argument, **Obj**, which must be a reference to a Visual Basic object whose **Tag** property is set to the tooltip string to be displayed. You make the call from a general procedure in the client application named, for example, **ApplyMethod**. The general procedure's code looks like Listing 15.4.

Listing 15.4 General procedure to call ShowToolTip method.

```
Sub ApplyMethod(Obj As Object)

    ' Variable.
    Static ToolTip As String

    If Obj.Tag <> ToolTip Then
        ToolTip = Obj.Tag
        ClientApp.ShowToolTip Obj:=Obj
    End If

End Sub
```

The **Static** variable **ToolTip** prevents the **ShowToolTip** method from being called more than once for each control object over which the mouse is moved. Only when the setting of **ToolTip** changes (that is, the mouse is moved over a new control object or the **Form** object) is the **ShowToolTip** method called again. The general procedure **ApplyMethod** is called from the **MouseMove** event procedure of any control object for which you want to display a tooltip, and from the **MouseMove** event procedure of the **Form** object itself (whose **Tag** property should be set to **vbNullString**). The call from **MouseMove** passes the **Name** property of the control or **Form** object to the general procedure named **ApplyMethod**.

The **ShowToolTip** method, which is shown in Listing 15.5, also takes several optional arguments that enable you to customize aspects of the display (the color of the tooltip, how long a delay there is before the tooltip appears, and how long the tooltip remains visible). If you do not pass any of its optional arguments, **ShowToolTip** defaults to the standard values employed by the Windows 95 operating system.

Listing 15.5 The ShowToolTip method's code.

```
Function ShowToolTip(Obj As Object, _
                     Optional Cancel, _
                     Optional Color, _
                     Optional Delay, _
                     Optional Hide)

    ' Constants for Windows API functions:
    Const HWND_TOPMOST = -1
    Const SWP_NOSIZE = &H1
    Const SWP_NOMOVE = &H2
    Const SW_SHOWNOACTIVATE = 4

    ' Constant for argument passed to member.
    Const PR_TAG = 1

    ' Constants for literals:
    Const PROC = "ShowToolTip"
    Const SYNTAX = True
    Const NO_TAG = vbNullString
    Const OFF_SCREEN = -20000
    Const DEF_DELAY = 1
    Const DEF_HIDE = 5

    ' Variables:
    Dim TwoParents  As Boolean
    Dim CurIndex    As Integer
    Dim Parent1     As Object
    Dim Parent2     As Object
```

```
' Enable error handler and do syntax checking:
On Error GoTo ET

If cDLLServer Then
    E.TrapSyntax 1, PROC, "ActiveX DLL component"
ElseIf cRAOServer Then
    E.TrapSyntax 1, PROC, "ActiveX RAO component"
ElseIf Not CL.HasProperty(Obj, PR_TAG) Then
    E.TrapSyntax 8, PROC, "Obj"
ElseIf Not IsMissing(Cancel) Then
    If Cancel <> True Then E.TrapSyntax 5, PROC, "Cancel"
End If

If Not IsMissing(Color) Then
    Select Case Color
        Case vbBlack, vbBlue, vbCyan, vbGreen, vbMagenta, _
            vbRed, vbWhite, vbYellow
        Case vbInfoBackground
            #If Win16 Then
                Color = vbYellow
            #End If
        Case Else
            E.TrapSyntax 5, PROC, "Color"
    End Select
    frmShowTip.BackColor = Color
    frmShowTip.lblShowTip.BackColor = Color
Else
    #If Win32 Then
        frmShowTip.BackColor = vbInfoBackground
        frmShowTip.lblShowTip.BackColor = vbInfoBackground
    #Else
        frmShowTip.BackColor = vbYellow
        frmShowTip.lblShowTip.BackColor = vbYellow
    #End If
End If

If Not IsMissing(Delay) Then

    Select Case Delay
        Case 0, 1, 2, 3
            frmShowTip.ToolTipDelay = Delay
        Case Else
            E.TrapSyntax 5, PROC, "Delay"
    End Select

Else
    frmShowTip.ToolTipDelay = DEF_DELAY
End If

If Not IsMissing(Hide) Then

    Select Case Hide
        Case 3, 4, 5, 6, 7
            frmShowTip.ToolTipHide = Hide
```

```
        Case Else
            E.TrapSyntax 5, PROC, "Hide"
    End Select

Else
    frmShowTip.ToolTipHide = DEF_HIDE
End If


If Not CL.IsForm(Obj) Then

    If Not CL.IsForm(Obj.Container) Then
        Set Parent1 = Obj.Container

        If CL.IsForm(Parent1.Container) Then
            Set Parent2 = Parent1.Container
            TwoParents = True
        Else
            E.TrapSyntax 31, PROC, "Obj"
        End If

    Else
        Set Parent1 = Obj.Container
    End If
End If

' * Initialize custom properties of container Form object.
With frmShowTip
    .ToolTipCancel = False
    .ToolTip = Obj.Tag

    ' If control object with tooltip is on Form object--
    ' * Set other custom properties of container Form object.
    ' * Start Timer object on frmShowTip to position tooltip.
    If Obj.Tag <> NO_TAG And Not TwoParents Then
        Set .Ctl = Obj
        Set .Parent1 = Parent1
        .tmrShowTip.Enabled = True
        .tmrHideTip.Enabled = True

    ' If control object with tooltip is layered on object--
    ' * Check if object is part of control array by seeing
    '   whether its Index property is set to some value:
    '   a) If it is not part of control array, runtime error
    '      343 occurs ("Object not an array") and is handled
    '      with more explanatory syntax error message.
    '   b) If it is part of control array:
    '      - Set custom properties of container Form object.
    '      - Start Timer object to position tooltip.
    ElseIf Obj.Tag <> NO_TAG And TwoParents Then
        On Error Resume Next
        CurIndex = Obj.Index

        If Err <> False Then
            On Error GoTo ET
```

```
        E.TrapSyntax 32, PROC, "Obj"
    End If

    On Error GoTo ET
    Set .Ctl = Obj
    Set .Parent1 = Parent1
    Set .Parent2 = Parent2
    .tmrShowTip.Enabled = True
    .tmrHideTip.Enabled = True

' If object has no tooltip attached (that is, it is
' Form object or some control object without tooltip):
' * Cancel display in tmrShowTip_Timer event procedure.
' * Initialize flag for toolbar button group.
' * Move tooltip off Screen object so it is not visible.
ElseIf Obj.Tag = NO_TAG Then
    .ToolTipCancel = True
    .SameBtnGroup = False
    .Top = OFF_SCREEN
    .Left = OFF_SCREEN
End If

' If not canceling, display tooltip Form object:
' * Keep tooltip form on top of all other windows.
' * Display tooltip form modelessly.
' * Immediately put focus back on client app's Form object.
' If client application is canceling:
' * Disable any currently executing threads.
' * Unload tooltip's associated Form object.
If IsMissing(Cancel) Then
    SetWindowPos .hWnd, HWND_TOPMOST, _
                vbEmpty, vbEmpty, vbEmpty, vbEmpty, _
                SWP_NOMOVE Or SWP_NOSIZE
    ShowWindow .hWnd, SW_SHOWNOACTIVATE

    If Not TwoParents Then

        If Obj.Tag <> NO_TAG Then
            Obj.Container.SetFocus
        Else
            Obj.SetFocus
        End If

    Else
        Parent2.SetFocus
    End If

Else
    .tmrHideTip.Enabled = False
    .tmrShowTip.Enabled = False
    Unload frmShowTip
End If

End With
```

```
    ShowToolTip = Array(True)
    Exit Function

ET:

    If Err = SYNTAX Then ShowToolTip = frmErrCodes.Codes
    If Err <> SYNTAX Then ShowToolTip = CL.TrapErr(PROC)

End Function
```

Our discussion of the **ShowToolTip** method's code will focus on these four issues:

- Handling different **ScaleMode** settings for the control object with the tooltip and its parent.
- Displaying the tooltip modelessly, on top, and without the focus.
- Running and aborting a threaded operation with a **Timer** object.
- Explicitly unloading a modeless **Form** object that was displayed from a class library.

HANDLING DIFFERENT SCALEMODE SETTINGS

When you write a member in an ActiveX component that takes a Visual Basic GUI object reference as one of its arguments, you never know what the settings of the various properties of that GUI object may be. Most of the time this is not a concern. However, if the member positions GUI objects on the screen, the setting of the **ScaleMode** property can affect the way the code of the member functions.

Consider a scenario where the **ShowToolTip** method displays a tooltip for an **Image** object (for instance, a toolbar button) that is layered on a **PictureBox** object (the toolbar) on a **Form** object. Because of the nature of the client application, the **ScaleMode** property of the **PictureBox** and **Form** objects of the client application might not be set to the default of 1 - Twip, or they might even be different settings altogether.

The **ShowToolTip** method positions the tooltip slightly below its control object and centered in relation to it. To compute the X and Y coordinates correctly, **ShowToolTip** needs to compare apples to apples in regard to **ScaleMode** property settings. To do this, the method follows these general steps:

- Uses **Property Set** procedures in the tooltip's **Form** object to store the object references for the control object and its container object(s). The

ShowToolTip method cannot display tooltips for control objects that are layered more than two levels deep.

- Starts two **Timer** objects on the tooltip's **Form** object. Code in their **Timer** event procedures positions the tooltip and implements the settings of the *Delay* and *Hide* arguments.

- Displays the tooltip's **Form** object modelessly, on top of all other windows, and without the focus. From here on, all the essential code executes in the **Timer** event procedures of the two **Timer** objects.

- Stores the original **ScaleMode** setting of the container object(s) and temporarily substitutes the setting of 1 - Twip (that is, the intrinsic constant **vbTwips**).

- Computes the X and Y coordinates of the top-left corner of the tooltip.

- Displays the tooltip at those coordinates.

- Restores the original **ScaleMode** setting of the control object's container object(s).

If the client application's user moves the mouse over another control object or its **Form** object, the **ShowToolTip** method is called again and the cycle starts over.

DISPLAYING THE TOOLTIP

These statements toward the bottom of the **ShowToolTip** method display the tooltip modelessly, keep it on top of the client application's **Form** object, and prevent it from getting the focus:

```
SetWindowPos .hWnd, HWND_TOPMOST, _
            vbEmpty, vbEmpty, vbEmpty, vbEmpty, _
            SWP_NOMOVE Or SWP_NOSIZE
ShowWindow .hWnd, SW_SHOWNOACTIVATE
```

The Windows API function **SetWindowPos** specifies the size, position, and z-order of a child, pop-up, or top-level window. Its first argument is the handle of the window to be positioned. When it is used to keep a window on top of all other windows, its second argument must be the HWND_TOPMOST constant; its last argument must be SWP_NOMOVE Or SWP_NOSIZE; and its other arguments must be set to zero (Null in C or **vbEmpty** in VB). The **ShowWindow** API function's first argument is the handle of the window to display modelessly. Its second argument provides more control over the display state of the window than the *style* argument of VB's **Show** method does. In this case, the constant SW_SHOWNO-ACTIVATE specifies that it is not to receive the focus.

RUNNING THREADED CODE WITH TIMER OBJECTS

The **ShowToolTip** method is one of the best examples in the book's class library of a member that implements a complex set of specifications and functionality, but does so with a simple public interface. This public interface, which has only one required argument, hides all the gory details of the implementation and encapsulates them inside the black box of the ActiveX component.

Most of the complexity of the **ShowToolTip** method is handled by the code for the two **Timer** objects on the tooltip's **Form** object. The code in the **Timer** event procedure of these two **Timer** objects implements the functionality associated with the method's *Delay* and *Hide* arguments. You can study the code at your leisure; it is well-commented. However, the most important thing to understand about this code are two concepts of ActiveX object-oriented programming that underlie the code and determine how you must write threaded, multitasking code.

A threaded, or asynchronous, routine is code that executes in another memory process (that is, out-of-process in relation to the client application's code), while allowing the client application's user to perform any other task that its code can do. If you want to run threaded or asynchronous code in a VB class library, you must use:

- An out-of-process ActiveX component (for VB4), or either an out-of-process or in-process ActiveX component (for VB5).

- A **Timer** object on an encapsulated, hidden **Form** object.

When a client application calls the **ShowToolTip** method, the member syntax checks its arguments, sets some custom properties on its associated tooltip **Form** object, starts two **Timer** objects, and loads the tooltip's **Form** object. At this point, the method returns a value to the client application (normally **True**). The client application's user regains control and can do something else (for example, move the mouse over the **Form** object, move it over another control object, or cause some other event to occur). Meanwhile, however, the two **Timer** objects in the ActiveX component are executing their routines asynchronously in two separate threads.

After the time specified by the *Delay* argument (or its default value of 1 second), the tmrShowTip's thread displays the loaded tooltip. If the user does not move the mouse off the original control in the client application within the time specified by the method's *Hide* argument (or its default value of 5 seconds), the tmrHideTip's thread removes the tooltip from the screen.

However, if the user moves the mouse off the control and over the **Form** object (which should have its **Tag** property set to **vbNullString**) before the tmrShowTip's thread can display the tooltip, then the **ShowToolTip** method is called again. At this point, early in the execution of the **ShowToolTip** method, there would be four separate threads running:

- The client application's thread.
- The **ShowToolTip** method's thread.
- The tmrShowTip **Timer** object's thread (from the previous call).
- The tmrHideTip **Timer** object's thread (from the previous call).

The **ShowToolTip** method reads that the **Tag** property of the **Form** object passed to it is set to **vbNullString** and reacts to this by executing this code:

```
ElseIf Obj.Tag = NO_TAG Then
    .ToolTipCancel = True
    .SameBtnGroup = False
    .Top = OFF_SCREEN
    .Left = OFF_SCREEN
End If
```

This code turns on the tooltip **Form** object's **ToolTipCancel** custom property, initializes the **SameBtnGroup** custom property's flag, and moves/hides the tooltip's **Form** object off the screen. Then both the **Timer** objects, which have been executing their code asynchronously in separate threads, read that the **ToolTipCancel** flag has been turned on and abort their routines. For example, the code in the **tmrHideTip_Timer** event procedure that reacts to the setting of the **fToolTipCancel** form-level flag is shown in Listing 15.6.

Listing 15.6   The Timer object's code thread.

```
Private Sub tmrHideTip_Timer()

    ' _____
    '
    ' Purpose of tmrHideTip is to track how long tooltip is
    ' displayed and to hide it after time specified by Hide
    ' argument has elapsed. Timer object's code runs
    ' asynchronously (that is, after ShowToolTip method's code
    ' has executed and returned value to client application).
    ' This is necessary so that previous call to display tooltip
    ' can be canceled if mouse moves over object without
    ' tooltip or new tooltip.
    ' _____
    '
    ' Constants for literals:
    Const OFF_SCREEN = -20000
```

```
' Variables:
Dim Start    As Long
Dim Finish   As Long

' * Get current time accurate to a millisecond.
' * Loop until hide time has elapsed or fToolTipCancel flag
'    was set to True (caused by mouse pointer moving over
'    Form or control object with Tag property set to
'    zero-length string).
' * If tooltip has not been canceled but hide time has
'    elapsed, hide tooltip by moving it off screen.
' * Turn Timer object off.
Start = TimeGetTime
Finish = Start + fToolTipDelay + fToolTipHide

Do Until TimeGetTime > Finish Or fToolTipCancel
    DoEvents
Loop

If Not fToolTipCancel Then
    Top = OFF_SCREEN
    Left = OFF_SCREEN
End If

tmrHideTip.Enabled = False

End Sub
```

If the mouse never moves off the original control, the tmrHideTip's empty loop executes for the length of time specified by the *Delay* and *Hide* arguments (while the tooltip is being displayed by the tmrShowTip's thread). Then the tmrHideTip's thread hides the tooltip by moving it off the **Screen** object and terminates its own thread. If the mouse does move off the original control, then the tmrShowTip's thread handles the situation and either displays another control's tooltip or reacts to the **fToolTipCancel** flag being turned on by terminating its own thread.

If this discussion has you a bit confused, don't worry. The concept of running threaded code in an out-of-process ActiveX component, using one or more **Timer** objects, is pretty complex. It can definitely be confusing when you first encounter it. To understand it better, run the example code calling the **ShowToolTip** method and carefully observe what happens.

Move the mouse over a **CommandButton** or **TextBox** object and leave it there. Count how many seconds it takes before the tooltip is removed from the screen. Which **Timer** object's thread removes it? Move the mouse over one of the controls and, after the tooltip is displayed, immediately move the mouse over the **Form** object and watch the tooltip being removed from the screen. Which **Timer** object's thread removes it? Finally, move the mouse over a control and, before the tooltip is displayed, move the mouse back over the **Form** object. Which **Timer** object's thread is canceled before it can display the tooltip?

IMPLICITLY LOADING AND EXPLICITLY UNLOADING A FORM

If a method in an out-of-process ActiveX component loads a **Form** object during its execution, the object instance of the method's class cannot be deinstantiated and the ActiveX component's EXE file cannot be terminated until that **Form** object is somehow unloaded. You saw this behavior before in Chapter 14, when you used the **WatchRAM**, **GetWindowInfo**, and **BrowseWinAPI** methods of the **Utility** class.

In the case of these three methods, it is obvious to the user that the **Form** object has to somehow be unloaded. Their forms not only remain on the screen after the methods are done executing, but they also remain on top of all other windows. Because each form is conspicuously displayed, the book's class library does not provide a way to unload these **Form** objects. The assumption is that the client application's user will close and unload them from their Control menus.

However, there are other methods in the book's class library (like **ShowToolTip**, **LoadStatusBar**, and **LoadToolBar**) that load a hidden **Form** object during their execution. In these cases, there is no way the client application's user can close the forms; in fact, to the user, they don't appear to be forms at all. Therefore, the class library must provide a way to explicitly unload the hidden **Form** object when the client application is done using its control.

The easiest way to do this is to provide an optional *Cancel* argument (as with the **ShowToolTip** method) or to specify a cancel value for the *Kind* argument (0 - SB_CANCEL or 0 - TB_CANCEL, as with the **LoadStatusBar** and **LoadToolBar** methods). The call to the class library's method to explicitly unload a hidden **Form** object should be made from the client application's **Form_Unload** event procedure. The code that does this for the **ShowToolTip** method is shown here:

```
Private Sub Form_Unload(Cancel As Integer)

   Dialog.ShowToolTip Obj:=Me, _
                   Cancel:=True

End Sub
```

It does not matter what object reference is passed to the *Obj* argument. If the optional *Cancel* argument is passed, all other arguments are ignored and the hidden **Form** object/tooltip is unloaded. The reason you should do this is because it is conventional Windows programming practice to free system resources when you are done using them, preventing memory leaks. If you do not explicitly make this call from the **Form_Unload** event procedure, the instance of the out-of-process ActiveX component will still appear on the Windows task list.

Returning An Object Reference

In this section, we'll examine the **LoadStatusBar** method, which enables a client application to display Microsoft's 32-bit **StatusBar** ActiveX control object. It illustrates a generic technique that, by returning an object reference to an ActiveX control encapsulated in a class library, enables a client application to use the ActiveX control as if it were its own. In the case of the **LoadStatusBar** method, the ActiveX control is a fairly simple one. But this same technique can be used with more complex ActiveX controls (see the **LoadToolBar** method, which is explained in Chapter 17) and can let you embody a very complex set of functional specifications within a single, easy-to-use method of an ActiveX component.

What The LoadStatusBar Method Does

Before we analyze the specifications of the **LoadStatusBar** method, it helps to see what it does first. To demonstrate the **LoadStatusBar** method, follow these steps:

1. Select File | New Project and open a Standard EXE project.

2. Add a **CommandButton** object and a **Timer** object to Form1.

3. Set the **Index** property of Command1 to zero.

4. Select Project | Components.

5. In the Controls tab, make sure that the Microsoft Windows Common Controls option is checked and then click on OK.

6. Open the class library's Help file (EFS.HLP), find the help topic for the **LoadStatusBar** method, click on its Example hotspot, and copy and paste the example code into the General Declarations section of Form1.

7. Run the project. The dialog box shown in Figure 15.5 is displayed.

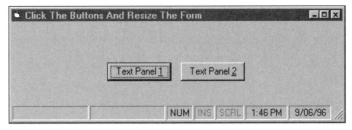

Figure 15.5 Dialog box to demo **LoadStatusBar** method.

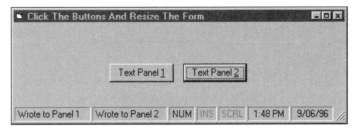

Figure 15.6 Client application sets properties of **StatusBar**.

8. Click on the buttons to write information to the two text panels on the **StatusBar** control, as shown in Figure 15.6.

LoadStatusBar Method's Specifications

The **LoadStatusBar** method embeds Microsoft's 32-bit ActiveX **StatusBar** control object on a **Form** object in a client application. The detailed functionality of the **LoadStatusBar** method is as follows:

The LoadStatusBar method's specifications.

SYNTAX

```
Object.LoadStatusBar(Kind, ParamArray Panels( ))
```

The **LoadStatusBar** method's syntax has the following object qualifier and arguments:

- *Object*. Required. **Object** data type. An expression that evaluates to an object in the Applies To pop-up list.

- *Kind.* Required. **Byte** data type. An expression specifying a value or constant which determines the type of status bar to display. Valid settings of *Kind* are 0 - SB_CANCEL, 1 - SB_TEXTONLY, 2 - SB_TIMEDATE, and 3 - SB_CUSTOM. If the *Panels( )* argument is passed, *Kind* is dependent on it and must be set to 3 - SB_CUSTOM.

- *Panels( ).* Optional. **Variant** data type. A **ParamArray** array containing one element that is passed in as a **Variant** array. This **Variant** array's lower bound can be any value and the array can contain from one to seven elements, which specify the customizable panels of the status bar. To specify any element, you must also specify all the elements preceding it in the array. If you want to skip an element/panel, sets its value to **False**. If you pass more than seven elements, the extraneous elements are ignored. See *Settings* for the data types and valid settings of the seven elements.

SETTINGS

The *Panels( )* argument's settings are:

- 1st element: **sbrText**. A numeric expression that specifies the number of text panels to include on the status bar. Valid settings are from 0 to 3. Any text panel(s) are displayed on the left side of the status bar. Code in the client application can display messages in these text panels.

- 2nd element: **sbrCaps**. A numeric expression that evaluates to either 1 or **False** and specifies whether or not the Caps Lock panel is displayed to the right of any previous panel(s).

- 3rd element: **sbrNum**. A numeric expression that evaluates to either 2 or **False** and specifies whether or not the Num Lock panel is displayed to the right of any previous panel(s).

- 4th element: **sbrIns**. A numeric expression that evaluates to either 3 or **False** and specifies whether or not the Insert panel is displayed to the right of any previous panel(s).

- 5th element: **sbrScrl**. A numeric expression that evaluates to either 4 or **False** and specifies whether or not the Scroll Lock panel is displayed to the right of any previous panel(s).

- 6th element: **sbrTime**. A numeric expression that evaluates to either 5 or **False** and specifies whether or not the time panel is displayed to the right of any previous panel(s).

- 7th element: **sbrDate**. A numeric expression that evaluates to either 5 or **False** and specifies whether or not the date panel is displayed to the right of any previous panel(s).

To use these constants you must pass the *Panels( )* argument a zero-based array, and the client application must have the Microsoft Windows Common Controls component referenced in its project. You do not have to pass the constants, however, and can instead just pass the specified numeric values.

If you use the Visual Basic constants, they do not have to be declared and are listed in the Object Browser. See the help topic titled *VB Constants: LoadStatusBar Method* for a detailed description of them.

CALLED

Normally from the **Form_Load** event procedure in a client application. If run from an out-of-process EXE component, **LoadStatusBar** must also be called from the **Form_Unload** event procedure (with the *Kind* argument set to 0 - SB_CANCEL).

RETURNS

Upon success, two elements in a **Variant**. The elements contain these subtypes:

- 0 - MBR_SUCCESS. A **Boolean** (**True**) that specifies the member executed successfully.

- 1 - MBR_STATUSBAR. An object expression that is the **Name** property of the **StatusBar** custom control object. The client application's programmer uses this object reference to apply the Windows API function **SetParent** to the status bar, to initially position it on the **Form** object, to reposition it when the user resizes the form, or to display a message in any of its text panel(s). If the optional *Cancel* argument is passed, **Nothing** is returned.

Upon failure, eight elements in a **Variant**. The elements contain the error codes that the class library returns when a runtime or syntax error occurs during the execution of one of its members.

REMARKS

- The **LoadStatusBar** method only runs under 32-bit Visual Basic because it uses Microsoft's **StatusBar** object, which only exists as a 32-bit ActiveX control.

- If the *Kind* argument is set to 3 - SB_CUSTOM, the *Panels( )* argument is dependent on it and must be passed.

- The object reference **LoadStatusBar** returns should be assigned by the client application's programmer to a previously declared form-level object variable with the **Set** statement. Once the object reference is assigned, the Windows API function **SetParent** must be called to change the parent window of the status bar to the client application's **Form** object. To see how to do this, click on the Example hotspot at the top of this help topic.

- To resize the status bar when the user resizes the client application's **Form** object, use a **Timer** object and code in its **Timer** event procedure. It is only necessary to do this if the **Form** object's **BorderStyle** property is set to 2 - Sizable, or its **MaxButton** or **MinButton** properties are set to **True**. To see how to do this, click on the Example hotspot at the top of this help topic.

- If the **LoadStatusBar** method is run from an out-of-process EXE component, it must be called from the **Form_Unload** event procedure of the client application's **Form** object and passed 0 - SB_CANCEL as its *Kind* argument. If the method's container **Form** object is not explicitly unloaded in this way, the **Terminate** event of its **CustomCtl** class does not occur and the status bar still appears on the screen.

- Because the **LoadStatusBar** method has a **ParamArray** optional argument, it cannot take named arguments. If you try to pass named arguments to it, Visual Basic displays OLE Automation runtime error 446 (Object doesn't support named arguments) or 448 (Named argument not found).

The LoadStatusBar Method's Code

When a client application calls the **LoadStatusBar** method, the frmShowSBar **Form** object itself is never displayed, but it is implicitly loaded when the method sets some properties of its **StatusBar** ActiveX control.

After the method selects the kind of status bar to display and sets its properties, it returns an object reference to it to the client application, which in turn assigns it to a form-level object variable. This approach enables the client application to set the status bar's properties and control its behavior. From this point on, the **StatusBar** control, which is actually encapsulated on a **Form** object in the class library, appears and behaves as if it were on the client application's **Form** object.

The code for the **LoadStatusBar** method is shown in Listing 15.7.

Listing 15.7   The LoadStatusBar method's code.

```
Function LoadStatusBar(Kind As Byte, _
                       ParamArray Panels())

    ' Constants for Kind argument:
    Const SB_CANCEL = 0
    Const SB_TEXTONLY = 1
    Const SB_TIMEDATE = 2
    Const SB_CUSTOM = 3

    ' Constants for literals:
    Const PROC = "LoadStatusBar"
    Const SYNTAX = True
    Const OFFSET = 1
    Const LOW_BOUND = 0
    Const MAX_PNLS = 7
    Const MAX_TXTPNLS = 3

    ' Variables:
    Dim NumEls          As Byte
    Dim NumPnls         As Byte
    Dim NumTxtPnls      As Byte
    Dim NumPnlsTested   As Byte
    Dim PnlValue        As Byte
    Dim El              As Variant
    Dim ElAdj           As Variant
    Dim Pnl             As Variant
    Dim Pnls            As Variant
    Dim FirstPnl        As Variant
    Dim LastPnl         As Variant
    Dim CapsPnl         As Variant
    Dim ValidTypes()    As Variant
```

```
#If Win32 Then
    Dim SBar          As Object
    Dim CstmPnl       As Object
#End If

' Enable error handler and do syntax checking:
On Error GoTo ET

#If Win16 Then
    E.TrapSyntax 1, PROC, "16-bit VB"
#ElseIf Win32 Then

    Select Case Kind
        Case SB_CANCEL, SB_TEXTONLY, SB_TIMEDATE, SB_CUSTOM

            If IsMissing(Panels()) Then

                Select Case Kind
                    Case SB_CUSTOM
                        E.TrapSyntax 28, PROC, "Kind", _
                                     "3 - SB_CUSTOM", "Panels()"
                End Select

            ElseIf Not IsMissing(Panels()) Then

                Select Case Kind
                    Case SB_CANCEL, SB_TEXTONLY, SB_TIMEDATE
                        E.TrapSyntax 21, PROC, "Panels()", _
                                     "Kind", "3 - SB_CUSTOM"
                End Select

            End If
        Case Else
            E.TrapSyntax 5, PROC, "Kind"
    End Select

' Check ParamArray Panels() argument--
' * Ensure it is Variant array.
' * Assign Panels() array to Variant Pnls. Passing as
'   Panels() causes "Invalid ParamArray use" error.
' * Ensure array is dimensioned.
' * Compute last element to check. It can be based on:
'   a) Maximum number of elements allowed, if same number of
'      elements were passed in.
'   b) Number of elements passed in, if that number is less
'      than maximum number of elements.
'   c) Maximum number of elements allowed, if number of
'      elements passed in is greater than maximum allowed.
' * Ensure valid value for text panel.
' * Specify valid data types for elements.
' * Call IsParamArray method to check ParamArray argument for:
'   a) Uninitialized element.
'   b) Element with invalid data type.
' * Ensure valid value for each panel.
```

```
If Kind = SB_CUSTOM Then
   Pnls = Panels(LOW_BOUND)

   If VarType(Panels) <> vbVariant + vbArray Then
      E.TrapSyntax 29, PROC, "Panels()"
   Else

      If Not CL.IsSized(Pnls) Then
         E.TrapSyntax 41, PROC, "Panels()"
      End If

   End If

   FirstPnl = LBound(Pnls)
   NumEls = UBound(Pnls) + OFFSET - LBound(Pnls)

   If NumEls = MAX_PNLS Then
      LastPnl = UBound(Pnls)
   ElseIf NumEls < MAX_PNLS Then
      LastPnl = FirstPnl + NumEls - OFFSET
   ElseIf NumEls > MAX_PNLS Then
      LastPnl = UBound(Pnls) - (NumEls - MAX_PNLS)
   End If

   NumTxtPnls = Pnls(FirstPnl)
   NumPnls = LastPnl - FirstPnl + NumTxtPnls
   CapsPnl = FirstPnl + 1

   Select Case NumTxtPnls
      Case 0, 1, 2, 3
      Case Else
         E.TrapSyntax 5, PROC, _
                     "Element " & CStr(FirstPnl) & _
                     " of Panels()"
   End Select

   On Error Resume Next
   ReDim ValidTypes(UBound(Pnls) - LBound(Pnls))

   For Each Pnl In Pnls
      ValidTypes(El) = vbLong
      El = El + 1
   Next Pnl

   For Pnl = FirstPnl To LastPnl
      Pnls(Pnl) = CLng(Pnls(Pnl))
   Next Pnl

   On Error GoTo ET
   CL.IsParamArray PROC, ValidTypes(), Pnls, MAX_PNLS
   PnlValue = 1

   For Pnl = CapsPnl To LastPnl
```

```
            If Pnls(Pnl) <> PnlValue And Pnls(Pnl) <> False Then
                E.TrapSyntax 5, PROC, _
                            "Element " & CStr(Pnl) & _
                            " of Panels()"
            End If

            PnlValue = PnlValue + 1
        Next Pnl

    End If


    ' * Clear/unload old status bar before displaying new one.
    ' * Assign references to object variables to abbreviate
    '   code below, make it more readable, and optimize it.
    ' * Depending on Kind of status bar selected, set appropriate
    '   properties and panels of StatusBar custom control object.
    ' * For custom status bar:
    '   a) Remove any unused text panels.
    '   b) Remove end panels not included in Panels() array.
    '   c) Remove panels with value set to False.
    If Kind <> SB_CANCEL Then
        Unload frmLoadSBar

        Select Case Kind
            Case SB_TEXTONLY
                Set SBar = frmLoadSBar.sbrTextOnly
            Case SB_TIMEDATE
                Set SBar = frmLoadSBar.sbrTimeDate
            Case SB_CUSTOM
                Set SBar = frmLoadSBar.sbrCustom
                Set CstmPnl = frmLoadSBar.sbrCustom.Panels

                For Pnl = MAX_TXTPNLS To NumTxtPnls Step -1
                    If Pnl > NumTxtPnls Then CstmPnl.Remove Pnl
                Next Pnl

                Do Until CstmPnl.Count = NumPnls
                    CstmPnl.Remove CstmPnl.Count
                Loop

                If LBound(Pnls) <> 0 Then
                    ElAdj = -LBound(Pnls) + NumTxtPnls
                Else
                    ElAdj = NumTxtPnls
                End If

                For Pnl = LastPnl To CapsPnl Step -1

                    If Pnls(Pnl) = False Then
                        CstmPnl.Remove Pnl + ElAdj
                    End If

                Next Pnl
        End Select
    End If
```

```
    ' Return results from method--
    ' * If client application is canceling status
    '   bar, return array and unload Form object.
    ' * If client application is displaying status bar, set
    '   object reference in returned array to custom control.
    ' * Free system resources associated with objects.
    If Kind = SB_CANCEL Then
        LoadStatusBar = Array(True, Nothing)
        Unload frmLoadSBar
    Else
        LoadStatusBar = Array(True, SBar)
    End If

    Set CstmPnl = Nothing
    Set SBar = Nothing
    Exit Function

#End If

ET:

    If Err = SYNTAX Then LoadStatusBar = frmErrCodes.Codes
    If Err <> SYNTAX Then LoadStatusBar = CL.TrapErr(PROC)

End Function
```

Our discussion of the **LoadStatusBar** method's code will focus on these three issues:

- Handling different custom panel configurations.
- Returning an object reference from a method.
- Changing the parent of a control in an ActiveX component.

HANDLING DIFFERENT CUSTOM PANEL CONFIGURATIONS

The most complex part of the **LoadStatusBar** method's code is the parsing routine that examines the values passed to the optional **ParamArray** *Panels( )* argument. The seven types of panels that Microsoft's **StatusBar** ActiveX control supports are actually **Panel** objects (all of which comprise the **Panels** collection), with each panel's **Style** property set to a different value.

The specifications of the **LoadStatusBar** method permit a client application to:

- Pass a **Variant** array containing the *Panels( )* argument's settings with any value (including negative numbers) as its lower bound.
- Display from zero to three text panels (that is, **Style** property set to **sbrText**).

- Display all or just some of the seven types of panels.
- Skip a panel by setting its value to **False**.

As you can imagine, writing the algorithm for a parsing routine to implement such flexible specifications is no trivial task. The major steps in this parsing routine include:

- Ensuring a valid value for the text panel's element (zero to three).
- Specifying the valid data types for the other elements in the *Panels( )* argument.
- Calling the **IsParamArray** method to check the *Panels( )* argument for uninitialized elements and invalid data types.
- Ensuring a valid value for each of the possible panels other than the text panel.
- Removing any text panels and end panels not specified by the client application (but which are part of the pre-defined **Panels** collection object on frmLoadStatusBar).
- Removing panels whose values are set to **False**.

The easiest way to comprehend the details of this parsing algorithm is to internally call the **LoadStatusBar** method from within the class library's ActiveX component project EFSE.EXE. You can use the example code found in the **LoadStatusBar** method's topic in EFS.HLP. Set a breakpoint and single step through the parsing code and watch what happens. Then, reduce the number of elements passed to the *Panels( )* argument or set some of their values to **False**, single step through the code again, and compare what happens to the first run through the code.

RETURNING AN OBJECT REFERENCE FROM AN ACTIVEX COMPONENT

Assuming that it executes successfully, the **LoadStatusBar** method returns two elements in the array in its **Variant** data type. The first element contains **True**. The second element contains an object reference to the **StatusBar** control object (its **Name** property). The object reference must be assigned to the element with the **Set** statement. The statement that returns the object reference from the **LoadStatusBar** method is

```
LoadStatusBar = Array(True, SBar)
```

where **SBar** is an object variable that was earlier assigned the **Name** property of the **StatusBar** control specified by the method's *Kind* argument.

The client application reads the values returned by the **LoadStatusBar** method and executes code like this:

```
Results = CustomCtl.LoadStatusBar(SB_CUSTOM, Panels())
Set fStatusBar = Results(MBR_STATUSBAR)
```

The form-level object variable **fStatusBar** is assigned the **Name** property of the **StatusBar** control. Then, in the **Timer** event procedure of a **Timer** object on the form (**Interval** property set to 1), the client application program has these two statements:

```
fStatusBar.Top = ScaleHeight - fStatusBar.Height
fStatusBar.Width = ScaleWidth
```

This **Timer** object in the client application is started at the end of the **Form_Load** event procedure, after the **LoadStatusBar** method has been called. The code is necessary if the **Form** object's **BorderStyle** property is set to 2 - Sizable, or its **MaxButton** or **MinButton** properties are set to **True**. If the user resizes the form, minimizes it, or maximizes it, the **Timer** object's code moves and resizes the status bar accordingly.

Returning an object reference

This technique of returning an object reference from an ActiveX component's method to a client application is a mirror image of passing an object reference from the client application to the ActiveX component's method. In both cases, the technique permits you to return and set almost any of the properties of the object which are read-and-write at runtime. In effect, there are no longer any boundaries or artificial barriers restricting the potential use of an object.

CHANGING THE PARENT OF A CONTROL

With the object reference returned from the **LoadStatusBar** method, the client application programmer can access almost any of the properties of the status bar (one strange exception will be noted in a moment). However, before you can see the status bar itself or any changes to its properties, you need to change the parent of the **StatusBar** custom control object.

If you read the value of Visual Basic's **Parent** property for the status bar after it is returned to the client application, the result is what you would expect (that is, frmShowSBar). The parent of the status bar is still its container **Form** object encapsulated in the class library. The **Parent** property is read-only at runtime so you cannot use it to change the status bar's parent. Instead, you must use the Windows API function **SetParent** to do this. The declaration for **SetParent**, in the General Declarations section of the client application's **Form** object, is shown here:

```
#If Win32 Then
    Private Declare Function SetParent& Lib "USER32" _
                            (ByVal hWndChild&, _
                            ByVal hWndParent&)
#End If
```

The call to **SetParent** is made in the **Form_Load** event procedure right after the returned object reference has been assigned to the form-level object variable **fStatusBar**:

```
Results = CustomCtl.LoadStatusBar(SB_CUSTOM, Panels())
Set fStatusBar = Results(MBR_STATUSBAR)
SetParent fStatusBar.hWnd, Me.hWnd
```

SetParent's first argument is the handle of the child object. Its second argument is the handle of the object that is to be the new parent. Once the parent is changed, the status bar is visible on the client application's **Form** object and the changes to *most* of its properties are visible. However, there are some interesting anomalies to note about the effects of changing the parent of the status bar with **SetParent**:

- Even though it is clearly visible, if you read its **Visible** property, it always returns **False**. Even if you explicitly set its **Visible** property to **True** (which does not cause a runtime error), reading it still returns **False**. And, if you use the Windows API function **IsWindowVisible** on it, Windows itself says it is not visible, despite the contrary evidence provided by your own eyes.

- If you read the value of the status bar's VB **Parent** property after having used the Windows API function **SetParent** to change it, it is the same as before (that is, frmShowSBar).

- However, if you use the Windows API function **GetParent**, you can see that Windows certainly thinks that the status bar has a new parent. The code shown next displays the message box in Figure 15.7:

```
If GetParent(fStatusBar.hWnd) = Me.hWnd Then
    MsgBox Me.Name
End If
```

Figure 15.7 Parent of **StatusBar** as read by **GetParent API** function.

These anomalies do not negatively affect the **LoadStatusBar** method, which works fine in spite of the discrepancies. However, it is important to pay attention to contradictions like these. The underlying capabilities of the ActiveX component software protocol, Microsoft's road map for the future of object-oriented programming, are extremely powerful and flexible. It is not surprising to find some unexpected twists and turns when you first start down a new road traveling in a foreign country. As always, those who pay attention to the signs along the way will probably enjoy the trip the most and reach their destination the soonest.

ActiveX Components And Other Applications

As you saw in Chapter 14, it is easy to write small utility applications and encapsulate them in an ActiveX component. All you need is a method in a class that displays a **Form** object, which is the GUI for the utility. These types of utility methods should be written to run under an out-of-process ActiveX EXE component for two reasons:

- An ActiveX EXE component can display modeless forms under VB4.

- An ActiveX EXE component can return control to the client application after the utility has begun to run in an out-of-process thread.

As you might imagine, it is also possible to write members in an ActiveX component that run applications that are not part of the class library. You can create members to implement classic algorithms, such as sorting and encryption, but, rather than write them in native Visual Basic code, you can call functions from external DLL files. These DLLs can be written in Assembly, C, or Fortran (or any other Windows programming language that supports pointers), and their implementations of such classic algorithms run many times faster than anything you could write with native Visual Basic code.

Since the release of VB4, the issue of performance has reared its ugly head again. When Borland released Delphi 1 (with its Pascal compiler) and then the upgrade to Delphi 2, all the programming magazines were inundated with letters arguing the relative merits of Delphi versus Visual Basic in the arena of performance. You also heard that writing ActiveX components with Visual Basic was not worth the time and effort. Many arguments were put forward, including:

- Both VB4 and VB5 are slower than VB3.
- The additional performance penalty associated with running an ActiveX component written with Visual Basic slows things down even more.
- Nobody wants to reuse slow objects.

There are many different perspectives from which you can view the issues of VB5's performance and the performance of an ActiveX component written with Visual Basic. Certainly, VB4 was not as fast as Delphi. Microsoft was well aware of this. In fact, it is reported that the VB5 development team had this sign etched on the wall, reminding them of their goal every time they glanced up: It's The Speed Issue, Stupid!

As we all know by now, VB5 supports the ability to create ActiveX controls and to create either interpreted (pcode) or compiled (native code) versions of applications. The Visual Basic development team would not have taken the pains required to do this if the performance of these ActiveX controls was not going to be competitive with those written with Delphi.

Also, Microsoft contends that the performance of the many OLE DLLs that are required to run ActiveX components will continue to improve, especially as the world of desktop computing inexorably switches from 16-bit Windows and 16/32-bit Windows 95 to 32-bit Windows NT. In case you haven't had the pleasure to see how fast 32-bit Visual Basic and the ActiveX components it creates run on Windows NT 4 and the new Pentium Pro chip, which is optimized for true 32-bit Windows, I'll let you in on the news: You're looking at an increase of 50 to 75 percent over Windows 95 and a Pentium chip with the same clock speed.

Meanwhile, if you have algorithms that you want to implement in an ActiveX component written with Visual Basic and you need the fastest performance possible, this chapter shows how easy it is to call functions from an external DLL file written with Assembly. The members in the book's class library that do this use Crescent Software's QuickPak Professional product (QPRO200.DLL for 16-bit Visual Basic and QPRO32.DLL for 32-bit Visual Basic).

The other techniques that we'll study in this chapter involve two different kinds of applications that can be run from a class library. The **GetSysInfo** method shows how to run an application that is distributed with Visual Basic and with the products that comprise the Microsoft Office suite (MSINFO.EXE for 16-bit Visual Basic or MSINFO32.EXE for 32-bit Visual Basic). Because at least 85 percent of all PCs that run Windows also run at least one of the Microsoft Office applications, this system information application is normally available. The **FormatDisk** method, on the other hand, shows how to run an application that is part of the Windows operating system itself. As a result, you can always count on such an application being available.

Calling DLL Assembly Routines

You call, from a class library, a routine or function in an external Assembly DLL exactly the same way as you call a Windows API function. First, you have to declare the functions you want to call. For the member of the book's class library that we will look at in this chapter, this is done in the General Declarations section of FILE.CLS. The conditionally compiled declarations required for the routines called from Crescent Software's QuickPak Professional product are in Listing 16.1.

Listing 16.1 QuickPak Professional DLL declarations.

```
' QPRO DLL Declarations in FILE.CLS:

#If Win32 Then

    Private Declare Function EncryptCL& Lib "QPRO32" _
                            Alias "Encrypt" _
                            (ByVal Work$, ByVal Password$)
    Private Declare Function Encrypt2& Lib "QPRO32" _
                            (ByVal Work$, ByVal Password$)
    Private Declare Function FClose& Lib "QPRO32" _
                            (ByVal hFile&)
    Private Declare Function FGet& Lib "QPRO32" _
                            (ByVal hFile&, ByVal Dest$)
    Private Declare Function FLof& Lib "QPRO32" _
                            (ByVal hFile&)
    Private Declare Function FOpen& Lib "QPRO32" _
                            Alias "CSFOpen" _
                            (ByVal FileName$, ByRef hFile&)
```

```
      Private Declare Function FPut& Lib "QPRO32" _
                              (ByVal hFile&, ByVal Source$)
      Private Declare Function FSeek& Lib "QPRO32" _
                              (ByVal hFile&, ByVal Location&)

#Else

      Private Declare Function EncryptCL% Lib "QPRO200" _
                              Alias "Encrypt" _
                              (ByVal Work$, ByVal Password$)
      Private Declare Function FClose% Lib "QPRO200" _
                              (ByVal hFile%)
      Private Declare Function FGet% Lib "QPRO200" _
                              (ByVal hFile%, Dest$)
      Private Declare Function FLof& Lib "QPRO200" _
                              (ByVal hFile%)
      Private Declare Function FOpen% Lib "QPRO200" _
                              (ByVal FileName$, hFile%)
      Private Declare Function FPut% Lib "QPRO200" _
                              (ByVal hFile%, Source$)
      Private Declare Function FSeek% Lib "QPRO200" _
                              (ByVal hFile%, Location&)
```

After making the required declarations, you write the members that use the third-party DLL and make the call to the DLL functions from there. The **Decrypt** and **Encrypt** methods are the two members in the **File** class of the book's class library that use these third-party DLLs. In order to see how much faster the Assembly encryption routine is than a routine written in native Visual Basic code, the **MiscExs** class has an **EncryptVB** method.

The Encrypt Method's Specifications

The **Encrypt** method encrypts one or more files, using Crescent Software's QuickPak Professional DLL. The detailed functionality of the **Encrypt** method is shown in the sidebar. The **Decrypt** method is a mirror image of the **Encrypt** method and actually calls the **Encrypt** method. **Decrypt** is given a different name in the class library just to make the public interface more understandable.

The Encrypt method's specifications.

SYNTAX

```
Object.Encrypt(FileSpec, Password, [DstPath])
```

The **Encrypt** method's syntax has the following object qualifier and named arguments:

- *Object.* Required. **Object** data type. An expression that evaluates to an object in the Applies To pop-up list.

- *FileSpec.* Required. **String** data type. An expression that evaluates to the string "FileDialog" or that specifies the path and name of a file or files to process. If "FileDialog" is passed, a common dialog box is displayed where the user can select one or more files or type a wildcard. If "FileDialog" is not passed, the **Encrypt** method parses the string for the path-and-file name formats that are supported. If more than one file name is passed, the path and file names must be delimited by **vbNullChar** (that is, a Null character) for 32-bit Visual Basic or a space character for 16-bit Visual Basic. The two types of delimiters cannot be mixed. See *Settings* below for a description of the supported formats.

- *Password.* Required. **String** data type. An expression that specifies the password to use to encrypt (and later decrypt) the file(s). *Password* cannot exceed 43 characters.

- *DstPath.* Optional. **Variant** data type whose subtype is a **String** expression that specifies the path for the encrypted file or files (for example, C:\NEWPATH\). If *DstPath* is passed, a copy of the original file is made and encrypted on *DstPath*. If *DstPath* is omitted, the path specified in *FileSpec* is used.

SETTINGS

The *FileSpec* argument's possible settings are:

- *CommonDlg.* **String** expression that evaluates to "FileDialog". The **Encrypt** method displays a common dialog box where the user can select one or more files, type a wildcard for a file type (for example, "•.CLS"), or type the wildcard for all files (that is, •.•).

- *One File.* **String** expression that evaluates to an existing path and file name. For example, "C:\VBCLSLIB\FILE.CLS".

- *File Type.* **String** expression that evaluates to an existing path and the wildcard for a file type. For example, "C:\VBCLSLIB\•.CLS".

- *All Files.* **String** expression that evaluates to an existing path and the wildcard for all files. For example, "C:\VBCLSLIB\•.•".

- *Several Files.* **String** expression that evaluates to an existing path and file names, with the path and file names separated by a delimiter. For example, "C:\VBCLSLIB\" & vbNullChar & "FILE.CLS" & vbNullChar & "DIALOG.CLS" or "C:\VBCLSLIB\ FILE.CLS DIALOG.CLS".

CALLED

From any procedure in a client application.

RETURNS

Upon success, two elements in a **Variant**. The elements contain these subtypes:

- 0 - MBR_SUCCESS. A **Boolean** (**True**) that specifies the member executed successfully.

- 1 - MBR_FILES. If the *FileSpec* argument specifies "FileDialog" and the user chooses Cancel from the common dialog box, **vbNullString** (that is, a zero-length string); otherwise, a **String** that specifies the path and file name(s) processed. If the *FileSpec* argument does not specify "FileDialog", a **String** that specifies the path and file name(s) processed. If the *FileSpec* argument specifies "FileDialog" and more than one file is processed, the path and file names returned are delimited either by **vbNullChar** (that is, a Null character) for 32-bit Visual Basic, or by a space character for 16-bit Visual Basic. For example, if two files on the C root drive are processed, the string would have this format when returned from the 32-bit ActiveX component: "C:\" & vbNullChar & "FILE1.TXT" & vbNullChar & "FILE2.TXT". When returned from the 16-bit ActiveX component, the string would have this format: "C:\ FILE1.TXT FILE2.TXT". The use of these delimiters to separate the path and file names is consistent with the delimiters used by the Open and Save As common dialog boxes for Windows 95/NT 4.0 and Windows 3.x.

Upon failure, eight elements in a **Variant**. The elements contain the error codes that the class library returns when a runtime or syntax error occurs during the execution of one of its members.

REMARKS

- If you pass its *FileSpec* argument the string "FileDialog", the **Encrypt** method's common dialog box supports multiple file selections.

- The **Encrypt** method can fail on very large files (greater than approximately 4 megabytes in size). If this occurs, the class library displays a syntax error message.

- If you try to use the **Encrypt** method on a currently open/locked file, it does not process the file; instead, it displays a message stating which file it cannot process and, if there are files remaining to be processed, asks whether it should continue the batch operation. The same approach is also used if some unexpected runtime error occurs while processing a file.

- If you call the **Encrypt** method from a **File** object instantiated from an out-of-process ActiveX component and pass its *FileSpec* argument the string "FileDialog", you should first apply Visual Basic's **Hide** method to the **Form** object in the client application from whose code you call the method. After the user closes the common dialog box, you can apply Visual Basic's **Show** method to redisplay the **Form** object. The reason this is necessary is because the out-of-process ActiveX component's **Encrypt** method displays the common dialog box modelessly, instead of modally as would be the case with the in-process ActiveX component. Hiding the client application's **Form** object prevents the user from calling another member in the ActiveX component (and thus getting the Component Request Pending message) until the common dialog box is closed.

The Encrypt Method's Code

The code for the **Encrypt** method, shown in Listing 16.2, consists of two parts. The first part is the code in the public member itself. The second part is the code in the **File** object's private **RunEncrypt** method. It is the **RunEncrypt** method's code that reuses the Assembly DLL functions. We will study the interface code of the **Decrypt** and **Encrypt** methods, which

is very similar to the interface code used by the other methods of the **File**
object, in Chapter 18.

Listing 16.2   The RunEncrypt method's code.

```
Private Sub RunEncrypt(File As String, _
                       Password As String, _
                       Path As String, _
                       Member As String)


' _____

' Purpose: Uses Assembler functions in Crescent Software's
'          QuickPak Professional DLLs to encrypt or decrypt
'          file.
'
' Called:  Internally from members of class library.
'
' Accepts: File:     String expression specifying path and
'                    file to be encrypted/decrypted.
'          Password: String expression specifying password
'                    to use as encryption/decryption key.
'                    Cannot be longer than 43 characters.
'          Path:     String expression specifying path
'                    portion of File argument.
'          Member:   String expression specifying name of
'                    member (Encrypt or Decrypt) from which
'                    this method is called.
' _____


' Constants for literals:
Const FOUR_SECTORS = 4096
Const ENC_PWRD1 = "~^!%@$#"
Const ENC_PWRD2 = "&|*+(_)"
Const ERR_HWND = -1


' Variables:
Dim Buff         As String
Dim TmpPassword  As String
Dim LenBuff      As Integer
Dim HWndFile16   As Integer
Dim HWndFile32   As Long
Dim FileSize     As Long
Dim AmtDone      As Long
Dim AmtLeft      As Long


' Execute method:
' * Double-encrypt copy of password.
' * Open file as binary and store its size.
' * Compute buffer size:
'    a) Initialize it at either 4,096 or no greater than size
'       of file.
'    b) Then ensure it is even multiple of password's length.
'    c) If even multiple resulted in size of zero, file is
'       very small. So reduce buffer to file size.
```

```
'   d) Size memory variable to size of buffer.
' * Until file is completely encrypted:
'   a) Get buffer-size piece of file and encrypt it.
'   b) Find start of piece and write encrypted data.
'   c) Update number of bytes encrypted.
'   d) If close to end of file (that is, unencrypted portion
'      is smaller than buffer size), set buffer size equal
'      to unencrypted portion.
'   e) Loop back and do next piece of file.
' * Close binary file.

TmpPassword = Password

#If Win32 Then
    Encrypt2 TmpPassword, ENC_PWRD1
    Encrypt2 TmpPassword, ENC_PWRD2
    FOpen File, HWndFile32
    FileSize = FLof(HWndFile32)
#Else
    EncryptCL TmpPassword, ENC_PWRD1
    EncryptCL TmpPassword, ENC_PWRD2
    FOpen File, HWndFile16
    FileSize = FLof(HWndFile16)
#End If

If HWndFile32 = ERR_HWND Or HWndFile16 = ERR_HWND Then
    CL.SetHourglass False
    File = Right$(File, Len(File) - Len(Path))
    E.TrapSyntax 46, Member, File
End If

LenBuff = FOUR_SECTORS

If FileSize < LenBuff Then LenBuff = FileSize

LenBuff = LenBuff - (FileSize Mod Len(Password))

If LenBuff = 0 Then LenBuff = FileSize

Buff = Space$(LenBuff)

Do While Len(Buff)

    #If Win32 Then
        FGet HWndFile32, Buff
        Encrypt2 Buff, TmpPassword
        FSeek HWndFile32, AmtDone
        FPut HWndFile32, Buff
    #Else
        FGet HWndFile16, Buff
        EncryptCL Buff, TmpPassword
        FSeek HWndFile16, AmtDone
        FPut HWndFile16, Buff
```

```
    #End If

    AmtDone = AmtDone + Len(Buff)
    AmtLeft = FileSize - AmtDone

    If AmtLeft < Len(Buff) Then Buff = Space$(AmtLeft)

Loop

#If Win32 Then
    FClose HWndFile32
#Else
    FClose HWndFile16
#End If

End Sub
```

If you are interested in the details of the encryption algorithm of the **RunEncrypt** method, you can study it at your leisure. However, there is one general point to note about the code in Listing 16.2. Although Crescent Software's documentation doesn't say so, there is a limit to the size of the file that its **FOpen** DLL function can handle. This failure point seems to vary, depending on the version of Windows that is running and the kind of file being encrypted. If this occurs, **FOpen** fails and returns -1 (that is, ERR_HWND). The class library then displays the syntax error message in Figure 16.1.

Relative Speeds Of Encrypt And EncryptVB Methods

The algorithm that the **EncryptVB** method of the **MiscExs** class uses is not comparable in sophistication or complexity to the Assembly-assisted **RunEncrypt** routine called by the **Encrypt** method. Nonetheless, as you would expect, the Assembly-assisted routine is much faster. My informal benchmarks show that, on a small 4 K file, the Assembly-assisted routine is five times faster. However, the larger the file being encrypted, the faster the Assembly-assisted routine is relative to the native-VB code routine. On a 38 K file, the **Encrypt** method is 37 times faster; on a 217 K file, it is 100 times faster.

This comparative demonstration of the speed of the two methods makes a couple important points about the general issue of Visual Basic's performance vis-à-vis the performance of other Windows programming languages. First, many algorithms (for example, encryption or sorting) should never be

Figure 16.1 The **Encrypt/Decrypt** method's syntax error 46.

run except under Assembly language implementations. Well-written Assembly routines will always run faster than any other language's implementation. Second, from its inception, Visual Basic was meant to be more than just a programming language; it was designed to be an extensible Windows development environment—an entirely different concept.

Traditionally, programmers focused on one or two languages and learned every trick in the book to use them effectively and squeeze performance out of them. However, the relatively recent ascendancy of the Windows operating system has changed the rules of the development game. Now it is just as important to understand all the different approaches and tools that are available to extend and enhance the Visual Basic development environment. In the future, as Microsoft's object-oriented, ActiveX component software protocol proliferates across hardware and software platforms, class libraries written as ActiveX components will become the most important way of extending Visual Basic (and Visual Basic for Applications) as a cross-platform development environment.

Running Microsoft's System Info Utility

For years, Microsoft has distributed a system information utility with Visual Basic and the products that comprise the Microsoft Office suite (MSINFO.EXE for 16-bit Visual Basic or MSINFO32.EXE for 32-bit Visual Basic). To see this utility, start VB5. Then select Help|About Microsoft Visual Basic, click on the System Info button, and Visual Basic displays the window shown in Figure 16.2. The type of window that is displayed and the kinds of system information that are available differ, depending on the Windows platform

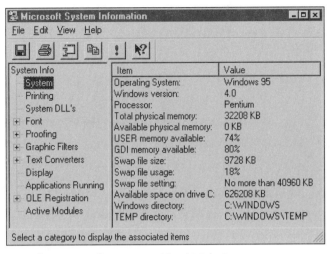

Figure 16.2 Microsoft System Information utility (32-bit).

you are running (32-bit versus 16-bit, or Windows 95 shell versus the old Windows NT 3.51 shell).

The key techniques that **GetSystemInfo** illustrates are how to read the WIN.INI file (for 16-bit Visual Basic) or the Windows registration database (for 32-bit Visual Basic) in order to determine where MSINFO.EXE or MSINFO32.EXE is located. Under 16-bit Windows, Microsoft recommended that a Windows programmer store information about an application in an initialization file. For a while, everybody wrote this information to WIN.INI, Windows own initialization file. Then, after WIN.INI got cluttered up with extraneous information, Microsoft recommended that each application should create its own initialization file upon installation.

Under 32-bit Windows, Microsoft is phasing out the initialization file approach for storing information. Although most of its own new application versions still use an initialization file for upward compatibility, Microsoft now wants all application-related information to be written to and read from the Windows registration database. Visual Basic has some functions specifically designed to do this. There are also some Windows API functions for writing to and reading from the Windows registration database, which are more powerful and flexible than Visual Basic's built-in functions. The **GetSystemInfo** method uses both types of syntax (its own

GetSetting function for the 16-bit code and the Windows API functions for the 32-bit code) to read where Microsoft's MSINFO.EXE or MSINFO32.EXE file is located.

The GetSystemInfo Method's Specifications

The detailed functionality of the **GetSystemInfo** method is shown in the following sidebar.

The GetSystemInfo method's specifications.

SYNTAX

```
Object.GetSystemInfo
```

The **GetSystemInfo** method's syntax has the following object qualifier:

- *Object*. Required. **Object** data type. An expression that evaluates to an object in the Applies To pop-up list.

CALLED

From any procedure in a client application.

RETURNS

Upon success, one element in a **Variant**. It contains a **Boolean** (**True**) that specifies the member executed successfully.

Upon failure, eight elements in a **Variant**. The elements contain the error codes that the class library returns when a runtime or syntax error occurs during the execution of one of its members.

The GetSystemInfo Method's Code

GetSystemInfo illustrates how to use Windows API functions to read entries stored in the Windows registration database. To understand how these Windows API functions work, you must first know how the registration database is structured. When you first open it, Windows 95's version of the Registry Editor application (REGEDIT.EXE) displays the window shown in Figure 16.3.

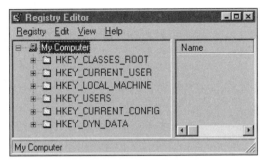

Figure 16.3 The Windows Registry Editor (initial view).

The Registry Editor uses the Windows 95 TreeView control to display its hierarchy of keys. The TreeView control works the same way that the Explorer or the File Manager does. Double clicking on a node or branch of the tree either expands it to show the nodes below it or collapses it to hide its nodes. In Figure 16.3, My Computer (which is always at the top of the hierarchy) has six nodes below it. The nodes directly below My Computer are referred to as *hives*.

The HKEY_LOCAL_MACHINE node contains the information the **GetSystemInfo** method requires. Double clicking on this node displays the nodes shown in Figure 16.4. The SOFTWARE node is where all information about files is stored. The location of the MSINFO32.EXE file is stored several more nodes down in the hierarchy, on the path SOFTWARE\Microsoft\Shared Tools\MSInfo.

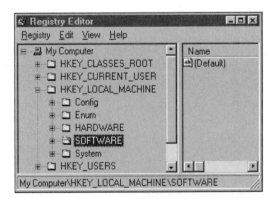

Figure 16.4 The Windows Registry Editor (nodes for local machine).

The specific path where any kind of information is located in the Windows registration database is determined by the application that writes it there. Microsoft provides general rules and recommendations about how the Windows registration database should be structured and where entries should be written; however, nothing will stop you from writing software information on the HARDWARE path.

The 32-bit portion of the **GetSystemInfo** method's code follows these steps:

- Specifies the top-level hive under which it wants to query information (HKEY_LOCAL_MACHINE).

- Specifies the SOFTWARE node and the path down it which contains the location of the MSINFO32.EXE. The entire path of SOFTWARE\ Microsoft\Shared Tools\MSInfo is called the *subkey*.

- Gets a handle to this subkey and queries/reads the value stored under the subkey's *Path* entry. Figure 16.5 shows how this looks in the Registry Editor.

- Stores the returned value in a fixed-length **String** and strips the trailing null characters from it.

- Closes the key/handle that was opened to free up system resources.

Listing 16.3 shows the code for the **GetSystemInfo** method.

Figure 16.5 Windows Registry Editor (Path entry for MS Info utility).

Listing 16.3   The GetSystemInfo method's code.

```
Function GetSystemInfo()

    ' Constants for Windows API functions:
    Const ERROR_SUCCESS = 0
    Const REG_SZ = 1
    Const KEY_QUERY_VALUE = &H1
    Const HKEY_LOCAL_MACHINE = &H80000002
    Const MSINFO_KEY = "SOFTWARE\Microsoft\Shared Tools\MSInfo"

    ' Constants for literals:
    Const PROC = "GetSystemInfo"
    Const SYNTAX = True

#If Win32 Then
    Const FILE_NAME = "File 'MSINFO32.EXE'"
#Else
    Const FILE_NAME = "File 'MSINFO.EXE'"
#End If

    ' Variables:
    Dim SysInfo    As String
    Dim Buff       As String * 256
    Dim HWndKey    As Long

    ' Enable error handler and do syntax checking:
    On Error GoTo ET

    If cRAOServer Then
        E.TrapSyntax 1, PROC, "ActiveX RAO component"
    End If

    ' Execute member's algorithm--
    ' * Read location of MSINFO32.EXE or MSINFO.EXE file:
    '    a) If 32-bit Windows, get from Windows registration
    '       database:
    '       - Return key entry from SYSTEM.DAT.
    '       - Open key in order to query it.
    '       - Return value stored under key's "Path" heading.
    '       - Close key so it can be opened/queried again.
    '    b) If 16-bit Windows, get from WIN.INI file with
    '       GetSetting function.
    ' * Depending on whether or not file exists--
    '    a) If it exists:
    '       - Run it.
    '       - Trap for possible runtime error 53 and, if it
    '          occurs, display more informative error message.
    '    b) If it does not exist, display syntax error message.

#If Win32 Then

    If RegOpenKeyEx(HKEY_LOCAL_MACHINE, MSINFO_KEY, _
                    vbEmpty, KEY_QUERY_VALUE, HWndKey) _
                    = ERROR_SUCCESS Then
```

```
            If RegQueryValueEx(HWndKey, "Path", vbEmpty, _
                              REG_SZ, Buff, Len(Buff)) _
                              = ERROR_SUCCESS Then
                SysInfo = Left$(Buff, Len(Buff) - 1)
            Else
                SysInfo = "NA"
            End If


            RegCloseKey HWndKey

        End If
    #Else
        SysInfo = GetSetting(AppName:="WIN.INI", _
                             Section:="Microsoft System Info", _
                             Key:="MSINFO", _
                             Default:="NA")
    #End If

    If SysInfo <> "NA" Then
        On Error Resume Next
        Shell SysInfo, vbNormalFocus

        If Err <> False Then
            E.TrapSyntax 48, PROC, FILE_NAME
        Else
            On Error GoTo ET
        End If

    Else
        E.TrapSyntax 48, PROC, FILE_NAME
    End If

    GetSystemInfo = Array(True)
    Exit Function

ET:

    If Err = SYNTAX Then GetSystemInfo = frmErrCodes.Codes
    If Err <> SYNTAX Then GetSystemInfo = CL.TrapErr(PROC)

End Function
```

There are three points to note about the 32-bit portion of the **GetSystemInfo** method's code. First, the Windows API function **RegOpenKeyEx**, which only exists in the 32-bit Windows API set, opens the specified key and subkey in the Windows registration database. Its first argument specifies one of the highest-level keys or hives. Its second argument specifies the path or subkey under the hive that contains the information you want. The third argument is reserved and must be zero (Null in C or **vbEmpty** in Visual Basic). The fourth argument (in this case, KEY_QUERY_VALUE) specifies the desired security access for the subkey. The fifth argument points to a variable that is assigned a handle to the opened subkey. Upon success, **RegOpenKeyEx** returns ERROR_SUCCESS (that is, zero); upon failure, it returns some other error code.

Second, after you have opened the subkey and have the handle to it, **RegQueryValueEx**, which also only exists in the 32-bit Windows API set, retrieves the data for the specified value name associated with it. Its first argument is the handle just returned by **RegOpenKeyEx**. Its second argument specifies the value to query. The third argument is reserved and must be zero. The fourth argument points to a fixed-string buffer that is filled with the value found by the query. The fifth argument specifies the length, in characters, of the fixed-string buffer. Upon success, **RegQueryValueEx** returns ERROR_SUCCESS; upon failure, it returns some other error code. Third, **RegCloseKey** releases the handle of the specified subkey, freeing the system resources associated with it.

The 16-bit portion of the method's code uses Visual Basic's **GetSetting** function to read the WIN.INI initialization file, where the location of the 16-bit MSINFO.EXE is written (its location is not written to the Windows registration database at all). You can also use **GetSetting** to read entries in the registration database; however, you are limited to reading entries on the hive HKEY_CURRENT_USER and under the subkey Software\Visual Basic and VBA Program Settings. This limitation also applies to the other three built-in Visual Basic functions for accessing the registration database (**DeleteSetting**, **GetAllSettings**, and **SaveSetting**).

After **GetSetting** returns the path, two kinds of exception scenarios can occur. The first case arises if Microsoft's system information file has never been installed on the current machine, and then the **String** variable **SysInfo** will have been set to "NA". The other situation occurs if the file was installed and the entry was written to the registration database or WIN.INI file, but it was later mistakenly deleted, moved, or renamed. Then Visual Basic's **Shell** function fails and runtime error 53 (File not found) occurs. Under either exception scenario, the method displays a syntax error message.

Using Other Registry API Functions

The **GetSystemInfo** method only reads from the Windows registration database. In this section, we'll see how to write your own entries to it and, later, read or delete them. Follow these steps to create a subkey in the Windows registration database, write the current time to it, read the value that was written, and delete the subkey:

1. Select File | New Project and open a Standard EXE project.

2. Add a **CommandButton** object to Form1 and set its **Index** property to 0.

3. Write the code in Listing 16.4. For the 32-bit Windows API declarations, you can use Visual Basic's 32-bit API Viewer utility to copy and paste the functions into Form1. Unfortunately, VB4's 16-bit API Text Viewer does not have the 16-bit versions of these functions; so, you will have to type those yourself or only run the exercise under 32-bit Visual Basic.

4. Run the project and click on the Write button to create the specified branch of subkeys below the HKEY_CURRENT_USER hive, write the current time to it, and print the message shown in Figure 16.6.

5. Click on the Read button to read the value written to the specified branch of subkeys and print the message shown in Figure 16.7.

6. Click on the Delete button to remove the specified branch of subkeys and print the message shown in Figure 16.8.

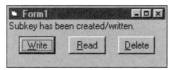

Figure 16.6 Time entry written to registration database.

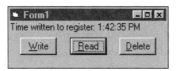

Figure 16.7 Time entry read from registration database.

Figure 16.8 Entry deleted from registration database.

Listing 16.4 Code to demo registry-related API functions.

```
' General Declarations Section:
' Windows API function constants:
Const ERROR_SUCCESS = 0
Const HKEY_CURRENT_USER = &H80000001
Const REG_SZ = 1

' Conditionally compile WIN API functions:
#If Win32 Then

    Private Declare Function RegCloseKey& Lib "ADVAPI32" _
                            (ByVal hKey&)
    Private Declare Function RegCreateKey& Lib "ADVAPI32" _
                            Alias "RegCreateKeyA" _
                            (ByVal hKey&, ByVal SubKey$, _
                            Result&)
    Private Declare Function RegDeleteKey& Lib "ADVAPI32" _
                            Alias "RegDeleteKeyA" _
                            (ByVal hKey&, ByVal SubKey$)
    Private Declare Function RegQueryValue& Lib "ADVAPI32" _
                            Alias "RegQueryValueA" _
                            (ByVal hKey&, ByVal SubKey$, _
                            ByVal ReturnStr$, LenReturnStr&)
    Private Declare Function RegSetValue& Lib "ADVAPI32" _
                            Alias "RegSetValueA" _
                            (ByVal hKey&, ByVal SubKey$, _
                            ByVal StrType&, ByVal KeyValue$, _
                            ByVal KeyLen&)

#Else

    Private Declare Function RegCloseKey& Lib "SHELL" _
                            (ByVal hKey&)
    Private Declare Function RegCreateKey& Lib "SHELL" _
                            (ByVal hKey&, ByVal SubKey$, _
                            Result&)
    Private Declare Function RegDeleteKey& Lib "SHELL" _
                            (ByVal hKey&, ByVal SubKey$)
    Private Declare Function RegQueryValue& Lib "SHELL" _
                            (ByVal hKey&, ByVal SubKey$, _
                            ByVal ReturnStr$, LenReturnStr&)
    Private Declare Function RegSetValue& Lib "SHELL" _
                            (ByVal hKey&, ByVal SubKey$, _
                            ByVal StrType&, ByVal KeyValue$, _
                            ByVal KeyLen&)

#End If

Private Sub Command1_Click(Index As Integer)

    ' Constants for elements in control array:
```

```vb
Const REG_WRITE = 0
Const REG_READ = 1
Const REG_DELETE = 2

' Variables:
Dim KeyHWnd      As Long
Dim HiveBranch   As String
Dim SubKeyName   As String
Dim Buffer       As String * 256
Dim Position     As Integer

Select Case Index
   Case REG_WRITE

      ' Create hive branch:
      HiveBranch = "Software\APIBrowser\RegTest\Initialization"
      RegCreateKey HKEY_CURRENT_USER, HiveBranch, KeyHWnd

      ' Create subkey and write current time to it:
      SubKeyName = "TimeLastRun"
      RegSetValue KeyHWnd, SubKeyName, REG_SZ, Time, Len(Time)

      ' Close registry key.
      RegCloseKey KeyHWnd
      Cls
      Print "Subkey has been created/written."

   Case REG_READ
      HiveBranch = "Software\APIBrowser\RegTest\Initialization"
      SubKeyName = "TimeLastRun"

      ' Get value for time that was written before.
      Cls

      If RegQueryValue(HKEY_CURRENT_USER, _
                    HiveBranch & "\" & SubKeyName, _
                    Buffer, Len(Buffer)) = ERROR_SUCCESS Then

         ' Parse and print entry:
         Position = InStr(Buffer, Chr$(0))
         Buffer = Mid$(Buffer, 1, Position - 1)
         Print "Time written to register: " & Buffer
      Else
         Print "Subkey does not exist."
      End If

   Case REG_DELETE
      ' Open Software branch of HKEY_CURRENT_USER hive:
      HiveBranch = "Software"
      RegCreateKey HKEY_CURRENT_USER, HiveBranch, KeyHWnd

      ' Delete APIBrowser subkey and everything below it.
      Cls
```

```
            If RegDeleteKey(KeyHWnd, "APIBrowser") = ERROR_SUCCESS Then
               Print "Subkey was deleted."
            Else
               Print "Subkey does not exist."
            End If

      End Select

   End Sub

   Private Sub Form_Load()

      ' Set properties of Form object and buttons:
      Command1(0).Height = 330
      Command1(0).Left = 200
      Command1(0).Top = 300
      Command1(0).Width = 700
      Load Command1(1)
      Command1(1).Visible = True
      Command1(1).Left = 1150
      Load Command1(2)
      Command1(2).Visible = True
      Command1(2).Left = 2100
      Command1(0).Caption = "&Write"
      Command1(1).Caption = "&Read"
      Command1(2).Caption = "&Delete"
      Width = 3120
      Height = 1200

   End Sub
```

I'd like to focus on the four Windows API functions used in this code: **RegCreateKey**, **RegSetValue**, **RegQueryValue**, and **RegDeleteKey**.

RegCreateKey creates the specified key or, if the key already exists in the registry, opens it. The first argument is the handle to a hive (HKEY_CURRENT_USER). The second argument specifies the name of the hive branch or subkey to open. The third argument points to a variable that is assigned a handle to the opened subkey.

RegSetValue associates a value, which must be a text string, with a specified subkey. The first argument is the handle just returned by **RegCreateKey**. The second argument is the text string to be associated with the subkey. The third argument specifies the type of information to be written and must be the REG_SZ type. The fourth argument specifies the value to be written (in this demonstration, returned by Visual Basic's **Time** function). The fifth argument is the length of the string to be written.

RegQueryValue retrieves the value associated with the specified key in the registry. The first argument specifies the hive. The second argument specifies the name of the subkey to query. The third argument points to a fixed-string buffer that is filled with the value found by the query. The fourth argument specifies the length, in characters, of the fixed-string buffer. Upon success, **RegQueryValue** returns ERROR_SUCESS (that is, zero); upon failure, it returns some other error code.

RegDeleteKey deletes the specified subkey. The first argument is the handle of a key just returned by **RegCreateKey**. The second argument specifies the subkey which is to be deleted. **RegDeleteKey** also deletes all subkeys in the hierarchy below the subkey specified by the second argument. Upon success, **RegDeleteKey** returns ERROR_SUCESS; upon failure, it returns some other error code.

> **Note:** *The registry demonstration code above (that is, the 32-bit API functions) works fine under Windows 95, but it does not work in the same way under Windows NT. If you run it under Windows NT, the values returned from **RegQueryKey** and **RegDeleteKey** upon failure are different than those returned under Windows 95. The code still writes, reads and deletes the entries under Windows NT, but its error codes are different. I did not bother to write additional code to handle this discrepancy.*

Running The Windows File Manager

The Windows operating system itself provides many reusable objects to the resourceful Visual Basic programmer. Throughout this book, you have seen that Windows API functions can be used in many different ways to enhance Visual Basic's capabilities. In a practical sense, these API functions (over 2,000 in 32-bit Windows) are analogous to methods of reusable objects. The details of how Microsoft has implemented any specific Windows API function (the so-called black box) will always be hidden from the Windows application programmer. All you need to know, in order to effectively reuse the function, is the information available about its public interface—the arguments it requires when it is called, and the values that it returns upon completion.

Another group of reusable objects that Windows provides falls under the general category of GUI-based system applications. Some obvious examples of this type of reusable object, which ship with every copy of Windows 95, include Calculator, Notepad, and Paint.

Typically, VB programmers use Visual Basic's **Shell** function to run one of these applications. However, suppose you want to enable a user to format a floppy disk from a Visual Basic application and you want to directly access the Format dialog box. You can use the **Shell** function to run either WINFILE.EXE (the File Manager, under either 16-bit or 32-bit Windows) or EXPLORER.EXE (the Explorer, under just 32-bit Windows). In either case, however, the user must take additional steps to access the dialog box that formats floppy disks.

For a user new to Windows 95, it is not easy to determine how to display the Format dialog box from the Explorer. There is a simple solution. The **FormatDisk** method of the **Utility** class uses several Windows API functions to directly access the Format dialog box from a Visual Basic client application. Let's take a look at how this works.

The FormatDisk Method's Specifications

The **FormatDisk** method starts the Windows File Manager (if it is not already running) and causes it to display its Format dialog box. It handles the different behaviors of 16-bit and 32-bit Windows and hides the gory details of the implementations from the client application's programmer. The detailed functionality of the **FormatDisk** method is shown in the sidebar.

The FormatDisk method's specifications.

SYNTAX

```
Object.FormatDisk
```

The **FormatDisk** method's syntax has the following object qualifier:

- *Object*. Required. **Object** data type. An expression that evaluates to an object in the Applies To pop-up list.

CALLED

From any procedure in a client application.

RETURNS

Upon success, one element in a **Variant**. It contains a **Boolean** (**True**) that specifies the member executed successfully.

Upon failure, eight elements in a **Variant**. The elements contain the error codes that the class library returns when a runtime or syntax error occurs during the execution of one of its members.

REMARKS

- The **FormatDisk** method displays the Format dialog box on top of all other windows. This is necessary because, given that it is displayed without the focus, it might not be visible to the user otherwise.

- It uses Microsoft's WINFILE.EXE file in the Windows directory. If this file is not available, the method displays a syntax error message to that effect.

The FormatDisk Method's Code

The code for the **FormatDisk** method is shown in Listing 16.5.

Listing 16.5   The FormatDisk method's code.

```
Function FormatDisk()

    ' Constants for Windows API functions:
    Const WM_COMMAND = &H111
    Const HWND_TOPMOST = -1
    Const SWP_NOSIZE = &H1
    Const SWP_NOMOVE = &H2

    ' Constants for elements in array:
    Const DRV_A35 = 0
    Const DRV_B35 = 1
    Const DRV_A525 = 2
    Const DRV_B525 = 3
    Const DRV_BOTH = 4

    ' Constants for literals:
    Const PROC = "FormatDisk"
    Const SYNTAX = True
    Const SHOW_FORMAT = &HCB
    Const CLS_NAME = "#32770"
```

```
' Variables:
Dim Drive        As Integer
Dim HWndFileMgr  As Variant
Dim HWndDlg(4)   As Variant


' Enable error handler and do syntax checking:
On Error GoTo ET

If cRAOServer Then
   E.TrapSyntax 1, PROC, "ActiveX RAO component"
End If


' Execute member's algorithm--
' * Depending on whether or not Explorer or File Manager
'   is running:
'   a) If not, try to start File Manager and store its handle.
'   b) If so, go to next step.
' * Tell File Manager to open its Format window.
' * Give focus to Format window.
HWndFileMgr = FindWindow("WFS_Frame", CLng(vbEmpty))

If HWndFileMgr = False Then
   On Error Resume Next
   Shell "WINFILE.EXE", vbMinimizedNoFocus

   If Err <> False Then
      E.TrapSyntax 48, PROC, "WINFILE.EXE"
   Else
      On Error GoTo ET
      HWndFileMgr = FindWindow("WFS_Frame", CLng(vbEmpty))
   End If

End If

PostMessage HWndFileMgr, WM_COMMAND, SHOW_FORMAT, vbEmpty

Do
   DoEvents
   HWndDlg(DRV_A35) = FindWindow(CLS_NAME, _
                                 "Format - 3 1/2_ Floppy (A:)")
   HWndDlg(DRV_B35) = FindWindow(CLS_NAME, _
                                 "Format - 3 1/2_ Floppy (B:)")
   HWndDlg(DRV_A525) = FindWindow(CLS_NAME, _
                                  "Format - 5 1/4_ Floppy (A:)")
   HWndDlg(DRV_B525) = FindWindow(CLS_NAME, _
                                  "Format - 5 1/4_ Floppy (B:)")
   HWndDlg(DRV_BOTH) = FindWindow(CLS_NAME, "Format Disk")

   For Drive = DRV_A35 To DRV_BOTH

      If HWndDlg(Drive) <> False Then
         SetWindowPos HWndDlg(Drive), HWND_TOPMOST, _
                      vbEmpty, vbEmpty, vbEmpty, vbEmpty, _
                      SWP_NOMOVE Or SWP_NOSIZE
```

```
            Exit Do
          End If
      Next Drive
    Loop

    FormatDisk = Array(True)
    Exit Function

ET:
    If Err = SYNTAX Then FormatDisk = frmErrCodes.Codes
    If Err <> SYNTAX Then FormatDisk = CL.TrapErr(PROC)

End Function
```

After its syntax checking is done, the **FormatDisk** method uses the Windows API function **FindWindow** to determine if a copy of the File Manager is already running. The function looks for the File Manager's distinctive class name (WFS_Frame) and, if it is running, returns the handle of the current instance of its window. If File Manager is not already running, **FindWindow** returns **False** and Visual Basic's **Shell** function is used to start it. Then, **FindWindow** again looks for the handle of the File Manager. In the unlikely event that the **Shell** statement would fail, runtime error 53 (File not found) occurs and the method's code displays a more explanatory syntax error message.

I'd like to cover several additional points about Windows API functions used by **FormatDisk**. **PostMessage** tells the File Manager to display its Format dialog box. Its first argument is the handle of the application to which to post the message. The second and third arguments specify the type of message (in this case, a command to display the Format dialog box). The fourth argument is unnecessary here and so zero is passed (Null in C or **vbEmpty** in Visual Basic).

Next, the method uses the **FindWindow** API function differently the second time than it did the first time. The first time it is used, **FindWindow** searches for the File Manager by a distinctive class name and, so, its second argument is set to zero. But, the second time it is used, the class name of the Format dialog box (CLS_NAME or #32770) is shared by other Windows objects; and, so, the second argument, which specifies the caption on the title bar of the dialog box, must also be used. You should note that there is no way of knowing in advance which one of five possible captions will be displayed on the title bar, so **FindWindow** checks all five possibilities.

Once one of the five possible windows is found (that is, the handle returned by **FindWindow** is not **False**/0), the code exits the **Do** loop and the

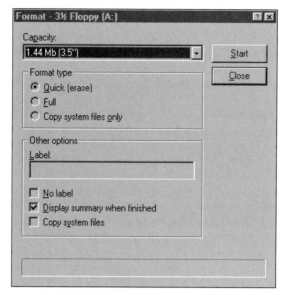

Figure 16.9   The Windows 95 Format dialog box.

method finishes up by returning **True**. Figure 16.9 shows the Format dialog box that is displayed from Windows 95.

Running A File's Application

The **File** class of the book's class library contains a **RunApp** method that starts the application associated with a particular file by Windows. This replicates the functionality of the Windows 95 Explorer or the Windows 3.x File Manager, which, when you double click on a file name, runs the application associated with the file and loads the file into the application. The **RunApp** method is a good example of how to reuse the complex functionality that is built into a single Windows API function.

The RunApp Method's Specifications

The detailed functionality of the **RunApp** method of the **File** class is shown in the sidebar.

The RunApp method's specifications.

SYNTAX

```
Object.RunApp(FileName)
```

The **RunApp** method's syntax has the following object qualifiers:

- *Object.* Required. **Object** data type. An expression that evaluates to an object in the Applies To pop-up list.

- *FileName.* Required. **String** data type. An expression that specifies the path and file name whose associated application is to be run.

CALLED

From any procedure in a client application.

RETURNS

Upon success, one element in a **Variant**. It contains a **Boolean** (**True**) that specifies the member executed successfully.

Upon failure, eight elements in a **Variant**. The elements contain the error codes that the class library returns when a runtime or syntax error occurs during the execution of one of its members.

REMARKS

If **RunApp** is unable to find and start the Windows application associated with the *FileName* argument, syntax error message 38 (RunApp method cannot run application) is displayed.

The RunApp Method's Code

Listing 16.6 shows the code for the **RunApp** method.

Listing 16.6   The RunApp method's code.

```
Function RunApp(FileName)

   ' Constants for Windows API functions:
   Const SW_SHOWNA = 8

   ' Constants for literals:
   Const PROC = "RunApp"
```

```
Const SYNTAX = True
Const ZERO = O&
Const SUCCESS = 33

' Variables:
Dim FilePath As String

' Enable error handler and do syntax checking:
On Error GoTo ET
CL.IsPath1 FileName, PROC, "FileName", FilePath
CL.IsFile FileName, FilePath, PROC, "FileName"

' Execute member's algorithm--
FilePath = Left$(FilePath, Len(FilePath) - 1)

If ShellExecute(ZERO, "Open", FileName, ZERO, _
    FilePath, SW_SHOWNA) < SUCCESS Then
    E.TrapSyntax 38, PROC
Else
    RunApp = Array(True)
End If

Exit Function

ET:
    If Err = SYNTAX Then RunApp = frmErrCodes.Codes
    If Err <> SYNTAX Then RunApp = CL.TrapErr(PROC)

End Function
```

When you call the **RunApp** method with the example code in its help topic, the example code first uses the **OpenCL** method of the **File** class to display the Open common dialog box, as shown in Figure 16.10.

After the user selects a file name (for example, BIBLIO.MDB), the **RunApp** method uses the Windows API function **ShellExecute** to run the application associated with the selected file (in this example, Microsoft Access 7, as shown in Figure 16.11).

The Windows API function **ShellExecute** resides in the DLL files SHELL32.DLL (32-bit) or SHELL.DLL (16-bit) and takes six arguments. As **ShellExecute** is used by the **RunApp** method, its first and fourth arguments are set to zero. The second argument is a **String** specifying the operation to perform, which can be either "Open" or "Print". The third argument specifies the name of the file, and the fifth argument specifies the file's path. The sixth and last argument specifies whether the file's application is shown when it is opened.

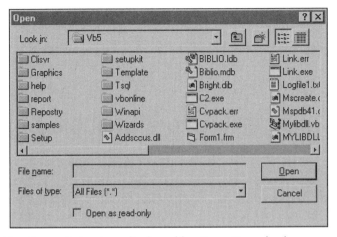

Figure 16.10   The Open dialog box displayed by **OpenCL** method.

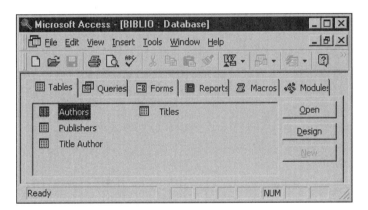

Figure 16.11   Access started with **RunApp** method (BIBLIO.MDB loaded).

17

POLLING AND
CALLBACK TECHNIQUES

As you have seen throughout this book, a client application can only communicate with an ActiveX component by instantiating one of its public classes, calling one of its members, and passing that member values as arguments (if it requires them). This communication from the client application to the ActiveX component is fundamentally the same whether the member in question is a method or a property. In turn, the ActiveX component normally communicates with the client application by having its member return some value(s) upon successful completion of its code, or some error code(s) upon failure. This two-way communication process between client and component is referred to as *messaging*. The entire possible set of members' arguments and returned values represents the component's public interface.

This messaging paradigm works well for most types of functionality that you can encapsulate in an ActiveX component. However, there is one generic type of function that ActiveX components can perform for which the typical messaging paradigm is insufficient—a member of an out-of-process or in-process component is called to run some type of batch-processing algorithm that takes a long time to complete. In this chapter, we will look at two techniques that can be used to communicate between a client application and an ActiveX component that is doing batch processing. These techniques are called *polling* and *callback*.

Messaging Between Client And Component

In Chapter 15, you saw that an ActiveX component can execute threaded, asynchronous code. The only restriction on this threaded code is that it must be run from the **Timer** event procedure of a **Timer** object in the class library. The **ShowToolTip** method's code starts up threads in two **Timer** objects, and when their asynchronous code is done running (in a matter of seconds), the original tooltip is hidden or another tooltip is displayed. The component's method does return **True**, just after it starts the two **Timer** objects' threads; but, there is no need to communicate anything back to the client when the threads themselves are done executing.

However, in the case of a threaded, batch-processing algorithm that takes a long time to complete and that may have some values to return to the client application, the typical messaging paradigm is inadequate. When the component runs a batch out-of-process, it returns **True** before starting the batch, allowing the client to regain control and continue to do other work. So, hours later, there needs to be another way for the out-of-process ActiveX component to tell the client application that it has finished the batch-processing operation and also to send back to the client any information or data relevant to the batch it just completed.

Visual Basic supports two generic techniques—polling and callback—that enable a client application to have the time of completion and the results of a threaded batch operation passed back to it. Polling consists of the client application periodically calling or polling the ActiveX EXE component to read the value of some property. This property or flag is **False** while the batch is running, but it is set to **True** by code in the **Timer** object when the threaded batch is finished.

In the case of a callback, it is the ActiveX EXE component that calls back to or notifies the client application. The component can do this in several possible ways. We will analyze these two callback techniques in this chapter:

- The ActiveX component calls back to the client by setting the property of an object reference (for example, a hidden **Label** object) that was passed to it as an argument. As you know by now, this approach has the same effect as setting the **Caption** property of the **Label** object back in the client application, which causes the **Change** event procedure of the **Label** object to occur. Code in that event procedure then reacts to whatever the new **Caption** property setting signifies (for example, that a batch operation is finished) and proceeds accordingly.

- The ActiveX component calls back to the client by calling the method of a **ClassModule** object in the client's application. An object reference to this **ClassModule** object is initially passed as an argument to the ActiveX EXE component's batch-processing method. Using this technique, the component can notify the client of any kind of action that occurs while the component is executing. Two general types of notification can be accomplished with this technique. First, an ActiveX component, which has been running a batch operation, can notify the client application that the batch is done and pass back values. Second, an ActiveX component, whose encapsulated ActiveX control is being used by a client application's **Form** object, can call back when the client application's user triggers one of the custom control's events (for example, the **ButtonClick** event of a **Toolbar** object).

Polling An ActiveX Component

The following steps make up the typical sequence of events that occurs when a client application calls an ActiveX component to run a batch-processing method and then, later, polls the component for the status of that batch operation:

1. The client application instantiates a class in an ActiveX component and calls one of its batch-processing members.

2. The member is typically a method and, after enabling an error handler and doing any necessary syntax checking, it enables a **Timer** object that is on a **Form** object encapsulated in the component. The **Form** object functions strictly as a container for the **Timer** object and is never displayed.

3. The method, having enabled the **Timer** object that contains the threaded, batch-processing code, returns **True** to the client application to signal that the method started the batch successfully.

4. The code in the **Timer** event procedure runs its threaded batch operation until completion.

5. Meanwhile, the client application does whatever its user wants, periodically calling (probably from code in a **Timer** object of its own) a **Property Get** procedure in the same instance of the ActiveX component that is running the batch operation. Most of the times the client application polls the component, the **Property Get** procedure returns **False**. It will only return **True** once, at which time the polling stops.

6. When the ActiveX component's batch operation is finally done, code in the **Timer** object does two things. First, it calls a **Property Let** procedure and sets a custom property flag to **True**. This is the flag whose value the client application has been periodically polling. Second, it terminates its own thread by setting its **Enabled** property to **False**.

7. When the client application's poll finally returns **True**, it knows that the batch operation in the ActiveX component is done.

Running The DemoPolling Example

The book's class library contains the **Thread** class, which has a method called **DemoPolling**. This method, in conjunction with example code in the book's class library Help file, illustrates the steps required for a client application to poll an ActiveX component and determine when a previously initiated batch-processing operation is finished. To run the example code that calls the **DemoPolling** method, follow these steps:

1. Select File | New Project and open a Standard EXE project.

2. Add a **CommandButton** object, **Label** object, and **Timer** object to Form1.

3. Set the **Index** property of Command1 to zero.

4. From the book's class library Help file (EFS.HLP), find the topic titled *Thread Object* and click on its Example hotspot.

5. From the secondary Help window, select the example code under the heading COPY/PASTE INTO FORM1 and copy and paste it into the General Declaration section of Form1.

6. Run the project. The dialog box shown in Figure 17.1 appears.

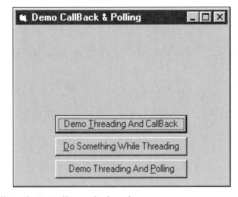

Figure 17.1   Demo CallBack & Polling dialog box.

How DemoPolling Works From The Client's Side

To run an example of the polling technique, click on the Demo Threading And Polling button. The code that makes the call to the **DemoPolling** method of the **Thread** object is shown in Listing 17.1.

Listing 17.1   Code that calls DemoPolling method.

```
Private Sub Command1_Click(Index As Integer)

    ' Variables:
    Dim Results As Variant

    ' Constant for literal.
    Const MBR_SUCCESS = 0

    Select Case Index
    . . .

        Case 2

            ' If call to method demonstrating polling technique
            ' succeeds:
            ' * Start executing code in Timer1_Timer event
            '    procedure (causing polling to take place).
            ' * Disable buttons calling methods.
            ' * Display initial message.
            Results = Thread.DemoPolling

            If Results(MBR_SUCCESS) Then
                Command1(0).Enabled = False
                Command1(2).Enabled = False
                Cls
                CurrentX = 200
```

```
        CurrentY = 200
        Print "Thread is executing for 10 seconds."
        CurrentX = 200
        Print "Will poll ActiveX server every 3 seconds."
        Timer1.Enabled = True
        Timer1.Interval = 3000
    Else
        SetFocus
        MsgBox "DemoPolling member failed.", vbInformation
    End If

    End Select

End Sub
```

In Listing 17.1, **Thread** is the name of the form-level object variable to which the instantiated **Thread** class was assigned in the **Form_Load** event procedure. The call to the **DemoPolling** method is made with the statement:

```
Results = Thread.DemoPolling
```

After the ActiveX component's method starts the batch in another thread controlled by its **Timer** object, it returns **True** to the client application. The client reads the returned value and reacts by printing the message shown in Figure 17.2.

Next, the following two lines of code, located toward the bottom of the button's **Click** event procedure, start a **Timer** object in the client that periodically polls the ActiveX component:

```
Timer1.Enabled = True
Timer1.Interval = 3000
```

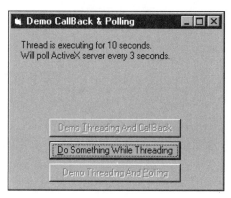

Figure 17.2 Polling demonstration has begun.

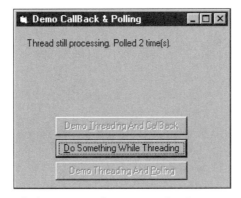

Figure 17.3   Poll of threaded operation that returned **False**.

The code in the **Timer** object polls the ActiveX component every three seconds and prints a message similar to the one shown in Figure 17.3 if the batch operation is not yet finished.

At any time, you can click on the Do Something While Threading button to show that the client application is able to perform its own thread's processing, even as its **Timer** object's polling code runs in another thread and the ActiveX's batch runs in a third thread. The client application's polling code is in Listing 17.2.

Listing 17.2   The Timer's code that polls DemoPolling's thread.

```
Private Sub Timer1_Timer()

    ' Variable.
    Static Polls As Integer

    If Not Thread.AsynchDone Then

        Polls = Polls + 1
        Cls
        CurrentX = 200
        CurrentY = 200
        Print "Thread still processing. Polled " & Polls & " time(s)."
        Beep

    Else

        Polls = Polls + 1
        Cls
        CurrentX = 200
        CurrentY = 100
        Print "Last poll " & "(#" & Polls & ") returned True."
```

```
        Print
        CurrentX = 200
        Print "This demo of threading and a polling"
        CurrentX = 200
        Print "technique works basically the same way"
        CurrentX = 200
        Print "with an RAO (Remote Automation Object)."
        Beep
        Polls = 0
        Command1(0).Enabled = True
        Command1(2).Enabled = True
        Timer1.Enabled = False

    End If

End Sub
```

In Listing 17.2, **Thread** is the name of the form-level object variable to which the instantiated **Thread** class was assigned in the **Form_Load** event procedure. **AsynchDone** is the name of a **Property Get** procedure in the **Thread** class where a flag is set to **True** when the batch processing is finished. If the batch is not yet done (if **AsynchDone** returns **False**), the client application's demonstration increments the polling counter, updates the polling message, and sounds the bell. Then the **Timer** object waits three seconds (its **Interval** property is set to 3000 milliseconds) and polls again.

When the out-of-process ActiveX component's batch is done (that is, when **AsynchDone** returns **True**), the client increments the polling counter for the last time, prints the message shown in Figure 17.4.

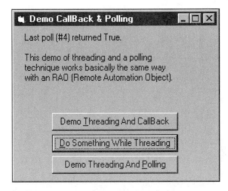

Figure 17.4 Poll of threaded operation that returned **True**.

How DemoPolling Works From The Component's Side

After the client application's code in Listing 17.1 calls the **DemoPolling** method, the code in Listing 17.3 in the ActiveX component executes.

Listing 17.3   The DemoPolling method's code.

```
Function DemoPolling()

    ' _____

    ' Purpose: Demonstrates polling technique from client
    '          application to ActiveX component
    '          (either local or remote).
    '
    ' Called:  From any procedure in client application.
    '
    ' Returns: Upon success, True. Upon failure, eight elements
    '          in array, whose subtypes contain codes for
    '          runtime or syntax error that occurred as
    '          DemoPolling method executed.
    '
    ' Notes:   a) DemoPolling method uses a technique that works
    '             either with local or remote ActiveX components.
    '          b) Real-world use of this technique would probably
    '             involve method that took some other arguments.
    ' _____


    ' Constants for literals:
    Const SYNTAX = True
    Const PROC = "DemoPolling"

    ' Enable error handler and do syntax checking:
    On Error GoTo ET

    If cDLLServer Then
        E.TrapSyntax 1, PROC, "ActiveX DLL component"
    End If

    ' Enable Timer object in frmThread which:
    ' * Simulates asynchronous, threaded polling routine.
    ' * Allows DemoPolling method to finish and return value.
    frmThread.tmrPolling.Enabled = True
    DemoPolling = Array(True)
    Exit Function

ET:

    If Err = SYNTAX Then DemoPolling = frmErrCodes.Codes
    If Err <> SYNTAX Then DemoPolling = CL.TrapErr(PROC)

End Function
```

There are two points to note about the **DemoPolling** method's code. First, this method's sole purpose is to start a **Timer** object on a **Form** object in the class library named frmThread. It is in the **Timer** event procedure that the threaded batch is run. Because the method's code refers to the **Timer** object on frmThread, the form is implicitly loaded but is never actually displayed. Second, for a brief time, two code threads are running in the ActiveX component. One is in the **Timer** event procedure and the other is in the **DemoPolling** method, which then returns **True** to the client application.

The code in the ActiveX component's tmrPolling **Timer** object is shown in Listing 17.4.

Listing 17.4   The DemoPolling method's Timer object code.

```
Private Sub tmrPolling_Timer()

    ' Constants for literals:
    Const TEN_SECS = 10000

    ' Variables:
    Dim Start As Long

    ' Simulate batch-type processing that takes just 10 seconds to
    ' complete. Real-world scenario could call any long-running
    ' procedure(s) that benefit from being run in this manner.
    Start = TimeGetTime

    Do Until TimeGetTime > Start + TEN_SECS
        DoEvents
    Loop

    ' Sequence of flags/reads:
    ' * frmThread's AsynchDone custom property is set to True to
    '    signal that asynchronous/threaded processing is done.
    ' * Client app polls Thread object's AsynchDone custom
    '    property.
    ' * Thread object then reads frmThread's AsynchDone custom
    '    property and, when it finds that it is True, it:
    '    a) Unloads frmThread.
    '    b) Returns True to client app.
    AsynchDone = True
    tmrPolling.Enabled = False

End Sub
```

The empty loop in the **Timer** object's code simulates a batch-processing operation (all 10 seconds of it). Each time the loop is executed, Visual

Basic's **DoEvents** statement executes. This enables code in another procedure of the ActiveX component (that is, the polling of the **Property Get AsynchDone** procedure) to run while batch processing goes on. Once the batch operation is done, the next two statements set an **AsynchDone** custom property in frmThread to **True** to signal completion and terminate the **Timer** object's thread. At this point, the frmThread **Form** object is still loaded and the instance of the ActiveX component is still running (although it is doing nothing).

Each time the client application polls the component, it calls the **Property Get AsynchDone** procedure in the **Thread** class (not to be confused with the similarly named custom property in the frmThread **Form** object). The complete code of the **Property Get AsynchDone** procedure in the **Thread** class is shown here:

```
Property Get AsynchDone()

   ' This is custom property that client application polls.
   If frmThread.AsynchDone Then
      AsynchDone = True
      Unload frmThread
   Else
      AsynchDone = False
   End If

End Property
```

Each time the client application polls or calls this **Property Get** procedure, its code reads the similarly named custom property in the **Form** object where the batch-processing code runs. Until the **Timer** object's batch algorithm is done, the **Property Get** procedure of the **Thread** class returns **False**. However, when the **Timer** object's batch is done, it turns on the **AsynchDone** custom property of frmThread (as you saw in Listing 17.4). Then, the next time the client application polls the ActiveX component, the **Property Get AsynchDone** procedure of the **Thread** class does two things:

1. It returns **True**, which tells the client to stop polling and go about its business.

2. It unloads the frmThread **Form** object. This is important to note because, unless the form is unloaded, an instance of the out-of-process ActiveX component continues to run and wastes system resources.

Calling Back To A Client's Property

The following steps make up the typical sequence of events that occurs when a client application calls an ActiveX component to run a batch-processing method and the component, when done, calls back to the client. In this example, the call back is done by setting the property of a **Label** object belonging to the client.

1. The client application instantiates a class in an ActiveX component.

2. It then calls a batch-processing member of the class, passing it a reference to a hidden **Label** object as one of its required arguments.

3. The member is typically a method and, after enabling an error handler and doing any necessary syntax checking, it does two things. First, it enables a **Timer** object that is on a **Form** object encapsulated in the component. The **Form** object functions strictly as a container for the **Timer** object and is never displayed. Second, it uses a **Set Property** procedure to set a custom property of the **Timer** object's form to refer to the client application's label.

4. The method, having enabled the **Timer** object that contains the threaded, batch-processing code, returns **True** to the client application to signal that the method started the batch successfully.

5. The client application does whatever its user wants.

6. Meanwhile, the code in the ActiveX component's **Timer** event procedure runs its threaded batch operation until completion.

7. When the batch operation is finally done, code in its **Timer** object sets a property of the **Label** object (that is, calls back to it), and triggers the **Change** event of that label back in the client application.

8. The **Timer** object's code then terminates its own thread, unloads its container **Form** object, and deinstantiates the ActiveX component.

9. Back in the client application, code in the **Change** event procedure of the **Label** object responds to the fact that the batch operation in the ActiveX component is done.

Running The DemoCallBack Example

The book's class library contains the **Thread** class, which has a method called **DemoCallBack**. This method, in conjunction with example code in the book's class library Help file, illustrates the steps required for an ActiveX component, which has finished a batch-processing operation, to call back to a client application's control by setting one of its properties and triggering an event. To run the example code that calls the **DemoCallBack** method, follow these steps:

1. Select File | New Project and open a Standard EXE project.

2. Add a **CommandButton** object, **Label** object, and **Timer** object to Form1.

3. Set the **Index** property of Command1 to zero.

4. From the book's class library Help file (EFS.HLP), find the topic titled *Thread Object* and click on its Example hotspot.

5. From the secondary Help window, select the example code under the heading COPY/PASTE INTO FORM1 and copy and paste it into the General Declaration section of Form1.

6. Run the project and click on the Demo Threading And CallBack button.

The code that makes the call to the **DemoCallBack** method of the **Thread** object is shown in Listing 17.5.

Listing 17.5   Code that calls DemoCallBack method.

```
Private Sub Command1_Click(Index As Integer)

    ' Variables:
    Dim Results As Variant

    ' Constant for literal.
    Const MBR_SUCCESS = 0

    Select Case Index

        Case 0

            Results = Thread.DemoCallBack(Lbl:=Label1)

            If Results(MBR_SUCCESS) Then
                Command1(0).Enabled = False
                Command1(2).Enabled = False
                Cls
                CurrentX = 200
                CurrentY = 200
                Print "Thread is executing for 10 seconds..."
            Else
                SetFocus
                MsgBox "DemoCallBack member failed.", vbInformation
            End If
```

. . .

```
    End Select

End Sub
```

Thread is the name of the form-level object variable to which the instanti-ated **Thread** class was assigned in the **Form_Load** event procedure. The call to the **DemoCallBack** method is made with the statement:

```
Results = Thread.DemoCallBack(Lbl:=Label1)
```

After the ActiveX component's method starts the batch in another thread controlled by its **Timer** object, it returns **True** to the client application. The client reads the returned value and reacts by printing the message shown in Figure 17.5. At any time, you can click on the Do Something While Thread-ing button to show that the client application is able to perform its own thread's processing, even as the ActiveX's batch runs in a separate thread.

When the ActiveX component's simulated batch (which takes all of 10 seconds to run) is done, it calls back to the client application by setting the **Caption** property of the hidden **Label** object to **AsynchDone**. Code in the **Label1_Change** event procedure reacts to the callback by printing the message in Figure 17.6. As you can see, there is nothing magical about the way this callback technique works. The key to the technique is that when you pass the **Name** property of a client application's control to an ActiveX component's member, the component can act upon that control just as if it were its own object.

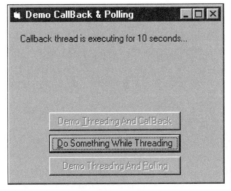

Figure 17.5 Callback demonstration has begun.

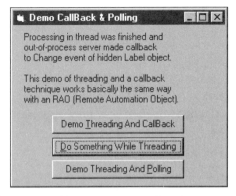

Figure 17.6   Callback from ActiveX component to client has occurred.

Calling Back To A Client's Method

The following example demonstrates the sequence of events that occurs when a client application calls the **LoadToolBar** method of the class library's **ActiveXCtl** class. Like the **LoadStatusBar** method we examined in Chapter 15, the **LoadToolBar** method returns object references to the client application. The two object references are to a **PictureBox** object (used as a container) and to Microsoft's 32-bit **Toolbar** ActiveX control (specified by the method's *Kind* argument).

After using the **SetParent** Windows API function to change the parent of the **PictureBox** object to the **Form** object in the client application, the user can click any of the toolbar's **Button** objects and trigger the **ButtonClick** event procedure of the toolbar. The code for the **ButtonClick** event procedure is in the ActiveX component's **Form** object, which is associated with the **LoadToolBar** method. The component responds to the clicking of the toolbar button and performs two tasks:

- Determines which button was clicked.
- Calls back to a predetermined method in a **ClassModule** object in the client application, passing values which specify the toolbar and button that was clicked. Based on those values, the client application's method then executes code appropriate for the clicked toolbar button.

The LoadToolBar Method's Specifications

The **LoadToolBar** method embeds Microsoft's 32-bit **Toolbar** ActiveX control on a **Form** object in a client application. The detailed functionality of the **LoadToolBar** method is shown in the sidebar.

The LoadToolBar method's specifications.

SYNTAX

```
Object.LoadToolBar(Class, Kind)
```

The **LoadToolBar** method's syntax has the following object qualifier and named arguments:

- *Object.* Required. **Object** data type. An expression that evaluates to an object in the Applies To pop-up list.

- *Class.* Required. **Object** data type. An expression that evaluates to the **Name** property of a **ClassModule** object in the client application. *Class* must contain a method, titled Sub TBarBtn_Click(Kind As Byte, Button As Integer). When the client application's user clicks a toolbar button, the class library's ActiveX component calls back to the **TBarBtn_Click** method in *Class*, passing the value of the *Kind* argument and the **Index** value of the clicked button as the *Button* argument. You use the values of *Kind* and *Button* to determine which routine to execute in the client application. See Tables 17.1 and 17.2 for the valid settings of the *Button* argument.

- *Kind.* Required. **Byte** data type. A numeric expression specifying a value or constant which determines the type of toolbar to display. Valid settings for *Kind* are 0 - TB_CANCEL, 1 - TB_EDIT, and 2 - TB_DRAW.

CALLED

Normally from the **Form_Load** event procedure in a client application. If run from an out-of-process ActiveX component, **LoadToolBar** must also be called from the **Form_Unload** event procedure (with the *Kind* argument set to 0 - TB_CANCEL).

RETURNS

Upon success, two elements in a **Variant**. The elements contain these subtypes:

- 0 - MBR_SUCCESS. A **Boolean** (**True**) that specifies the member executed successfully.

- 1 - MBR_PICBOX. An object expression that is the **Name** property of the **PictureBox** object which the **Toolbar** ActiveX control object is layered on. The client application's programmer uses this object reference to write code to resize the container **PictureBox** object when the user resizes the form. If the *Kind* argument is set to TB_CANCEL, **Nothing** is returned.

- 2 - MBR_TOOLBAR. An object expression that is the **Name** property of the **Toolbar** ActiveX control object. The client application's programmer uses this object reference to write code to resize the **Toolbar** object when the user resizes the form. If the *Kind* argument is set to TB_CANCEL, **Nothing** is returned.

Upon failure, eight elements in a **Variant**. The elements contain the error codes that the class library returns when a runtime or syntax error occurs during the execution of one of its members.

REMARKS

- The **LoadToolBar** method only runs under 32-bit Visual Basic because it uses Microsoft's **Toolbar** object, which only exists as a 32-bit ActiveX control.

- The object references that **LoadToolBar** returns should be assigned by the client application's programmer to previously declared form-level object variables with the **Set** statement. Once the object references are assigned, the Windows API function **SetParent** must be called to change the parent window of the container **PictureBox** object to the client application's **Form** object.

- To resize the toolbar when the user resizes the client application's **Form** object, use a **Timer** object and code in its **Timer** event procedure. It is only necessary to do this if the **Form** object's **BorderStyle** property is set to 2 - Sizable, or its **MaxButton** or **MinButton** properties are set to **True**.

- If the **LoadToolBar** method is run from an out-of-process ActiveX component, it must be called from the **Form_Unload** event procedure of the client application's **Form** object and passed 0 - TB_CANCEL as its *Kind* argument. If the method's container **Form** object is not explicitly unloaded in this way, the **Terminate** event of its **ActiveXCtl** class does not occur and the toolbar still appears on the screen.

- Visual Basic cannot generically determine if an **Object** data type contains a reference to a **ClassModule** object. Visual Basic's **TypeName** function returns only the **ClassModule** object's **Name** property; its **TypeOf** function does not recognize a **ClassModule** object and results in a syntax error (User-defined type not defined). If you try to read the values of any of its properties (**Instancing**, **Name**, or **Public**), you get runtime error 438 (Object doesn't support this property or method). The class library uses its **HasHandle** method, in the private **CL** class, to test whether an object reference is to a **ClassModule** object or not.

Running The LoadToolBar Example

To run the example code that calls the **LoadToolBar** method, follow these steps:

1. Start Visual Basic.
2. Select File | New Project and open a Standard EXE project.
3. Add a **Timer** object to Form1.

Table 17.1 Edit toolbar's Button argument settings.

Value	Constant
2	TB_NEW
3	TB_OPEN
4	TB_SAVE
6	TB_UNDO
7	TB_CUT
8	TB_COPY
9	TB_PASTE
11	TB_BOLD
12	TB_ITALIC
13	TB_UNDERLINE

Table 17.2 Draw toolbar's Button argument settings.

Value	Constant
2	TB_NEW
3	TB_OPEN
4	TB_SAVE
6	TB_ARC
7	TB_ELLIPSE
8	TB_LINE
9	TB_RECTANGLE

4. Select Project | Add Class Module.

5. From the book's class library Help file (EFS.HLP), find the topic titled *LoadToolBar Method* and click on its Example hotspot.

6. From the secondary Help window, select the example code under the heading COPY/PASTE INTO CLASS1 and paste it into the General Declarations section of Class1.

7. Copy and paste the code under the heading COPY/PASTE INTO FORM1 into the General Declarations section of Form1.

8. Run the project. The dialog box shown in Figure 17.7 appears. Click on the toolbar buttons, double click on the toolbar itself, or resize the **Form** object and observe the behavior of the toolbar.

The LoadToolBar Example From The Client's Side

When the dialog box in Figure 17.7 loads, code in its **Form_Load** event procedure calls the **LoadToolBar** method, passing it an object reference to Class1 and a value specifying the kind of toolbar to display:

```
Results = ActiveXCtl.LoadToolBar(Class:=Class1, Kind:=TB_EDIT)
```

Figure 17.7 Dialog box to demo **LoadToolBar** method.

The **LoadToolBar** method returns an array of values in a **Variant** from which the client application's **Form_Load** event procedure reads the object references. The client then calls the **SetParent** Windows API function to change the parent of the container **PictureBox** object:

```
Set fPicBox = Results(MBR_PICBOX)
Set fToolBar = Results(MBR_TOOLBAR)
SetParent fPicBox.hWnd, hWnd
Timer1.Interval = 1
```

Finally, code in a **Timer** object positions the **Toolbar** object and its container **PictureBox** object at the top of the client application's **Form** object and keeps them there:

```
Private Sub Timer1_Timer()

    ' Resize/position toolbar when user
    ' resizes/moves client's Form object:
    fPicBox.Top = 0
    fPicBox.Width = ScaleWidth
    fToolBar.Width = ScaleWidth

End Sub
```

When the user clicks on one of the toolbar's buttons, code in the ActiveX component takes control.

The LoadToolBar Example From The Component's Side

The **LoadToolBar** method's code is in Listing 17.6.

Listing 17.6   The LoadToolBar method's code.

```
Function LoadToolBar(Class As Object, _
                     Kind As Byte)

    ' Constants for Kind argument:
    Const TB_CANCEL = 0
    Const TB_EDIT = 1
    Const TB_DRAW = 2

    ' Constants for literals:
    Const PROC = "LoadToolBar"
    Const SYNTAX = True

    ' Variables:
    #If Win32 Then
        Dim PBox   As Object
```

```
    Dim TBar    As Object
#End If

' Enable error handler and do syntax checking:
On Error GoTo ET

#If Win16 Then
    E.TrapSyntax 1, PROC, "16-bit VB"
#Else

    If CL.HasHandle(Class) <> "ClassModule" Then
        E.TrapSyntax 8, PROC, "Class"
    Else
        Select Case Kind
            Case TB_CANCEL, TB_EDIT, TB_DRAW
            Case Else
                E.TrapSyntax 5, PROC, "Kind"
        End Select
    End If

    ' Execute member's algorithm:
    ' * Unload old toolbar before displaying new one.
    ' * Assign PictureBox object holding toolbar to variable to
    '   abbreviate code, make it more readable, and optimize it.
    ' * Set custom property in container Form object to store
    '   Class argument passed from client application, in order
    '   to know which object to make callback to from ButtonClick
    '   event procedures in frmLoadTBar Form object.
    If Kind <> TB_CANCEL Then
        Unload frmLoadTBar

        If Kind = TB_EDIT Then
            Set PBox = frmLoadTBar.picEdit
            Set TBar = frmLoadTBar.tbrEdit
        Else
            Set PBox = frmLoadTBar.picDraw
            Set TBar = frmLoadTBar.tbrDraw
        End If

        Set frmLoadTBar.CallBackCls = Class
    End If

    ' Return results from member:
    ' * If client application is canceling toolbar,
    '   return array and unload Form object.
    ' * If client application is displaying toolbar, set
    '   object references in returned array to controls.
    ' * Free system resources associated with objects.
    Select Case Kind
        Case TB_CANCEL
            LoadToolBar = Array(True, Nothing, Nothing)
            Unload frmLoadTBar
        Case Else
            LoadToolBar = Array(True, PBox, TBar)
```

```
        End Select

        Set PBox = Nothing
        Set TBar = Nothing
        Exit Function
    #End If

ET:

    If Err = SYNTAX Then LoadToolBar = frmErrCodes.Codes
    If Err <> SYNTAX Then LoadToolBar = CL.TrapErr(PROC)

End Function
```

There are four points to note about the **LoadToolBar** method's code in Listing 17.6. First, it calls the **HasHandle** method of the private **CL** class to determine if the object reference passed to the *Class* argument is a **ClassModule** object. Second, depending on the *Kind* argument's value, it selects the appropriate object references for the **Toolbar** ActiveX control and its container **PictureBox** object. Third, it sets a custom property of the toolbar's **Form** object (**CallBackCls**) to refer to the client application's **ClassModule** object, based on the value of the *Class* argument. Fourth, after it has returned the object references to the client application and the **LoadToolBar** method is done executing, the frmLoadTBar **Form** object remains loaded (even though it is never displayed).

When the client application's user clicks a button on the Edit toolbar, the code in Listing 17.7 executes in the loaded frmLoadTBar. The value (**Button.Index**) that gets passed back to the client application, as part of the callback to its **ClassModule** object's **TBarBtn_Click** method, is the element of the clicked **Button** object in the toolbar's **Buttons** collection.

Listing 17.7   Toolbar control's ButtonClick event code.

```
Private Sub tbrEdit_ButtonClick(ByVal Button As Button)

    ' Constants for literals:
    Const TB_EDIT = 1

    ' Enable in-line error handler to handle scenario where
    ' class with TBarBtn_Click method did not get passed in.
    ' Then call back to method in class in client application.
    On Error Resume Next
    fCallBackCls.TBarBtn_Click TB_EDIT, Button.Index
    Button.Value = tbrUnpressed

End Sub
```

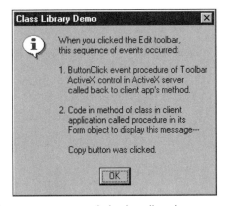

Figure 17.8 Client application reacts to clicked toolbar button.

At this point, all the example's client application does with the index value of the clicked toolbar button is to read the button's number and display an appropriate message, like the one in Figure 17.8. A real-world client application would execute the appropriate routine (for example, a procedure to cut, copy, or paste to or from the clipboard). You could use the **Edit** method of the book's class library **Text** class to do this, as you will see in Chapter 21 of the final section of this book.

It is also important to understand two other points about the implications of the **LoadToolBar** method (and of the **LoadStatusBar** method we discussed in Chapter 15). First, both of these ActiveX controls happen to have been developed by Microsoft and are distributed with Visual Basic. So, because everybody who programs with Visual Basic has them, they were the logical ActiveX controls to use in this book's class library. However, the same kinds of techniques that these two methods illustrate can be used with any ActiveX control manufactured by third-party software vendors. Second, any functionality associated with an ActiveX control in an ActiveX component's class library can be used by the client application. For example, if the **Toolbar** ActiveX control's **AllowCustomize** property is set to **True**, the user can customize the toolbar. This is the case with the book's class library toolbar; if you double click on the toolbar itself, the Customize Toolbar dialog box shown in Figure 17.9 is displayed.

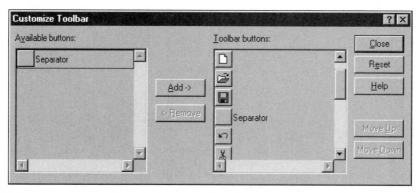

Figure 17.9 Customize Toolbar dialog box of Toolbar ActiveX control.

18

REUSABLE APPLICATION
FRAMEWORKS, PART 1

U ntil now, we have been discussing the object-oriented programming syntax and techniques that VB5 supports. I have demonstrated, using the ActiveX component class library that comes with this book, how to write many different kinds of reusable objects and public members and call them from a client application.

In this chapter, we will go one step further and show you how to begin to write reusable application frameworks. In the context of this book, the application framework is specifically the Windows operating system itself. In a more general sense, an application framework is the overarching concept or context that defines how parts/members should be organized and combined to make reusable objects.

A great book on reuse, *Framing Software Reuse: Lessons From The Real World* by Paul G. Bassett, was recently published by Prentice Hall (ISBN 0-13-327859). I strongly suggest you locate this resource. Ed Yourdon, an authority on software development, says in the book's foreword that Bassett "has written the best book about reuse I've seen in my career." Early in *Framing Software Reuse*, Bassett cites the following statistics:

- The traditional reuse techniques, properly implemented using the object-oriented development methodology, typically achieve reuse rates of anywhere from 10 percent to 50 percent of the code in an entire project.

- Component-based application frameworks, when properly designed and implemented in conjunction with object-oriented programming, can achieve reuse rates of up to 80 percent of a project's code.

- A study of 15 projects from 9 different companies found that component-based application frameworks, on average, reduced schedules by 70 percent and development costs by 84 percent, compared to industry norms.

In Chapters 18 and 19, you will learn how to create parts of a Windows application framework using the object-oriented programming syntax and techniques that VB5 supports. Specifically, we will focus on two reusable objects in the book's class library: the **File** class in Chapter 18 and the **Text** class in Chapter 19. We have looked at a couple of the methods of the **File** class in previous chapters, but here we'll examine it in more depth. The **File** class does tasks related to files for a client application (compressing, copying, deleting, encrypting, expanding, opening and saving them, and so on).

In this chapter, you will also see specific examples of OOP techniques and tricks that show you how to:

- Display, under Windows 95, the various common dialog boxes by directly calling 32-bit Windows API functions and thus speed up their performance.

- Subclass and customize the appearance and functionality of common dialog boxes, beyond anything that merely setting their properties permits you to do.

- Start a separate executable from a class library to implement threading/asynchronous processing under Windows 3.x and Windows NT, and achieve effects not possible with an ActiveX component alone.

- Implement a file finder by calling the one that is displayed from the Windows Explorer application.

- Create your own file finder in the form of a reusable object in an ActiveX component.

Understanding The Design Of The File Class

The **File** class in the book's ActiveX component is designed to serve two general purposes. First, it includes public members that perform the functions conventionally associated with the File menu items of the Windows operating system. Second, it includes public members that perform many of the file-related tasks conventionally done with the Windows Explorer or File Manager.

To meet these two objectives, the **File** class is composed of 13 public members. The name of each public member and a description of its purpose is shown in Table 18.1

Table 18.1 The public members of the **File** class.

Member	Description
Browse	Displays the conventional Windows file browser common dialog box and returns the user's selection(s).
Compress	Compresses one or more files using COMPRESS.EXE, the utility included with Visual Basic's Setup Wizard (32-bit only).
Copy	Copies one or more files from one directory to another.
Decrypt	Decrypts one or more files encrypted with the Encrypt method of the File object.
Delete	Deletes one or more files from a directory.
Encrypt	Encrypts one or more files.
Expand	Expands one or more files that were compressed with COMPRESS.EXE, the utility included with Visual Basic's Setup Wizard (32-bit only).
Find	Finds every instance of a file or type of file on a drive and path.
Move	Moves one or more files from one directory to another.
OpenCL	Displays the Open common dialog box and returns the user's selection(s).
PrintCL	Displays the Print common dialog box and returns the user's selection(s).
RunApp	Runs the application associated with a file and opens the file.
SaveAs	Displays the Save As common dialog box and returns the user's selection(s).

There are two major points to note about the **File** class, from the viewpoint of its design. First, consider the **OpenCL** and **SaveAs** members, which use the appropriate common dialog boxes to return a **String** specifying the path and file name the user wants to open or save. However, these members do not actually do the open and save operations; instead, files are opened and saved by the **Load** and **Save** methods of the **Graphic**, **List**, and **Text** classes. This is a design decision on my part that was largely determined by my desire to implement the **Load** and **Save** methods in a polymorphic fashion. Another developer, using another set of assumptions or in another context, might have made a different design decision. The moral of the story is this: Designing the architecture of an application framework, while mostly a science (that is, rules-based and consistent with the existing Windows framework), is also to some degree an art.

Second, the time and effort that you must invest in creating an elaborate framework, such as the **File** class, suggests that your design objectives should be ambitious. The functionality associated with such public members as **Browse**, **OpenCL**, and **SaveAs** should, if at all possible, improve upon the functionality embodied in the **CommonDialog** ActiveX control (for example, center the dialog box, support wildcard entries, customize the caption of the default button, and so on). Likewise, the **Copy** and **Move** methods ought to support wildcard entries to improve upon their counterparts in the Explorer or File Manager. The essential point here is that the greater the frequency with which a public member is reused, the greater the justification for a more complex set of specifications and an elegant implementation.

Displaying Common Dialogs With Windows API Functions

In Chapter 15, we saw how the **CommonDialog** ActiveX control could be encapsulated in a class library and reused from a client application. The example we used was the **SelectFont** method of the **Text** class. You may have noticed that the performance of this technique is a little slow. Although it is not well known, under Windows 95, you can display four of the common dialog boxes (Color, Open, Printer, and Save As) by calling 32-bit Windows API functions from Visual Basic.

Displaying common dialog boxes with the Windows API under Windows 95 has these advantages:

- Because you are calling COMDLG32.DLL directly, the four common dialog boxes are displayed about twice as fast as when displayed using the **CommonDialog** ActiveX control.
- The size of the ActiveX component's file is reduced.
- It is possible to customize the appearance and behavior of the Open and Save As common dialog boxes displayed by the Windows API calls by running an asynchronous thread in a hidden **Form** object in the class library. This asynchronous thread essentially subclasses the common dialog boxes.

To see how the book's class library uses Windows API functions to display common dialog boxes, we will look at the **Browse** member of the **File** class. Once you understand how **Browse** works, you will easily grasp the other common dialog-related members of the class library (**SelectColor**, **OpenCL**, **PrintCL**, and **SaveAs**).

The Browse Method's Specifications

The **Browse** method displays the conventional Windows file browser common dialog box and returns the user's selection(s). The detailed functionality of the **Browse** method is shown in the sidebar.

The Browse method's specifications.

SYNTAX

```
Object.Browse([Filter], [Title])
```

The **Browse** method's syntax has the following object qualifier and named arguments:

- *Object.* Required. **Object** data type. An expression that evaluates to an object in the Applies To pop-up list.

- *Filter.* Optional. **Variant** data type whose subtype is a **String** expression that specifies the filter displayed in the Type list of the dialog box. If omitted, the default setting for Filter is "All Files (*.*)|*.*". For more information about the setting of *Filter*, see the help topic in the Visual Basic Help file titled *Filter Property (Common Dialog)*.

- *Title*. Optional. **Variant** data type whose subtype is a **String** expression that specifies the caption to be displayed in the title bar of the dialog box. If omitted, the default setting for *Title* is *Browse*.

CALLED

From any procedure in a client application.

RETURNS

Upon success, two elements in a **Variant**. The elements contain these subtypes:

- 0 - MBR_SUCCESS. A **Boolean** (**True**) that specifies the member executed successfully.

- 1 - MBR_FILES. A **String** that specifies the selected path and file name or, if the user chooses Cancel, **vbNullString** (that is, a zero-length string). If more than one file is selected or a wildcard is typed, the path and file names returned are delimited either by **vbNullChar** (that is, a Null character) for 32-bit Visual Basic, or by a space character for 16-bit Visual Basic. For example, if two files on the C root drive are selected, the string would have this format when returned from the 32-bit ActiveX component: "C:\" & vbNullChar & "FILE1.TXT" & vbNullChar & "FILE2.TXT". When returned from the 16-bit ActiveX component, the string would have this format: "C:\ FILE1.TXT FILE2.TXT". The use of these delimiters to separate the path and file names is consistent with the delimiters used and returned by the Open and Save As common dialog boxes for Windows 95/NT 4.0 and Windows 3.x.

Upon failure, eight elements in a **Variant**. The elements contain the error codes that the class library returns when a runtime or syntax error occurs during the execution of one of its members.

REMARKS

- The **Browse** method's common dialog box supports multiple file selections and wildcards. You can type a wildcard for a specific file type (for example, *.CLS) or for all files (that is, *.*), choose the Browse button, and return all the file names matching the wildcard on the current path.

- If you pass an invalid setting to the *Filter* argument, the **Browse** method ignores it. However, the files on the current path may not be displayed properly.

- If you call the **Browse** method from a **File** object instantiated from an out-of-process ActiveX component, you should first apply Visual Basic's **Hide** method to the **Form** object in the client application from whose code you call the method. After the user closes the common dialog box, you can apply Visual Basic's **Show** method to redisplay the **Form** object. The reason this is necessary is because the out-of-process ActiveX component's **Browse** method displays the common dialog box modelessly, instead of modally as would be the case with the in-process ActiveX component. Hiding the client application's **Form** object prevents the user from calling another member in the ActiveX component (and thus getting the *Component Request Pending* message) until the common dialog box is closed.

The Browse Method's Code

There are three major points that our analysis of the **Browse** method's code will focus on. First, the way the **GetOpenFileName** Windows API function and its associated user-defined data type is declared and called. Second, the way the asynchronous thread that subclasses the common dialog box works. Third, the way the **Browse** method parses the value returned from the common dialog box and returns it to the client application. This **String** value can specify a single path and file name, a path and multiple file names, or a wildcard that represents all files or files of a certain kind on a given path.

DECLARING AND CALLING THE GETOPENFILENAME API FUNCTION

The **GetOpenFileName** function exists in the 32-bit Windows API in the file COMDLG32.DLL. It takes just one argument, which is the user-defined data type OPENFILENAME. They are both declared in the General Declarations section of FILE.CLS, as shown in Listing 18.1.

Listing 18.1   API declarations for the Browse method.

```
#If Win32 Then

    Private Type OPENFILENAME
        TypeSize As Long
        Owner As Long
        Inst As Long
        Filter As String
        CustomFilter As String
        MaxCustFilter As Long
        FilterIndex As Long
        FileName As String
        MaxFileName As Long
        FileTitle As String
        MaxFileTitle As Long
        InitDir As String
        DialogTitle As String
        Flags As Long
        FileOffset As Integer
        FileExtension As Integer
        DefaultExt As String
        CustData As Long
        Hook As Long
        TemplateName As String
    End Type

    Private Declare Function GetOpenFileName& Lib "COMDLG32" _
                        Alias "GetOpenFileNameA" _
                        (FileName As OPENFILENAME)

#End If
```

In Listing 18.1, you can see that the **OPENFILENAME** user-defined data type is a complex one, with 20 different data elements. You should note that I've deleted the C-language data type prefixes (l, lpstr, n, lpfn, and so on) from the element names, which the Text API Viewer that comes with VB includes. I've also renamed some of the data elements to correspond to the property names used by the **CommonDialog** ActiveX control (**FileName**, **MaxFileName**, **InitDir**, **DialogTitle**, and so on). Eliminating the prefixes and renaming the data elements does not affect the call to the **GetOpenFileName** function and it makes for more consistent, English-like and readable code in the **Browse** method.

> *Note: The **GetSaveFileName** Windows API function is declared the same way as the **GetOpenFileName** function and uses the same OPENFILENAME user-defined data type. The only difference is that **GetSaveFileName** displays the Save As common dialog box when it is called.*

In the **Browse** method itself, the code is broken up into five major parts:

- The syntax-checking code block.
- The code block that displays the Windows 95-related common dialog box.
- The code block that displays the Windows NT-related common dialog box.
- The code block that displays the Windows 3.x-related common dialog box.
- The code block that parses the **String** value returned from the common dialog box and returns it to the client application.

Next, we will analyze the code block that displays the Windows 95-related common dialog box, which is shown in Listing 18.2.

Listing 18.2   The Browse method's Windows 95 -related code.

```
Function Browse(Optional Filter, _
                Optional Title)

    ' Variables:
    #If Win32 Then
        Dim Cdl As OPENFILENAME
    #End If
    . . .

    Flags = cdlOFNAllowMultiselect + cdlOFNHideReadOnly + _
            cdlOFNPathMustExist

    #If Win32 Then

        If Not CL.IsWinNT Then
            LockWindowUpdate GetDesktopWindow
            Cdl.TypeSize = Len(Cdl)
            Cdl.FileName = Space$(512)
            Cdl.MaxFileName = 512
            Cdl.Filter = Filter
            Cdl.Flags = Flags + cdlOFNExplorer
            Cdl.DialogTitle = Title
            frm32ComDlg.DlgCaption = Title
            frm32ComDlg.BtnCaption = Title
            frm32ComDlg.tmrSetProps.Interval = 1

            If GetOpenFileName(Cdl) Then
                FileSpec = Trim$(Cdl.FileName)
```

```
        Do Until Right$(FileSpec, 1) <> vbNullChar
            FileSpec = Left$(FileSpec, Len(FileSpec) - 1)
        Loop

    Else
        Browse = Array(True, vbNullString)
    End If

Else

    . . .

End If
    . . .

End Function
```

The portion of the **Browse** method in Listing 18.2 works in this order:

1. Two Windows API functions are used to disable screen redrawing. **GetDesktopWindow** returns the handle of the screen and **LockWindowUpdate** uses that handle to temporarily prevent screen flicker.

2. Several elements of the user-defined data type OPENFILENAME (represented here by the variable **Cdl**) are initialized. The elements required to be set to display the Open common dialog box are **TypeSize**, **FileName**, **MaxFileName**, **Filter**, and **Title**. The **Flags** element is optional, but the **Browse** method sets it to enable multifile selection and other capabilities appropriate to a Browse dialog box.

3. Two custom properties of a **Form** object associated with the **Browse** method, **DlgCaption** and **BtnCaption**, are set to either the value of the **Title** argument or to the default **String** value of "Browse".

4. A **Timer** object is started to run the asynchronous thread that will customize the appearance and behavior of the Open dialog box.

5. The **GetOpenFileName** Windows API function displays the dialog box, and code execution in the method pauses on that line to await the returned **String** value.

If you run the example code for the **Browse** method in the class library's Help file (EFS.HLP) under Windows 95, the customized/subclassed common dialog box shown in Figure 18.1 is displayed.

There are several noteworthy subclassed features of the common dialog box in Figure 18.1. First, it is displayed in the center of the screen. Second, the default button has the caption *Browse* (the normal caption is *Open*).

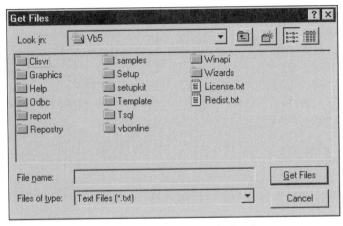

Figure 18.1   **Browse** method's customized common dialog box.

Third, if you type a backslash character or a semicolon in the file name text box, the common dialog box displays the message box in Figure 18.2. Fourth, you can type a wildcard entry in the file name text box (for example, *.DIB) and, when you select the Browse button, the common dialog box closes and returns a **String** value that is parsed by the **Browse** method and returned to the client application where it can be read, as in Figure 18.3.

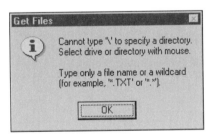

Figure 18.2   **Browse** method's warning message box.

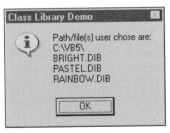

Figure 18.3   Wildcard selection returned from **Browse** method.

Every Windows programmer familiar with the behavior of the Open common dialog box knows that the four characteristics just described are not part of its normal behavior. How does the **Browse** method do this and, in effect, subclass features of a common dialog box over which it supposedly can have no control? I'll explain how this is done in the next section.

Subclassing The Common Dialog Box

The code that subclasses the behavior of the Open common dialog box is in the **Timer** object in frm32ComDlg. This **Timer** object's code starts an asynchronous thread before the common dialog box is displayed and is triggered by the following statement in the **Browse** method:

```
frm32ComDlg.tmrSetProps.Interval = 1
```

The code in the **Timer** event procedure of the **Timer** object is shown in Listing 18.3. There are three general points that you need to understand about this code. First, it is used by many of the methods of the **File** object. Second, it is only used when the book's ActiveX component is run under Windows 95. Other code and techniques are used when the operating system is Windows NT or Windows 3.x. Third, the **Form** object containing the **Timer** is loaded but never displayed.

Listing 18.3   Timer object's code that runs customization thread.

```
Private Sub tmrSetProps_Timer()

    ' Constants for Windows API functions:
    Const GW_CHILD = 5
    Const GW_HWNDNEXT = 2
    Const SWP_NOSIZE = &H1
    Const SWP_NOZORDER = &H4
    Const WM_GETTEXT = &HD
    Const WM_SETTEXT = &HC

    ' Constants for literals:
    Const ONE_HALF = 0.5

    ' Variables:
    Dim Msg          As String
    Dim DlgCapt      As String
    Dim BtnCapt      As String
    Dim Files        As String
    Dim PrevText     As String
    Dim Buff         As String * 200
    Dim Pos1         As Byte
    Dim Pos2         As Byte
```

```
Dim Centered    As Boolean
Dim WildCard    As Boolean
Dim Warning     As Boolean
Dim X           As Long
Dim Y           As Long
Dim HWndCmDlg   As Long
Dim HWndCtl     As Long
Dim HWndBtn     As Long
Dim HWndEdit    As Long
Dim Wnd         As RECT
Dim Scr         As RECT

DlgCapt = fDlgCaption

If DlgCapt = "Find" Then
    BtnCapt = "F&ind"
Else
    BtnCapt = "&" & fBtnCaption
End If

Do
    DoEvents

    If Not Centered Then
        HWndCmDlg = FindWindow("#32770", DlgCapt)
        If HWndCmDlg <> False Then
            SetForegroundWindow HWndCmDlg
            GetWindowRect HWndCmDlg, Wnd
            GetWindowRect GetDesktopWindow, Scr
            X = ((Scr.Rgt - Scr.Lft) - (Wnd.Rgt - Wnd.Lft)) _
                * ONE_HALF
            Y = ((Scr.Bot - Scr.Top) - (Wnd.Bot - Wnd.Top)) _
                * ONE_HALF
            SetWindowPos HWndCmDlg, vbEmpty, _
                        X, Y, vbEmpty, vbEmpty, _
                        SWP_NOZORDER Or SWP_NOSIZE
            Centered = True

            If BtnCapt = "&Color" Or BtnCapt = "&Print" Then
                LockWindowUpdate False
                GoTo Finish
            Else
                Exit Do
            End If
        End If
    End If
Loop

HWndCtl = GetWindow(HWndCmDlg, GW_CHILD)

Do
    DoEvents
    SendMsg HWndCtl, WM_GETTEXT, Len(Buff), Buff
```

```
        If Left$(Buff, 5) = "&Open" Or _
            Left$(Buff, 5) = "&Save" Then
                HWndBtn = HWndCtl
                SendMsg HWndBtn, WM_SETTEXT, vbEmpty, BtnCapt
                LockWindowUpdate False

                If fMultiSelect = "N" Then
                   GoTo Finish
                Else
                    Exit Do
                End If

        End If

    HWndCtl = GetWindow(HWndCtl, GW_HWNDNEXT)
Loop

HWndCtl = GetWindow(HWndCmDlg, GW_CHILD)

Do
    DoEvents
    GetClassName HWndCtl, Buff, Len(Buff)

    If Left$(Buff, 4) = "Edit" Then
        HWndEdit = HWndCtl
        Exit Do
    End If

    HWndCtl = GetWindow(HWndCtl, GW_HWNDNEXT)
Loop

Do Until IsWindowVisible(HWndCmDlg) = False
    DoEvents
    SendMsg HWndEdit, WM_GETTEXT, Len(Buff), Buff
    Pos1 = InStr(Buff, "\")
    Pos2 = InStr(Buff, ":")

    If Pos1 <> False Then
        Msg = "Cannot type '\' to specify a directory."
        Warning = True
    ElseIf Pos2 <> False Then
        Msg = "Cannot type ':' to specify a drive."
        Warning = True
    End If

    If Warning Then
        Msg = Msg & vbCr
        Msg = Msg & "Select drive or directory with mouse."
        Msg = Msg & vbCr & vbCr
        Msg = Msg & "Type only a file name or a wildcard"
        Msg = Msg & vbCr
        Msg = Msg & "(for example, '*.TXT' or '*.*')."
        MsgBox Msg, vbInformation, DlgCapt
        SetForegroundWindow HWndCmDlg
```

```
        If Pos1 <> False Then
            PrevText = Left$(Buff, Pos1 - 1)
        ElseIf Pos2 <> False Then
            PrevText = Left$(Buff, Pos2 - 1)
        End If

        SendMsg HWndEdit, WM_SETTEXT, vbEmpty, PrevText
        SetFocusAPI HWndEdit
        SendKeys "{END}", True
        Warning = False
    End If

    If GetFocus = HWndBtn Then
        SendMsg HWndEdit, WM_GETTEXT, Len(Buff), Buff

        If Left$(Buff, 3) = "*.*" And _
            Mid$(Buff, 4, 1) = vbNullChar Then
                WildCard = True
                Files = "WILDCARD.ALL"
        ElseIf Left$(Buff, 2) = "*." And _
            Mid$(Buff, 6, 1) = vbNullChar Then
                WildCard = True
                Files = Left$(Buff, 5)
                Files = "WILDCARD." & Right$(Files, 3)
        End If

        If WildCard Then
            LockWindowUpdate HWndCmDlg
            SendMsg HWndEdit, WM_SETTEXT, vbEmpty, Files
            LockWindowUpdate False
            SendKeys "{ENTER}", True
        End If
    End If
    Loop

Finish:

    tmrSetProps.Enabled = False
    Unload Me

End Sub
```

The **Timer** object's code in Listing 18.3 works in this order:

1. It reads the settings of frm32ComDlg's two custom properties, **DlgCaption** and **BtnCaption**, and uses them to determine which method is running and what captions are to be used.

2. The code in the first **Do** loop uses the Windows API function **FindWindow** to begin searching for the common dialog box's window by class name (#32770) and caption. When the **GetOpenFileName** Windows API function back in the **Browse** method displays the

dialog box, the **Do** loop finds the window and centers it. We have discussed the **GetWindowRect**, **GetDesktopWindow**, and **SetWindowPos** API functions before. However, there is one new API function that is used in the first **Do** loop, **SetForegroundWindow**, which puts the thread that created the common dialog box's window (specified by the argument's handle, **HWndCmDlg**) into the foreground and activates the window. *Note: If the common dialog box being centered is Color or Printer, code execution is rerouted to the line label Finish and the* **Timer** *object's asynchronous thread is terminated because these two dialog boxes don't require additional subclassing.*

3. The code in the second **Do** loop searches through all the child windows of the common dialog box (its control objects in VB terminology), looking for the button that has the caption *Open* or *Save*. In the case of the **Browse** method, it finds the Open button and changes its caption to *Browse. Note: If the method being run does not require multiselect file capability, additional subclassing is not required and the asynchronous thread is terminated.*

4. The code in the third **Do** loop searches through all the child windows again, looking this time for the one with the class name of **Edit** (that is, the file name text box). When it finds the window, the **Do** loop stores its handle for later use. It is also at this point that screen redrawing is enabled again (remember that it was disabled back in the **Browse** method).

5. The code in the fourth and last **Do** loop runs as long as the common dialog box's window is displayed. It does two things. First, it watches for invalid keystrokes in the file name text box (backslash or semicolon) and, if the user types either one, displays the warning message box. Second, it uses the Windows API function **GetFocus** to determine when the Browse button is clicked. When the user clicks on Browse to close the common dialog box, the loop's code examines the contents of the file name text box. If there is a valid wildcard entry in it, the code changes the entry to one of two arbitrary **String** values (for example, "WILDCARD.ALL") that the **Browse** method's code will recognize and react to. If the entry is the more typical case of a file name or names, it returns them. If the user clicks on Cancel, the loop code also recognizes that the common dialog box's window is closed.

6. When the **Do** loop is done, the two statements under the Finish line label execute and terminate the asynchronous thread.

When you watch, in realtime mode, how the **Browse** method's call to the **GetOpenFileName** Windows API function and the code in the **Timer** object work together, it almost seems like magic! Not only is the code able to subclass the appearance and behavior of a Windows object that is not even part of the class library's ActiveX component, but the speed at which the common dialog box is displayed is improved by about 100 percent.

When the user finally clicks on the Browse or Cancel button and the modal common dialog box is closed, code execution resumes back in the **Browse** method. We'll discuss the portion of the code there that parses the **String** value returned from the **GetOpenFileName** Windows API function next.

PARSING THE COMMON DIALOG BOX'S STRING

When the user clicks on Browse or Cancel in the Browse common dialog box, his or her selection is returned in the **FileName** element of the OPENFILENAME user-defined data type. After the selection is trimmed of spaces and Null characters, it is assigned to the variable **FileSpec**. **FileSpec** can be one of these four general kinds of **String** values:

- "WILDCARD.ALL", signifying all file names on the current path.
- "WILDCARD.*" (for example, WILDCARD.HLP), signifying all file names matching the specified file extension.
- "" or **vbNullString**, signifying that the user selected Cancel.
- The path and name of a file or files.

The code in Listing 18.4 deals with these four possible cases and does the appropriate parsing.

Listing 18.4   Code that parses the string returned from the common dialog.

```
Function Browse(Optional Filter, _
                Optional Title)

    . . .

    If InStr(FileSpec, "WILDCARD.ALL") Then

        WildCard = True
        Pos = InStr(FileSpec, "WILDCARD.ALL")
        Src = Left$(FileSpec, Pos - 1) & "*.*"
        SrcPath = Left$(FileSpec, Pos - 1)

    ElseIf InStr(FileSpec, "WILDCARD") Then
```

```
        WildCard = True
        Pos = InStr(FileSpec, "WILDCARD")
        Src = Left$(FileSpec, Pos - 1) & "*." & Right$(FileSpec, 3)
        SrcPath = Left$(FileSpec, Pos - 1)

    End If

    If WildCard Then
        CL.ParseFiles1 Src, SrcPath, PROC, vbNullString, Files()
        InitializeVars Delimiter, SrcPath, FilesDone

        For Each File In Files
            UpdateInfo File, Src, SrcPath, Delimiter, _
                      UBound(Files), NumDone, FileDone, FilesDone
        Next File

        Browse = ReturnFiles(NumDone, FileDone, FilesDone)

    ElseIf FileSpec <> NONE Then

        AddSlashToRetPath FileSpec
        Browse = Array(True, FileSpec)

    ElseIf FileSpec = NONE Then
        Browse = Array(True, FileSpec)
    End If

    Exit Function

ET:

    If Err = SYNTAX Then Browse = frmErrCodes.Codes
    If Err <> SYNTAX Then Browse = CL.TrapErr(PROC)

End Function
```

The parsing code block in Listing 18.4 (or something very similar to it) is used by almost all the public members of the **File** object. I am not going to discuss it in detail because it does not demonstrate any new OOP techniques or Windows API functions, and it is fairly straightforward. It calls the **ParseFiles1** method of the **CL** class and several private methods of the **File** object (**InitializeVars**, **UpdateInfo**, and **AddSlashToRetPath**). These methods are also used by other members of the **File** object.

The end result of this parsing code block is to return a **String** value to the client application that conforms to the specification for the second element returned from the **Browse** method (the first element being **True** to signify that the method succeeded). This specification and the use of the Null character (32-bit) or space character (16-bit) as a delimiter is consistent with the delimiters used and returned by the Open and Save As common dialog boxes for Windows 95/NT 4 and Windows 3.x.

Of course, the client application's programmer has to write a little code to check the **String** value returned in the second element, see if it has any delimiters in it, and parse them out if required. But, even if you used the **CommonDialog** ActiveX control, you would still have to do this. The important point here is that when you write a member that is part of a reusable application framework, you should always write the code so that the way it behaves is consistent with the conventional, existing usage for that part of the application framework.

It would have been easier for me to write the **Browse** method to always return the **String** value with a **vbNullChar** delimiter, regardless of whether it ran under 32-bit or 16-bit Windows. However, then the **Browse** method would not have been as easy to reuse for the client application programmer, who expects the 16-bit **CommonDialog** ActiveX control to return a **String** value delimited by the space character.

Implementing An ActiveX Component's Thread With A Separate EXE File

As I mentioned earlier in the chapter, the **GetOpenFileName** and **GetSaveFileName** Windows API functions do not work under Windows NT. When I try to call them, the common dialog box is not displayed and **False** is returned, just as if the user had selected Cancel. Then, when I call the Windows API function **CommDlgExtendedError** to get more detailed error information, it returns an error code (2 - CDERR_INITIALIZATION). The Visual C++ Help file API32.HLP says that the error code CDERR_INITIAL-IZATION means that some kind of out-of-memory condition was encountered, causing the Windows API function to fail.

This error code explanation is nonsense (I have plenty of RAM and a huge swap file on my PC) and reminds me of the old days with Microsoft Word for Windows 2.0, when any runtime error that could not be specifically pinned down by the Microsoft development team was attributed to a lack of memory. If anyone out there knows the real problem (and, preferably, a workaround) with calling **GetOpenFileName** or **GetSaveFileName** from Windows NT, I'd love to hear about it via email.

Sometimes, however, necessity turns out to be the mother of invention (as the clever mother of some programmer must have once said). Although I cannot call the API functions from Windows NT, I can use the **CommonDialog** ActiveX control contained on the frmComDlg **Form** object, in the same way as the **SelectFont** method used it. In order to subclass the appearance and behavior of the common dialog boxes, I use essentially the same code as you saw in Listing 18.3; but, instead of putting it in a **Timer** object within the class library's ActiveX component, I wrote it in a separate executable file.

The **Browse** method runs this executable, NTCOMDLG.EXE, with VB's **Shell** function, just before it displays the Open or Save As common dialog boxes from frmComDlg. When it runs the executable, it passes to it, as part of its command line, the captions for the title bar and default button of the common dialog box. The code that runs NTCOMDLG.EXE and passes these caption **String** values is shown here:

```
DlgCapt = Title
BtnCapt = "|" & PROC
Shell App.Path & "\NTCOMDLG " & DlgCapt & BtnCapt & "|Y"
```

A statement in the **Sub Main** procedure of NTCOMDLG.EXE starts a **Timer** object that is contained by a **Form** object that is never displayed. From there, the code in the **Timer** object's **Timer** event procedure runs exactly the same as the code shown in Listing 18.3, except for the first few lines. These few lines of code, shown in Listing 18.5, parse the captions passed in as part of the command line of the executable and assign them to variables that are used by the rest of the routine. These variables serve the same purpose as the custom properties **DlgCaption** and **BtnCaption** do when the **Browse** method is called from Windows 95.

Listing 18.5   Code that parses the command line of NTCOMDLG.EXE.

```
Private Sub tmrSetProps_Timer()

    . . .

    If Right$(Command, 2) = "|Y" Then
        MultiSelect = True
        CommandStr = Left$(Command, Len(Command) - 2)
    ElseIf Right$(Command, 2) = "|N" Then
        CommandStr = Left$(Command, Len(Command) - 2)
    Else
        CommandStr = Command
    End If

    Pos1 = InStr(CommandStr, PIPE)
```

```
DlgCapt = Mid$(CommandStr, 1, Pos1 - OFFSET)
BtnCapt = Mid$(CommandStr, Pos1 + OFFSET)


 . . .


End Sub
```

This technique of implementing an ActiveX component's thread with a separate EXE file is used by many of the other members of the **File** class when they need the services of a common dialog box and are being called from Windows NT. If you're running the class library from 16-bit VB4 and Windows 3.x, the name of the executable that is called is 16COMDLG.EXE.

This technique is obviously an inelegant kludge; but it works and, in some cases, it may be the best solution available. For example, another situation where this approach might come in handy would be to display, from an ActiveX component, the percentages of system resources available under Windows 95. The 16-bit Windows API provided the **GetFreeSystemResources** function to do this, but it was not included in the 32-bit API. Under the Windows NT architecture, this doesn't matter because the three kinds of system resources (USER, GDI, and system) all remain unchanged at 90 percent. Under Windows 95, however, these percentages gradually decrease as you open more applications.

One way that you could find these percentages would be to write a small EXE file with 16-bit VB that uses the **GetFreeSystemResources** function to determine their values. You would then call this executable from a public member of a 32-bit ActiveX component and run a loop within the member until the percentages were determined by the EXE file and copied to the Windows clipboard in a string. The member's looping code would keep reading the contents of the clipboard until it found the percentages/string and would then return them to the client application.

Displaying Explorer's File Finder

As we have discussed before, creating an application framework for Windows dictates that you reuse as much of the operating system's existing functionality as possible. As an ActiveX component developer, you want to do this for two reasons. First, the user is familiar with the Windows operating system and expects that any Windows application will conform with its conventions and resources. Second, using existing functionality reduces the size of your ActiveX class library and the amount of time required to develop it.

A good example of an existing Windows application that can easily be called and reused from an ActiveX component is the File Finder application included with Windows 95 and Windows NT 4. Most users of the Windows 95-style shell open the File Finder window from the Explorer and then use it to find the location of a single file or files of any kind. To do this from the book's class library, you can call the **FindFile** public method of the **Utility** class. Its code is shown in Listing 18.6.

Listing 18.6   The FindFile method's code.

```
Function FindFile()

    ' Constants for Windows API functions:
    Const SW_RESTORE = 9

    ' Constants for literals:
    Const PROC = "FindFile"
    Const SYNTAX = True

    ' Variables:
    Dim WasIconic     As Boolean
    Dim HWndExplorer  As Variant

    ' Enable error handler and do syntax checking:
    On Error GoTo ET

    If cRAOServer Then
        E.TrapSyntax 1, PROC, "ActiveX RAO component"
    ElseIf Not CL.IsWin95Shell Then
        E.TrapSyntax 1, PROC, "old Windows shell"
    End If


    ' Execute member's algorithm--
    ' * Try to find Explorer's handle.
    ' * If it does not exist, open it and find handle.
    ' * If it does exist:
    '     a) If it is iconized, restore it to normal display state.
    '     b) Give it focus.
    '     c) Send it menu accelerator keystrokes to open utility.
    '     d) If it was previously iconized, minimize it again.
    HWndExplorer = FindWindow("ExploreWClass", 0&)

    If HWndExplorer = False Then
        WinExec "EXPLORER.EXE", vbNormalFocus

        Do Until HWndExplorer <> False
            HWndExplorer = FindWindow("ExploreWClass", 0&)
        Loop
    Else

        If IsIconic(HWndExplorer) Then
            WasIconic = True
```

```
        ShowWindow HWndExplorer, SW_RESTORE
    End If
End If

SetForegroundWindow HWndExplorer
SendKeys "%(TFF)", True

If WasIconic Then ShowWindow HWndExplorer, vbMinimizedNoFocus

FindFile = Array(True)
Exit Function

ET:

If Err = SYNTAX Then FindFile = frmErrCodes.Codes
If Err <> SYNTAX Then FindFile = CL.TrapErr(PROC)

End Function
```

The **FindFile** method's code is really quite easy to understand. After doing some syntax checking, it checks whether the Explorer is running or not. If it is running, Windows API functions (**IsIconic** and **ShowWindow**) check if Explorer is minimized and, if so, display it normally. If it is not running, the Windows API function **WinExec** starts it. At this point, **SetForegroundWindow** gives the Explorer window the focus. Then, I use the simple but effective syntax of VB's **SendKeys** statement to select its Tools I Find I Files or Folders menu command, which displays the Find: All Files window shown in Figure 18.4. Finally, the **FindFile** method returns control to the client application that called it.

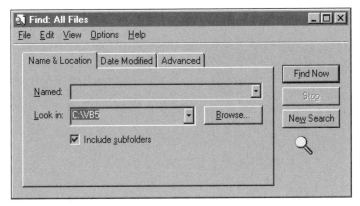

Figure 18.4 Explorer's File Finder window.

In some situations, the **FindFile** method may be all the client application's user needs. However, as it is currently coded, **FindFile** has no way of returning a string specifying the location of any file(s) found by the Explorer's File Finder. It might be possible to write some clever code that would enhance the **FindFile** method and enable it to read the locations that were found. But I decided not to try this approach. Instead, I wrote the **Find** method in the **File** class to create my own customized file finder. We will look at how it works in the next section.

Writing A Custom File Finder

The **Find** method of the **File** class searches for every instance of a file or type of file on a drive and path and returns the information found to the client application. The detailed functionality of the **Find** method is shown in the sidebar.

The Find method's specifications.

SYNTAX

```
Object.Find(FileSpec)
```

The **Find** method's syntax has the following object qualifier and named argument:

- *Object*. Required. **Object** data type. An expression that evaluates to an object in the Applies To pop-up list.

- *FileSpec*. Required. **String** data type. An expression that evaluates to the string "FileDialog" or that specifies the path and name of a file or type of file to process. If "FileDialog" is passed, a common dialog box is displayed from where the user can select the drive and root path and type the file name or file wildcard. If "FileDialog" is not passed, the **Find** method parses the string for the path-and-file name formats that are supported. See *Settings* for a description of the supported formats.

SETTINGS

The *FileSpec* argument's possible settings are:

- Common Dlg. **String** expression that evaluates to "FileDialog". The **Find** method displays a common dialog box where the user can select the drive and root path and type the file name or wildcard (for example, "*.CLS" or "*.*").

- One File. **String** expression that evaluates to an existing path and file name. For example, "C:\FILE.CLS" finds all instances of the file named FILE.CLS on the root path of drive C and any of its subdirectories; or "C:\VBCLSLIB\FILE.CLS" finds all instances of the file named FILE.CLS on the path C:\VBCLSLIB\ and any of its subdirectories (if they exist).

- File Type. **String** expression that evaluates to an existing path and a wildcard. For example, "C:*.CLS" finds all instances of files with the extension .CLS on the root path of drive C and any of its subdirectories; or "C:\VBCLSLIB*.*" finds all files on the path C:\VBCLSLIB\ and any of its subdirectories (if they exist).

CALLED

From any procedure in a client application.

RETURNS

Upon success, two elements in a **Variant**. The elements contain these subtypes:

- 0 - MBR_SUCCESS. A **Boolean** (**True**) that specifies the member executed successfully.

- 1 - MBR_FILES. If the *FileSpec* argument specifies "FileDialog" and the user chooses Cancel from the common dialog box, the return value is **vbNullString** (that is, a zero-length string); otherwise, a **String** that specifies the instance(s) of the file name or type of file found. If no instance is found, **vbNullString**. If the *FileSpec* argument specifies "FileDialog" and more than one instance is found, the file names returned are delimited either by **vbNullChar** (that is, a Null character) for 32-bit Visual Basic, or by a space character for 16-bit Visual Basic. The use of these delimiters to separate the file names is consistent with the delimiters used by the Open and Save As common dialog boxes for Windows 95/NT 4.0 and Windows 3.x.

Upon failure, eight elements in a **Variant**. The elements contain the error codes that the class library returns when a runtime or syntax error occurs during the execution of one of its members.

REMARKS

- If you pass its *FileSpec* argument the string "FileDialog", the **Find** method's common dialog box does not allow you to type a drive and/or path. You must select the drive and path with the mouse. Also, you must type the file name (or a wildcard) because the common dialog box does not allow you to select a file name with the mouse.

- While the **Find** method does its search, it displays a modal dialog box with a progress bar and a Cancel button. If you cancel the search, the **Find** method returns **vbNullString** in its MBR_FILES element.

- If you call the **Find** method from a **File** object instantiated from an out-of-process ActiveX component and pass its *FileSpec* argument the string "FileDialog", you should first apply Visual Basic's **Hide** method to the **Form** object in the client application from whose code you call the method. After the user closes the common dialog box, you can apply Visual Basic's **Show** method to redisplay the **Form** object. The reason this is necessary is because the out-of-process ActiveX component's **Find** method displays the common dialog box modelessly, instead of modally as would be the case with the in-process ActiveX component. Hiding the client application's **Form** object prevents the user from calling another member in the ActiveX component (and thus getting the *Component Request Pending* message) until the common dialog box is closed.

Understanding The Find Method's Code

Although the specifications of the **Find** method appear to be pretty complicated, the way the code works is fairly easy to understand. In its most common usage with the **FileSpec** argument set to "FileDialog", it runs the same kind of code we covered under the **Browse** method. In the case of the **Find** method, however, this code is contained in the separate private **GetFiles** method of the **File** object and it displays a specially subclassed Find common dialog box, as shown in Figure 18.5. You should note that this subclassed common dialog box does not show any file names and displays the customized message *Select path and type file name/wildcard* in the Files of type list. These visual indicators prompt the user that this common dialog box is being used as a File Finder.

After the user types the file name or a wildcard and clicks on the Find button, the **Find** method parses the **String** value returned from the subclassed common dialog box and calls a routine in its frmFind associated **Form** object. This routine uses a recursive search algorithm and, while it is running, displays the progress bar shown in Figure 18.6.

After the recursive search run by its associated **Form** object is done, the **Find** method parses the paths and names of all the instances of the file or file type that were found and returns them as a **String** value to the client application.

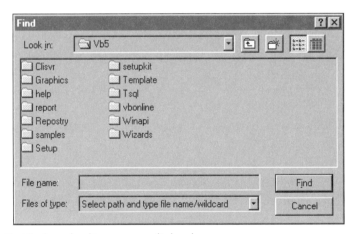

Figure 18.5   **Find** method's common dialog box.

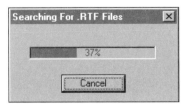

Figure 18.6   **Find** method's progress bar.

Because the code that calls and performs the recursive search is the only part of the **Find** method and its associated **Form** object that uses techniques you haven't seen before in the book; that's what we'll focus on in this chapter.

After the **Find** method has the path and file/file type to search for, which it gets either from the common dialog box or passed in as the **FileSpec** argument, it sets a **Boolean** flag named **Continue** to **True**. The rest of the code in the **Find** method, which displays its associated progress bar **Form** object and reads the returned value, is shown in Listing 18.7.

Listing 18.7   The Find method's code that displays the progress bar.

```
Function Find(FileSpec As String)

    . . .

    If Continue Then

        If SrcPath = vbNullString Then SrcPath = CurDir

        SrcPath = CL.AddSlashToDir(SrcPath)
        frmFind.CurPath = SrcPath
        frmFind.FileName = Mid$(FileNames, Len(SrcPath) + 1)

        #If Win32 Then
            frmFind.Delimiter = vbNullChar
        #Else
            frmFind.Delimiter = Chr$(vbKeySpace)
        #End If

        frmFind.Show vbModal
        FilesFound = frmFind.FileNames

        If FilesFound <> NONE Then
            FilesFound = Left$(FilesFound, Len(FilesFound) - 1)
        End If

        Unload frmFind
    End If

    Find = Array(True, FilesFound)
    Exit Function

ET:
    If Err = SYNTAX Then Find = frmErrCodes.Codes
    If Err <> SYNTAX Then Find = CL.TrapErr(PROC)

End Function
```

Before the **Find** method displays the frmFind **Form** object, whose code runs the recursive search, it first sets the **CurPath**, **FileName**, and **Delimiter** custom properties of frmFind. Then it displays the frmFind progress bar modally. Once the progress bar's form is loaded and displayed, code execution reroutes itself to the **dirFind_Change** event procedure, where the actual recursion routine is located. This recursion code is pretty complex; so, rather than put it all in one uninterrupted code listing, we'll analyze it piece by piece.

The first thing the recursion routine does is declare its constants and variables:

```
Private Sub dirFind_Change()

    ' Constants for literals:
    Const NONE = vbNullString
    Const ATTRBS = vbHidden + vbSystem

    ' Variables:
    Dim Path           As String
    Dim File           As String
    Dim PathFile       As String
    Dim SubDir         As Integer
    Dim NumSubDirs     As Integer
    Static DoneOnce    As Boolean
    Static NumDirs     As Integer
    Static Progress    As Integer
    Static Dirs()      As String

    . . .
```

Then, after ensuring that the current setting of the **DirListBox** object's **Path** property ends with a backslash character, it uses VB's **Dir$** function to check for the existence of a file (including system and hidden files) on the current directory which matches the file or file type specified by the **FileName** custom property. If there is a match, its path and name is stored in the form-level variable **fFileNames**:

```
    . . .

    Path = dirFind.Path

    If Right$(Path, 1) <> "\" Then Path = Path + "\"

    PathFile = Path & fFileName
    File = Dir$(PathFile, ATTRBS)
```

```
If File <> NONE Then
   fFileNames = fFileNames & Path & File & fDelimiter
End If
```

. . .

The following code repeats the **Dir$** function and continues to check for other matches in the current directory, concatenating/assigning any matches to **fFileNames**. The routine then gets the number of subdirectories on the current directory and sizes the dynamic array **SubDirs()** to hold them:

. . .

```
Do While File <> NONE

   File = Dir$

   If File <> NONE Then
      fFileNames = fFileNames & Path & File & fDelimiter
   End If

Loop

NumSubDirs = dirFind.ListCount
ReDim SubDirs(NumSubDirs) As String
```

. . .

If it is the first time through the recursion algorithm, the routine gets the number of directories on the root directory being searched and stores them in the dynamic **Dirs()** array. This number is later used to update the progress bar each time a directory on the root directory is searched:

. . .

```
If Not DoneOnce Then

   NumDirs = dirFind.ListCount
   ReDim Preserve Dirs(NumDirs) As String

   For SubDir = 0 To NumDirs - 1
      Dirs(SubDir) = dirFind.List(SubDir)
   Next SubDir

   DoneOnce = True

End If
```

. . .

If the current directory is on the root directory of the search, the progress bar is updated and the counter is incremented. There is a separate subroutine called **UpdateBar** that uses a **PictureBox** object and the Windows API function **BitBlt** to update the progress bar (see Listing 18.8 at the end of the chapter for **UpdateBar**'s code):

```
. . .

For SubDir = 0 To NumDirs - 1

   If dirFind.Path = Dirs(SubDir) Then
      UpdateBar picProgress, NumDirs
      Progress = Progress + 1
   End If

Next SubDir

. . .
```

Next, the routine stores all subdirectory names on the current directory in the **SubDirs()** array:

```
. . .

For SubDir = 0 To NumSubDirs - 1
   SubDirs(SubDir) = dirFind.List(SubDir)
Next SubDir

. . .
```

The last loop in the routine actually executes and calls the recursion. Each time the path of the **DirListBox** object dirFind is changed to another subdirectory with the **dirFind.Path = SubDirs(SubDir)** statement, the **dirFind_Change** event procedure is called again. This recursive search continues until the routine has drilled down to the last subdirectory on the root search path:

```
. . .

For SubDir = 0 To NumSubDirs - 1

   DoEvents

   If fCancel Then
      fFileNames = vbNullString
      Exit Sub
   End If

   dirFind.Path = SubDirs(SubDir)
```

```
Next SubDir

    . . .

End Sub
```

You should note that, in the last loop, there is a **DoEvents** statement that permits the user to select the Cancel button on the progress bar form and terminate the search. If this happens, code in the **cmdCancel_Click** event procedure sets the form-level flag **fCancel** to **True**. The last loop would then read this flag and exit the **dirFind_Change** event procedure.

Depending on how the recursive search is completed, code in either the **cmdCancel_Click** or the **Form_Resize** event procedure applies VB's **Hide** method to the progress bar **Form** object. Invoking the **Hide** method causes code execution to revert to the statement in the **Find** method immediately following the statement that modally displayed the progress bar's form. It's then a simple matter for the **Find** method to read the **FileNames** custom property of **frmFind** (where all the found instances were stored), unload frmFind, and return the concatenated/delimited **String** value to the client application, which then reads the **String** value and uses it as is appropriate.

The example code contained in the **Find** method's help topic in EFS.HLP parses the **String** value and displays the found instances in a **ListBox** object, as shown in Figure 18.7. If you are interested in seeing how to create a progress bar without using Microsoft's 32-bit **ProgressBar** ActiveX custom control, check out the code in Listing 18.8.

That about does it for this chapter. If you worked your way through this chapter's examples from the **File** object, you should have learned a lot about the concept of an OOP application framework for Windows and

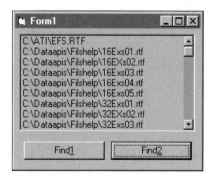

Figure 18.7 Results of search by **Find** method.

how to implement a portion of one. There are several more methods of the **File** object that we did not specifically look at in this or preceding chapters. However, they all utilize the same fundamental techniques that you have already seen. Next up is the portion of the Windows application framework implemented in the **Text** object of this book's ActiveX component. Stay tuned.

Listing 18.8   UpdateBar procedure in frmFind.

```
Sub UpdateBar(Pic As PictureBox, _
              Steps As Integer)

   ' Constants for Windows API functions:
   Const SRCCOPY = &HCC0020

   ' Constants for literals:
   Const ONE_HALF = 0.5
   Const HUNDRED = 100

   ' Variables:
   Dim Lbl         As String
   Dim PrctgPts    As Integer
   Static Progress As Long

   ' * Initialize/update progress bar variables and parameters.
   ' * Adjust CurrentX and CurrentY settings of progress bar.
   ' * Print updated percentage.
   ' * Update line marker.
   ' * Update color band.
   Pic.Cls
   Pic.ScaleWidth = HUNDRED
   PrctgPts = Pic.ScaleWidth / Steps
   Progress = Progress + PrctgPts

   If Progress > Pic.ScaleWidth Then Progress = Pic.ScaleWidth

   Lbl = Format$((Progress / Pic.ScaleWidth * HUNDRED)) + "%"

   Pic.CurrentX = (Pic.ScaleWidth - Pic.TextWidth(Lbl)) * _
                  ONE_HALF
   Pic.CurrentY = (Pic.ScaleHeight - Pic.TextHeight(Lbl)) * _
                  ONE_HALF

   Pic.Print Lbl
   Pic.Line (vbEmpty, vbEmpty)-(Progress, Pic.ScaleHeight), _
            Pic.ForeColor, BF

   If Progress = HUNDRED Then
      Exit Sub
   Else
      BitBlt Pic.hDC, vbEmpty, vbEmpty, Pic.ScaleWidth, _
             Pic.ScaleHeight, Pic.hDC, vbEmpty, vbEmpty, SRCCOPY
   End If

End Sub
```

19

REUSABLE APPLICATION FRAMEWORKS, PART 2

In Chapter 18, we looked at the **File** object, which is part of a reusable application framework designed for the Windows operating system. In this chapter, we will continue to explore how VB5 and the OOP programming methodology can support the development of application frameworks by focusing on the **Text** class of the book's ActiveX component. The **Text** class subclasses and manipulates Visual Basic objects that contain text and performs the tasks related to the conventional Windows Edit and Format menus for a client application.

In particular, we will study the **Edit** and **Format** methods of the **Text** class. At this point in the evolution of Windows, everyone should be pretty familiar with the conventional Edit and Format menus of a Windows application, but just in case you've had a severe memory lapse, take a look at Figure 19.1, which shows the Word for Windows Edit menu.

The **Edit** method of the book's class library demonstrates how far you can carry the concept of reusable application frameworks by replicating all of the essential functionality of

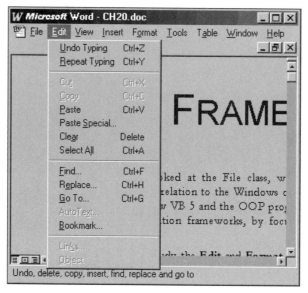

Figure 19.1 The Word for Windows Edit menu.

the Edit menu used in Word for Windows. Likewise, the **Format** method implements many of the standard formatting features that Windows users have come to expect in a rich text editor application.

In this chapter, we will also use several members of the **Text** class to discuss individual OOP techniques and tricks. Specifically, you will see how to:

- Use the **SendMessage** Windows API function, instead of VB's **Clipboard** object-related methods, to implement the Undo, Cut, Copy, and Paste commands.
- Create reusable, full-featured find-and-replace dialog boxes that are encapsulated in an ActiveX component.
- Create reusable, full-featured Go To and Change Case dialog boxes that are encapsulated in an ActiveX component.

Understanding The Design Of The Text Class

The **Text** class in the book's ActiveX component is designed to serve three general purposes. First, it performs the functions conventionally associated with the Edit and Format menu items of the Windows operating system. Second, it loads files into text-related control objects and saves the contents of these control objects to files. Third, it manipulates the contents of **String** variables.

To meet these three objectives, the **Text** class is currently composed of 10 public members, which are described in detail in Table 19.1.

With regard to its design, there are several interesting points to note about the **Text** class. First, consider its **Save** and **Load** members, which do file I/O on text-related control objects. These members perform the functions of the Windows File menu's Save command and the loading of a recently used file (the path and name of which are typically displayed at the bottom of the File menu). I bet you're wondering why I put these members in the **Text** class if they perform file-related functions. The answer is quite simple: The design decision was largely determined by my desire to implement the **Load** and **Save** methods in a polymorphic fashion (they also apply to the **Graphic** and **List** objects of the book's class library).

Table 19.1   The public members of the **Text** class.

Member	Description
Edit	Performs the conventional operations of the Windows Edit menu (Undo, Redo, Cut, Copy, Paste, Find, Replace, and so on); 32-bit only.
Format	Performs the conventional operations of the Windows Format menu (select a font; set text to bold, italic, underline, and so on; set the case of text).
IsModified	Checks if the contents of a text-related control object have been changed.
Load	Loads a file into a text-related control object.
Replace	Replaces all instances of a string within the contents of a text-related control object (or within a String variable) with another string.
Reverse	Reverses the characters of the contents of a text-related control object or in a String variable.
Save	Saves the contents of a text-related control object to a file.
SelectFont	Displays the Font common dialog box and returns information about the user's selection(s).
SetModify	Turns a text-related control object's modify flag on or off.
SetReadOnly	Turns a text-related control object's read-only flag on or off.

Second, most of the members of the **Text** class are described as applying to text-containing control objects. In their current implementation, this includes VB's **RichTextBox** and **TextBox** objects. But, because of the design of the public interface of these members, I can easily add code to them in the future that would enable them to work with other objects (for example, a third-party software vendor's ActiveX control that processes text or the **Microsoft Word Document** ActiveX control).

This second point suggests a broader definition and use of the term polymorphism. In the technical OOP sense, if two or more classes (for example, **Graphic**, **List**, and **Text**) have methods that share the same name, take the same arguments, and have the same basic purpose but are implemented differently, the methods (**Load** and **Save**) are said to be polymorphic. But a kind of polymorphism can also be built in to individual methods (for example, **Edit**, **Format**, and **Replace**) that enables them to be applied to several possible VB control objects. We could coin the terms *primary polymorphism* and *secondary polymorphism* to describe these two different kinds of polymorphism.

Microsoft has an interesting discussion of polymorphism in the VB *Programmer's Guide*. In the section titled *How Visual Basic Provides Polymorphism*, the Guide stresses that VB doesn't use inheritance to provide polymorphism. Instead, it states that VB provides polymorphism through multiple ActiveX interfaces or controls (for example, the **RichTextBox**, **TextBox**, and **Microsoft Word Document** control objects). The term *secondary polymorphism*, as I use it in the preceding paragraph, is akin to Microsoft's description of polymorphism in the VB *Programmer's Guide*.

Third, most of the methods of the **Text** class (**IsModified**, **Load**, **Replace**, **Reverse**, **Save**, **SetModify**, and **SetReadOnly**) are similar to the methods of the **List** class in one generic respect. Just as the methods of the **List** class subclassed VB's **ListBox** and **ComboBox** objects, the methods of the **Text** class subclass VB's **RichTextBox** and **TextBox** control objects by adding functionality to them that Microsoft's VB development team did not implement.

Implementing The Windows Edit Menu

Of all the methods in the book's class library, the one that exhibits the most complex and powerful functionality and yet has a simple and easy-to-use public interface is the **Edit** method of the **Text** object. The design and implementation of the **Edit** method is a classic example of the aesthetic choices that a developer must make when writing a class library.

If you asked six different VB developers to implement the functionality of the Windows Edit menu as part of a class library and application framework, you can imagine just how diverse the eventual results would be. The key issue is not whether one implementation is right and another is wrong; rather, it is which implementation best promotes the high-level objective of the OOP methodology, which is to foster reuse of the code by as many VB application developers as possible.

Demonstrating The Edit Method

Before we analyze the specifications of the **Edit** method, it helps to actually see what it does first. This way, its specifications make more sense. To demonstrate the **Edit** method, follow these steps:

1. Start VB5 and select the Existing tab of the New Project dialog box.

2. Select the project file EDIT.VBP, which should be on the path C:\VBOOPEFS\VBCLSDEM, and click on Open.

3. Select Run|Start and the demo code displays a **Form** object with an **Edit** menu, **RichTextBox** and **TextBox** control objects, and a Load File button.

4. Select the Edit menu and let it drop down. The form appears as shown in Figure 19.2.

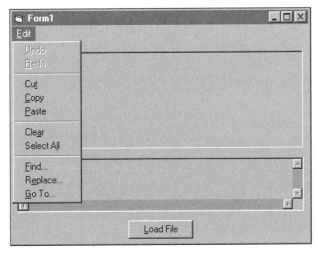

Figure 19.2 The **Edit** method demo's form and menu.

> *Note: The demonstration code in EDIT.VBP is the same as the Example code for the **Edit** method in the book's class library Help file (EFS.HLP). Because the setup of the **Edit** method's example code is a little tricky and requires the creation of two **Menu** control objects, it's easier the first time you run it to use the EDIT.VBP demo project that you installed from the book's CD-ROM.*

If you click on the Load File button, it first calls the **OpenCL** method of the **File** class to display the Open common dialog box. You can select any RTF or TXT file you wish and, after the **OpenCL** method returns a **String** value specifying the selected path and file name, the demo code calls the **Load** method, passing to it values for its two required arguments (that is, the **Name** property of the **RichTextBox** object and the file's name). Note that if you select an RTF file, the **Load** method (as implemented for the **Text** object) displays the message box shown in Figure 19.3, which gives you the option of loading the RTF file in either rich text or plain text format. The corresponding **Save** method also gives you this same option. However, for this demonstration, it doesn't matter how you load the file.

CALLING THE EDIT METHOD

If you look at the code in the **mnuEdit_Click** event procedure of Form1 of EDIT.VBP, shown in Listing 19.1, you can see how simple it is to call the **Edit** method. All you need to do is implement the Edit menu items in your client application as a control array (done in this demonstration in the **Form_Load** event procedure) and use a form-level flag to track which text-related control object has the focus. The flag is set with a single line of code in the **MouseDown** event procedure of each of the text-related controls.

Figure 19.3 Rich text/plain text selection option dialog box.

Listing 19.1   Code to call the Edit method.

```
Private Sub mnuEdit_Click(Index As Integer)

    ' Variables:
    Dim Ctl As Control

    If GotFocus = 1 Then
        Set Ctl = RichTextBox1
    Else
        Set Ctl = Text1
    End If

    ' Call object's member using named arguments:
    Text.Edit TextCtl:=Ctl, Kind:=Index

End Sub
```

REUSING THE CLIPBOARD-RELATED FUNCTIONS

Once a file is loaded, you can select the different Edit menu items to demonstrate how the **Edit** method works. To give the clipboard-related functions a workout, follow this sequence:

1. Select some text and then select Edit|Cut. The **Edit** method removes the selected text from the **RichTextBox** object and copies it to the clipboard.

2. Whoops! You decide you didn't really want to cut that text, so select Edit|Undo Cut and the **Edit** method undoes the Cut operation.

3. Select some text and then select Edit|Copy. The **Edit** method copies the selected text to the clipboard. Then click on the **TextBox** object at the bottom of the form and select Edit|Paste. The **Edit** method pastes the text copied from the **RichTextBox** object into the **TextBox** object.

4. Select Edit|Redo Paste and the **Edit** method repeats the Paste operation.

You can continue in this manner as long as you like, going back and forth between the two text-related controls or working with just one of them.

REUSING THE FIND-AND-REPLACE FUNCTIONS

To put the find-and-replace functions of the **Edit** method through their paces, follow this sequence:

1. Select the **RichTextBox** object at the top of the form.

2. Click on the Load File button and open the file MAPI32.TXT, which is located in the WINAPI subdirectory of the VB5 path.

3. Select Edit | Find. The **Edit** method displays the Find dialog box encapsulated in the book's ActiveX component, as shown in Figure 19.4.

4. Enter the word *Global* in the Find What text box. The Find and Replace buttons are then enabled, as shown in Figure 19.5.

5. Click on the Find button once and watch as the code in the ActiveX component finds the first instance of the word *Global* in the **RichTextBox** object. Each time an instance is found, it is selected and the client application's **Form** object is given the focus (Figure 19.6).

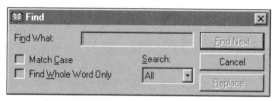

Figure 19.4 Find dialog box as initially displayed.

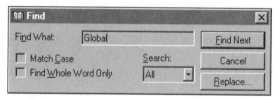

Figure 19.5 Find dialog box after entering a string to find.

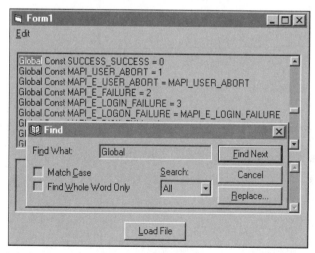

Figure 19.6 Find dialog box and client app's form after string is found.

6. If you click on the Replace button, the Find dialog box expands to the Replace dialog box, as shown in Figure 19.7.

7. Enter the word *Public* in the Replace With text box and click on the Replace All button. The code in the ActiveX component replaces all instances of *Global* with *Public*. At the end of the routine, the message box in Figure 19.8 displays how many replacements were made.

You can continue in this manner as long as you like, moving the focus back and forth between the client application's **Form** object and the Find or Replace dialog box. When you are done, click on Cancel to close the dialog box. You can close the client application's **Form** object while the **Edit** method's Find or Replace dialog box is still open, but, the dialog box will remain open until you close it.

REUSING THE GO TO FUNCTION

To see the Go To function of the **Edit** method in action, follow this sequence:

1. Select the **RichTextBox** object at the top of the form and load it with an RTF or TXT file.

2. Select Edit | Go To. The **Edit** method displays the Go To dialog box encapsulated in the book's ActiveX component, as shown in Figure 19.9.

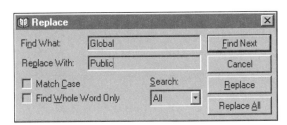

Figure 19.7 Replace dialog box as initially displayed.

Figure 19.8 Message box displaying how many replacements were made.

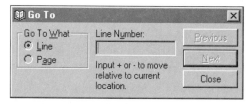

Figure 19.9 Go To dialog box as initially displayed.

3. Enter a line number or a + or - sign followed by the number of lines you want to scroll the text in the **RichTextBox** object.

4. Click on the Go To, Next, or Previous button and watch as the code in the ActiveX component scrolls to the appropriate line, as shown in Figure 19.10.

You can continue in this manner as long as you like, moving the focus back and forth between the client application's **Form** object and the Go To dialog box. When you are done, click on Cancel to close the dialog box.

After working through these demonstrations of the **Text** object's **Edit** method, I think you'll agree that it's a pretty slick implementation and very easy to reuse. At this point, you need to dig into the specifications and code of the **Edit** method to see how this part of the book's reusable application framework was designed and coded. The detailed functionality of the **Edit** method is shown in the sidebar.

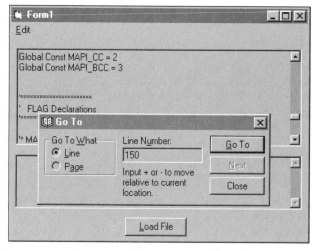

Figure 19.10 The Go To dialog box and client application's form after scrolling to the specified line number.

Edit method's specifications.

SYNTAX

```
Object.Edit(TextCtl, Kind, [Mnu])
```

The **Edit** method's syntax has the following object qualifier and named arguments:

- *Object*. Required. **Object** data type. An expression that evaluates to an object in the Applies To pop-up list.

- *TextCtl*. Required. **Object** data type. An expression that evaluates to the **Name** property of a Visual Basic **RichTextBox** or **TextBox** object.

- *Kind*. Required. **Integer** data type. A value or constant which determines the kind of editing to be done. See *Settings* below for the valid settings of *Kind*.

- *Mnu*. Optional. **Variant** data type whose subtype is an **Object** expression that evaluates to a **Menu** object. *Mnu* is passed if the user wants to have Undo and Redo menu items on an Edit menu; when it is passed, *Kind* must be set to -2 (ED_SETUNDO) or -1 (ED_SETREDO). If omitted, there is no Undo or Redo capability associated with the Cut, Copy, Paste, and Clear operations.

SETTINGS

The *Kind* argument's settings are:

- -2 - ED_SETUNDO. Stores a reference to the **Menu** object for the Undo item. Should be called/passed from the **Form_Load** event procedure.

- -1 - ED_SETREDO. Stores a reference to the **Menu** object for the Redo item. Should be called/passed from the **Form_Load** event procedure.

- 0 - ED_UNDO. Undoes the previous Cut, Copy, Paste, or Clear operation.

- 1 - ED_REDO. Redoes the previous Cut, Copy, Paste, Clear, or Select All operation.

- 3 - ED_CUT. Cuts the selected text from a **TextBox** or **RichTextBox** object to the Windows clipboard.

- 4 - ED_COPY. Copies the selected text from a **TextBox** or **RichTextBox** object to the Windows clipboard.

- 5 - ED_PASTE. Pastes the text from the Windows clipboard to a **TextBox** or **RichTextBox** object.

- 7 - ED_CLEAR. Deletes the selected text from a **TextBox** or **RichTextBox** object.

- 8 - ED_SELALL. Selects all the text in a **TextBox** or **RichTextBox** object.

- 10 - ED_FIND. Displays a dialog box from which you can find the next instance of a string within the text in a **TextBox** or **RichTextBox** object. Must be done from an out-of-process ActiveX component.

- 11 - ED_REPL. Displays a dialog box from which you can replace either the next instance or all instances of a string within the text in a **TextBox** or **RichTextBox** object with another string. Must be done from an out-of-process ActiveX component.

- 12 - ED_GOTO. Displays a dialog box from which you can scroll to the next line(s) or page(s) or to a specified line or page in a **TextBox** or **RichTextBox** object. Must be done from an out-of-process ActiveX component.

CALLED

From any procedure in a client application.

RETURNS

Upon success, one element in a **Variant**. It contains a **Boolean** (**True**) that specifies the member executed successfully.

Upon failure, eight elements in a **Variant**. The elements contain the error codes that the class library returns when a runtime or syntax error occurs during the execution of one of its members.

REMARKS

- Because of limitations in the way the **TextBox** object behaves under 16-bit Visual Basic, the **Edit** method is designed to work only under 32-bit Visual Basic.

- If the *Kind* argument of the **Edit** method is set to 10 - ED_FIND, 11 - ED_REPL, or 12 - ED_GOTO, the **Text** class must be instantiated from an out-of-process ActiveX component. This is because these three settings of the *Kind* argument display a modeless dialog box, and an in-process ActiveX component cannot display a modeless **Form** object under Visual Basic 4.0.

- If the *Kind* argument of the **Edit** method is set to 10 - ED_FIND or 11 - ED_REPL, if it is passed a reference to a **RichTextBox** control object as its *TextCtl* argument, and if the **RichTextBox** contains an RTF file, the Replace All button on the Find/Replace dialog box is disabled. To replace all instances of a string in an RTF file, use the **Load** method of the **Text** object to open the RTF file in plain text format. After making changes/replacements in the file with the **Edit** method, use the **Save** method of the **Text** object to save it either in rich text or plain text format.

The Edit Method's Code

Our analysis of the **Edit** method's code will focus on the three functional groupings of its **Kind** argument, as demonstrated in the previous section. First, we will examine how the **Edit** method uses the **SendMessage** Windows API function to easily implement the clipboard-related cut, copy, and paste functions. Second, we will see how **Edit** displays its associated Find/Replace dialog box and how the routines contained in it work. Third, we'll look at the code that the Go To dialog box uses.

WORKING WITH THE WINDOWS CLIPBOARD

Every VB developer is familiar with VB's **Clipboard** global object and its associated properties and methods. It is not tremendously difficult to write native-VB code that uses the **Clipboard** object's members to implement the cut, copy, paste, and clear algorithms. However, it's so much easier to use the Windows API function **SendMessage** to perform these operations that it's almost a crime that Microsoft does not document this capability somewhere in Visual Basic's Help file or printed documentation.

Before we examine the code in the **Edit** method that actually cuts, copies, pastes, clears, undoes, and redoes, we should look at the initial declarations, the syntax-checking code, and the setup code for the Undo and Redo menu commands. This code is shown in Listing 19.2.

Listing 19.2   The Edit method's initialization code.

```
Function Edit(TextCtl As Object, _
              Kind As Integer, _
              Optional Mnu)

    ' Constants for Windows API functions:
    Const WM_CUT = &H300
    Const WM_COPY = &H301
    Const WM_PASTE = &H302
    Const WM_CLEAR = &H303
    Const WM_UNDO = &H304
    Const WM_SETREDRAW = &HB
    Const EM_GETSEL = &HB0
    Const EM_SETSEL = &HB1
    Const EM_UNDO = &HC7

    ' Constants for Kind argument:
    Const ED_SETUNDO = -2
    Const ED_SETREDO = -1
    Const ED_UNDO = 0
    Const ED_REDO = 1
    Const ED_CUT = 3
    Const ED_COPY = 4
    Const ED_PASTE = 5
    Const ED_CLEAR = 7
    Const ED_SELALL = 8
    Const ED_FIND = 10
    Const ED_REPL = 11
    Const ED_GOTO = 12

    ' Constants for literals:
    Const PROC = "Edit"
    Const SYNTAX = True
    Const NONE = vbNullString

    ' Variables:
    Dim KindOfRedo      As String
    Dim KindOfUndo      As String
    Dim SelTxt          As String
    Dim ClsName         As String
    Dim Operation       As Long
    Static Undo         As Boolean
```

```
Static Redo        As Boolean
Static UndoMenu    As Object
Static RedoMenu    As Object

' Enable error handler and do syntax checking:
On Error GoTo ET

#If Win16 Then
    E.TrapSyntax 1, PROC, "16-bit VB"
#End If

ClsName = TypeName(TextCtl)

Select Case ClsName
    Case "RichTextBox", "TextBox"
    Case Else
        E.TrapSyntax 5, PROC, "TextCtl"
End Select

Select Case Kind
    Case ED_SETUNDO, ED_SETREDO

        If IsMissing(Mnu) Then
            E.TrapSyntax 28, PROC, "Kind", _
                        "-2 (ED_SETUNDO) or -1 (ED_SETREDO)", _
                        "Mnu"
        End If

    Case ED_UNDO, ED_REDO, ED_CUT, ED_COPY, ED_PASTE, ED_CLEAR
    Case ED_SELALL, ED_FIND, ED_REPL, ED_GOTO
    Case Else
        E.TrapSyntax 5, PROC, "Kind"
End Select

If Not IsMissing(Mnu) Then

    If TypeName(Mnu) <> "Menu" Then
        E.TrapSyntax 8, PROC, "Mnu"
    End If

    If Kind <> ED_SETUNDO And _
        Kind <> ED_SETREDO Then
            E.TrapSyntax 21, PROC, "Mnu", "Kind", _
                        "-2 (ED_SETUNDO) or -1 (ED_SETREDO)"
    End If
End If

Select Case Kind
    Case ED_FIND, ED_REPL, ED_GOTO
        If cDLLServer Then
            E.TrapSyntax 1, PROC, "ActiveX DLL component"
        ElseIf cRAOServer Then
            E.TrapSyntax 1, PROC, "ActiveX RAO component"
        End If
```

```
        CL.IsQPro32DLL PROC
End Select

' Execute method and kind of operation:
SendMessage TextCtl.hWnd, WM_SETREDRAW, False, vbEmpty
CL.SetHourglass True

Select Case Kind

    Case ED_SETUNDO
        Set UndoMenu = Mnu
        UndoMenu = False
        Undo = True

    Case ED_SETREDO
        Set RedoMenu = Mnu
        RedoMenu = False
        Redo = True

SendMessage TextCtl.hWnd, WM_SETREDRAW, True, vbEmpty

    . . .

End Function
```

Three points about this code are worthy of discussion. First, Microsoft recommends that you always use constants to make your code more readable. Throughout the class library, I have followed this recommendation, and the **Edit** method clearly illustrates the advantage of doing so. This method's code is pretty extensive and uses many nested control structures. If numeric literals were used instead of the constants, the code would be literally (pardon the lousy pun) unreadable.

Second, the syntax-checking code disallows the use of a local or remote, out-of-process ActiveX component when the Find, Replace, and Go To functions of the **Edit** method are being called. I must emphasize again that this restriction is implemented throughout the book's class library for any method that displays a dialog box. I took this approach only because one of the design objectives of the book's class library was that its source code be able to be compiled under both VB4 and VB5. Remember, though, that VB5 (unlike VB4) also allows you to display modeless dialog boxes from an in-process ActiveX component.

Third, the optional **Mnu** argument of the **Edit** method is not required to implement the cut, copy, paste, and clear functions. In fact, an Edit menu in a client application is not required either (you can also call **Edit** from the event procedures of a toolbar's buttons). You only need to pass **Mnu** if you also want to reuse the Undo and Redo capabilities of the **Edit** method. However, if you do pass **Mnu**, the **Kind** argument must be set to either -2 (ED_SETUNDO) or -1 (ED_SETREDO). Likewise, when the **Kind** argument is set to either -2 (ED_SETUNDO) or -1 (ED_SETREDO), the **Mnu** argument is no longer treated as optional. These kinds of dependent relationships between arguments need to be clearly spelled out via feedback from the method's syntax-checking routine.

The code in the **Edit** method that actually cuts, copies, pastes, and clears is shown in Listing 19.3. As you will see, the Windows API function **SendMessage** does all four of these functions with the same statement. The only variable that changes is the third argument of **SendMessage**, which is set to one of four different Windows API constants that specifies the operation to be done. The majority of the code in Listing 19.3 customizes the captions of the Undo and Redo menu items (if they were earlier passed in to the **Edit** method).

Listing 19.3 The Edit method's cut, copy, paste, and clear code.

```
Function Edit(TextCtl As Object, _
            Kind As Integer, _
            Optional Mnu)

    . . .

    Case ED_CUT, ED_COPY, ED_CLEAR, ED_PASTE

      SelTxt = TextCtl.SelText

      If Kind = ED_CUT Or _
         Kind = ED_COPY Or _
         Kind = ED_CLEAR Then

          If SelTxt <> NONE Then

              If Kind = ED_CUT Then
                 Operation = WM_CUT
              ElseIf Kind = ED_COPY Then
                 Operation = WM_COPY
              Else
                 Operation = WM_CLEAR
              End If
          End If

      ElseIf Kind = ED_PASTE Then

          If Clipboard.GetFormat(vbCFText) Then
             Operation = WM_PASTE
          End If
      End If
```

```
        SendMessage TextCtl.hWnd, Operation, vbEmpty, vbEmpty

    If Undo Then

        UndoMenu = True

        If Kind = ED_CUT Or _
            Kind = ED_CLEAR Then

                If SelTxt <> NONE Then

                    If Kind = ED_CUT Then
                        UndoMenu.Caption = "&Undo Cut"
                    Else
                        UndoMenu.Caption = "&Undo Clear"
                    End If
                End If

        ElseIf Kind = ED_PASTE Then

            If Clipboard.GetFormat(vbCFText) Then
                UndoMenu.Caption = "&Undo Paste"
            End If

        ElseIf Kind = ED_COPY Then
            UndoMenu.Caption = "Can't &Undo"
            UndoMenu = False
        End If
    End If

    If Redo Then

        RedoMenu = True

        If Kind = ED_CUT Then
            RedoMenu.Caption = "&Redo Cut"
        ElseIf Kind = ED_COPY Then
            RedoMenu.Caption = "&Redo Copy"
        ElseIf Kind = ED_PASTE Then

            If Clipboard.GetFormat(vbCFText) Then
                RedoMenu.Caption = "&Redo Paste"
            End If

        ElseIf Kind = ED_CLEAR Then
            RedoMenu.Caption = "&Redo Clear"
        End If
    End If

    If TypeName(TextCtl) = "RichTextBox" Then
        TextCtl.SetFocus
    End If


    . . .


End Function
```

The code that undoes or redoes a previously executed cut, copy, paste, or clear operation is in Listing 19.4. The reversal of an operation is done with the same **SendMessage** Windows API function used in Listing 19.3. The only difference is that its third argument is set to the API constant WM_UNDO. One major advantage of using **SendMessage** instead of VB's **Clipboard**-related syntax is that when you undo an operation, the original selection status of the text that was cut, copied, pasted, or cleared is exactly restored. You would have to write many lines of VB **Clipboard**-related code to achieve this same restoration effect. The repetition of an operation is easily done by recursively calling the **Edit** method itself and setting its **Kind** argument to the constant ED_CUT, ED_COPY, ED_CLEAR, or ED_PASTE.

Listing 19.4 The Edit method's undo and redo code.

```
Function Edit(TextCtl As Object, _
            Kind As Integer, _
            Optional Mnu)


    . . .

    Case ED_UNDO

        If Undo Then

            SendMessage TextCtl.hWnd, WM_UNDO, vbEmpty, vbEmpty

            RedoMenu = True
            KindOfUndo = Mid$(UndoMenu.Caption, 7)
            RedoMenu.Caption = "&Redo " & KindOfUndo
            UndoMenu.Caption = "Can't &Undo"
            UndoMenu = False

            If TypeName(TextCtl) = "RichTextBox" Then
               TextCtl.SetFocus
               TextCtl.Refresh
            End If
        End If

    Case ED_REDO

        If Redo Then
            KindOfRedo = Mid$(RedoMenu.Caption, 7)

            Select Case KindOfRedo
               Case "Cut"
                  Edit TextCtl, ED_CUT
               Case "Copy"
                  Edit TextCtl, ED_COPY
               Case "Paste"
                  Edit TextCtl, ED_PASTE
```

```
            Case "Clear"
                Edit TextCtl, ED_CLEAR
            Case "Select All"
                Edit TextCtl, ED_SELALL
        End Select

        UndoMenu = True
        UndoMenu.Caption = "&Undo " & KindOfRedo

        If TypeName(TextCtl) = "RichTextBox" Then
            TextCtl.SetFocus
        End If

    End If


    . . .


End Function
```

IMPLEMENTING A REUSABLE FIND-AND-REPLACE DIALOG BOX

If the **Kind** argument of the **Edit** method is set to 10 - ED_FIND or 11 - ED_REPL, the Find/Replace **Form** object that is encapsulated in the book's ActiveX component is displayed modelessly. I want to emphasize at the outset of our discussion of these features of the **Edit** method that the slickest aspect of this functionality is not how sophisticated and diverse the find-and-replace routines are (for example, that they provide support for case-sensitive or whole-word searches and for different directions such as all, down, and up). Rather, it is the design of the **Edit** method's public interface, which is very simple and consistent and yet at the same time allows a client application's programmer to access and reuse such sophisticated and diverse features, that is the really cool aspect of how the find-and-replace functionality is implemented.

The code that modelessly displays the find-and-replace **Form** object, shown in Listing 19.5, is straightforward and should be second nature to you at this point in the book. If the **Edit** method's **Kind** argument is set to 10 - ED_FIND, the custom property **TextCtl** of the frmFindReplace **Form** object is assigned the object reference passed to the **TextCtl** argument. This object reference can currently be the **Name** property of either VB's **RichTextBox** or **TextBox** control object. As I mentioned earlier in the chapter, it would be quite easy in the future to enhance the **Edit** method's code to accept another text-related control object, without breaking the existing public interface. If the **Edit** method's **Kind** argument is set to 11 - ED_REPL, an additional **Boolean** custom property named **ReplaceMode** is set to **True**. This form-level flag signals that the frmFindReplace **Form** object is to be displayed as the Replace dialog box.

Listing 19.5   The Edit method's find-and-replace code.

```
Function Edit(TextCtl As Object, _
             Kind As Integer, _
             Optional Mnu)

   . . .

     Case ED_FIND
        Set frmFindReplace.TextCtl = TextCtl
        frmFindReplace.Show

     Case ED_REPL
        Set frmFindReplace.TextCtl = TextCtl
        frmFindReplace.ReplaceMode = True
        frmFindReplace.Show

   . . .


End Function
```

The single frmFindReplace **Form** object can be displayed as either the Find or the Replace dialog box. The way this is done is via the code in its **Form_Load** event procedure, which reads the value of the **ReplaceMode** custom property and displays the Find dialog box if it is **False** or the Replace dialog box if it is **True**. The **ReplaceMode** custom property can be set to **True** by the **Edit** method when its **Kind** argument is 11- ED_REPL, or when the user clicks on the Replace button in the Find dialog box. The **Form_Load** event procedure's code is shown in Listing 19.6.

Listing 19.6   The Form_Load event procedure of
Find/Replace dialog box.

```
Private Sub Form_Load()

   ' Constants for literals:
   Const CL_BOLD = 0
   Const CL_DLG = 1
   Const CL_ONTOP = 2
   Const ONE_HALF = 0.5

   ' Variables:
   Static Loaded      As Boolean
   Dim Properties(2)   As Boolean

   ' This Form object serves as both Find and Replace dialog
   ' box. Form-level flag, set by calling member or in
   ' cmdReplace_Click event procedure, signals to Form_Load
   ' event procedure which property settings to make. Code
   ' at bottom of procedure, which subclasses Form object,
   ' is run only once.
```

```
If fReplaceMode Then
   Caption = "Replace"
   lblReplace.Visible = True
   txtReplace.Visible = True
   cmdReplaceAll.Visible = True
   chkCase.Top = 900
   lblSearch.Top = 870
   cboOrder.Top = 1125
   cboOrder = cboOrder.List(2)
   chkWholeWord.Top = 1170
   Height = 2050
   cmdReplace.Caption = "&Replace"
Else
   Caption = "Find"
   lblReplace.Visible = False
   txtReplace.Visible = False
   cmdReplaceAll.Visible = False
   chkCase.Top = 540
   lblSearch.Top = 510
   cboOrder.Top = 765
   cboOrder = cboOrder.List(2)
   chkWholeWord.Top = 810
   Height = 1630
End If

If Not Loaded Then
   Loaded = True
   Properties(CL_BOLD) = True
   Properties(CL_DLG) = True
   Properties(CL_ONTOP) = True
   Dialog.ShowCL Me, Properties()
   Move (Screen.Width - Width) * ONE_HALF, _
        (Screen.Height - Height) * ONE_HALF
End If

End Sub
```

Two long routines implement the actual find-and-replace algorithms: the **Find** procedure of the frmFindReplace **Form** object and the **Replace** method of the **Edit** object. We will not analyze either of these routines in depth. Both of them are well written in English-like code and clearly commented. You will have no problem understanding either routine if you take the time to single step through the code in Debug mode. I will, however, highlight the following key points about how they are implemented and work:

- The complexity of the **Find** procedure's algorithm is primarily due to its support of searches in three different directions (all, down, and up).

- The **Replace** method of the **Text** object is called (rather than a Replace procedure in the frmFindReplace **Form** object) to demonstrate two points. First, it is possible to call back from a **Form** object to a different method of the same class which displayed the **Form** object in the first place. Second, this approach illustrates how far you can extend the concept of secondary polymorphism we referred to at the beginning of this chapter. The **Replace** method's **Text** argument, which is declared as the default data type **Variant**, can be passed a **RichTextBox** object reference, a **TextBox** object reference, or a **String** variable. However, in a commercial implementation of this find-and-replace functionality, I would opt for greater speed and call a dedicated **Replace** procedure in the frmFindReplace **Form** object.

- The Replace All button of the Replace dialog box is disabled when a **RichTextBox** control object is being operated on and the **RichTextBox** contains an RTF file. The reason for this is that the **Replace** method, in order to maximize performance, operates on a **String** variable that has been assigned the contents of the **Text** argument. This works fine for a **TextBox** control object, but it would destroy the formatting of the text in a **RichTextBox** object. To replace all instances of a string in an RTF file loaded in a **RichTextBox** object, you can use the **Load** method of the **Text** object to open the RTF file in plain text format. After making all replacements in the file with the **Edit** method, use the **Save** method of the **Text** object to save the changes either in rich text or in plain text format.

- The Replace All algorithm uses calls to a few functions in Crescent Software's QuickPak Professional Assembly DLL to optimize performance. These calls to a third-party DLL, in conjunction with a finely tuned algorithm, result in performance that approaches that of the find-and-replace algorithms of Microsoft's Word for Windows.

- I am not satisfied with the speed of the routines that I am currently using to refresh the positions of the caret and scroll bar when a find-and-replace operation is in process. This slow performance is especially evident when you run a find-and-replace operation on a very large RTF file in a **RichTextBox** object. Ah well! We all need to have something on our to-do list to stay motivated, don't we?

IMPLEMENTING A REUSABLE GO TO DIALOG BOX

If the **Kind** argument of the **Edit** method is set to 12 - ED_GOTO, the Go To **Form** object that is encapsulated in the book's ActiveX component is displayed modelessly. The way this form works and calls its supporting routines is a piece of cake to understand compared to the Find/Replace dialog box. After the **Edit** method sets the custom property **TextCtl** and modelessly displays the frmGoTo dialog box, the code that calls the supporting routines is in the **Click** event procedures of the cmdNext and cmdPrevious **CommandButton** objects. This code, in turn, calls one of four possible members of the **CL** class. The names of the four members and a description of their purposes is shown in Table 19.2.

Again, it is easy enough to see what these four members of the **CL** class do by observing their behavior when you call the **Edit** method and pass its **Kind** argument the value 12 - ED_GOTO. All four of them use different variations of the **SendMessage** Windows API function to handle the scrolling. If you are interested in writing this kind of code, you can study the implementations in the book's class library and imitate them.

Implementing The Windows Format Menu

Once you have grasped the essentials of how the **Edit** method of the **Text** object works, understanding its **Format** method is simple. Like the **Edit** method, **Format** takes two required arguments, **TextCtl** and **Kind**. However, the **Format** method has no optional **Mnu** argument because there is no need to provide Undo or Redo menu capabilities. The entire code of the **Format** method is shown in Listing 19.7.

Table 19.2 Members of the **CL** class called by frmGoTo.

Member	Description
ScrollToLine	Scrolls a RichTextBox or TextBox control object to a specified line number.
ScrollToPage	Scrolls a RichTextBox or TextBox control object to a specified page number.
ScrollLines	Scrolls a RichTextBox or TextBox control object a specified number of lines down or up.
ScrollPages	Scrolls a RichTextBox or TextBox control object a specified number of pages down or up.

Listing 19.7   The Format method's code.

```
Function Format(TextCtl As Object, _
                Kind As Integer)

    ' Constants for Kind argument:
    Const FM_FONT = 0
    Const FM_BOLD = 2
    Const FM_ITALIC = 3
    Const FM_STRIKE = 4
    Const FM_UNDER = 5
    Const FM_COLOR = 6
    Const FM_CASE = 7

    ' Constants for literals:
    Const PROC = "Format"
    Const SYNTAX = True

    ' Constants for elements returned from members:
    Const MBR_CHOICE = 1
    Const CF_NAME = 1
    Const CF_SIZE = 2
    Const CF_BOLD = 3
    Const CF_ITALIC = 4
    Const CF_STRIKE = 5
    Const CF_UNDER = 6
    Const CF_COLOR = 7

    ' Variables:
    Dim Msg         As String
    Dim RichText    As Boolean
    Dim PlainText   As Boolean
    Dim Results     As Variant

    ' Enable error handler and do syntax checking:
    On Error GoTo ET

    If TypeName(TextCtl) = "RichTextBox" Then
        RichText = True
    ElseIf TypeName(TextCtl) = "TextBox" Then
        PlainText = True
    Else
        E.TrapSyntax 8, PROC, "TextCtl"
    End If

    Select Case Kind
        Case FM_FONT, FM_BOLD, FM_ITALIC, FM_STRIKE, _
            FM_UNDER, FM_COLOR, FM_CASE
        Case Else
            E.TrapSyntax 5, PROC, "Kind"
    End Select

    Select Case Kind
        Case FM_FONT, FM_COLOR, FM_CASE
```

```
        If cRAOServer Then
            E.TrapSyntax 1, PROC, "ActiveX RAO component"
        End If
End Select

' Execute method and kind of operation:
Select Case Kind

    Case FM_FONT
        Results = SelectFont(cdlCFBoth + cdlCFEffects)

        If Results(CF_NAME) <> vbNullString Then

            If RichText Then
                TextCtl.SelFontName = Results(CF_NAME)
                TextCtl.SelFontSize = Results(CF_SIZE)
                TextCtl.SelBold = Results(CF_BOLD)
                TextCtl.SelItalic = Results(CF_ITALIC)
                TextCtl.SelStrikeThru = Results(CF_STRIKE)
                TextCtl.SelUnderline = Results(CF_UNDER)
                TextCtl.SelColor = Results(CF_COLOR)
            Else
                TextCtl.FontName = Results(CF_NAME)
                TextCtl.FontSize = Results(CF_SIZE)
                TextCtl.FontBold = Results(CF_BOLD)
                TextCtl.FontItalic = Results(CF_ITALIC)
                TextCtl.FontStrikethru = Results(CF_STRIKE)
                TextCtl.FontUnderline = Results(CF_UNDER)
                TextCtl.ForeColor = Results(CF_COLOR)
            End If
        End If

    Case FM_BOLD

        If RichText Then
            TextCtl.SelBold = Not TextCtl.SelBold
        Else
            TextCtl.FontBold = Not TextCtl.FontBold
        End If

    Case FM_ITALIC

        If RichText Then
            TextCtl.SelItalic = Not TextCtl.SelItalic
        Else
            TextCtl.FontItalic = Not TextCtl.FontItalic
        End If

    Case FM_STRIKE

        If RichText Then
            TextCtl.SelStrikeThru = Not TextCtl.SelStrikeThru
        Else
```

```
                    TextCtl.FontStrikethru = Not TextCtl.FontStrikethru
                End If

            Case FM_UNDER

                If RichText Then
                    TextCtl.SelUnderline = Not TextCtl.SelUnderline
                Else
                    TextCtl.FontUnderline = Not TextCtl.FontUnderline
                End If

            Case FM_COLOR
                Results = ClientApp.SelectColor

                If Results(MBR_CHOICE) <> vbNullString Then

                    If RichText Then
                        TextCtl.SelColor = Results(MBR_CHOICE)
                    Else
                        TextCtl.ForeColor = Results(MBR_CHOICE)
                    End If

                End If

            Case FM_CASE
                Set frmChangeCase.TextCtl = TextCtl

                If RichText And TextCtl.SelLength <> 0 Or PlainText Then
                    frmChangeCase.Show vbModal
                    TextCtl.Container.SetFocus
                Else
                    Msg = "You must first select some text" & vbCr
                    Msg = Msg & "in the RichTextBox object."
                    ClientApp.ShowMsg Msg, vbInformation, "Change Case"
                End If

        End Select

        Format = Array(True)
        Exit Function

ET:

        If Err = SYNTAX Then Format = frmErrCodes.Codes
        If Err <> SYNTAX Then Format = CL.TrapErr(PROC)

End Function
```

Let's review some of the key points about how the **Format** method works:

- The method can take either a **RichTextBox** or **TextBox** object reference as its **TextCtl** argument. If it is a **RichTextBox** control, the
  Format method's operation works on the control's selected text. If it is
  a **TextBox** control, the operation works on all the text in the control.

- If its **Kind** argument is set to 0 - FM_FONT, the **Format** method in turn calls the **SelectFont** method of the **Text** class and applies the selections the user returns to the appropriate text in the **RichTextBox** or **TextBox** control.

- If its **Kind** argument is set to 6 - FM_COLOR, the **Format** method in turn calls the **SelectColor** method of the **ClientApp** class and applies the selection the user returns to the appropriate text in the **RichTextBox** or **TextBox** control.

- If its **Kind** argument is set to 7 - FM_CASE, the **Format** method modally displays its associated frmChangeCase **Form** object, which appears in Figure 19.11. Select one of the option buttons on frmChangeCase and click on OK to change the case of the appropriate text in the **RichTextBox** or **TextBox** control.

Well, that's it for Chapter 19 and our examination of how to create parts of a reusable Windows application framework. If you are interested in any of the members of the **Text** class that we did not discuss in this chapter, you can run the example code for them from EFS.HLP. Compared to the members we did focus on, the others are all very easy to understand and reuse. In the last chapter of this book, Chapter 21, we will look at a full-fledged Rich Text Editor client application that demonstrates just how much reusability a well-designed and implemented Windows application framework can provide. But, before we get to that, we need to examine some of the different ways that VB5 enables you to extend the IDE of Visual Basic itself by creating and using ActiveX controls, add-ins, Wizards, and so on.

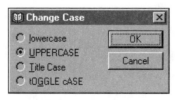

Figure 19.11 Change Case dialog box.

20

EXTENDING VISUAL BASIC'S IDE

When VB1 was first released, Microsoft had high hopes for its new Windows programming language. Yet, even the company's chairman, Bill Gates, admits that he was surprised by the overwhelming success of the product right from the outset. Gates, who rightly considers himself an authority on the BASIC language (after all, he did help write the first BASIC interpreter for a microprocessor), has been quoted several times during the 1990s as saying that the single biggest factor contributing to the early success of VB was its ability to use third-party VBX custom controls.

Extensibility is the characteristic that allows any programmer to enhance the feature set of the language after a version of the language has been released. VBX custom controls were the first example of VB's extensibility architecture. Because VB is a Windows programming language, you could also extend it by calling and reusing functions in the Windows API and in third-party DLLs. After VBX custom controls, the next significant milestone in the extensibility of VB was Sheridan Software's clever VBAssist product, which enhanced the capabilities of VB's menu structure and Properties window.

Through the release of VB3, you had to typically be a C or C++ developer in order to extend the language. With the release of VB4, however, the rules of the game governing the language's extensibility were changed forever. VB4 allowed the VB developer to extend the IDE by creating OLE Automation servers (now ActiveX components). And, you could write these OLE servers in different ways (as class libraries, add-ins, Wizards, and so on). In order for an OLE server written with VB4 to be snapped on to VB's own menu structure as an add-in, the language itself was rewritten as an OLE Automation server. Because of this change, VB4 could expose its own selected public objects and members, like the Add-Ins menu, to VB developers at design time.

With the release of VB5, VB's extensibility architecture has been enhanced even further. Some of the new features that fall into the category of extensions to the IDE and that we'll discuss in this chapter include:

- The ability to create ActiveX controls (formerly known as OCX custom controls) that can be added to VB4 or VB5's Toolbox, or to any other ActiveX control-compliant language.

- Additions to and revisions of its VB4 Add-In extensibility model. Creating add-ins with VB4 was not as easy or flexible as it should have been. VB5 has made great progress in this area and includes many new add-in Wizards that illustrate how add-ins can be used.

- Visual Basic Books Online. You'll never have to take the shrink-wrap packaging off of VB's technical manuals again because every page can be found in the new Visual Basic Books Online; and, of course, you can search by any topic or keyword to find what you're looking for.

- Project and module templates, which are especially useful to the veteran programmer who is new to VB or to the ActiveX software paradigm.

Creating VB5 ActiveX Controls

For the last two to three years, the question most frequently asked by VB developers has been "Will Microsoft ever make it possible to create custom controls with Visual Basic?" Well, with the arrival of VB5, that question has been answered in the affirmative. You can now use VB to develop your own ActiveX controls (formerly known as OLE/OCX custom controls under VB4 and VBX custom controls under VB3), compile them to native code, use them in your applications, and distribute them for reuse to other Windows developers.

VB5 supports several features to help you easily create ActiveX controls:

- Designing an ActiveX control is almost as easy as designing a VB **Form** object. You can use familiar Visual Basic commands to draw your control or create a control group using existing controls.

- ActiveX controls can be debugged in-process, allowing you to step directly from the code for your test form into the code for the ActiveX control project.

- You can add data-binding to an ActiveX control. Using the **Data** control object, a user can easily bind the individual fields within the control to the appropriate fields in a database.

- VB5 makes it easy to create professional-looking ActiveX control packages by providing Wizards to help you add property pages, named constants, and events to your controls.

- You can compile your ActiveX controls directly into your application's executable or into OCX files that can be used by other ActiveX-compliant languages (Visual C++, Delphi 2, PowerBuilder 5, and so on), with applications such as Microsoft Office, or on the Internet.

VB5 also includes a new IDE tool called a *designer*. A designer is an add-in Wizard that provides a visual design window in VB5's IDE. You can use this window to design new classes visually. VB5 has built-in designers for forms, ActiveX controls, and documents. Objects you create from classes you designed with a designer have separate design-time and runtime behaviors and appearances, although many objects (for example, forms and controls) look very similar in the two modes.

In addition to its built-in designers, VB5 allows developers to create designers for use in the VB5 IDE. These *ActiveX designers* work just like the built-in designers in VB5, making them easy to learn and use. There is an ActiveX Designer SDK that comes with the Professional and Enterprise Editions of VB5. Unfortunately, using the ActiveX Designer SDK requires a C++ compiler, such as Visual C++. ActiveX designers cannot be written using VB5, but the add-in Wizard-type of designer can be.

Probably the best systematic way to learn how to use VB5 to create an ActiveX control is to work your way through the chapter in Visual Basic Books Online titled *Creating An ActiveX Control*. Leading you through a series of procedures, it shows you how to create a simple ActiveX control called **ShapeLabel**. I could fill up the rest of this chapter by simply replicating this material in Visual Basic Books Online, but I don't think you'd feel like you were getting your money's worth if I did that.

Instead, what I want to do is examine two ActiveX controls that I built with the Beta2 release of VB5. These two ActiveX controls:

- Are fully functional components that you can reuse.
- Illustrate useful techniques that you can use in creating your own ActiveX controls.
- Give you a feel for how similar the underlying software architectures are for ActiveX controls and the ActiveX components/servers that this book is primarily about.

General Steps To Follow

The first thing you need to know to create an ActiveX control is the general steps to perform. The list of steps that follows will create a simple ActiveX control that does not require a user interface and does not contain any associated control objects. Although these steps are generic, specific settings reflect the settings for the **TBIcon** ActiveX control (which we'll discuss in the next section):

1. Start VB5 and, from the New Project dialog box, double click the ActiveX Control icon. VB loads a project that contains a UserControl (CTL) module. The **UserControl** object is new to VB5 and is the basic form you use to create an ActiveX control. A new **UserControl** object appears as shown in Figure 20.1.

2. Make the following entries in the General tab of the Project Properties dialog box: Project Type (ActiveX Control), Startup Object (None),

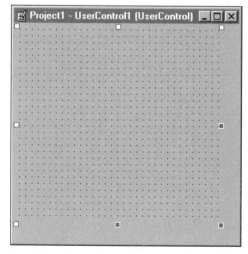

Figure 20.1 Newly loaded **UserControl** object.

Project Name (TBarIcon), and Project Description (Taskbar Icon Control). The Project Description is the entry that later appears in the list of ActiveX controls in the Components dialog box.

3. Make the following entries in the Properties window: Name (TBIcon—the name of the class that appears when you move the mouse pointer over the ActiveX control on VB's Toolbox), InvisibleAtRuntime (True for ActiveX controls that do not require a runtime GUI interface, like TBIcon), and ToolboxBitmap (the path to a specially sized, 16×15 pixels BMP file that appears on the ActiveX control's Toolbox icon).

4. Make any module-level declarations in the General Declarations section of the **UserControl** object.

5. Declare any members (properties, methods, or events) that the **UserControl** object will require and write their procedures.

6. Select Project|TBarIcon Properties, click on the Compile tab, and select Compile to Native Code (Optimize for Fast Code). You need all the speed you can get for ActiveX controls.

7. Save the ActiveX control's project.

8. Select File|Make TBarIcon.OCX to make and register the new ActiveX control.

At this point, you could open a new Standard EXE project and check the list of ActiveX controls (Project|Components) to ensure that your ActiveX control is registered and available for reuse. You should find it listed alphabetically by its Project Description entry on the Controls tab of the Components dialog box, as shown in Figure 20.2.

When you select the new ActiveX control and click on OK, the icon, specified by its **ToolboxBitmap** property's setting, appears in VB's Toolbox, as shown in Figure 20.3.

Double click the ActiveX control's icon to instantiate it on Form1. If you select the ActiveX control and its **InvisibleAtRuntime** property is set to **True**, the Properties window should appear similar to the one shown in Figure 20.4.

At this point, if you know how to use its members, you could test the ActiveX control. For example, if you set TBIcon1's **Picture** property to an icon and call its **Add** method with the statement

```
TBIcon1.AddIcon "New tooltip"
```

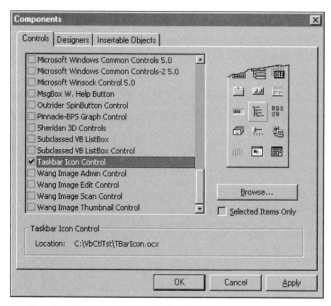

Figure 20.2 Controls tab of Components dialog box.

Figure 20.3 VB's Toolbox after **TBIcon** ActiveX control is added to it.

Figure 20.4 Properties window with **TBIcon** ActiveX control selected.

the **TBIcon** ActiveX control adds an icon with the specified tooltip to the right side of the Windows 95-style shell's Taskbar.

The Taskbar Icon ActiveX Control

Of course, as someone said a long time ago, the devil is always found in the details. To really get a good feel for the various techniques involved in creating ActiveX controls, we need to take a closer look at the general declarations, properties, methods, and events that make up specific ActiveX controls. We will do this first for the **TBIcon** ActiveX control.

What the **TBIcon** ActiveX control does for an application is to add an icon with a specified tooltip to the right side of the Windows 95-style shell's Taskbar. While the application is running, you can change the tooltip associated with the icon, which is displayed when the mouse moves over the icon. The **TBIcon** ActiveX control also causes the Taskbar's icon to react to left and right mouse button clicks and to return a value to the application. This value signals which button was clicked. The key to this functionality is the use of the Windows API function **Shell_NotifyIcon**, found in the file SHELL32.DLL.

If you installed the files for the ActiveX controls contained on the book's CD-ROM when you ran SETUP.EXE, they should be on the path C:\VBOOPEFS\ACTXCTLS. What you should do now is open up the VB project for the **TBIcon** ActiveX control (TBARICON.VBP). Then we'll analyze its source code in the following sections. The total amount of code, including declarations, is only about 60 lines. It consists of procedures for four methods, one property, and three events (one being a developer-declared event, a new syntactical element that VB5 supports).

> **Note:** To register the **TBIcon** ActiveX control on your machine, open the TBARICON.VBP project and select File|Make TBARICON.-OCX. Accept all the current settings and then save the project TBARICON.VBP.

THE TASKBAR ICON'S GENERAL DECLARATIONS

The general declarations for the Taskbar icon's **UserControl** object are shown in Listing 20.1.

Listing 20.1   General declarations for the TBIcon ActiveX control.

```
' User-defined data types:
Private Type ICONDATA
   TypeSize As Long
   HWnd As Long
   ID As Long
   Flags As Long
   CallBackMsg As Long
   Graphic As Long
   ToolTip As String * 64
End Type

' DLL functions:
Private Declare Function Shell_NotifyIcon& Lib "SHELL32" _
                    Alias "Shell_NotifyIconA" _
                    (ByVal Action&, Info As ICONDATA)

' Events:
Event MouseMove(Button As Integer, Shift As Integer, _
                X As Single, Y As Single)

' Module-level variables:
Private uIcon As ICONDATA
```

There are two major points you need to understand about the code in Listing 20.1. First, the Windows API function **Shell_NotifyIcon** uses the ICONDATA user-defined data type and only takes two arguments. The initial argument is a **Long** value or API constant that specifies the action to be taken and the other argument is the user-defined data type. Second, the developer-declared **MouseMove** event must be declared in the General Declarations section of the module. As you will see a little later in this section, there is a difference between the declaration of a developer-declared event and its corresponding event procedure.

THE TASKBAR ICON'S PROPERTIES

Listing 20.2 shows the **Property** procedures for the **Picture** property of the Taskbar icon's **UserControl** object. Even though a **UserControl** object has a **Picture** property at design time, you have to explicitly create a proxy **Picture** property with **Property** procedures in order for it to apply to the ActiveX control in an application.

Listing 20.2   Properties of the TBIcon ActiveX control.

```
Property Get Picture() As Picture

   ' Read by Add method of UserControl object.
   Set Picture = UserControl.Picture
```

```
End Property

Property Set Picture(ByVal Setting As Picture)

    ' Can be set in Properties window or at runtime.
    ' PropertyChanged method applies to UserControl
    ' object and notifies it that one of its properties
    ' has changed. This way it can synchronize its
    ' property window with new setting of property.
    Set UserControl.Picture = Setting
    UserControl.PropertyChanged Picture

End Property
```

You should note three points about the **Property** procedures in Listing 20.2. First, they must be declared as the object data type **Picture**. Second, the **Setting** argument of the **Property Set** procedure must be declared **ByVal**. Third, VB5's new **PropertyChanged** method, which applies to the **UserControl** and **UserDocument** objects, changes the setting of the ActiveX control's **Picture** property in the Properties window, if you change its setting at design time in an application. If you change its setting with code at runtime, the **PropertyChanged** method has no effect.

THE TASKBAR ICON'S METHODS

The four methods that apply to the Taskbar icon's **UserControl** object are shown in Listing 20.3. Their names—**Add**, **ChangeTip**, **Delete**, and **GetBtnClicked**—clearly denote their functionality.

Listing 20.3 Methods of the TBIcon ActiveX control.

```
Sub Add(ToolTip As String)

    ' Constants for Windows API functions:
    Const NIF_MESSAGE = &H1
    Const NIF_ICON = &H2
    Const NIF_TIP = &H4
    Const NIM_ADD = &H0
    Const WM_MOUSEMOVE = &H200

    ' Size user-defined data type and
    ' assign values to its elements.
    ' ID element can be any Long value.
    uIcon.TypeSize = Len(uIcon)
    uIcon.ID = 1000
    uIcon.Flags = NIF_MESSAGE + NIF_ICON + NIF_TIP
    uIcon.HWnd = HWnd
    uIcon.CallBackMsg = WM_MOUSEMOVE
    uIcon.Graphic = Picture
    uIcon.ToolTip = ToolTip & vbNullChar
```

```
    ' Call Windows API function to add icon specified by
    ' Picture property of ActiveX control to taskbar.
    Shell_NotifyIcon NIM_ADD, uIcon

End Sub

Sub ChangeTip(ToolTip As String)

    ' Constants for Windows API functions:
    Const NIF_TIP = &H4
    Const NIM_MODIFY = &H1

    ' Assign values to elements of user-defined data type:
    uIcon.Flags = NIF_TIP
    uIcon.ToolTip = ToolTip & vbNullChar

    ' Change tooltip of icon on taskbar.
    Shell_NotifyIcon NIM_MODIFY, uIcon

End Sub

Sub Delete()

    ' Constants for Windows API functions:
    Const NIM_DELETE = &H2

    ' Delete icon from taskbar.
    Shell_NotifyIcon NIM_DELETE, uIcon

End Sub

Function GetBtnClicked(X As Single) As Integer

    ' Constants for Windows API functions:
    Const WM_LBUTTONDOWN = &H201
    Const WM_RBUTTONDOWN = &H204
    Const WM_MBUTTONDOWN = &H207

    ' Variables:
    Dim Btn As Integer

    ' Convert twips to pixels.
    Btn = X \ Screen.TwipsPerPixelX

    ' Convert Windows API constant to VB intrinsic constant:
    Select Case Btn
        Case WM_LBUTTONDOWN
            Btn = vbLeftButton
        Case WM_RBUTTONDOWN
            Btn = vbRightButton
        Case WM_MBUTTONDOWN
            Btn = vbMiddleButton
```

```
    End Select
    GetBtnClicked = Btn

End Function
```

The code for the four methods in Listing 20.3 is pretty straightforward, but a couple points do require some explanation. First, you might wonder why the **CallBackMsg** element of the user-defined data type is assigned the constant WM_MOUSEMOVE in the **Add** method. After the Windows API function **Shell_NotifyIcon** adds an icon to the Taskbar, either Windows 95 or NT 4 automatically sends back a Windows message to the **TBIcon** ActiveX control (identified by its **hWnd** property) that signifies the mouse event that occurred over the icon (left click, right click, mouse move, and so on). However, VB's architecture does not permit you to read the message directly because it does not explicitly support Windows callbacks. Instead, VB maps certain Windows messages into events. In this case, the message WM_MOUSEMOVE works best because it responds to all three possible kinds of mouse button clicks (left, right, and middle) and because it maps back to an event (**MouseMove**) that VB supports and that has been developer-declared for the ActiveX control.

Second, it is not obvious what the purpose of the **GetBtnClicked** method is. **GetBtnClicked** is called from the **MouseMove** event procedure of the **TBIcon** ActiveX control. It exists primarily to save the application programmer the trouble of writing such conversion code in the control's **MouseMove** event procedure. The actual button that gets clicked on the Taskbar's icon is mapped by VB into the **X** argument of **MouseMove** and must be converted from twips to pixels to match up with the Windows API constants (WM_LBUTTONDOWN, WM_RBUTTONDOWN, and so on). Most VB programmers don't write this kind of code on a day-to-day basis, so it's just a lot easier to provide the **GetBtnClicked** method for them and have it return the familiar intrinsic VB constants (**vbLeftButton**, **vbRightButton**, or **vbMiddleButton**). The typical code in the ActiveX control's **MouseMove** event procedure that calls the **GetBtnClicked** method looks like that shown in Listing 20.4.

Listing 20.4   Code to call the GetBtnClicked method.

```
Private Sub TBIcon1_MouseMove(Button As Integer, _
                      Shift As Integer, _
                      X As Single, _
                      Y As Single)
```

```
' Variables:
Dim Msg As String

SetFocus

Select Case TBIcon1.GetBtnClicked(X)
   Case vbLeftButton
      Msg = "You clicked left button on taskbar's icon."
   Case vbRightButton
      Msg = "You clicked right button on taskbar's icon."
   Case vbMiddleButton
      Msg = "You clicked middle button on taskbar's icon."
   Case Else
      Msg = vbNullString
End Select

If Msg <> vbNullString Then
   MsgBox Msg, vbInformation, "TBIcon ActiveX Control Demo"
End If

End Sub
```

THE TASKBAR ICON'S EVENTS

The three events of the Taskbar icon's **UserControl** object that contain code—**MouseMove**, **ReadProperties**, and **WriteProperties**—are shown in Listing 20.5. Of these three, only the developer-declared **MouseMove** event procedure is accessible at runtime in an application.

Listing 20.5 Event procedures of TBIcon's UserControl object.

```
Private Sub UserControl_MouseMove(Button As Integer, _
                                  Shift As Integer, _
                                  X As Single, _
                                  Y As Single)

   ' Use VB5's new RaiseEvent method to trigger
   ' MouseMove event of TBIcon ActiveX control.
   RaiseEvent MouseMove(Button, Shift, X, Y)

End Sub

Private Sub UserControl_ReadProperties(PropBag As PropertyBag)

   ' Variables:
   Dim Msg As String

   ' Read property's setting from storage:
   On Error Resume Next

   Set Picture = PropBag.ReadProperty("Picture", Nothing)

   If Err <> False Then
```

```
      Msg = "VB run-time error " & Err & " ---" & vbCr
      Msg = Msg & Error(Err)
      MsgBox Error(Err), vbExclamation, "ReadProperties Procedure"
   End If

End Sub

Private Sub UserControl_WriteProperties(PropBag As PropertyBag)

   ' Write property's setting to storage.
   PropBag.WriteProperty "Picture", Picture, Nothing

End Sub
```

To understand the **MouseMove** event procedure's code, you must appreciate that it is the second step in a three-step process required to create and use a developer-declared event for an ActiveX control. Let's take a moment to review these steps:

- In the General Declarations section of the **UserControl** object, use the **Event** statement to declare the developer-declared event.

- In the corresponding event procedure of the **UserControl** object, use the **RaiseEvent** method to trigger the developer-declared event in the ActiveX control at runtime.

- At runtime in the application's ActiveX control, write a procedure in the developer-declared event, which is the only kind of event an instantiated ActiveX control supports, that reacts to the event, like the code in Listing 20.4.

The **ReadProperties** and **WriteProperties** event procedures are new to VB5 and definitely require some explanation. The new syntactical elements that they use are listed and explained in Table 20.1.

Table 20.1   New VB5 syntax related to **ReadProperties** and **WriteProperties** events.

Syntax	Description
WriteProperties	An event that occurs when an ActiveX UserControl or UserDocument object is saved. The developer of the component can save the settings of its properties when the WriteProperties event occurs. The one argument of WriteProperties must be declared as a PropertyBag object.
ReadProperties	An event that occurs when loading an ActiveX UserControl or UserDocument object that has previously saved the settings of its properties. This event occurs after the control's Initialize event.

continued

Table 20.1 New VB5 syntax related to **ReadProperties** and **WriteProperties** events (continued).

Syntax	Description
	You should always include error trapping in the ReadProperties event procedure to protect the control from invalid property values that may have been entered by users editing the FRM file with text editors. The one argument of ReadProperties must be declared as a PropertyBag object.
PropertyBag	An object that holds settings of properties that are to be saved across invocations of an ActiveX UserControl or UserDocument object. A Property Bag object is passed into a control through the Read Properties or the WriteProperties event and it has ReadProperty and WriteProperty methods.
WriteProperty	A method of the PropertyBag object that saves the settings of a property of an ActiveX UserControl or UserDocument object. The WriteProperty method writes a setting to the property bag and associates it with the String value in its first argument (that is, the name of the property). This String value is then used to read the setting when the ReadProperty method is called from the ReadProperties event procedure.
ReadProperty	A method of the PropertyBag object that returns the property setting of an ActiveX UserControl or UserDocument object that was previously saved with the WriteProperty method. The ReadProperty method returns the setting of the property associated with the String value of its argument (the name of the property). This String value must match the String value used when the property's setting was saved.

USING THE TASKBAR ICON'S ACTIVEX CONTROL

Open up the demo VB project that uses the **TBIcon** ActiveX control (DEMOTBAR.VBP) so we can examine its source code and watch how it works.

> *Note: When you open DEMOTBAR.VBP, Visual Basic will display the message "Version 47.0 of TBARICON.OCX is not registered. The control will be upgraded to version 48.0." Click on OK to clear the message box and upgrade the ActiveX control. This presumes, of course, that you previously registered the TBIcon ActiveX control on you r PC as an earlier note prompted you to do.*

After you have added the newly registered **TBIcon** ActiveX control to Form1, you can add an icon to the ActiveX control by setting its **Picture** property in the Properties window to some new icon. Its tooltip text is set based on the entry in the **TextBox** control object. Select Run|Start and note that this ActiveX control does not appear at runtime; remember, we set its **InvisibleAtRuntime** property to **True** when we created it. Click on the Add Icon button and watch what happens to the right side of the Windows 95-style shell's Taskbar. Move the mouse over the icon on the Taskbar and watch as the tooltip is displayed. Click on the icon to see the code in the **MouseMove** event procedure of the ActiveX control display a message box like the one shown in Figure 20.5. Next, change the entry in the **TextBox** object and click on the Change Tip button, or click on the Delete Icon button to call those methods of **TBIcon**.

The code in Form1 of DEMOTBAR.VBP is simple. The only procedure that we'll specifically note is the **TBIcon1_MouseMove** event procedure in Listing 20.4. It contains the code that takes the event procedure's **X** argument and passes it to the **GetBtnClicked** method of the ActiveX control. This method then converts the Windows pixels/constant value to a VB twips/intrinsic constant value and returns the number of the button (**vbLeftButton**, **vbRightButton**, or **vbMiddleButton**).

That's all there is to say about the **TBIcon** ActiveX control. At this point, I think you'll have to admit that it's a slick little reusable component. Little? Did I say little? Well, okay, maybe not so little. Even a modest ActiveX control like this one takes up quite a bit of space on your hard drive. VB5 generates eight files with eight different extensions when it creates and registers the **TBIcon** ActiveX control. The two major files—TBARICON.OCX and TBARICON.OCA—weigh in at 16 K and 17 K, respectively. The other five files add another 13 K, for a total of almost 50 K.

It's also a good idea to remember exactly what kind of animal the COM/OLE software protocol considers an ActiveX control to be. When I was

Figure 20.5 Message box displayed by clicking the icon on the Taskbar.

developing **TBIcon**, I looked in the Windows registry and found the entry displayed in Figure 20.6 for it. It turns out that an ActiveX control is just another variation on our old friend the in-process server/component, albeit one that provides a more developer-friendly interface in the form of the Properties window.

It would be a good exercise for you to consider whether and how you could implement the functionality of the **TBIcon** ActiveX control as a reusable object in an ActiveX DLL component. How would you design its public interface? Would it run at the same speed? Would it be harder to reuse? How much hard drive space would it require?

We could spend a lot of time discussing and analyzing these kinds of questions, but we still have a lot of ground to cover in this chapter. Next up is an example of an ActiveX control that subclasses the functionality of an existing, built-in VB control object. I am referring to the **ListSC** ActiveX control, which illustrates some other interesting techniques you can use when creating ActiveX controls.

The Subclassed VB ListBox ActiveX Control

Open up the VB project for the **ListSC** ActiveX control (LSTBOXSC.VBP). In the following sections, we'll analyze its source code.

> **Note:** To register the **ListSC** ActiveX control on your machine, select File|Make LSTBOXSC.OCX and accept all the current settings. Save the project LSTBOXSC.VBP.

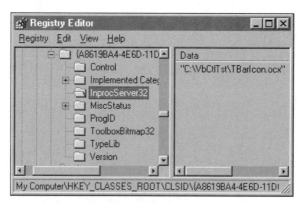

Figure 20.6 Windows registry entry for the **TBIcon** ActiveX control.

At this point in the book, understanding the **ListSC** ActiveX control's functionality and most of its procedures will be easy for you because it simply replicates most of the different methods of the **List** object in the book's class library. However, the **ListSC** methods do not require you to pass in the **Name** property of a **ListBox** control object as an argument. The reason why you can dispense with the object reference to a **ListBox** is that the **ListSC** ActiveX control's **UserControl** object actually contains an encapsulated **ListBox** object. At design time, the **UserControl** object of **ListSC** appears as shown in Figure 20.7. The object with the handles is the **UserControl**. It, in turn, contains a **ListBox** object with a **Name** property setting of List1.

This relationship between a **UserControl** object and a VB control object that is layered on it looks to be the same as the relationship between a **Form** object and a VB control object that it contains. However, there is a fundamental difference. If you have a **ListBox** object layered on a **Form** object, you can access a member of that **ListBox** object with a statement like:

```
Form1.List1.Clear
```

As you know, this statement allows you to apply the **Clear** method of the **ListBox** object even from another code module in the project. But, in the case of a **ListBox** object layered on a **UserControl** object in an ActiveX control, this kind of syntax does not work. You can never directly refer to the encapsulated **ListBox** object by its **Name** property or directly apply any of its other properties or methods. Instead, all references must be to the instance of the **UserControl** object (for example, ListSC1) that contains the **ListBox**.

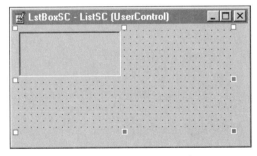

Figure 20.7 **UserControl** object of LSTBOXSC.VBP at design time.

To the application programmer who is reusing the **ListSC** ActiveX control, it appears as if she is referencing a **ListBox** object, but the reality of what's going on inside the "black box" that is the ActiveX control is quite different. The analysis of the **ListSC** ActiveX control that follows in this chapter will focus on the aspects of its implementation that enable it to contain a subclassed VB **ListBox** object, whose members can be transparently accessed by an application programmer. I will not repeat the material covered in Chapter 10, where we studied the functionality and implementation of the members of the **List** object of the book's class library.

CREATING PROXY MEMBERS FOR LISTSC1

Because the programmer who reuses the **ListSC** ActiveX control can never directly refer to the **ListBox** object it contains, any existing members of the **ListBox** object (that is, properties and methods) that you want to apply must be declared as custom members of the **UserControl** object. The proxy custom members that I created for the **ListSC** ActiveX control are shown in Listing 20.6.

Listing 20.6 Proxy members of the ListSC ActiveX control.

```
Property Get List(Index)
   List = List1.List(Index)
End Property

Property Get ListCount()
   ListCount = List1.ListCount
End Property

Property Get ListIndex()
   ListIndex = List1.ListIndex
End Property

Property Get TopIndex()
   TopIndex = List1.TopIndex
End Property

Sub AddItem(Item, _
            Optional Index)
   If IsMissing(Index) Then
      List1.AddItem Item
   Else
      List1.AddItem Item, Index
   End If
End Sub

Sub Clear()
   List1.Clear
```

```
End Sub

Sub Refresh()
   List1.Refresh
End Sub
```

When you look at the proxy members in Listing 20.6, please keep in mind that the **ListSC** ActiveX control is only meant to be a demonstration version, and, as a result, the proxy members that I created for it do not constitute a complete set. Also, I declared the four proxy properties to be read-only; again, this is for demonstration purposes only.

Now, you might think that this process of creating proxy members for an ActiveX control to replicate the members of the built-in VB control that it contains is awkward and tedious. Couldn't Microsoft's VB5 development team have come up with a simpler approach? Well, first of all, there is an add-in Wizard included with VB5 (the ActiveX Control Interface Wizard, which we'll look at later in this chapter) that helps to automate the creation of proxy members. Second, when you're subclassing a VB control object with an ActiveX control, this proxy approach is necessary in order to give you the freedom to decide which intrinsic properties of the VB control you want to replicate and which ones you want to override. We will discuss how you can override the behavior of an intrinsic property in the next section.

OVERRIDING THE INTRINSIC SORTED PROPERTY OF A LISTBOX

As you saw in Chapter 10, the approach to subclassing that is used in the **List** object of the book's class library does not allow you to completely override the behavior of the intrinsic **Sorted** property of VB's **ListBox** object. If **Sorted** is set to **False**, anything is possible (sort ascending, sort descending, don't sort). However, if **Sorted** is set to **True** and you pass an object reference to that **ListBox** to the **FillWithDAO** or **FillWithDataCtl** method of the **List** object, you can neither suspend the sort nor sort in descending order. Because **Sorted** is read-only at runtime, you are stuck with the behavior that its design-time setting of **True** dictates (that is, sort in ascending order).

The approach to subclassing that a **UserControl** object containing a **ListBox** object permits overcomes the restriction discussed in the previous paragraph. The following steps are required to override the behavior of the intrinsic **Sorted** property:

1. Declare a custom **Property Let** procedure named **Sorted** for the **UserControl** object.

2. In this **Property Let** procedure, specify the possible settings of the argument of the custom **Sorted** property (0 - SORT_NONE, 1 - SORT_ASC, 2 - SORT_DSC).

3. If the argument is set to SORT_NONE (or any setting other than SORT_ASC or SORT_DSC), do nothing and exit the procedure.

4. If the argument is set to SORT_ASC or SORT_DSC, run the algorithm shown in Listing 20.7.

Listing 20.7   Sorted custom property of the ListSC ActiveX control.

```
Property Let Sorted(Setting)

   '  _____
   '
   ' Sorted property is write-only at runtime. It demonstrates
   ' how to override built-in property of VB control object
   ' that is encapsulated inside UserControl object.
   '  _____


   ' Constants for Windows API functions:
   Const WM_SETREDRAW = &HB
   ' Constants for Setting argument:
   Const SORT_NONE = 0
   Const SORT_ASC = 1
   Const SORT_DSC = 2

   ' Variables:
   Dim Tmp      As String
   Dim El       As Long
   Dim Item     As Long
   Dim Items()  As String

   If Setting <> SORT_ASC And Setting <> SORT_DSC Then
      Exit Property
   Else

      SendMessage List1.hWnd, WM_SETREDRAW, False, vbEmpty

      For Item = 0 To List1.ListCount - 1
         ReDim Preserve Items(Item)
         Items(Item) = List1.List(Item)
      Next Item

      List1.Clear

      For El = LBound(Items) To UBound(Items) - 1

         If Setting = SORT_ASC Then

            For Item = UBound(Items) To El + 1 Step -1
```

```
                If UCase$(Items(Item)) < UCase$(Items(Item - 1)) Then
                    Tmp = Items(Item)
                    Items(Item) = Items(Item - 1)
                    Items(Item - 1) = Tmp
                End If
            Next Item

        Else

            For Item = UBound(Items) To El + 1 Step -1

                If UCase$(Items(Item)) >= UCase$(Items(Item - 1)) Then
                    Tmp = Items(Item)
                    Items(Item) = Items(Item - 1)
                    Items(Item - 1) = Tmp
                End If

            Next Item
        End If
    Next El

    For Item = 0 To UBound(Items)
        List1.AddItem Items(Item)
    Next Item

    SendMessage List1.hWnd, WM_SETREDRAW, True, vbEmpty
    End If

End Property
```

If **Sorted** is set to 1 - SORT_ASC or 2 - SORT_DSC, the procedure in Listing 20.7 follows these steps: It suspends redrawing of the **ListBox** object to speed up the process; then, it assigns the items in the **ListBox** to a dynamic **String** array, clears the **ListBox**, and sorts the elements of the **String** array in the specified order; finally, it uses the **AddItem** method of the **ListBox**, implemented as a proxy method, to reload it with the sorted items from the array and then redraws the **ListBox**. If **Sorted** is set to 0 - SORT_NONE, nothing happens and the items remain in their current order.

The sort routine in Listing 20.7 works, but it is not very fast. I used to have some sorting methods in the book's class library that used Crescent Software's QuickPak Professional Assembly sort routines. They ran fine under VB4 and were 100 times faster than anything you could write in native VB code. Unfortunately, the Beta1 and Beta2 releases of VB5 have "broken" those Assembly-based sorts. The moral of this story is twofold: First, not all code that runs under VB4 will be upwardly compatible with VB5; second, Crescent Software's developers better get to work and upgrade their DLL library.

> *Note: When you create an ActiveX control that subclasses a VB control object, you can use the same kind of technique used with the **Sorted** property of the **ListBox** on any intrinsic property of any control object that is normally read-only at runtime.*

SIZING A CONTROL LAYERED ON A USERCONTROL OBJECT

One other technique you need to understand is how to enable an application programmer to size a VB control object that is layered on a **UserControl** object in an ActiveX control. In this example of the subclassed **ListBox** object, here is the dilemma: The **UserControl** object has **Height** and **Width** properties, which appear in the Properties window when an application reuses the ActiveX control. The **ListBox** object does not have **ScaleHeight** and **ScaleWidth** properties, which are the ones you need to set when an application reuses the ActiveX control.

But, you might ask, why can't you just set the **Height** and **Width** properties of the **ListBox** object? The answer is that when an application reuses the ActiveX control, the **Height** and **Width** properties of the **ListSC** ActiveX control govern the dimensions of the container or non-client area of the **ListBox**. What you need to do is declare custom **ScaleHeight** and **ScaleWidth** properties for the **ListBox** (which are not intrinsic properties of a **ListBox**), which govern the dimensions of the client area of the **ListBox**.

The general declarations, **Property** procedures, and event procedures that are needed to size the **ListBox** object of the ActiveX control at runtime are shown in Listing 20.8.

Listing 20.8   Procedures to size the client area of a subclassed ListBox.

```
' General declarations:

' Module-level custom property variables:
Private uScaleHeight   As Integer
Private uScaleWidth    As Integer

Property Let ScaleHeight(ByVal Setting)

    ' Store setting of custom property and set Height
    ' of ListBox equal to ScaleHeight. Then call
    ' PropertyChanged method to notify UserControl
    ' object that property has been changed and
    ' to trigger WriteProperties event.
```

```
      uScaleHeight = Setting
      List1.Height = Setting
      PropertyChanged ScaleHeight

End Property

Property Get ScaleHeight()
   ScaleHeight = uScaleHeight
End Property

Property Let ScaleWidth(ByVal Setting)

   ' Store setting of custom property and set Width
   ' of ListBox equal to ScaleWidth. Then call
   ' PropertyChanged method to notify UserControl
   ' object that property has been changed and
   ' to trigger WriteProperties event.

   uScaleWidth = Setting
   List1.Width = Setting
   PropertyChanged ScaleWidth

End Property

Property Get ScaleWidth()
   ScaleWidth = uScaleWidth
End Property

Private Sub UserControl_WriteProperties(PropBag As PropertyBag)

   ' Write settings of properties to storage:
   PropBag.WriteProperty "ScaleHeight", ScaleHeight, 0
   PropBag.WriteProperty "ScaleWidth", ScaleWidth, 0

End Sub

Private Sub UserControl_ReadProperties(PropBag As PropertyBag)

   ' Variables:
   Dim Msg As String

   ' Read settings of properties from storage:
   On Error Resume Next
   ScaleHeight = PropBag.ReadProperty("ScaleHeight", 0)
   ScaleWidth = PropBag.ReadProperty("ScaleWidth", 0)

   If Err <> False Then
      Msg = "VB run-time error " & Err & " ---" & vbCr
      Msg = Msg & Error(Err)
      MsgBox Error(Err), vbExclamation, "ReadProperties Procedure"
   End If

End Sub
```

Using The Subclassed ListBox's ActiveX Control

Open up the demo VB project that uses the **ListSC** ActiveX control (DEMOLBSC.VBP). In this section, we'll examine some of its source code and watch how it works.

> **Note:** *When you open DEMOLBSC.VBP, Visual Basic will display the message "Version 55.0 of LSTBOXSC.OCX is not registered. The control will be upgraded to version 56.0." Click on OK to clear the message box and upgrade the ActiveX control. This presumes, of course, that you previously registered the **ListSC** ActiveX control on your PC as an earlier note prompted you to do.*

When you look at Form1 of DEMOLBSC.VBP at design time, it appears as shown in Figure 20.8. Note that the **ListSC** ActiveX control on Form1 looks pretty much the same as it does in its own LSTBOXSC.VBP project (displayed previously in Figure 20.7).

The procedures in Listing 20.8 enable the application programmer to size the client area of ListSC1 in one of two ways:

- At design time in the Properties window, explicitly set its **ScaleHeight** and **ScaleWidth** properties to the same values as its **Height** and **Width** properties (which, remember, are really the **Height** and **Width** properties of the **UserControl** container object).

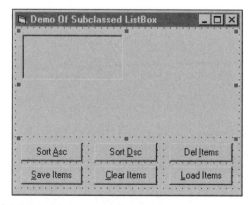

Figure 20.8 Form1 of DEMOLBSC.VBP at design time.

- At runtime in the **Form_Load** event procedure, set its **ScaleHeight** and **ScaleWidth** properties equal to its **Height** and **Width** properties with these two lines of code:

```
ListSC1.ScaleWidth = ListSC1.Width
ListSC1.ScaleHeight = ListSC1.Height
```

I took the second approach in DEMOLBSC.VBP. When you select Run | Start, code in the **Form_Load** event procedure calls the **FillWithDAO** method of ListSC1. That method is passed values that tell it to fill the ActiveX control's subclassed **ListBox** with a field from VB's BIBLIO.MDB. When the method is done loading the **ListBox**, Form1 appears as shown in Figure 20.9.

From here on in the demonstration project, you can click the various buttons and watch the subclassed members of the **ListBox** object encapsulated in the ActiveX control do their thing. As I said earlier in the chapter, I'm not going to repeat the material from Chapter 10, which explains how the **FillWithDAO**, **DeleteItems**, **Save**, and **Load** subclassed methods work.

You should also remember that, for this demonstration version of **ListSC**, I didn't implement the proxy properties and the **Sorted** custom property as writeable at design time. But, from the examples of the **ScaleHeight** and **ScaleWidth** properties here (and the **Picture** property of the **TBIcon** ActiveX control), you should now understand how to do this.

ActiveX Controls Vs. ActiveX Servers

I want to finish up this chapter's discussion of ActiveX controls by emphasizing again what an ActiveX control is at a lower level of abstraction. To the COM/OLE software protocol, an ActiveX control is just another kind of in-

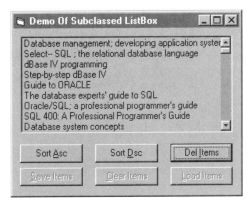

Figure 20.9 Form1 of DEMOLBSC.VBP at runtime.

process server/component. There are three kinds of special features that an ActiveX control component supports, which an ActiveX server component can't provide:

- An ActiveX control presents à friendlier public interface, in the form of its Properties window, to the developer who wants to reuse it.

- An ActiveX control can also be connected to a *property page,* which displays the control's properties in an alternate format. Each property page you connect to your control becomes one tab on a tabbed Properties dialog box. VB5 handles all the details of presenting the pages as a tabbed dialog box, and manages the OK, Cancel, and Apply buttons. All you have to do is lay out the controls that will be used to set the property values. Property pages are useful when a group of properties interact in a complex fashion, as with the **Toolbar** ActiveX control included with Visual Basic. They're also useful for controls that will be distributed internationally because the captions can be localized for different languages.

- An ActiveX control can enable you to completely override the normal behavior of an intrinsic property of a VB control object (as in the example of the **Sorted** property of the **ListSC** ActiveX control).

> **Note:** It used to be the case that only ActiveX controls could support developer-declared events. Although I did not use any developer-declared events in the book's ActiveX component server, VB5 now supports that capability.

My opinion of VB5-created ActiveX controls, based on playing around with them for a relatively short period of time, is that they are a pretty cool addition to the toolkit of the VB OOP developer. If you or your company need a very specialized kind of functionality that no third-party vendor of ActiveX controls currently provides, you now have an easy-to-develop and easy-to-maintain solution available in VB5.

However, don't be fooled by the hype about speed. Even if you compile a VB5-written ActiveX control to native code, it will always run significantly slower than a third-party software manufacturer's ActiveX control that encapsulates the same functionality. VB5-compiled native code, even in its final released version, will definitely not be as fast as C or C++, no matter what Microsoft's PR evangelists say.

There are three other issues that you should be aware of regarding the tradeoffs between developing reusable objects as ActiveX controls versus ActiveX servers. First, my experiences developing the **ListSC** ActiveX control and the **List** object of the ActiveX server component indicate that an ActiveX control takes significantly more time and effort than the same functionality in the form of an ActiveX server component. This is especially the case if you are subclassing one of VB's intrinsic control objects because of the need to replicate and test the proxy properties and methods of the control object.

Second, I find the debugging and testing process for ActiveX controls, which I do not have the space to elaborate on here, to be far more awkward and cumbersome than the process for debugging ActiveX server components. To find out what's involved in testing an ActiveX control, see the topic *Running The ShapeLabel Control At Design Time* in Visual Basic Books Online.

Third, some developers may try to tell you that an ActiveX control implementation runs dramatically faster than the same functionality encapsulated in an ActiveX server component. They will argue that an ActiveX control has to be much faster because it is actually part of the application that reuses its services. However, this is definitely not the case, and the reason is related to what you saw in Figure 20.6, which showed the Windows registry entry for the **TBIcon** ActiveX control. You must always remember that at a lower level of abstraction in the COM/OLE software architecture, an ActiveX control is just another kind of in-process ActiveX component.

To demonstrate my point about the relative performance of an ActiveX control versus an ActiveX DLL server component, I have set up two demonstration executables—DEMOCTL.EXE and DEMODLL.EXE. If you installed them when you used the book's CD-ROM setup routine, they are on the path C:\VBOOPEFS\ACTXCTLS. Both executables reuse the same three members (**FillWithDAO**, **Sort**, and **Save**) on about 250 records from BIBLIO.MDB. However, DEMCTL.EXE reuses them from the **ListSC** ActiveX control and DEMODLL.EXE reuses them from the **List** object of the book's class library.

I benchmarked these two implementations and the results are listed in Table 20.2. Each of the five sets of timings was done from a complete reboot of Windows NT 4 so that I could rule out any caching effects. I used the **TimeGetTime** Windows API function (which is accurate to 10 milliseconds when called under Windows NT) for the timings. In the case of the ActiveX server component, I used the in-process version and early binding

Table 20.2 Total milliseconds required to instantiate, load, and reuse.

Control	DLL Server	Control Faster/(Slower)
3515	3665	4.3%
3524	3625	2.9%
3534	3635	2.8%
3645	3705	1.6%
3594	3635	1.1%

to get as much speed as possible and to have an apples-to-apples comparison. The results clearly show that although the ActiveX control implementation is faster overall, the difference is slight. The average of the five timings indicates that the ActiveX control implementation is only 2.5 percent faster.

However, you have to remember that the server component's implementation is part of a much larger DLL file. Also, its members have quite a bit of syntax checking code that I did not bother to put into the demonstration version of the **ListSC** ActiveX control. And, finally, the **ListSC** ActiveX control would be slightly slower if I had implemented all of the **ListBox** object's proxy members and properties. So, in the end, the ActiveX control's edge over the server component is probably only about 1.5 to 2.0 percent.

VB5 And Add-Ins

For those readers who are upgrading to VB5 from VB3 or who are first working with the language in its latest VB5 release, add-ins may be a totally new concept. Even those developers who have been using VB4 over the last year may not be too familiar with them. Add-ins are tools (actually, a special kind of ActiveX DLL or EXE component) that you can create programmatically by using objects and collections in VB5's extensibility object model to customize and extend VB's IDE. The primary goal of an add-in is to enable you to automate something in VB's IDE that is difficult or tedious to accomplish manually.

Table 20.3 lists the four kinds of add-ins you can create with VB5.

Most add-ins used with VB4 were visible; that is, they appeared as commands in menus or as buttons on toolbars in the IDE. Now, add-ins don't

Table 20.3 Kinds of VB5 add-ins.

Name	Description
Add-In	The generic term for a program you develop that performs task(s) within the IDE, often in response to certain events (such as a mouse click or a form opening). Its actions may or may not be visible to the user.
Wizard	A special type of add-in that leads a user step-by-step through a task, often an especially complex or tricky one. A Wizard consists of a sequence of Form objects, each one containing an image in the upper-left corner, a label description to the right of the image, and an optional area near the bottom in which other control objects (such as ListBox or CommandButton objects) can be placed. To help you create Wizards, VB5 comes with an add-in called the Wizard Manager.
Utility	A kind of add-in, sometimes a rather large one, that doesn't necessarily require VB to run. This means that it is compiled as an ActiveX EXE component, but it retains the ability to also be called as an add-in in VB's IDE. VISDATA.EXE is an example of a utility add-in that comes with VB5's sample code. APIBRWS.EXE is an example of a utility add-in that comes with this book's CD-ROM.
Builder	A kind of add-in that helps a user to view or set properties of a control, or properties that several controls have in common. Builders were useful in VB4, but they aren't normally created as add-ins anymore for VB5 because these capabilities are now available through the PropertyPage object.

necessarily have to be visible; instead, they can remain hidden in the background and do things like:

- Respond to events such as the sizing of a form or control.
- Reset a **Timer** control object when a certain project loads.

Writing Your Own VB5 Add-Ins

Just as with ActiveX controls, there are many third-party software vendors who write elaborate add-ins for VB. One of the best is Sheridan Software, whose VBAssist, ClassAssist, and sp_Assist products are well known among VB developers. However, up until recently, most of these commercial add-ins (written in C or C++ by the way, not VB) have been commodity-priced. This is starting to change as vendors like LogicWorks (the ERwin product) and Rational Software Corp. (the Rational Rose and Visual Test products) have migrated their client/server, OOP modeling tools from C++ and

PowerBuilder to VB5. The ERwin and Rational Rose add-in products start at $3,000 and can cost quite a bit more than that if you purchase all the bells-and-whistles extras.

The documentation that came with VB4 on how to write add-ins was pretty poor. Luckily, VB5's add-in documentation is better, and the topic *Creating A Basic Add-In* in Visual Basic Books Online can help you work your way through a step-by-step example of how to create an add-in. There is one major difference between VB4 and VB5 add-ins that you need to keep in mind, especially if you spent a significant amount of time developing them with VB4. The extensibility object hierarchy in VB5 has changed significantly from its predecessor, and it is now more powerful and complex than it used to be.

Although the focus of this book is not on add-ins, I did include two simple examples of utility add-ins on the book's CD-ROM. If you installed the files for these add-ins when you ran the CD-ROM's SETUP.EXE, they should be on the path C:\VBOOPEFS\VBADDINS.

Both these add-ins, described in Table 20.4, run under VB4 and VB5. If you are interested in seeing how they are written and work, follow these steps for each one:

1. Open up the add-in's project in VB5 (WINDINFO.VBP or APIBRWS.VBP).
2. Select Run | Start to make the necessary entries in VB's INI file. The code that does this is in **Sub Main**.
3. Select File | Make EXE to remake and register the add-in, accepting the current EXE name. VB automatically registers the ActiveX EXE add-in in the Windows registry.
4. Select File | Save Project to save the changes.

After you have registered the two add-ins, select Add-Ins | Add-In Manager to display the available add-ins. Check the two items at the bottom of the list, Window Info Utility and Windows API Browser Utility, as shown in Figure 20.10.

Click on OK and VB connects the two add-in items to the bottom of its own Add-Ins menu, as shown in Figure 20.11. Select either item from the Add-Ins menu to see it in action. I hope you find the book's two add-ins useful. I also hope you order the full-featured, 32-bit version of the Windows API Browser. I guarantee that if you liked the code that came with this book and feel you got your money's worth, you'll definitely like the Windows API Browser utility!

Table 20.4 Add-ins included on the book's CD-ROM.

Project Name	Description
WINDINFO.VBP	The ActiveX EXE component WINDINFO.EXE, with the add-in title of Window Info Utility, displays information for the window (handle, class name, caption, and so on) currently under the mouse pointer. It is found in the book's class library as the GetWindowInfo method of the Utility object.
APIBRWS.VBP	The ActiveX EXE component APIBRWS.EXE, with the add-in title of Windows API Browser Utility, runs a demo version of my Windows API Browser utility. The full-featured 16/32-bit version of the utility costs only $9.99 plus $5.00 S/H.

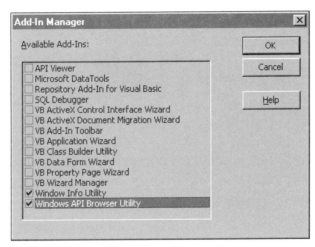

Figure 20.10 VB's Add-In Manager dialog box.

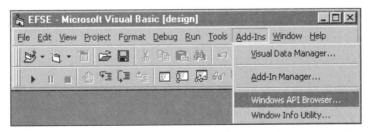

Figure 20.11 VB's Add-In menu, with book's two Add-In utilities connected.

Add-In Wizards That Come With VB5

There are almost a dozen add-ins that are installed and registered when you install VB5. Many of these add-ins are Wizards that help you do various complex development tasks within VB's IDE. Table 20.5 lists the most important of these Wizards.

To help you learn how to write your own add-in Wizards, VB5 comes with a Wizard Template project titled WIZARD.VBP. Installed on the \WIZARDS\TEMPLATE path of VB5, this project contains source code that will be helpful to anyone trying to create an initial Wizard add-in. Needless to say, a comprehensive treatment of the subject of VB add-ins (Wizards or otherwise) could itself fill an entire book. At this time, I don't know of anyone who is writing such a book. Who knows, maybe that'll be my next project, after I've spent a couple months recuperating from the burnout I've experienced writing this book.

Other VB5 IDE Extensions (Real And Rumored)

I'm going to finish up this chapter by highlighting a few other extensions to VB5's IDE, which are meant to make your life as a VB developer easier and more fun. In no particular order, some of the most important ones are as follows:

- *Visual Basic Books Online*—For the first time, VB comes with a set of online files that contains all of its documentation in one location. Books Online also includes multimedia demonstrations and topics that aren't available in the printed documentation. You can find all the topics available on any subject in VB5's documentation, print or online, with a single search. This is a great addition to the programming language's IDE! As a long-time advocate of Windows Help files as the way to document applications, I heartily applaud Microsoft for adding Visual Basic Books Online to the product.

- *Project and Module templates*—As I indicated in the Introduction to the book, because VB5 now supports the development of so many different kinds of applications, the IDE can be very bewildering to someone new to the language. The addition of the Project and Module templates (displayed as icons in the New Project, Add Form, Add Module, and other Add dialog boxes) helps to rationalize and organize the IDE at a high level of abstraction.

Table 20.5 Major Wizard Add-Ins included with VB5.

Wizard Name	Description
ActiveX Control Interface	Although the topic for this Wizard was blank in Visual Basic Books Online for the Beta2 release of VB5, the Wizard itself and its associated Help file were functional. It helps you define the public interface for an ActiveX control by writing the stubs for the procedures that will comprise its properties, methods and event, and also to write some of the code for the procedures. Using this Wizard is the only way to go when you're trying to develop your first ActiveX control. It can be used in conjunction with/before the use of the Property Page Wizard.
Property Page	This Wizard helps you create property pages for an existing UserControl object that will be made into an ActiveX control. It can be used in conjunction with/after the use of the ActiveX Control Interface Wizard.
ActiveX Document Migration	This Wizard helps you change an existing Form object into an ActiveX Document object. An ActiveX Document is a specific type of ActiveX object that can be placed and activated within ActiveX Document containers, such as the Microsoft Internet Explorer. When you convert a form to an ActiveX Document, the Wizard helps you: copy the form's properties to a new user document, retaining all Menu items; copy all controls, retaining the same names and properties; and convert form event handlers into ActiveX Document object event handlers as the code is being copied.
Application	This Wizard helps you to create a new, fully functioning application. After the Wizard is done, you can edit the forms, and then view and modify the code it creates. This is a great tool for programmers who are new to VB.
Data Form	This Wizard is a new-and-improved version of the Data Form Designer add-in that comes with VB4. The Data Form Wizard automatically generates a Visual Basic form that contains individual data-bound controls and the procedures needed to manage information derived from local or remote data sources.

- *New toolbars*—The new toolbars that come with VB5 and the ability to dock them or let them float free are nice additions.

I have left one of these extensions, the VB Class Builder utility add-in, to the end of this discussion. It is also the feature I am referring to in this section's title when I use the word *rumored*. For the last few months, the word on the VB grapevine was that VB5 was finally going to add inheritance to its IDE. Whether or not this was going to include the capability for multiple inheritance, no one was sure, but everyone was hoping that at least simple inheritance would be supported. I'm sorry to say that it appears, from the Beta2 release, that VB5 still will not support inheritance.

I think what sparked the inheritance rumors was the inclusion of the VB Class Builder utility add-in in the Beta1 release. The Class Builder utility is meant to help you build a class and collection hierarchy for your VB5 project. It keeps track of the hierarchy and generates the framework code necessary to implement the relationships between the classes and collections.

If the Class Builder utility is invoked for the first time in a project that already has existing classes and collections, they will all initially appear at the root of the hierarchy because the Class Builder does not yet have information about the hierarchy. You can arrange the existing classes and collections using drag-and-drop; the Class Builder will remember this arrangement. When you start the Class Builder add-in utility in a new project without any **ClassModule** objects, it appears as shown in Figure 20.12.

When you select File | New | Class, you can add a **ClassModule** object (for example, Rectngle). Then, when you click on Rectngle in the Classes pane and select File | New | Class again, you can add another **ClassModule** object at the next level of the hierarchy (for example, Square). You can also add the stubs for procedures (properties, methods, and events) to these classes. Figure 20.13 shows how this two-level hierarchy will appear in the Class Builder dialog box.

Figure 20.12   Initial appearance of the Class Builder dialog box.

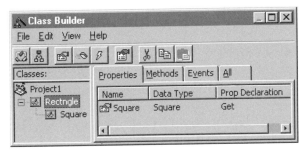

Figure 20.13 Class Builder dialog box with two-level hierarchy.

At first glance, I can see how the rumors about inheritance got started, but on closer observation, what you find is disappointing. What the Class Builder add-in actually does (as a modal dialog box, unfortunately) is to help you implement the kind of hierarchy that Visual Basic Books Online refers to as an *object model*, as opposed to the kind traditionally referred to by the term *inheritance*. Inheritance is the technique by which a subclass is derived from a base or super class, in the process automatically inheriting the members of the base class. An object model, on the other hand, is a hierarchy that implements *containment*. Containment is the technique by which complex collections/objects contain simpler collections/objects.

Well, containment is not new to VB5, and compared to the inheritance methodology that languages like Smalltalk, Delphi 2, and PowerBuilder 5 support, it's an inelegant kludge. Yes, containment is better than nothing, but it's certainly nothing to brag about at this stage of VB's evolution. And, so, the one extension to the VB IDE that client/server development shops we're hoping for the most has not been included in VB5.

You should keep in mind, though, that a containment hierarchy that goes deeper than two to three levels really starts to degrade performance. Microsoft itself has belatedly realized that its own Office suite applications, although designed and implemented as OLE servers (soon to be ActiveX components with Office 97), do not have their public objects and members reused very much by non-Microsoft applications. The main reason for this is their poor performance, partly because you often have to instantiate four to five levels of containment classes to reach the public member you want to reuse. Another bad feature of an overly complex containment hierarchy is the mind-numbing syntax that you have to remember to drill down through the multiple levels.

However, as we conclude our discussion, let's focus on the fact that with all of its new IDE extensions, VB5's glass is still way more than half full. Yes, maybe the missing feature of inheritance means that it's 10 to 15 percent empty for some developers. But, for those who need simple inheritance, Sheridan Software's ClassAssist add-in utility is available. For the rest of us, there is plenty to like and learn about VB5's new IDE. As someone was supposed to have said during World War II (and I paraphrase him here), "Damn the inheritance, full speed ahead."

THE FINISHING TOUCHES 21

Chapter 21 concludes our study of object-oriented programming and the development of ActiveX components with VB5. I'll bet that when you started working your way through this book, you had no idea of what you were letting yourself in for. But you made it; and I hope that, at this point, you'll agree both that VB5 is a really cool tool for OOP and ActiveX development and that this book was well worth the money you paid for it.

What we want to do in this final chapter is look at some miscellaneous issues related to ActiveX components that I've grouped together under the title of *Finishing Touches*. These issues are of two general kinds. First, there are some advanced topics that are best left to the end of a book like this because they require that you advance your learning curve to the point where you can better understand them. The topics in this chapter that fall into this category are:

- Calling ActiveX components from other programming languages.

- Running an out-of-process ActiveX component as a standalone executable.

- Maintaining compatibility among different versions of an ActiveX component.

Second, some issues related to making and registering ActiveX components with VB5 only come into play at the very end of the development cycle. These kinds of issues are also best left to the end of a book like this. The topics in this chapter that fall into this category are:

- Compiling an ActiveX component (p-code versus native code).
- Creating a Windows Help file for an ActiveX component.
- Using VB5's Setup Wizard to install ActiveX components.

Calling VB ActiveX Components From Other Languages

Because Microsoft's ActiveX component software protocol is cross-platform and cross-language compatible, components that you write with Visual Basic can expose their objects and members to other ActiveX component-compliant languages. These other languages can call any public members of public classes in your Visual Basic-created component. You need to understand the implications of this fact when you use VB5 to design and write methods for ActiveX components, and when you try to call methods in components that were written with other ActiveX-compliant languages (for example, Delphi 2, PowerBuilder 5, Visual C++, and so on).

All ActiveX-compliant languages support the traditional string and numeric data types, so they can call any member of a Visual Basic class library whose arguments use only those data types (**String**, **Integer**, **Long**, **Single**, and **Double**). Most of these languages also support the **Variant** data type (or something equivalent), so they should be able to read the results or error codes returned from members of the book's class library.

Where it starts to get more problematic is when a language like Delphi 2 or, as you will see shortly, Excel 7's Visual Basic for Applications calls a member that requires a non-traditional data type as an argument. In the book's class library, the most obvious example of this situation is where a member's argument is declared as the OLE Automation data type **Object**.

All ActiveX-compliant languages support the underlying OLE Automation data type **IDispatch**. **IDispatch**, at a lower level of abstraction, corresponds to Visual Basic's OLE Automation **Object** data type. So for example, Delphi 2 or Excel 7 VBA has no problem calling the **DeleteItems** method of the **List** class of the book's class library. **DeleteItems** takes the *CboOrLst* argument, which is declared **As Object** (that is, **IDispatch**). Where the problem arises is in the **DeleteItems** method's code itself. That code references certain properties and methods that Visual Basic's built-in **ComboBox** and **ListBox** objects support.

We need to concern ourselves with these two key questions:

- Will Delphi's list-related objects and Excel VBA's list-related objects support the same members as Visual Basic's list objects do (for example, the **hWnd** and **MultiSelect** properties and the **RemoveItem** method)?

- If Delphi's list objects and Excel VBA's list objects do support the same properties and methods, will the functionality of those members adhere to the same specifications as Visual Basic's members?

It turns out that you must deal with these two questions on a case-by-case basis. The easiest way to demonstrate this problem of handling **Object** data types as arguments in ActiveX component members is to use Excel VBA and the class library's **DeleteItems** method as an example.

Calling The DeleteItems Method From Excel 7

To work through this demonstration, you must have a copy of Microsoft Excel 7.

1. Start Excel 7.

2. Select File|Open, find the file DELITEM.XLS (located on C:\VBOOPEFS\VBCLSDEM), and open it.

3. Select Tools|Run Dialog to display the Demo Of DeleteItems Method dialog box, which is shown in Figure 21.1.

4. Click on the Fill With Items button. VBA code fills the **ListBox** object with integers from 1 to 250 and selects the odd ones.

5. Click on the DeleteItems button. VBA code declares an object variable, uses the **CreateObject** function to instantiate the **List** class of the book's class library, calls the **DeleteItems** method to remove the selected items, and displays the message box shown in Figure 21.2.

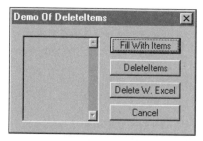

Figure 21.1 Excel dialog box to demo call to **DeleteItems** method.

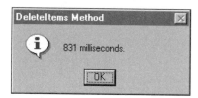

Figure 21.2 Time required to delete items with **DeleteItems** method.

This dialog box shows how long, in milliseconds, the **DeleteItems** method took.

6. Click on OK to clear the message box, then choose Fill Items again. VBA refills the **ListBox** object.

7. Click on the Delete W. Excel button. VBA removes the selected items with its native code and displays the message box shown in Figure 21.3, which indicates how long native Excel-VBA code took.

8. Click Cancel when you are done running the demonstration.

As you would imagine, the native Excel-VBA code is faster than calling the method in the book's class library. However, once the ActiveX component is cached, the difference between the two times is significantly reduced. The comparative timings in Table 21.1 show the component to be only slightly slower (all timings in the table were made with the ActiveX component cached).

The average difference of the five sets of timings in Table 21.1 shows the call to the method in the ActiveX component to be just 1.7 percent slower than the native VBA code. All timings were done on a 166 MHz Pentium under Windows 95. The in-process EFSD.DLL version of the book's ActiveX component was used. Interestingly enough, on the same Pentium 166 MHz PC under Windows NT 4.0, the times using both approaches were on average 40 percent faster than under Windows 95. Your absolute times will

Figure 21.3 Time required to delete items with Excel-VBA code.

differ, depending on your processor's speed, but the percentage differences should be about the same. This demonstration illustrates three points:

- From Excel VBA's ActiveX-compliant programming language, you *can* call a method in a Visual Basic class library whose argument is declared as the **Object** data type.
- The called method's performance is pretty competitive with native Excel-VBA code.
- 32-bit VB5 and VBA code runs significantly faster under Windows NT 4.0 than under Windows 95.

What this demonstration does not show is the extra effort that was required to write the **DeleteItems** method so it would work with Excel's **ComboBox** or **ListBox** object.

The DeleteItems Method's Excel-Related Code

Listing 21.1 shows the code in the **DeleteItems** method that ensures the method works with Excel's **ComboBox** and **ListBox** objects.

Table 21.1 Comparative times to delete items from Excel list.

Excel-VBA Time	DeleteItems Method's Time
1537	1559
1540	1556
1539	1569
1536	1569
1538	1562

Listing 21.1 DeleteItems method's Excel-related code.

```
Function DeleteItems(CboOrLst As Object)

    . . .

    ' Enable error handler and do syntax checking:
    On Error GoTo ET

    If TypeName(CboOrLst) <> "ListBox" And _
        TypeName(CboOrLst) <> "ComboBox" Then
        E.TrapSyntax 8, PROC, "CboOrLst"
    End If

    ' Execute member's algorithm--
    ' * If it is Excel ComboBox or ListBox object, use this
    '    code because you cannot get handle for these objects:
    If CL.IsExcelObj(CboOrLst) Then

        For Item = CboOrLst.ListCount To 1 Step -1

            If CboOrLst.Selected(Item) Then
                CboOrLst.RemoveItem Item
            End If

        Next Item

    . . .

    End If

End Sub
```

I'd like to focus on several points that this code illustrates. First, Visual Basic's **TypeName** function returns many of the same class names for Excel VBA objects as it does for Visual Basic's own objects; so, the syntax checking code can validate that the object reference passed to the *CboOrLst* argument is a **ListBox** object. What it cannot determine is whether it is an Excel **ListBox** object. This is done with the **IsExcelObj** method of the **CL** class, in a way similar to the approach used by the **IsForm** and **IsMDIForm** methods, which we discussed earlier in the book. If you pass an Excel object other than a **ComboBox** or **ListBox** to the *CboOrLst* argument, the **DeleteItems** method displays its usual syntax error message.

Second, if it is an Excel **ListBox** object, the **DeleteItems** method executes a **For...Next** loop in native Visual Basic for Applications code to delete the selected items. You must use native-VBA code for an Excel **ListBox** because code further down in the **DeleteItems** method refers to the object's **hWnd** property (to call the **SendMessage** Windows API function), and Excel's objects do not support the **hWnd** property.

Third, the native-VBA code in the Excel-related **For...Next** loop is slightly different than the native-VB code you could write for a Visual Basic **ComboBox** or **ListBox** object. The difference is that the array of items in Excel's lists is one-based, but the array of items in Visual Basic's lists is zero-based. So, the **For** statement for a Visual Basic list would read:

```
For Item = CboOrLst.ListCount - 1 To 0 Step -1
```

On the other hand, the **For** statement for an Excel **ListBox**, as in Listing 21.1, reads:

```
For Item = CboOrLst.ListCount To 1 Step -1
```

This example of tailoring the **DeleteItems** method of the **List** class to work with Excel's list-related objects should be enough to show you the care required to make members, which take the **Object** data type as arguments, reusable by more than just Visual Basic itself.

The other thing to remember about the general issue of calling VB-written ActiveX components from other languages is that you cannot stop a programmer in another language from trying to call one of your Visual Basic methods. If the method is a public member of a public class, it can be called. For example, you could comment out all the code in Listing 21.1 that checks for and handles Excel's **ComboBox** or **ListBox** object, and then remake the component. However, if you took this approach and then called the **DeleteItems** method from the demonstration code in DELITEM.XLS, the book's class library would display the runtime error message shown in Figure 21.4.

If you wrote the **DeleteItems** method, *you* know that the runtime error occurred on the statement:

```
NumSel = SendMessage(CboOrLst.hWnd, LB_GETSELCOUNT, _
                     vbEmpty, vbEmpty)
```

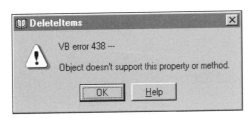

Figure 21.4 VB runtime error 438.

What caused the runtime error was the reference to the **hWnd** property, which none of Excel's objects support. So code execution is rerouted to the enabled error handler at the bottom of the method, and the class library's **Error** class displays the error message. If, however, you are not privy to the **DeleteItems** method's code, the error message would be true but not too helpful. All that really matters, though, is that the error is handled gracefully and that the ActiveX component does not crash and bring down the client application with it. In a nutshell, because any programmer in the ActiveX universe can call public members of your component, it is *your* responsibility to ensure that the worst that can happen is that an error message is displayed.

One last issue worth mentioning about calling a VB5 ActiveX component's methods from some other programming language is related to performance. As you saw earlier in the book, for traditional algorithms that do encryptions, sorts, and mathematical/financial calculations, nothing runs faster than Assembly. Because these kinds of algorithms normally require only the traditional string and numeric data types, an ActiveX component's method that relies on a call to a third-party Assembly DLL like Crescent Software's QuickPak Professional product can be called from any ActiveX-compliant language.

Compiling An ActiveX Component

One of the exciting new features that VB5 supports is its ability to compile any kind of VB project, including ActiveX components, to either p-code or to native code. The settings that allow you to switch between compilation modes are on the Compile tab of the Project Properties dialog box. If you start VB5 and open EFSD.DLL, you can find these settings by selecting Project|EFSD Properties and clicking the Compile tab. The Project Properties dialog box should then appear as in Figure 21.5.

You may not have noticed it before, but the book's ActiveX component compilation switch was set to p-code when you installed it from the CD-ROM. If you did not change the setting to native code, any time you remade and registered the book's class library while working through this book, you were compiling the p-code version. For almost the entire development cycle of an ActiveX component, the p-code compilation setting is what you should use. There are three reasons for this:

- It takes significantly longer to compile to native code (300 to 400 percent longer with the book's class library).

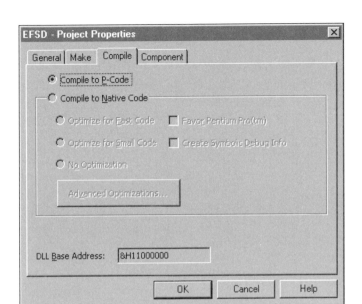

Figure 21.5 Compile tab of Project Properties dialog box.

- The native-code DLL or EXE file is 80 to 85 percent larger than under p-code compilation and takes up that much more space on your hard drive.
- There is no good reason to compile a native-code version until you are ready to use VB5's Setup Wizard to create the distribution disks for the ActiveX component.

However, you definitely should set the compilation switch to native code when you make the final version. From the informal benchmarks that I have run, it is clear that, although compiling to native code does not result in dramatic performance gains, you can expect to realize an average increase in speed of 15 to 30 percent. The actual increase is dependent on the specific mix of functionality and code in your ActiveX component or standard EXE project. It may also be the case that the final version of VB5, stripped of its debug code, will produce slightly faster native code than the Beta2 release that I am working with does.

When you do select the Compile To Native Code option button on the Compile tab, the other possible selections related to native compilation are enabled. These native-code options and their meanings are listed in Table 21.2.

Table 21.2 Native-code compilation options.

Setting	Description
Optimize for Fast Code	Maximizes the speed of the EXE or DLL file by instructing VB5's compiler to favor speed over size. The compiler can reduce many constructs to functionally similar sequences of machine code. In some cases, the differences offer a trade-off of size versus speed. If you select this option, you will have code that is larger in size but is the fastest possible version of your project for a 486 or 586 processor.
Optimize for Small Code	Minimizes the size of the EXE or DLL file by instructing the compiler to favor size over speed. The compiler can reduce many constructs to functionally similar sequences of machine code. If you select this option, you will have code that is smaller in size but that runs slower than if the Optimize for Fast Code switch is set.
No Optimization	Compile without optimizations. Results in an EXE or DLL file that is a compromise between the compilations achieved by the Fast Code and Small Code optimizations.
Favor Pentium Pro	Optimizes the code created to favor the Pentium Pro™ processor. Use this option for programs meant only for the Pentium Pro™ processor. Code generated with this option will still run on earlier processors, but it does not perform as well. Selecting this checkbox, in conjunction with selecting Optimize for Fast Code, results in the fastest possible version of your project for the Pentium Pro™ processor.
Create Symbolic Debug Info	Generates symbolic debug information in the EXE or DLL file. An executable file created using this option can be debugged using Visual C++ or debuggers that use the CodeView style of debug information. Setting this option generates a PDB file with the symbol information for your executable.
Advanced Optimizations	Displays the Advanced Optimizations dialog box. See the next paragraph for a discussion of these features.
DLL Base Address	Sets a base address for the program, overriding the default location for a DLL file (at 0X10000000). The operating system first attempts to load a program at its specified or default address. If there is insufficient space, the system relocates the program. This option is only enabled for in-process DLL ActiveX components.

When you click the Advanced Optimizations button on the Compile tab, VB5 displays the Advanced Optimizations dialog box shown in Figure 21.6. If you're thinking of using these advanced settings, take heed of the Microsoft VB development team's warning in Visual Basic's Help file. They explicitly state that "enabling these optimizations may prevent the correct execution of your program." My advice is to not use them (too much hassle for too little payoff) and, if you do use them, to test your ActiveX component very carefully before distributing it. If you want more information about these settings, click the Help button on the Advanced Optimizations dialog box.

The bottom-line answer to the question of whether to have VB5 compile your standard or ActiveX component project to native code is a resounding Yes! No matter what kind of VB applications you write, they will run faster when compiled to native code. However, given my experience with the Beta2 release, compiling to native code is nowhere close to being a panacea for all the potential performance bottlenecks in VB applications. If your application runs like a snail because it uses too many ActiveX controls, or it doesn't take advantage of Windows API function calls when appropriate, or the poor I/O performance of the server database you're linked to is the real culprit, then compiling to native code won't solve your performance problem. But all other factors being equal, it will speed up your VB applications by 15 to 30 percent.

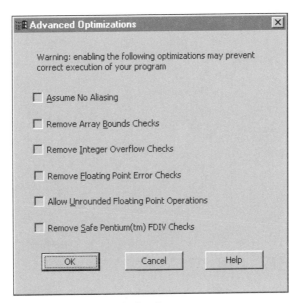

Figure 21.6 Advanced Optimizations dialog box.

Compatible ActiveX Components

On the Project tab of the Options dialog box of VB4 (Tools | Options), there is a Compatible OLE Component entry. VB5 has replaced this one entry with three possible compatibility settings. If you start VB5 and open EFSE.EXE, you can find these settings by selecting Project | EFSE Properties and clicking the Component tab. The Project Properties dialog box should then appear as in Figure 21.7. VB5 uses these compatibility settings to monitor whether you are breaking the existing public interface of your ActiveX component and to warn you when you are about to do so.

The three possible compatibility settings and their meanings are in Table 21.3.

The Location box setting, if you use it, must point to the path and name of the DLL or EXE file that is your ActiveX component. You can only make the entry after you have first made/compiled an initial version of the in-process or out-of-process component. Visual Basic then uses the setting to warn you when you try to make a new version of the component that is incompatible with the previous version. If it detects an incompatibility, it displays the dialog box shown in Figure 21.8.

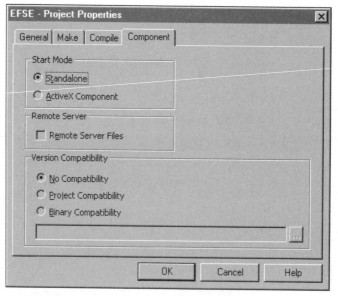

Figure 21.7 Component tab of Project Properties dialog box.

Table 21.3   Version Compatibility settings.

Setting	Description
No Compatibility	Version compatibility is not enforced and the Location box at the bottom of the tab is disabled.
Project Compatibility	If checked, the Location box is enabled. Use the Location box to search for the ActiveX component's EXE or DLL file with which the current version of the component is to be compatible, when it is compiled. This setting is for an ActiveX component that has been compiled to p-code.
Binary Compatibility	If checked, the Location box is enabled. Use the Location box to search for the ActiveX component's EXE or DLL file with which the current version of the component is to be compatible, when it is compiled. This setting is for an ActiveX component that has been compiled to native code.

Here is a list of some of the things that you can do to an ActiveX component's project that will render it incompatible with the previously compiled version:

- Change the name of an existing project, class, or member.
- Change the declaration of a public class or member to a private one.
- Remove arguments or change the order of arguments in the declaration of a member.
- Change a custom property from read and write (that is, it has both **Property Let** and **Property Get** procedures) to read-only or write-only.

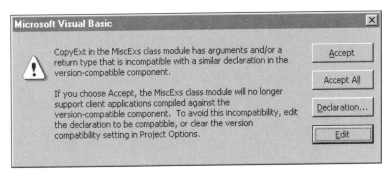

Figure 21.8   Component incompatibility alert message.

- Change an optional argument to a required argument in the declaration of a member.

- Add a required argument to the declaration of a member.

Visual Basic uses the Version Compatibility setting to maintain the same registration number, the GUID or global unique ID, for the ActiveX component and in the Windows registration database when you build a new version of the ActiveX component. If you do not keep the same registration number, the registration database gradually gets cluttered up with outdated GUIDs.

Also, if the GUID for the ActiveX component changes and you or some other developer previously hard-coded a reference to an ActiveX component in a client application (that is, used early binding), the reference will no longer be valid and the client application will no longer run correctly. This is why most Visual Basic ActiveX component developers only use the **CreateObject** function approach (that is, late binding) to test their components from a client application. **CreateObject** instantiates the class regardless of how many outdated GUIDs there are in the registry. The only time it fails is if there is no valid programmatic ID string in the registry at all.

Unless you are extremely disciplined in the way you design classes and their members, you will in the course of development make many changes that render the previous version of the component incompatible. Whether or not you want Visual Basic to warn you each time it detects such an incompatibility is questionable. Different Visual Basic ActiveX component developers have different philosophies about using the Version Compatibility settings; however, based on my experience, I must agree with Deborah Kurata, who says in her book *Doing Objects In Microsoft Visual Basic 4.0* that only an actual released version of the ActiveX component should be listed (under the Version Compatibility entry), not an interim build version. The hassle of always seeing and having to clear the message box in Figure 21.8, by selecting Accept All, is intolerable.

There are different techniques you can use to periodically clean up the registration database. You can manually delete outdated entries with the Registry Editor (REGEDIT.EXE); or you can store clean versions of the two registry DAT files under different names and manually replace the cluttered-up versions of the DAT files with the clean versions. Finally, you can also try using some of the tools that come on the Visual Basic CD-ROM, such as REGCLEAN.EXE and REGCLN16.EXE (located in \TOOLS\PSS). However, in my experience, these tools do not clean out all the outdated entries.

Running An ActiveX EXE In Standalone Mode

As you have seen earlier in the book, an out-of-process ActiveX EXE component has special capabilities that the in-process ActiveX DLL component does not support. One of those capabilities, which we have not yet looked at, is to run the ActiveX EXE component in two different modes:

- As an ActiveX component, whose objects expose their members for reuse by a client application.
- As a normal, executable application.

It is interesting to note that all of the Microsoft Office 7 applications also have this capability. Excel 7, arguably the greatest Windows application that has ever been written, is a spreadsheet that everyone knows how to run in standalone mode. When you run it this way, it normally starts by displaying an MDI parent window and one MDI child window (actually, a **Worksheet** object of the **Sheets** collection).

Because Excel 7 is, at a lower level of abstraction, an OLE Automation server (soon to be an ActiveX component in Excel 97), any ActiveX-compliant programming language can avail itself of the reusable objects that comprise Excel 7. The client application's programmer does this in the same way as when reusing objects written with VB5, by following the usual three-step process:

- Declare a module-level object variable.
- Instantiate the class to be reused with the **CreateObject** function and assign the object instance to the object variable with the **Set** statement.
- Call the member of the object that you want to reuse.

One of the aesthetically elegant features of the ActiveX component architecture, as implemented in VB5, is how similar its behavior is to Microsoft's own applications. One of these similarities is that you can design an out-of-process ActiveX EXE component so that it can be run either as a component with reusable objects, as we have done throughout this book, or as a standalone executable. Although the book's class library is not really designed to do this, it does have some code in its Startup Object (the **Sub Main** procedure in STARTUP.BAS, which is shown in Listing 21.2) that simulates this dual functionality and gives you a sense of how it would work on a more complex scale.

Listing 21.2   Sub Main procedure of book's class library.

```
Sub Main()

    ' Simulate dual capacity of ActiveX EXE component--
    ' * If ActiveX EXE component is started in typical way,
    '   as library of reusable objects, do nothing here in
    '   Sub Main. Instead, proceed to Initialize event
    '   procedure of class that is being instantiated.
    ' * But if it is started as standalone EXE:
    '   a) Check how it is being started by calling Windows
    '       API function.
    '   b) If it is being tested in VB's IDE, display Form1
    '       (which is used to simulated client application).
    '   c) If it is being started as standalone executable
    '       (for example, by double clicking it from Explorer
    '       or running it with VB's Shell function), simulate
    '       different kind of behavior by modelessly showing
    '       mock startup Form object. Code in frmStartEXE's
    '       Form_DblClick event procedure demos ability to:
    '       - Reuse ActiveX component's objects internally.
    '       - Or run any other kind of Visual Basic code.

    ' Variables:
    Dim RunningInIDE As Boolean

    If App.StartMode = vbSModeAutomation Then
        Exit Sub
    ElseIf App.StartMode = vbSModeStandalone Then

        #If Win32 Then

            If GetModuleHandle("VB32.EXE") Or _
              GetModuleHandle("VB5.EXE") Then
                RunningInIDE = True
            End If

        #Else
            If GetModuleHandle("VB.EXE") Then RunningInIDE = True
        #End If

        If RunningInIDE Then
            Form1.Show
        Else
            frmStartEXE.Show
        End If

    End If

End Sub
```

In Listing 21.2, the **StartMode** property of Visual Basic's **App** object (that is, the book's ActiveX component) returns a value at runtime that determines whether it is being started as a standalone project or as an ActiveX component. **StartMode** can have two settings:

- **vbSModeAutomation** - 1. The application is started as an ActiveX component.

- **vbSModeStandalone** - 0. The application is started as a standalone executable by running it inside VB's IDE or running it from a command line (double-clicking it in Explorer, using VB's **Shell** function, selecting Start | Run from the taskbar, and so on).

If it is being run as an ActiveX component, **Sub Main** does nothing and the code exits the procedure. If it is being run standalone, the book's ActiveX component's **Sub Main** code can do one of two things. It can detect that the ActiveX component is being run:

- In VB's IDE (that is, being tested internally) and display the simulated client application's Form1. This technique only works if Start Mode on the Component tab of the Project Properties dialog box is set to Standalone.

- From a command line and display, in this simulated mockup, the modeless dialog box shown in Figure 21.9. When you double click on the **Form** object in Figure 21.9, the code in Listing 21.3 executes.

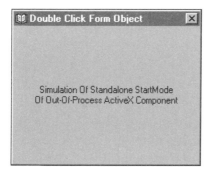

Figure 21.9 Simulation of standalone executable's startup form.

Listing 21.3   Code in standalone executable's startup form.

```
Private Sub Form_DblClick()

    ' Variables:
    Dim Msg     As String
    Dim Title   As String

    Title = "Demo Of Dual Capability"

    Msg = "This demo shows how an ActiveX EXE component," & vbCr
    Msg = Msg & "when it's run as a standalone executable, "
    Msg = Msg & "can" & vbCr
    Msg = Msg & "call methods internally or run any other "
    Msg = Msg & "kind of " & vbCr
    Msg = Msg & "Visual Basic code, application or program."
    Msg = Msg & vbCr & vbCr
    Msg = Msg & "The ShowMsg method displayed this message."

    ClientApp.ShowMsg Msg, vbInformation, Title

    Msg = "VB's MsgBox function displayed this message." & vbCr
    Msg = Msg & vbCr
    Msg = Msg & "When you choose OK, code in the Form_DblClick"
    Msg = Msg & vbCr
    Msg = Msg & "event procedure of this demo form will unload"
    Msg = Msg & vbCr
    Msg = Msg & "the form and terminate the executable."

    MsgBox Msg, vbInformation, Title

    Unload Me

End Sub
```

The code in Listing 21.3 simply displays two message boxes. The first message box, shown in Figure 21.10, is displayed using the class library's **ShowMsg** method (the **ClientApp** class was instantiated in the General Declarations section of frmStartEXE so that its members could be reused). After you clear the first message box, Visual Basic's **MsgBox** function is used to display the second message box, which is shown in Figure 21.11. After you clear this message box, the **Unload** statement triggers the **Form_Unload** event, which deinstantiates any objects, frees system resources, and terminates the standalone executable.

This simple simulation demonstrates how easy it is to design and write an ActiveX component that can function in this dual fashion. Remember, however, that this technique only works with the out-of-process EXE version of an ActiveX component. The same code in the **Sub Main** procedure in

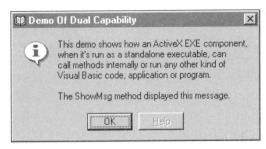

Figure 21.10   Standalone EXE displaying message with **ShowMsg** method.

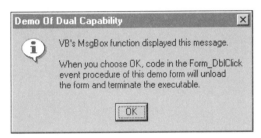

Figure 21.11   Standalone EXE displaying message with **MsgBox** function.

Listing 21.2 is also compiled and made into the in-process DLL version of the book's class library. However, because Windows treats a dynamically linked library file differently than it does an executable file, you cannot start EFSD.DLL in standalone mode. If you try to do this, Windows displays the message box shown in Figure 21.12.

> **Note:** An application's actual **StartMode** setting is determined by how that application is started at runtime, not by its nominal setting on the Component tab of the Project Properties dialog box when you create an executable file. Also, only an EXE ActiveX component can use the Start Mode setting on the Component tab at design time; this setting is disabled for a DLL ActiveX component.

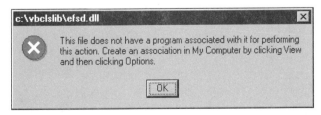

Figure 21.12   Warning when you try to run a DLL file in standalone mode.

Using VB's Setup Wizard On ActiveX Components

You can use the Setup Wizard that Microsoft distributes with VB5 to create a set of distribution disks for an ActiveX component's file(s). In this section, we'll focus on issues concerning how the Setup Wizard works with an ActiveX component that differ from how it was used in VB3 or from how it is used in VB5 with a normal Visual Basic project. All references in this section and screen shots are related to the book's class library.

The Select Project dialog box, shown in Figure 21.13, asks you to select the Visual Basic project file for the application that you want to distribute. It doesn't matter if you have been making more than one kind of ActiveX component from the same set of source code and have more than one project file (for example, EFSD.VBP, EFSE.VBP, and so on). Select one of the project files by clicking the Browse button.

As shown in Figure 21.14, VB5's Setup Wizard now supports three distribution modes: floppy disk, single directory, and disk directories (\Disk1, \Disk2, and so on). You can distribute an ActiveX component under any one of the three modes.

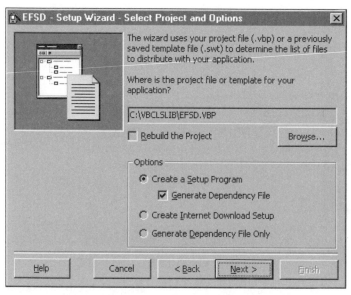

Figure 21.13 The Setup Wizard's Select Project dialog box.

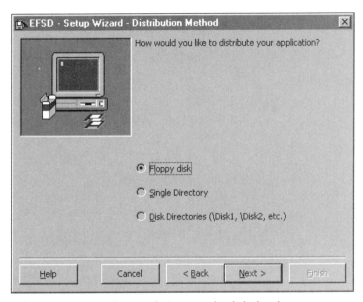

Figure 21.14 The Setup Wizard's Distribution Method dialog box.

When you reach the ActiveX Components dialog box, shown in Figure 21.15, it always displays the message "The Wizard has determined that your application does not use any ActiveX components." This message can be a little confusing. The Wizard knows that the selected project (for example, EFSD.VBP) is itself an ActiveX component; what the message means is that Setup Wizard did not detect any references/calls to other, external ActiveX components in the code of this component's project.

The book's class library does not have any references to such an external ActiveX component. However, there are three separate ActiveX components that the single set of source code supports under 32-bit Windows (EFSD.DLL, EFSE.EXE, and EFSR.EXE). Simply click on the Add Local button to select these three files.

After you have selected EFSD.DLL, EFSE.EXE, and EFSR.EXE and clicked the Next button on the ActiveX Components dialog box, the Wizard displays an Unable To Locate Dependency Information message box. Select the Never warn me checkbox and click Yes. The Wizard will then warn you about EFSR.EXE; again, select the Never warn me checkbox and click Yes. You can safely ignore these dependency warnings because all versions of the book's ActiveX component use the same files.

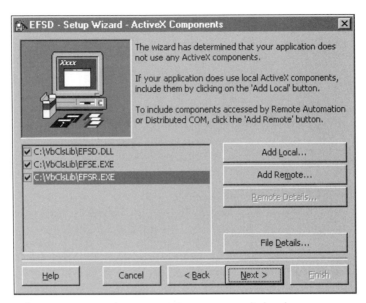

Figure 21.15 The Setup Wizard's ActiveX Components dialog box.

> ***Note:*** *Under VB4, the Setup Wizard at this point displayed a Shared Components dialog box that allowed you to specify the path on which the DLL or EXE file would be installed (either the shared path \PROGRAM FILES\COMMON FILES\OLESVR or another path). This dialog box no longer appears in VB5's Wizard, and it later automatically installs the DLL or EXE files on the shared components path.*

The File Summary dialog box, shown in Figure 21.16, enables you to add to the distribution disks any files that the Setup Wizard missed. You have to know whether the ActiveX component(s) uses any Help files, database files, or third-party DLL files which the Wizard did not list and manually add them.

Then you complete the work of the Setup Wizard by following these steps:

1. Select Next to move to the Finished dialog box.

2. Select Save Template to save the Setup Wizard configuration information for the ActiveX component(s) to a template (.SWT) file. You can retrieve the information stored in this template file later by clicking the Open Template button when you next use the Setup Wizard.

3. Select Finish to complete the compression of the files and the creation of the distribution disks.

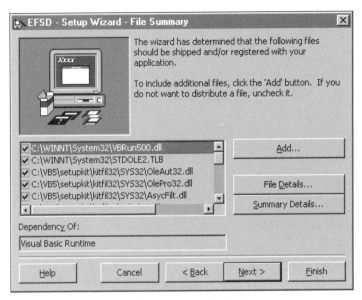

Figure 21.16 The Setup Wizard's File Summary dialog box.

When you actually install an ActiveX component(s) from a set of distribution disks by double clicking on the file SETUP.EXE from the Explorer or the File Manager, there is no way to specify the path. The installation routine automatically:

- Installs the ActiveX component and any related Help files or database files on the path for shared components. Again, on Windows 95 and NT 4, this directory is \PROGRAM FILES\COMMON FILES\OLESVR.

- Installs all other DLL or EXE files on the Windows System path.

Visual Basic's Setup Wizard also supports the Uninstall feature required to be part of any 32-bit application that wants to display the *Designed for Microsoft Windows 95* logo. If you have installed a 32-bit ActiveX component from a set of distribution disks, this Uninstall feature is the easiest and safest way to remove its files (and all its related entries in the Windows registration database) from the system.

To use the Uninstall feature, open the Windows Control Panel and double click on the Add/Remove Programs icon. From the Add/Remove Programs dialog box, select the name of the project file under which you created the distribution disks for the ActiveX component(s) and click on the Add/Remove button. A series of dialog boxes leads you through the Uninstall process. At a certain point, you will be asked whether you want to remove all shared components or only selected ones. With this question, the Uninstall process is reminding you that ActiveX components can be shared and used by many different applications. Don't panic! Removing all shared components means only those ActiveX components that were installed as part of the single installation routine to which this Uninstall process applies. The normal selection would be to remove all shared components.

Creating An ActiveX Component's Help File

One of the essential features that every ActiveX component should have is its own Windows Help file that documents the public interface of its reusable objects and members. This book is not meant to teach you how to write and compile a Windows Help file from scratch. There are several excellent books devoted to this subject. The most complete and current book is *Developing Online Help For Windows 95* by Boggan, Farkas & Welinske (International Thompson Computer Press, 1996).

If you have had no experience writing Help files, this book will get you up to speed pretty quickly on the technical issues involved. I can assure you that we're not talking rocket science here.

What I would like to do in this section is to describe the design issues specific to creating a good Windows Help file for an ActiveX component. My recommendations here reflect both my own years of experience in writing Help files (including a portion of VB4's own Help file) and Microsoft's standards for documenting their ActiveX components. Take my word for it: When it comes to ActiveX components, Microsoft writes the best Help files in the business.

All of the files that comprise the book's ActiveX component's Help file (EFS.HLP) are on the CD-ROM. If you chose to install them as part of the CD-ROM's setup routine, these files should be on the path C:\VBOOPEFS-\VBCLSHLP. Among these files, there are a lot of graphics files that support the bitmaps used by EFS.HLP; but, the major files used to compile EFS.HLP are listed and described in Table 21.4.

The major design objectives of an ActiveX component's Help file are few in number and straightforward in concept. I summarize them in the following list of bullet points:

• Each public class/object needs a topic to describe the object's general purpose.

Table 21.4 Major files used to compile EFS.HLP.

Name	Description
CONTENTS.RTF	Contents topic (Windows 3.x style).
CLASSLIB.RTF	Main file that contains all topics for objects and their members.
SYNTAX.RTF	File that contains new VB4 and VB5 syntax information.
GLOSSARY.RTF	File that contains glossary of OOP and Windows terms.
ERRMSGS.RTF	File that contains 48 syntax error messages.
OBJECT.RTF	Sample file that contains four topics used to document an object (ActiveXCtl).
MEMBER.RTF	Sample file that contains four topics used to document a member (LoadStatusBar).
EFS.HPJ	Project file that compiler reads for settings, paths, and so on.
HCP.EXE	Windows 3.x-style Help compiler.
HCP.ERR	Help compiler's error file.
*.BMP	Miscellaneous bitmap files.

- Each public class/object's topic has three jumps, located at the top of the topic and kept with the topic's title as the topic is scrolled. These jumps are titled Methods, Properties, and See Also. If any of your objects have developer-declared events, you should also have a fourth jump for Events. These jumps are to topics which list all the methods and properties that apply to the object, and to other topics related to the object. Including the object's topic, this results in four topics per object (five if you need one for Events). To see a sample of a four-topic set for an object, open OBJECT.RTF with Microsoft Word for Windows.

- Each public member needs a topic to document the member's purpose, syntax, where it can be called from, the values it can return, and miscellaneous remarks.

- Each public member's topic has three jumps, again located at the top of the topic and kept with the topic's title as the topic is scrolled. These jumps are titled Example, Applies To, and See Also. The Example topic appears in a secondary Help window and contains the example code for how to call and reuse the member. The Applies To topic lists the objects in the ActiveX component to which the member applies. The See Also jump is to other topics related to the member. Including the member's topic, this results in four topics per member. To see a sample of a four-topic set for a member, open MEMBER.RTF.

- There should be a set of syntax error message topics that document any syntax errors raised by the ActiveX component. To see how these are done, open ERRMSGS.RTF.

Once you get in the habit of documenting an ActiveX component's reusable objects and members in a Windows Help file, you'll wonder why you ever tried to do it any other way. If you organize the Help file in compliance with the design objectives listed in Table 21.4, you will find it easy to add the necessary topics for new objects and members as you develop them. You will also find it much easier to revise and maintain the documentation for existing objects and members. Most important, if your ActiveX component is distributed with a good Help file, you will find that other developers will be much more likely to reuse your ActiveX component.

Creating An Application With Reusable Objects

In Chapter 18, which introduced the concept of the reusable application framework, I cited some statistics from Paul G. Bassett's book *Framing Software Reuse: Lessons From The Real World*. The statistics documented the percentage of reuse achieved through the proper use of an OOP methodology and application frameworks. The claims were quite impressive. But, as we all know in the hype-dominated world of computer programming and development, statistics can be made to say or do almost anything.

In order to give you a better sense of the degree of reuse that can be achieved by using VB5 and OOP/ActiveX component techniques, I wrote a full-featured Rich Text Editor client application. If you installed it from the book's CD-ROM, its files should be on the path C:\VBOOPEFS\CLINTAPP. You can open up the source code from the VB5 project file RTFEDIT.VBP and run the client application from there, or you can double click the executable RTFEDIT.EXE from the Explorer or File Manager.

When you do run this Rich Text Editor, you will first be greeted by a splash screen and then a security password dialog box. Once you clear them, you can use the File menu or the appropriate toolbar button to open a rich text or plain text file and load it into the **RichTextBox** control on the form. At this point, the client application will appear as in Figure 21.17. Take some time to try the various menu items and toolbar buttons of this Rich Text Editor; give it a real workout.

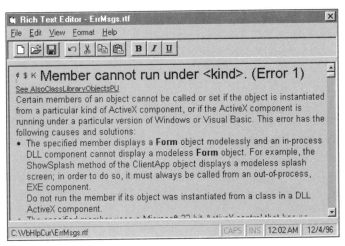

Figure 21.17 Rich Text Editor's form with RTF file loaded.

I want to make two key points about this Rich Text Editor client application. First, almost all of its functionality is the result of calling reusable objects and members from the book's ActiveX component. Second, the size of the EXE file is only 24 K. Of this 24 K, only about 10 K is related to code. The other 14 K is related to the **Form** object and its **Menu** and **RichTextBox** control objects. In other words, you would use this 14 K regardless of how you implemented the functionality of the application. I leave it to you to estimate how much VB5 code you would have to write to replicate all the functionality of this Rich Text Editor, without calling any reusable objects in an ActiveX component.

When you run this client application on your PC, you may have some concerns about its speed. As far as performance is concerned, you have to appreciate two things about this client application. First, as it is currently written, it uses the **CreateObject** function and late binding to instantiate classes from the book's ActiveX component. In a stable environment, where the ActiveX component was installed via distribution disks and I was sure its GUID could not change, I would have used early binding and the **Dim As New** syntax to improve performance.

Second, VB5 (unlike VB4) can create an ActiveX DLL component that displays modeless forms. Because of my desire to have the book's source code run under either VB4 or VB5, I did not take advantage of this new VB5 capability. However, it is fairly easy to go through EFSD.DLL and change certain methods (like the **Edit** method of the **Text** object) to display modeless forms and delete the syntax checking code that forbids them to be run from a DLL ActiveX component. After you recompiled EFSD.DLL with VB5, this change, in conjunction with the early binding approach to instantiation discussed in the previous paragraph, would speed up the performance of the Rich Text Editor application to more than acceptable levels.

The Future Of OOP And ActiveX Components

The details of how to use the polling and callback techniques we demonstrated in Chapter 17 are admittedly tedious and complex. Still, if you are willing to invest the time and effort required, you can learn how to replicate the techniques used in the **DemoPolling**, **DemoCallBack**, and **LoadToolBar** methods.

What is at least as important as learning the techniques of polling and callbacks, however, is to understand the major implications they have for the future of OOP development and ActiveX components. If we assume that Microsoft will maintain its dominance of the PC operating system platform well into the future, then the next logical step is that the ActiveX component model will soon come to dominate object-oriented development.

Object-oriented analysis, design, and development is not a passing fancy. In conjunction with the client/server, three-tier, and distributed objects models, object-oriented programming will be the dominant development methodology for large-scale projects for the next couple decades. You cannot find any major figure in software manufacturing or computer science, from Bill Gates to Steve Jobs to Edward Yourdon to Donald Knuth, who does not wholeheartedly believe that this is the best way to write software.

Visual Basic has changed significantly over its lifetime of about six years. It started out as simply an easier way to write bare-bones Windows applications; but, it has now evolved to the point where its Enterprise Edition can support even the largest-scale development projects that embody these features:

- Client-server, three-tier, and distributed objects architectures
- Object-oriented analysis, design, and development
- ActiveX controls
- ActiveX components/servers

The last feature, ActiveX components, is the most important one of the four. If you consider, for example, what a three-tier or distributed objects architecture involves, you can visualize the separate hardware platforms running three different kinds of software models: the client's GUI, the server's data warehouse, and the middle tier's business rules.

However, what is most important to understand about this three-tier model is that each tier (including the nominal client), at a lower level of abstraction, is actually going to be written and programmed as an ActiveX component. Each tier will conform to a different model and serve a different business purpose, but, in Microsoft's vision of the object-oriented future, each tier will have in common with the other two the fact that it is implemented as an ActiveX component.

There will be no exceptions to this ActiveX component-dominated model. The operating system, personal-use applications like the Microsoft Office suite, departmental/divisional or enterprise networks, data repositories, programming languages, and development tools will all be written to the ActiveX software protocol. Sure, one software entity will be called a server and another will be called a client or controller and, in the long run, who knows what other names, but, at an easily understood and high level of abstraction, each one will function and communicate with the others in the same fundamental ways:

- By messaging (the passing in of arguments to members and the returning of values back from them)
- By polling
- By callbacks

In the near future, it will be a truism that this communications process among ActiveX components, residing on local/distributed/remote hardware platforms, cannot really be said to have a beginning (client) or ending (server) point, or orientation.

Developers have always enjoyed debating which is the best programming language. For all practical purposes, in two to three years, that debate will be strictly academic. The answer to that question will be equivalent to the answer to this question: What is the easiest way to write and develop an ActiveX component?

The purpose of this book has been to guide you through the new syntax and tools that the Professional Edition of VB5 provides to create ActiveX components. The techniques you have learned will work unchanged with the Enterprise Edition of Visual Basic. The only essential difference between using an out-of-process component locally or using it remotely (that is, as a Remote Automation Object) has nothing to do with Visual Basic's syntax rather, it is strictly a function of how the two ActiveX components (client and remote) are registered.

When you have mastered the techniques that this book's class library demonstrates, you will be on the cutting edge of Visual Basic object-oriented development. I'm guessing that it will probably take another year or two for project managers to fully understand and become comfortable with the many capabilities of Active X components as Visual Basic embodies them. When project managers (and IS management personnel) have reached that point, a two-tier, wage-scale model will become the norm for Visual Basic programmers. The lower tier will consist of the majority of Visual Basic programmers—those who can write decent code but lack the training and experience required to write robust, commercial-quality ActiveX components. The upper tier will consist of a minority of Visual Basic object-oriented developers, whose value in the marketplace is commensurate with their superior skills and development methodology. Which tier will you occupy?

INDEX

D

H

I

O

P

T